VERDI

VERDI

A DOCUMENTARY STUDY

compiled, edited and

translated by

William Weaver

318 illustrations, 54 in colour

THAMES AND HUDSON

FRONTISPIECE
Verdi with an autograph quotation from *La forza del destino*
(1862). Cover of *The Graphic*, London, 8 March 1873. William
Weaver Collection, Monte San Savino (AR).

Text filmset in Great Britain by Keyspools Ltd, Golborne, Lancs.
Printed and bound in Italy by Amilcare Pizzi S.p.a., Milan.

Contents

IN MEMORIAM
Richard Miller
(1920–1971)

Prefatory note

Traditionally, in presenting his work, the anthologist offers an explanation of his choices. In the case of Verdi documents, such an explanation is difficult. I believe the reader will be able to see for himself why I have included the letters, pictures, reviews, biographical excerpts that will be found here. Verdi could not write a really dull letter, and – like Falstaff – he seemed to spark the intelligence of those around him. What is less easy for me to explain are the omissions. Though this book is big, it still had limitations of space, so my saddest task was cutting. Compiling this book was largely a process of resisting temptation. An example: the furnishing of the Villa Sant'Agata was a long process. The furniture and other objects had to be found in Milan, Genoa, Paris. Shamelessly, Verdi involved his friends in the process, first the long-suffering conductor Mariani, then the publisher Ricordi. There are long, fascinating letters about the billiard-table still to be seen on the ground-floor of the villa. Verdi was as fastidious in the choice of the table as he was in the casting of a role. Poor Ricordi had to make the purchase, find just the right kind of lamp to be hung over the table, and so on. I am sorry to say none of these letters is included here, though, taken all together, they certainly illustrate a facet of Verdi's character and they tell us what was on his mind for a fairly extended period.

More seriously, and after more painful inner debate, I have omitted many letters to his librettists (many, however, are included). These are not only fascinating, but invaluable to a study of the operas. But they must be read as a whole, and with the finished libretto and the score at hand. One day we can hope there will be complete, annotated editions of this correspondence. As I write, two such volumes are about to be published: Professor Hans Busch's mammoth study of *Aida*, which will include every available document on the opera's gestation and first productions; and the edition of the Verdi-Boito correspondence being prepared at the Istituto di studi verdiani in Parma. In presenting, all the same, a generous sample of the correspondence with Cammarano, Piave, Ghislanzoni and Boito, I hope I have indicated the tone of each of these relationships and, more importantly, the extent to which Verdi took advice and, more often, gave it, sometimes in a peremptory tone. Every writer on Verdi has said that the composer was, in a large measure, the co-author or even author of the texts he set. The proof lies in his letters.

I think it is safe to say that if Verdi, for some reason, had not studied music, he would still have left his mark on nineteenth-century Italy. If – to venture one hypothesis – he had studied law at the University of Parma, as his father had originally wished, he might well have become a statesman like his friends Piroli and Arrivabene. For that matter, he *did* become a member of parliament, and though no laws bore his name, his presence in that assembly lent allure and dignity to the government of the newly-forged nation. He might also have been a leader in the field of agronomy; his farmlands, in fact, were famous in his day because of his wise introduction of the latest farming methods, some picked up on his journeys abroad and his visits to great exhibitions. He might even have been an art critic. From a fairly early age, he enjoyed the company of painters and sculptors; he regularly went to look at works of art, new and old; and he was, to some degree, a collector. As the wheel of taste in painting turns, his paintings by Palizzi and Morelli – to say nothing of his Gemito sculptures – have proved as sound an investment as his fields and farms in the fertile Po valley.

Among the illustrations in this book I have included not only Morelli, Palizzi and Gemito, but also works by other artists of the period; in this selection, I was led by a wish to give some notion of the visual world in which Verdi lived, the sort of paintings he saw, and the sort of subjects that were painted. The subjects – *La battaglia di Legnano, I due Foscari, I vespri siciliani* – speak for themselves: the painter and the composer, in Risorgimento Italy, drew on the same sources of inspiration.

A word about the translations. Obviously, Verdi was not writing his letters to posterity, but to collaborators and friends (or enemies). He used words with facility, but sometimes with a freedom that a professional writer can only envy. The addressees knew what he meant. Sometimes, for us, the meaning must be dug out. He uses, for instance, the word *lasciare* (i.e. 'to leave') sometimes to mean 'leave in', sometimes to mean 'leave out'. The translator has to choose, basing his choice on the context. Similarly the word *costumi* can mean either 'costumes' or 'customs' (*moeurs*). I have translated it, in different contexts, in different ways. In a famous letter about *La traviata* in which the word occurs, I have opted for 'costumes', since the question of the contemporary dress of the characters was much on Verdi's mind. If, however, another translator were to say 'behaviour' or something of the sort, I would not strenuously object.

In preparing the translations, I have tried, as far as possible, to work from original sources and not from published transcriptions. In many cases, however, only the published texts were available. Where I have been able to compare the autograph with the transcriptions, I must say that, except for a very few instances, the differences were slight. Omissions are shown thus: [. . .].

As the reader will see, the documents are presented here with a bare minimum of comment. I have avoided nudging. Verdi and his contemporaries speak for themselves. At times they are contradictory; the reader will judge on the evidence, which, I believe, is sufficiently eloquent.

Podere Tarucolo   W. W.
Monte San Savino (Arezzo)

Acknowledgments and sources

In preparing this volume, I have naturally drawn on previous biographies and studies of Verdi, and my first debt of gratitude is to their authors, living and dead. I have also received generous assistance from numerous libraries, galleries, archives, museums; they are listed below or in the captions of the illustrations.

Many individuals have also helped me, and it is a pleasure for me to thank them here. I list them by cities.

In London, Gertrude Buckman, Julian Budden, and my publishers, especially my editor.

In New York, Claire Brook, John Freeman, Dorle and Dario Soria, David Stivender, Helen Wolff.

In Milan, Giancarlo Costa (responsible for many of the photographs), Giampiero Tintori, Lorenzo Siliotto, Luciana Pestalozza, Fausto Broussard, Renata Vercesi, Natale Gallini, Sergio Dragoni.

In Florence, Lamberto Scotti, Harold Barnes.

In Rome, Dina Zanetti, Emilia Zanetti, Michele Corradi.

In Parma, Mario Medici, Marcello Conati, Gustavo Marchesi, Marisa Casati, Lina Re.

In Busseto, Mary Jane Phillips Matz, Corrado Mingardi.

In Siena, Rita Toninelli.

In Ferrara, Giuseppe Minerbi, Paolo Ravenna, Giorgio Bassani.

Inevitably, my Verdian neighbours in Tuscany have been particularly involved in the long genesis of this book. Some have contributed material to it, some have lent me rare books, all have been exploited for advice and moral support. In Monte San Savino, Andrew Porter, Floriano Vecchi, Giuseppe Greghi. In Cortona, John Ross. In Panzano, Michael Rose. In Camigliano Santa Gemma, John Fleming and Hugh Honour.

In the course of working on this book, I have also made extensive use of Elvidio Surian's Verdi Chronology, to be published shortly in *The Verdi Companion*, edited by Martin Chusid and myself.

AB	Abbiati, Franco, *Giuseppe Verdi*, Ricordi, Milan, 1959.
AD	Adami, Giuseppe, *Giulio Ricordi*, Domus, Milan, 1945.
ADC	Accademia dei Concordi, Rovigo.
ALB	Alberti, Annibale, *Verdi intimo*, Mondadori, Milan, 1931.
AMC	Accademia Musicale Chigiana, Siena.
AN	Archivio Notarile, Parma.
ANL	Accademia Nazionale dei Lincei, Rome.
AS	Archivio di Stato.
ASR	Archivio storico Ricordi, Milan.
ATLF	Archivio Teatro la Fenice, Venice.
ATTI	*Atti dei congressi internazionali di studi verdiani*, Istituto di studi verdiani, Parma.
BARB	Barbiera, Raffaello, *Il salotto della Contessa Maffei*, Baldini, Castoldi & C., Milan, 1903.
BASEVI	Basevi, Abramo, *Studio sulle opere di Giuseppe Verdi*, Tofani, Florence, 1859.
BC	Biblioteca del Conservatorio 'S. Pietro a Majella', Naples.
BERLIOZ	Bernard, Daniel, *Correspondance inédite de Hector Berlioz*, Bernard, Paris, n.d.
BIB	Biblioteca del Monte di Pietà, Busseto.
BIB VATICANA	Biblioteca Vaticana, Rome.
BLP	Biblioteca Lucchesi-Palli, Naples.
BNB	Biblioteca Nazionale Braidense, Milan.
BNC	Biblioteca Nazionale Centrale, Florence.
BONG	Bongiovanni, Giannetto, *Dal Carteggio inedito Verdi-Vigna*, Edizioni 'Giornale d'Italia', Rome, 1941.
BQ	Biblioteca Queriniana, Brescia.
BSV	*Bollettino dell'Istituto di studi verdiani*, Parma.
BU	Biblioteca universitaria, Pisa.
BÜLOW	Bülow, Hans von, *Briefe und Schriften*, Leipzig 1895–1908.
BUR	Burckhardt, Jacob, *Briefe*, Kröner, Leipzig, 1935.
CIMGD	Civico Istituto Musicale 'Gaetano Donizetti', Bergamo.
CONATI	Conati, Marcello, 'L'Oberto, conte di San Bonifacio, in due recensioni straniere poco note e in una lettera inedita di Verdi', *Atti* I, Istituto di studi verdiani, Parma.
COP	Cesari e Luzio, *I copialettere di Giuseppe Verdi*, Comune di Milano, 1913.
CV	Luzio, Alessandro, *Carteggi verdiani*, Accademia Nazionale, Rome, 1935–47.
D'AN	D'Annunzio, Gabriele, 'In morte di Giuseppe Verdi' (1901) in *G. Verdi*, La Scala, Milan, 1951.
DE A	De Amicis, *Nuovi Ritratti Letterari ed Artistici*, Treves, Milan, 1908.
DE R	De Rensis, Raffaello, *Franco Faccio e Verdi*, Treves, Milan, 1934.
DREI	Drei, Giovanni, 'Il Concorso di Verdi a Busseto secondo nuovi documenti', *Aurea Parma*, Fasc. iv–v, 1939.
DUPRÉ	Dupré, Giovanni, *Ricordi autobiografici*, Imperia, Milan, 1924.
EREDI CESARI	Cesari estate, Parma.
EREDI MAFFEI	Maffei estate, Milan.
ESC	Escudier, Léon, *Mes Souvenirs*, Dentu, Paris, 1863.
FOL	Pougin, Arthur, *Giuseppe Verdi, vita aneddotica con note ed aggiunte di Folchetto (Jacopo Caponi)*, Ricordi, Milan, 1881.
GAR	Garibaldi, Luigi, *Giuseppe Verdi nelle lettere di Emanuele Muzio ad Antonio Barezzi*, Treves, Milan, 1931.
GATTI	Gatti, Carlo, *Verdi*, Mondadori, Milan, 1953.

GHIS   Ghislanzoni, Antonio, 'Storia di Milano dal 1836 al 1848', in *In chiave di baritono*, Milan, 1882.

GHIS LS   Ghislanzoni, Antonio, *Libro serio*, Tipografia Editrice Lombarda, Milan, 1879.

GODEFROY   Godefroy, Vincent, *The Dramatic Genius of Verdi*, vol. I, Gollancz, London, 1975.

ISV   Istituto di studi verdiani, Parma.

LUMLEY   Lumley, Benjamin, *Reminiscences of the Opera*, Hurst and Blackett, London, 1864.

MARC   Marchesi, Gustavo, *Giuseppe Verdi e il conservatorio di Parma*, La Ducale, Parma, 1976.

MART   Martinelli, Amilcare, *Verdi, raggi e penombre*, Studio editoriale Genovese, Genoa, 1926.

MARTIN   Martin, George, *Verdi*, Macmillan, London, 1965.

MARV   Marchesi, Gustavo, *Verdi*, UTET, Turin, 1970.

MCP   Monte di credito su pegno, Busseto.

MM   Filippi, Filippo, *Musica e musicisti*, Milan, 1876.

MONALDI   Monaldi, Gino, *Verdi 1839–1898*, Bocca, Milan, 1943.

MTS   Museo Teatrale alla Scala, Milan.

NARDI   Nardi, Piero, *Vita di Arrigo Boito*, Mondadori, Milan, 1942.

NICOLAI   Nicolai, Otto, *Tagebücher*, Leipzig, 1892.

OPERA   Bibliothèque de l'Opéra, Paris.

PAN   Panzacchi, Enrico, *Riccardo Wagner*, Zanichelli, Bologna, 1883.

PANIZ   Panizzardi, Mario, *Wagner in Italia*, Progresso, Genoa, 1923.

PASC   Pascolato, Alessandro, *Re Lear e Ballo in Maschera*, Lapi, Città di Castello, 1913.

PIZZI   Pizzi, Italo, *Ricordi verdiani inediti*, Turin, 1901.

PL   Pleasants, Henry, *Vienna's Golden Years of Music*, Gollancz, London, 1951.

PORT   Porter, Andrew, '*Don Carlos* and the Monk-Emperor' in *Musical Newsletter*, New York, vol. II, no. 4, October 1972.

QISV   *Quaderni*, Istituto di studi verdiani, Parma.

RDM   *Revue des deux mondes*, Paris.

RES   Resasco, Ferdinando, *Verdi a Genova*, Pagano, Genoa, 1901.

REY   Reyer, Ernest, *Notes de Musique*, Charpentier, Paris, 1875.

RO   Rossi, Adolfo, *Roncole Verdi, guida storica*, Arte Grafica, Fidenza, 1969.

ROOS   Roosevelt, Blanche, *Verdi: Milan and 'Othello'*, Ward and Downey, London, 1887.

SANTLEY   Santley, Charles, *Student and Singer*, London, 1892.

SHAW   Shaw, Bernard, *Music in London*, 3 vols, Constable, London, 1932.

SOLERA   Solera, Temistocle, 'Giuseppina Strepponi', in *Strenna Teatrale Europea*, III, Milan, 1840.

STAN   Stanford, C. V., *Studies and Memories*, Constable, London, 1908.

TAL   *Teatri Arte e Letturatura*, Bologna.

TIMES   *The Times*, London.

VELF   *Verdi e la Fenice*, La Fenice, Venice, 1951.

VER   *Verdi e Roma*, Teatro dell'Opera di Roma, Rome, 1951.

VSA   Villa Sant'Agata, Busseto.

WAL   Walker, Frank, *The Man Verdi*, Knopf, New York, 1962.

ZAVADINI   Zavadini, Guidi, *Donizetti, Vita – Musiche – Epistolario*, Istituto Italiano d'Arti Grafiche, Bergamo, 1948.

Verdi's autobiographical narrative

In the late 1870s an 'anecdotal biography' of Verdi appeared serially in a French paper, *Le Ménestrel*. Its author was Arthur Pougin. Promptly an Italian translation was commissioned by Verdi's publisher, Ricordi, who assigned the job to Jacopo Caponi, a journalist who signed himself 'Folchetto'. As the translator began his task, he soon realized there were lacunae in Pougin's story, and some of the best anecdotes about Verdi – by then internationally famous and, in Italy, virtually a folk-hero – had been omitted. So to Pougin's text he added long, chatty notes of his own.

The longest of these notes and the most fascinating is an 'autobiographical narrative' which Verdi himself dictated to Ricordi at the Villa Sant'Agata in the autumn of 1879. Verdi, who claimed not to like publicity, biographies, newspapers, invasions of privacy, agreed to recount the details of his early career in the interest of accuracy. In the event, his narrative is factually inaccurate to a remarkable degree.

The composer skates lightly over the dates of composition of his first performed opera, *Oberto conte di San Bonifacio*, omitting any mention of the opera *Rocester*, which may or may not be the same work. Musicologists and Verdi specialists are still trying to untangle this puzzle, which Verdi himself complicated.

But even more surprisingly, Verdi confuses the dates of the deaths of his two children, and even the order of their dying. In his narrative, it is the boy – Icilio – who dies first, followed by the girl, Virginia. In reality, Virginia died in Busseto, in 1838, a month after Icilio's birth. Icilio died on 22 October 1839. Margherita, Verdi's young wife, followed her children to the grave on 18 June 1840. Verdi has the three deaths occur in the space of two and a half months.

He also gives a mistaken impression when he says that, after these deaths and the crushing failure of his second opera, *Un giorno di regno*, in September 1840, he completely abandoned the theatre. Beyond any doubt, he went through a period of black depression and even of aversion to the stage. But that period was much shorter than he remembered. On 17 October 1840, five weeks after the terrible fiasco, Verdi was conducting a revival of *Oberto* at La Scala. A few weeks later he supervised a production of the same opera in Genoa, and for that production he composed new music. So his pen – like the baton – was not long from his hand.

But the autobiographical narrative must be read, not as a source of dates and facts, but as a self-portrait. This is how *Verdi* saw the facts. This is how he wanted others to think of him. There is emotional, if not always literal, truth in these pages.

Verdi was a proud man. He was especially proud of being self-made, and he tended to exaggerate the humility of his origins, the poverty of his childhood.

Our present knowledge – partial though it still is – of the true situation of Verdi's young manhood does not make his rise to celebrity the less striking or admirable. Verdi fought hard; he had a right to enjoy his victory.

But in the autumn of 1879 that victory may still not have seemed definitive to him. True, he had personally tasted his wide fame, conducting his *Messa da Requiem* in major European cities, even in Germany, the land of Wagner. But at the same time, Wagner's operas had begun, however cautiously, to make their way into the Italian repertory. So Verdi may well have allowed, even encouraged the publication of the Pougin-Folchetto hagiography as further ammunition in his battle.

That autumn of 1879 is significant in Verdi's life for another reason. He had not composed an opera since *Aida* in 1871. At the end of June, the idea of an opera on Shakespeare's *Othello* had been slyly broached by Ricordi. In September, Boito had completed the sketch of the libretto. On 18 November – weeks after his autobiographical monologue to the publisher – Verdi went to Milan, met Boito, and began discussing the opera more seriously. As the sixty-six-year-old musician recalled the struggles of forty years before, he was preparing himself for a return to the arena.

Verdi's autobiographical narrative to Giulio Ricordi, Sant'Agata, 19 October 1879

In 1833 or 34 there existed in Milan a Società filarmonica, made up of good voices: it was directed by one Mas[s]ini, a man who, if not very learned, was at least tenacious and patient: therefore just what was needed for a society of amateurs. They were organizing at the Teatro Filodrammatico the performance of an oratorio by Haydn, *The Creation*: my teacher Lavigna asked me if, for my instruction, I wanted to follow the rehearsals, and I accepted with pleasure.

Nobody paid any attention to the youth modestly seated in a corner. The rehearsals were conducted by three maestri: Perelli, Bonoldi, and Almasio; but one fine day, by a strange twist of fate, all three conductors were absent from a rehearsal. The ladies and gentlemen were growing impatient, when Maestro Masini, who did not feel himself capable of sitting at the piano and accompanying with the score, addressed me, asking me to serve as accompanist, and, perhaps unconvinced of the knowledge of the young and unknown artist, he said to me: 'It is enough just to accompany with the bass.' My studies then were still fresh in my mind, and I certainly did not find myself in difficulty, facing an orchestral score. I accepted, I sat down at the piano to begin the rehearsal. I well remember some little ironic smiles from the amateurs, ladies and gentlemen, and it seems that my youthful form, thin and none too elegant in dress, was such as to inspire scant faith.

In short we began rehearsing, and little by little, warming and growing excited, I did not limit myself only to accompanying, but began also to conduct with my right hand, playing only with my left: I had a real success, all the greater for being unexpected. When the rehearsal was over, compliments, congratulations on all sides, and especially from Count Pompeo Belgiojoso and Count Renato Borromeo.

Finally, whether because the three maestri mentioned above had too many concerns and could not therefore attend to the job, or whether for other reasons, in the end they entrusted the concert entirely to me. The public performance took place, with such success that it was repeated in the grand salon of the Casino de' Nobili, in the presence of the Archduke and Archduchess Rainer and all the grand society of that time.

A little later Count Renato Borromeo gave me the assignment of composing the music for a cantata for voices and orchestra, I believe on the occasion of the marriage of some member of his family. Mind you, however, that from all this I earned nothing, since these were all quite gratuitous assignments.

Masini, who apparently had faith in the young musician, then suggested to me that I write an opera for the Teatro Filodrammatico, which he directed, and he handed me a libretto which then, partly modified by Solera, became *Oberto di San Bonifacio*.

I accepted the offer with pleasure and went back to Busseto, where I was engaged in the position of organist. I remained in Busseto about three years; having completed the opera, I again undertook the journey to Milan, taking with me the entire score in perfect order, having gone to the trouble of copying and extracting on my own all the singers' parts.

But here the difficulties began. Masini was no longer director at the Filodrammatico: therefore it was no longer possible to give my opera. However, whether because Masini really did have faith in me, or whether because he wanted somehow to show his gratitude to me, since after Haydn's *Creation*, I had assisted him several other times, preparing and conducting various performances (including *La Cenerentola*) without ever demanding any compensation, he did not lose heart at this obstacle, but said to me that he would do all he could to have my opera performed at La Scala on the occasion of the benefit for the Pio Istituto. Count Borromeo and the lawyer Pasetti promised Masini their support, but out of my love for the truth I must say that, to my knowledge, this support did not extend beyond a few words of recommendation. On the other hand, Maestro Masini went to a great deal of trouble, strongly assisted by the violoncellist Merighi, who, having made my acquaintance when he was part of the orchestra of the Filodrammatico, apparently had faith in the young maestro.

Finally everything was arranged for the spring of 1839; and in the event I had the double good fortune of staging my work at the Teatro alla Scala on the occasion of the performances for the benefit of the Pio Istituto, and of having four truly extraordinary performers: la Strepponi, the tenor Moriani, the baritone Giorgio Ronconi, and the bass Marini.

When the parts had been distributed and the vocal rehearsals barely begun, Moriani fell seriously ill! . . . so all was interrupted and there could be no more thought of giving my opera! . . . I was therefore left high and dry and was thinking of going back to Busseto, when then one morning a servant from the Teatro alla Scala comes to me and quite brusquely says: 'Are you that Maestro from Parma who was supposed to give an opera for the Pio Istituto? . . . Come to the theatre, because the Impresario wants you.' 'Is that possible?!' I interjected – and the man replied: 'Yes, sir, he ordered me to call the maestro from Parma who was supposed to give an opera: if that is you, then come.' And I went.

The impresario then was Bartolomeo Merelli: one evening on the stage of the theatre he had heard a conversation between Signora Strepponi and Giorgio Ronconi, in which the former was speaking very favourably about the music of *Oberto*, and this impression was also shared by Ronconi.

I introduced myself then to Merelli, who promptly told me that, after the favourable report he had received about my music, he would like to give it during the coming season: if I were to accept, however, I would have to make some adjustments to the tessitura, since there would not be all four of the artists as before. It was a handsome offer: young, unknown, I encountered an impresario who dared stage a new work without asking me for any kind of indemnification – an indemnification which, for that matter, I would have been unable to give. Risking on his own all the expenses of the production, Merelli simply proposed that we divide half-and-half the sum I would make if, in the case of success, I sold the opera. Nor must you believe that he was making a disadvantageous proposal: it was the opera of a beginner! . . . And the fact remains that, after the success, the publisher Giovanni Ricordi bought the rights for two thousand Austrian lire.

Oberto di San Bonifacio had not a very great success, but one sufficient to receive a fair number of performances, which Merelli decided to extend, giving more than those established by subscription. The opera was performed by la Marini, mezzosoprano, Salvi, tenor, and the bass Marini, and as I mentioned, I had here and there to modify the music for reasons of tessitura and write a new number, the quartet, whose dramatic position was suggested by Merelli himself, and I had it versified by Solera: this quartet proved one of the best numbers in the opera!

Merelli then made me an offer that was munificent for those times; he offered me, that is, a contract for three operas to be written at eight-month intervals, to be performed at La Scala or at the Vienna theatre, of which he was also impresario. In return he would pay me 4000 Austrian lire per opera, sharing equally the profit from the sale of the scores. I accepted the contract at once, and a little later, as Merelli was leaving for Vienna, he gave the poet Rossi the assignment of supplying me with the libretto, and this was *Il proscritto*; however, I was not completely satisfied with it, and I had not even begun to set it to music, when Merelli returned to Milan in the first months of 1840 and told me that for the autumn he absolutely needed an opera buffa, and this because of special reasons of his repertory: he would seek out a libretto for me immediately, and then later I would set *Il proscritto*. I did not refuse the invitation, and Merelli gave me to read various librettos by Romani, which, either because of scant success or for other reasons, were lying forgotten. I read and reread, I liked none of them, but, with pressure being put on me, I selected the one that seemed least bad to me, and it was *Il finto Stanislao*, then baptized *Un giorno di regno*.

I was living at that time in a small, humble apartment near the Porta Ticinese, and I had with me my little family, that is to say my young wife Margherita Barezzi and two little children. As soon as I set to work, I was afflicted by a serious angina, which kept me for long days in bed; as soon as my convalescence began, I remembered that in three days the rent fell due, for which 50 scudi was needed. At that time, though for me this was no small sum, it could not be called grave, either; but my painful illness had prevented me from making timely provision, nor did the communications then with Busseto (the post left twice a week) allow me to write to my excellent father-in-law Barezzi to send the said amount at once. I wanted at all costs to pay the rent on the set date, therefore, though it irked me to have to recur to third parties, I decided nevertheless to charge the engineer Pasetti with asking Merelli for the necessary 50 scudi. It upset me to allow the due date of the rent to pass without paying it, even for a few days, and my wife, seeing my torments, takes the few gold objects of her property, leaves the house, manages I do not know how to collect the mentioned sum, and gives it to me: I was moved by this affectionate act, promising myself to give it all back to my wife, which I would be able to do shortly by virtue of the contract that I already had in hand.

But here serious misfortunes begin: my little boy falls ill at the beginning of April: the doctors cannot understand what his disease is, and the poor child languishes and dies in the arms of his despairing mother. Nor does that suffice: after a few days the little girl falls ill in her turn!... and the illness also has a mortal end!... but that is still not enough: in the first days of June my young wife is struck by a violent encephalitis, and on 19 June 1840 a third coffin leaves my house!... I was alone!... alone!... In the space of about two months three persons dear to me had disappeared forever: my family was destroyed!... In the midst of this terrible anguish, to maintain the commitment assumed, I had to write and complete an opera buffa!!... *Un giorno di regno* did not please: some of the blame surely lay with the music, but some also lay with the performance. My spirit tormented by my domestic woes, exacerbated by the failure of my work, I became convinced that it would be vain to expect consolation from art, and I decided never to compose again!... In fact I wrote to the engineer Pasetti (who since the failure of *Un giorno di regno* had not been in touch with me), asking him to have Merelli dissolve the contract.

Merelli had me summoned and treated me as a capricious boy!... He refused to accept that I could so lose heart because of one setback, etc. etc.: but I stood my ground, so that, returning the contract to me, Merelli said to me:

'Listen, Verdi, I cannot force you to compose!... My faith in you is not lessened: who knows but that one day you may decide to take up your pen again!... You have only to let me know two months in advance of a season, and I promise you that your opera will be staged.'

I thanked him, but these words were unable to budge me from my decision, and I left. – I settled in Milan near the Corsia de' Servi: I had lost faith, and thought no more of music, when one winter evening, coming out of the Galleria De Cristoforis, I run into Merelli, who was going to the theatre. It was snowing in broad flakes, and taking me by the arm he invites me to accompany him to the backstage of La Scala. Along the way we chat, and he tells me he is an awkward position about the new opera he must put on: he had given the assignment to Nicolai, but the latter was not satisfied with the libretto.

'Imagine!' Merelli says, 'a libretto by Solera, stupendous!!... Magnificent!!... Extraordinary!... Effective, grandiose dramatic situations: beautiful verses!... But that stubborn composer will not hear of it and declares it is an impossible libretto!... I am at a loss to find him another promptly.'

'I will save you the trouble.' I added. 'Did you not have *Il proscritto* written for me? I have not written a note of it: I put it at your disposal.'

'Oh! bravo... that is really good luck.'

Saying this, we had reached the theatre: Merelli calls Bassi, the poet, stage-director, bouncer, librarian, etc. etc., and tells him to look at once in the archive to see if he can find a copy of *Il proscritto*: the copy is there. But at the same time Merelli picks up another manuscript and, showing it to me, exclaims:

'Look, here is Solera's libretto! Such a beautiful subject, and to refuse it!... Take it... read it.'

'What the devil am I to do with it?... No, no, I have no desire to read librettos.'

'Oh... it won't do you any harm!... Read it and then bring it back to me.' And he hands me the manuscript: it was a thick script in big letters, as was the custom then. I roll it up and, saying good evening to Merelli, I go off to my house.

Along the way I felt a kind of vague uneasiness upon me, a supreme sadness, an anguish which swelled the heart!... I went home and with an almost violent gesture, I threw the manuscript on the table, stopping, erect in front of it. Falling on the table, the sheaf opened on its own; without knowing how, my eyes stare at the page that lay before me, and this verse appears to me:

'Va, pensiero, sull'ali dorate...'

[Go, thought, on golden wings...]

I glance over the following verses and I receive a deep impression from them, especially since they were almost a paraphrase of the Bible, which I always found pleasure in reading.

I read a passage, I read two: then steadfast in my intention of not composing, I make an effort of will and force myself to close the script, and I go off to bed!... No good... *Nabucco* was trotting about my head!... Sleep would not come: I get up and read the libretto, not once, but two, three times, so often that in the morning you could say I knew Solera's entire libretto by heart.

All the same I did not feel like going back on my decision, and during the day I return to the theatre and give the manuscript back to Merelli.

'Beautiful, eh?'... he says to me.

'Very beautiful.'

'Eh!... Then set it to music!...'

'Not on your life.... I won't hear of it.'

'Set it to music, set it to music!...'

And, saying this, he takes the libretto and jams it into the pocket of my overcoat, grabs me by the shoulders, and not only shoves me out of his office, but shuts the door in my face and turns the key.

What to do?

I returned home with *Nabucco* in my pocket: one day a verse, one day another, one time a note, another a phrase ... little by little the opera was composed.

It was the autumn of 1841, and recalling Merelli's promise, I went to him, announcing that *Nabucco* was written, and therefore could be staged during the next Carnival-Lent season.

Merelli declared himself ready to keep the promise, but at the same time he pointed out to me that it was impossible to give the opera in the coming season, because three new operas by renowned composers were already fixed; to give a fourth opera by a quasi-beginner was dangerous for all concerned, but especially for me: it was therefore wise to wait for spring, a period for which he had no commitments, assuring me that he would engage good artists. But I refused; either during Carnival or never again . . . and I had my good reasons, since it would not be possible to find two other artists more suited to my work than la Strepponi and Ronconi, who I knew were engaged, and on whom I was therefore counting greatly.

Merelli, though he was ready to satisfy me, was not entirely wrong as an impresario: four new operas in a single season was a great risk! . . . But I had good artistic arguments on my side. In short, amid yeses and nos, embarrassments, half-promises, the programme of La Scala is posted . . . but *Nabucco* was not announced.

I was young, I had hot blood!! . . . I wrote a furious letter to Merelli, in which I gave free rein to all my bitterness – I confess that as soon as it was sent I felt a kind of remorse! . . . and I feared that everything would be ruined.

Merelli sends for me and, seeing me, exclaims gruffly:

'Is this the way to write to a friend? . . . Come now, you are right: we will give this *Nabucco*: you must consider, however, that I will have very heavy expenses for the other new operas; I cannot have costumes or sets specially made for *Nabucco*! . . . and I'll have to patch up as best I can the most suitable material I find in the storeroom.'

I agreed to everything, as what was important to me was that the opera be given. A new poster came out on which finally I read: NABUCCO! . . .

I remember a comical scene I had with Solera a short time before: in the third act he had made a love duet between Fenena and Ismaele: I didn't like it because it cooled the action and seemed to me to diminish somewhat the Biblical grandeur that characterized the drama: one morning when Solera was at my house I mentioned this to him: but he wouldn't consider my remark, not so much because he didn't find it correct, but because it irritated him to redo what had once been done: both of us argued, presenting our reasons; I held fast and so did he. He asked me what I wanted in place of the duet, and I suggested then that he make a prophecy for the Prophet Zaccaria: he did not find the idea bad, and with ifs and buts, he said he would think it over and would write it later. That was not what I wanted, because I knew that many, many days would go by before Solera would make up his mind to write a verse. I locked the door, put the key in my pocket, and half-serious, half-joking, I said to Solera: 'You are not leaving here until you have written the prophecy: here's the Bible, you have the words all ready-made.' Solera, furious by nature, did not take this sally of mine well: a flash of wrath gleamed in his eyes; I had a nasty moment because the poet was a big man who could quickly have overpowered the stubborn maestro, but suddenly he sits at the table and a quarter of an hour later the prophecy was written! . . .

Finally, at the end of February 1842, the rehearsals began; and in twelve days from the day of the first piano rehearsal we reached the first performance, which took place on 9 March, having as interpreters Signora Strepponi and Signora Bellinzaghi, and the Signori Ronconi, Miraglia and Derivis.

With this opera it can truly be said that my artistic career began: and, though I had to battle against so many adversities, it is nevertheless certain that *Nabucco* was born under a lucky star, since even everything that could have been bad contributed instead in a favourable sense. In fact: I write an enraged letter to Merelli, it was therefore probable that the impresario would send the young maestro to the devil: the opposite happens.

The costumes, patched together in haste, proved splendid! . . .

Old sets, repaired by the painter Perroni, have an extraordinary effect: the first scene of the temple in particular produces such a great effect that the applause of the audience lasts for a good ten minutes! . . .

At the dress rehearsal we didn't even know how and when to have the band appear on the stage: Maestro Tutsch was at a loss: I indicate a bar to him: and at the first performance the band enters on stage so in time, on the crescendo, that the audience bursts into applause! . . .

. . . .

But it is not always a good thing to trust in lucky stars! . . . and experience showed me later how accurate is the proverb: *To trust is good, but not to trust is better!* . . .

FOL, 40–6

Plates

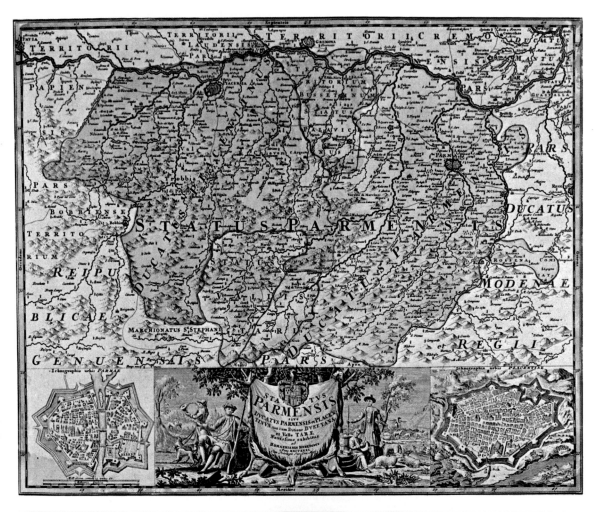

1 Map of the State of Parma, 18th c. Raccolta Bertarelli, Milan.

When Verdi was born, in 1813, Parma was under French domination. After the treaty of Vienna two years later, the State became, with Piacenza and Guastalla, a duchy ruled over by Marie-Louise, separated wife of Napoleon. Verdi's birthplace, the hamlet of Roncole, is near Busseto, north-west of the city of Parma.

2 Verdi's birthplace at Roncole. Painting by Achille Formis (1832–1906). Museo teatrale alla Scala, Milan.

Carlo Verdi, the composer's father, was a small landowner and the proprietor of the tavern at Roncole. Giuseppe was born in a bedroom on the upper floor of the house, where he lived until, at the age of ten, he moved to nearby Busseto to pursue his studies.

3 Baptismal register, 1813. San Michele Arcangelo, Roncole. The ledger, in Latin, records Verdi's baptism on 11 October 1813. The words 'born yesterday' have led to some confusion about the composer's birthday. At that time days were counted from one sunset to the next, so Verdi seems to have been born on 9 October – feast of San Donnino – the day he always celebrated.

4 Birth register, 1813. Comune, Busseto. At nine a.m. on 12 October, Carlo Verdi appeared at the Busseto registry office, to report the birth of his son. Because of the Napoleonic rule, the event is recorded in French. The composer's names are Joseph Fortunin François. His father's occupation is given as innkeeper (*aubergiste*); his mother's as spinner (*fileuse*).

5 Parish church of San Michele Arcangelo, Roncole. Photograph.
Verdi was baptized in this church, and here, according to legend, his mother saved his life in 1814, by hiding in the belfry with her son in her arms, when Russian troops invaded the area, pillaging and killing.

6 Parish church of San Michele Arcangelo, Roncole. Interior. Photograph.
Verdi received his early musical instruction on the organ of San Michele (visible at left in the photograph). Later he served as organist, and in the final year of his life he arranged for the instrument to be repaired.

prete che domandava le ampolline. La domanda fu ripetuta un paio di volte, ma invano; allora il celebrante, che non era veramente un esemplare di pazienza, si voltò, diè de uno spintone al piccolo servente e lo mandò ruzzolone in un canto. Il fanciullo non ebbe che una pèsca alla fronte, ma fu lì per lì stordito dal colpo, svenne, e fu necessario spruzzargli d'acqua la testa, per

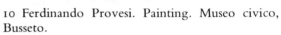

10 Ferdinando Provesi. Painting. Museo civico, Busseto.
Verdi's music teacher in Busseto, Provesi (1770–1833) was also the town organist and a prolific professional composer. He died before his gifted pupil's career had begun.

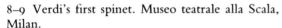

8–9 Verdi's first spinet. Museo teatrale alla Scala, Milan.
At Giuseppe's insistence, his father encouraged his musical instruction and, in 1820 or 1821, bought the boy this primitive spinet. Verdi kept it with him all his life (it was in his Villa Sant'Agata at his death), and bequeathed it to the Casa di Riposo, the home for needy musicians he had founded.

11 Pietro Seletti. Painting. Museo civico, Busseto.
Besides his musical instruction, Verdi studied at the Ginnasio, the Busseto high school, where his professor of Italian was the distinguished Don Pietro Seletti. Verdi also studied Latin, humanities and rhetoric, receiving the traditional classical education of his time.

<7 Verdi's childhood misadventure as an altar-boy. Caricatures and text by Melchiorre Delfico. Collezione Gallini, Milan.
Verdi's great friend, the Neapolitan caricaturist Melchiorre Delfico (1825–95), left an incomplete, handwritten, illustrated biography of the composer, still unpublished. This page narrates a favourite story of how the young Giuseppe, enchanted by the sound of the organ, forgot his duties in serving Mass and was reprimanded by a swift kick from the celebrant. The child had to be brought round with sprinkled water, then bandaged.

12 House of Antonio Barezzi. Busseto. Photograph.
During his first years in Busseto, Verdi lodged with a cobbler nicknamed Pugnatta, a native of Roncole. Then, in 1831, he went to live in the home of Antonio Barezzi (1787–1867), a well-to-do local merchant and amateur musician. The Barezzi house is on the main square of the town.

13 Antonio Barezzi. Photograph. Istituto di studi verdiani, Parma.
Barezzi – here seen in later life – allowed his young daughter Margherita to take music-lessons from Verdi, who was eventually to marry her. After her early death, Verdi continued to regard Barezzi as a second father; in fact, they were closer than Verdi and his real father were.

(*Opposite*)

16 Rocca di Busseto. Painting by Marchesi. Museo teatrale alla Scala, Milan.
Barezzi's house faced, at the opposite end of the long square, the Rocca – or castle – of Busseto, a handsome thirteenth-century fort, altered in the Cinquecento and again in the nineteenth century. The building houses the city offices and, in one wing, the Teatro Verdi, constructed in 1868 despite the composer's fierce objections. A monument to Verdi was erected in the square in 1913 (accidentally, no doubt, but aptly, Verdi turns his back on the theatre).

14 Certificate of Verdi's studies from his teacher Provesi. Monte di credito su pegno, Busseto.

It soon became clear that Verdi's talents required a kind of advanced instruction not available in Busseto. At the end of 1831, he began thinking of Milan. For this move, he needed financial support, and his admiring teacher gave him a recommendation, mentioning his exceptional talent (*genio singolare*). This document, by the way, is not in Provesi's hand. It is a copy by Giuseppe Demaldè, made in the 1840s or 1850s when he was collecting notes for a biography of Verdi.

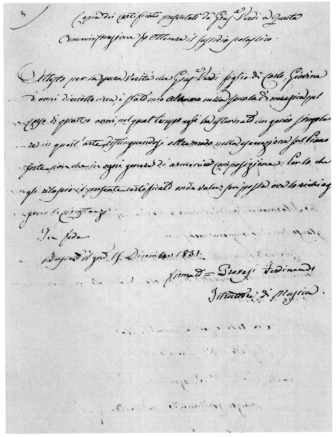

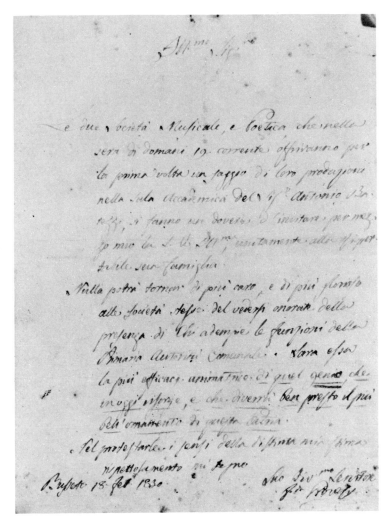

15 Provesi invites the mayor of Busseto to a concert, 1830. Museo civico, Busseto.

Meanwhile, Verdi's gifts had been amply recognized (and exploited) by the local Società musicale, the Filarmonici, of which Barezzi was a leading member. To one of their concerts, Provesi invited the city's mayor, referring to Verdi's nascent genius.

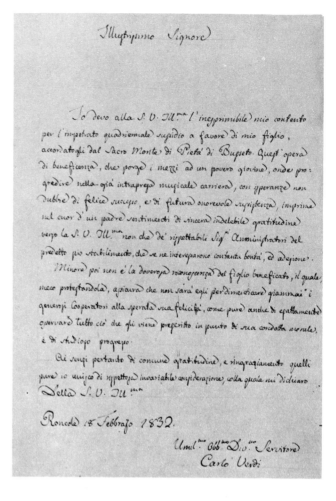

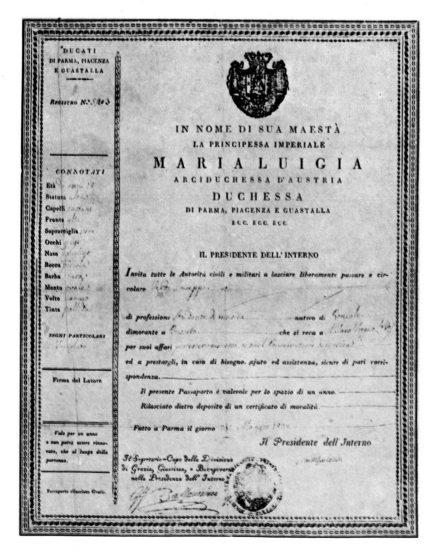

17 Monte di pietà (now Monte di credito su pegno), Busseto. Interior. Photograph.
A local charitable organization, the Monte di pietà, earning its income by pawnbroking, provided the city with an excellent free public library (still in operation) and offered a certain number of scholarships for deserving youths. Verdi applied for one and was eventually granted it.

18 Letter from Carlo Verdi, 1832. Monte di credito su pegno, Busseto.
Verdi's father (whom certain careless biographers have called illiterate) expressed his thanks to the head of the Monte di pietà in this carefully written letter of 18 February 1832.

19 Verdi's first passport, 1832, Museo civico, Busseto.
Finally, on 22 May 1832, Verdi was issued a passport by the government of Marie-Louise (Maria Luigia), allowing him to travel from the Duchy of Parma to neighbouring Lombardy, then under Austrian rule. The document supplies a contemporary physical description of the eighteen-year-old musician: Hair – brown; eyes – grey; forehead – high [. . .] distinguishing features – pock-marked.

20 Milan, Piazza del Duomo. Print, c. 1840. Raccolta Bertarelli, Milan.
Centre of the city's religious life, the Duomo, when Verdi first saw it in the 1830s, was still incomplete.

21 Milan, Teatro alla Scala. Painting by Angelo Inganni (1807–80). Museo teatrale alla Scala, Milan.
Social life centred on La Scala, whose exterior – despite Second World War damage – has changed little in the past century and a half.

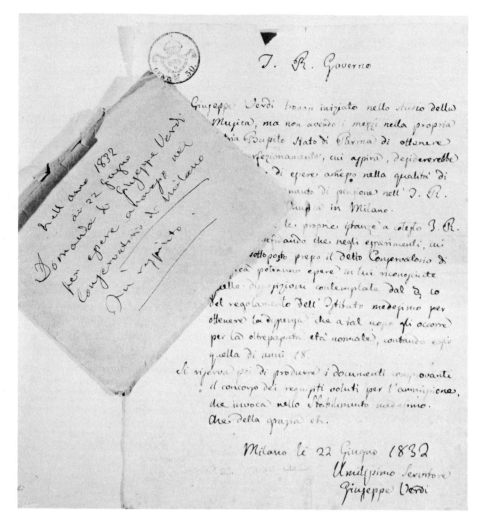

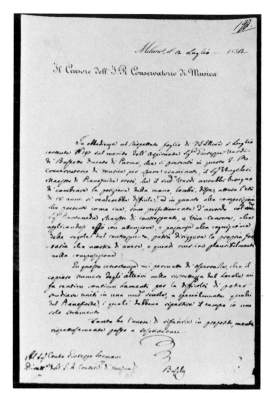

22 Verdi's application for admission to the Milan Conservatory, 1832. Villa Sant'Agata, Busseto.
Shortly after his arrival in Milan, Verdi submitted an application to the Conservatory. He was given entrance examinations, but was rejected for several reasons: he was over-age, he was a foreigner, there were few vacancies in the school, and the examiners disapproved of the way he played the piano. Years later, the application was returned to him, but the refusal still rankled. He wrote on the envelope: *Fui respinto* ('I was rejected').

23 Letter of Francesco Basily to Count Sormani Andreani, 1832. Conservatorio 'G. Verdi', Milan.
Francesco Basily, who headed the examining committee, wrote on 2 July 1832 to Count Giuseppe Sormani Andreani, the director of the Conservatory, explaining the rejection of Verdi and, at the same time, recognizing the young man's possibility of future success as a composer.

24 Alessandro Rolla. Engraving. Raccolta Bertarelli, Milan.
A friend of Provesi's, Alessandro Rolla (1757–1841) had been from 1782 till 1802 concertmaster of the ducal orchestra of Parma, where Paganini had studied with him. After that he was in Milan, where in 1832 he was conductor at La Scala, professor at the Conservatory, and a respected composer. Though even his considerable influence was not enough to win Verdi admission to the Conservatory, he gave the young man good advice and was helpful in the selection of Verdi's private teacher, Vincenzo Lavigna (1776–1836).

25 Giuseppe Seletti. Lithograph. Museo civico, Busseto.

Nephew of Verdi's teacher in Busseto, Giuseppe Seletti was also a teacher, at the Ginnasio di Santa Marta in Milan. He was a close friend of the Barezzi family and, out of friendship for them, he accepted the young Verdi as a lodger.

26 Seletti's house, Milan. Photograph. Istituto di studi verdiani, Parma.

Seletti lived in the Via Santa Marta (almost completely destroyed in 1943), not far from La Scala. Verdi, from his landlord's point of view, was a far from ideal tenant, and eventually Seletti insisted that Verdi move elsewhere.

27 Seletti's list of expenditures for Verdi, 1832. Museo teatrale alla Scala, Milan.

At Barezzi's request, Seletti looked after Verdi's day-to-day needs, paying for his lessons and for the postage on his letters home, and even buying clothes for him. Lavigna received 4 Austrian lire per lesson.

28 Announcement of competition for the post of Maestro di Musica, Busseto, 1836.

The tale of Verdi's appointment as Maestro di musica in Busseto is long, complex, and, today, of only moderate interest. After several years of bitter wrangling in the town, public pressure forced the mayor to announce a competition for the post at the beginning of 1836. The mayor makes his position clear by saying that he is carrying out orders from above (*in eseguimento degli ordini superiori*).

29 Certificate by Lavigna of Verdi's studies in Milan, 1834. Monte di credito su pegno, Busseto.

In presenting his application for the Busseto post, Verdi submitted a declaration from his teacher Lavigna, who praised not only the young man's musical talent, but also his 'good moral conduct' (*morigerata condotta*). Lavigna also told a helpful lie, saying Verdi had begun his studies in June 1832; the actual date was August.

30 Chapel in the Chiesa Collegiata di San Bartolomeo, Busseto. Photograph.

As a result of his appointment, Verdi was able to marry Margherita Barezzi. The wedding took place on 4 May 1836 in the little Cappella della SS. Trinità, part of the Chiesa Collegiata di San Bartolomeo, a few steps from Barezzi's house.

31–32 Verdi as a young man. Pencil drawing by Stefano Barezzi. Private collection, Busseto.

Perhaps on the occasion of Verdi's marriage in 1836, his portrait was drawn by Stefano Barezzi, brother of Antonio and a successful painter (he discovered a system for detaching frescoes from walls, and worked on one of the many restorations of Leonardo's *Last Supper* in Milan). He signed the drawing on the back.

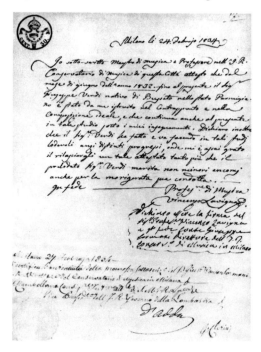

33 Margherita Barezzi. Painting. Museo teatrale alla Scala, Milan.

Stefano Barezzi also made a companion pencil drawing, now lost, of his niece. After her death, this oil portrait was painted from it.

34 Marriage register, 1836. Chiesa Collegiata di San Bartolomeo, Busseto.

Verdi's marriage to Margherita is recorded on the right-hand page.

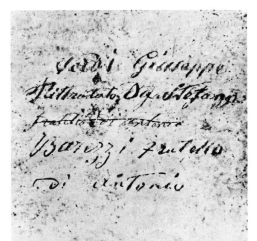

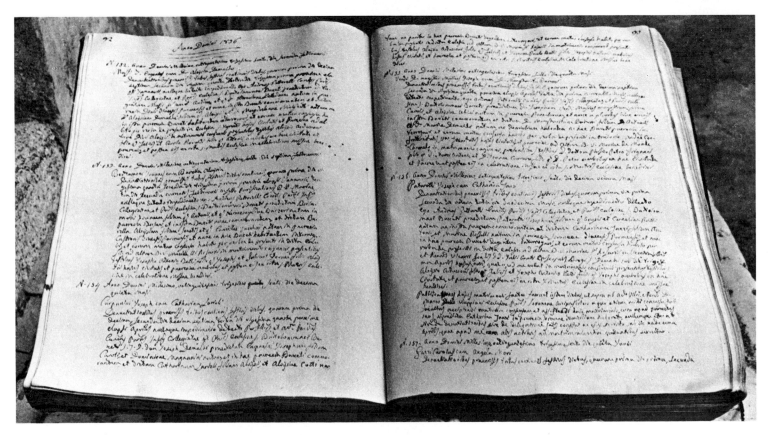

35–36 Verdi, *Scena lirica*, 'Io la vidi'. Autograph. Pierpont Morgan Library, Mary Flagler Cary music collection, New York.

These are the first two pages of a very early Verdi work, his earliest surviving manuscript. Though it is headed 'aria', it is a fully developed operatic scena, for tenor and bass. The piece cannot be dated definitely, but probably belongs to the mid 1830s, before Verdi returned to Milan, to settle there with Margherita.

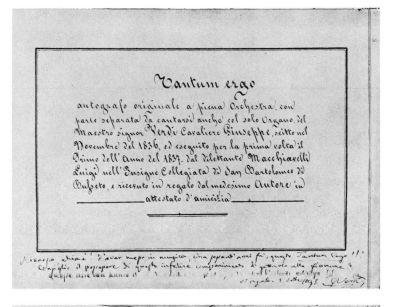

37 Expense-sheet by Antonio Barezzi, 1835. Museo teatrale alla Scala, Milan.

The meticulous Barezzi kept careful accounts, not only in his business, but also in his private life. This is a list of his expenses during a journey to Milan in 1835 to see Verdi. His passion for the theatre is evident. He journeyed by way of Lodi, where he stopped and attended a performance (4 Austrian lire). And in Milan he went to La Scala twice, and to the Teatro Carcano and the Teatro della Canobbiana.

38–40 Verdi, *Tantum ergo*. Title-page and first two pages of autograph, 1836. Museo teatrale alla Scala, Milan.

From Verdi's period as Maestro di musica in Busseto, this *Tantum ergo* survives. Written in November 1836, it was first performed on New Year's Day 1837. Many years later, in 1893, the owner of the autograph asked Verdi to authenticate it. He did so, writing at the foot of the elegantly penned title-page, 'I admit, alas, to having set to music, about sixty years ago, this *Tantum ergo*!!! I advise the owner of this unhappy composition to throw it into the fire. These notes have not the slightest musical value, nor any shadow of religious hue.'

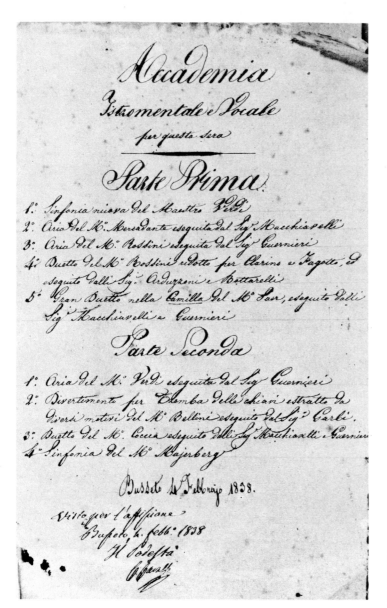

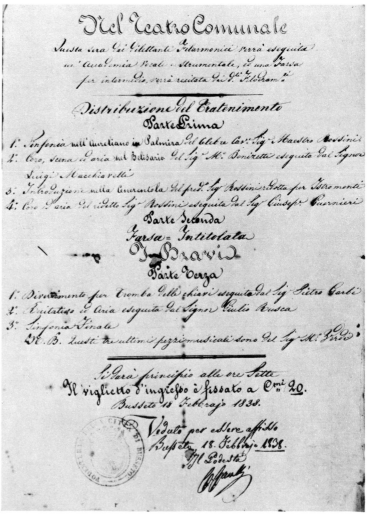

41–44 Programmes of concerts given by the Filarmonici in Busseto, 1838. Museo civico, Busseto.

The programmes of the Filarmonici, while Verdi was their director, give an indication of the musical taste of the time. There are works by Mercadante, Rossini, Paër, Coccia, Meyerbeer, Pavesi. There are also pieces by Verdi (all presumably lost), including a Capriccio for horn, an Introduction and variations for bassoon, and a *duetto buffo*. The Filarmonici were also amateur actors. One programme included *La Soffitta degli Artisti* (*La Mansarde des Artistes*, 1824), a one-act farce by Scribe (see ill. 146), who was later to be Verdi's librettist.

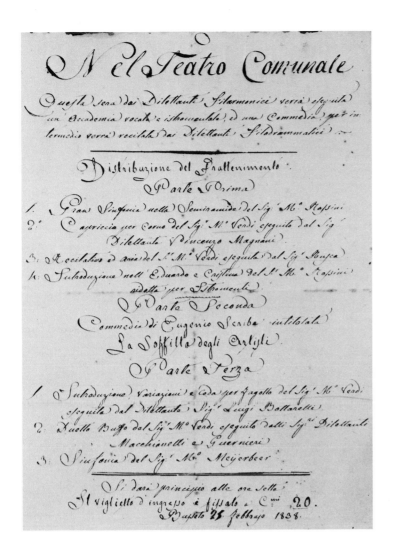

45 Verdi's resignation as Maestro di musica, 1838. Museo civico, Busseto.

At the end of October 1838, though his contract still had some months to run, Verdi submitted his resignation to the mayor, who accepted it. Verdi's letter is superficially deferential, but clearly bitter. He says, at one point, 'The need to earn enough to nourish my family forces me to seek elsewhere that which I cannot have in my homeland.'

46 Solemn entry of Ferdinand I into Milan, 1838. Raccolta Bertarelli, Milan.
Even before the acceptance of his resignation, Verdi had gone to Milan, where he hoped to have an opera produced. His arrival coincided with that of Emperor Ferdinand I of Austria, who had come to have himself crowned King of Lombardy-Venetia. Verdi and Margherita witnessed the parades, reviews, and other festivities, which he described in a letter as an uproar (*bordello*).

47–48 Verdi, *Notturno* for soprano, tenor, bass, with flute obbligato, 1838. Museo teatrale alla Scala, Milan.
Written in 1838, published the following year, this vocal work was, exceptionally, reviewed in the *Gazzetta privilegiata di Milano* in glowing terms: 'a new work that is an inspiration, an enchantment of delicate feeling'.

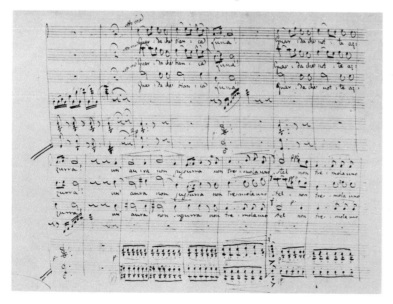

49 Bartolomeo Merelli. Painting. Museo teatrale alla Scala, Milan.

Merelli (1793–1879) was one of the most important Italian impresarios during the early years of Verdi's career. His influence extended also to Vienna, Paris, London, and Berlin. At La Scala, which he directed from 1836 to 1850 (and again in 1861–63), he presented Verdi's first operas. Later the composer resented Merelli's skimping on productions, and for many years Verdi refused to have his new works given at the theatre.

50 Giuseppina Strepponi in the title role of Paisiello's *Nina, o sia La pazza per amore*. Engraving. Museo teatrale alla Scala, Milan.

Giuseppina Strepponi (1815–97) made her debut in 1834. In 1839, she was engaged at La Scala, where she sang the leading role in Donizetti's *Lucia di Lammermoor, Elisir d'amore* and *Pia de' Tolomei*, and in Bellini's *I puritani*. Her enthusiasm for Verdi's music led Merelli to produce *Oberto*, the composer's first staged opera. Later she created the role of Abigaille in his *Nabucco*, and she was eventually to become his second wife.

51 Verdi, *Sei romanze*. Cover of sheet music, 1838.

Verdi's first published work was this collection of six songs, composed in Busseto. They include two settings from Goethe's *Faust*, translated by the composer's Busseto friend, the distinguished doctor Luigi Balestra (1808–63), his schoolmate at the Ginnasio. The publisher of the album, Giovanni Canti, also brought out Verdi's *Notturno*.

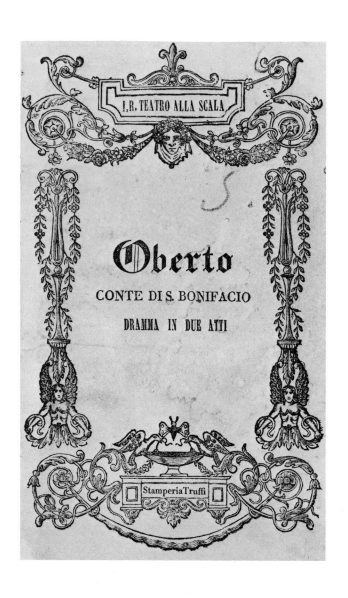

52 Libretto of *Oberto, conte di San Bonifacio*. Title-page, 1839. Conservatorio 'G. Verdi', Milan.
Verdi's *Oberto* was presented at La Scala on 17 November 1839 with encouraging success. The rights to the score were bought – for the handsome sum of 2000 Austrian lire – by the firm of Ricordi.

53 Giovanni Ricordi. Drawing by Bignami. Museo teatrale alla Scala, Milan.
Giovanni Ricordi (1785–1853) was the founder of the music-publishing firm which still bears his name and flourishes today. Ricordi – like his son Tito (1811–88) and his grandson Giulio (1840–1912) – not only published Verdi's operas, but also fostered their production and diffusion.

55 Funeral expenses of Margherita Verdi, 1840. Museo teatrale alla Scala, Milan.
Margherita Barezzi Verdi died on 18 June 1840, eight months after the premiere of *Oberto*, while Verdi was composing his comic opera *Un giorno di regno*. Her funeral, 'private, second-class, solemn' – according to the bill above – cost 522.12 Milanese lire.

< 54 *Oberto*. Sketch for a set design by Giuseppe Bertoja, 1840. Biblioteca Correr, Venice.
From 1831 to his death over forty years later, Giuseppe Bertoja (1808–73) was the leading designer at the Teatro La Fenice in Venice. He also worked for other theatres; and for the carnival season of 1840 at the Teatro Regio, Turin, he designed *Oberto*, shortly after the opera's success at La Scala.

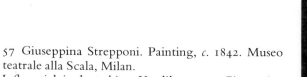

56 Giorgio Ronconi, Erminia Frezzolini, Antonio Poggi. Engraving. Raccolta Bertarelli, Milan.

The baritone Giorgio Ronconi (1810–90) created the title role in Verdi's third opera *Nabucco* in 1842 and was one of Verdi's favourite singers. Other early Verdi interpreters were the soprano Erminia Frezzolini (1818–84), who sang in the premieres of *I lombardi*, 1843, and *Giovanna d'Arco*, 1845, and her first husband, the tenor Antonio Poggi (the first Carlo in *Giovanna d'Arco*).

57 Giuseppina Strepponi. Painting, *c.* 1842. Museo teatrale alla Scala, Milan.

Influential in launching Verdi's career, Giuseppina Strepponi was already nearing the end of her own professional life when she sang Abigaille in *Nabucco*, a taxing role unsuited to her voice. Nevertheless, the opera meant a great deal to her and she was painted with its score in her hands.

58 Verdi, *Nabucco*, 'Va, pensiero'. Autograph score, 1842. Archivio storico Ricordi, Milan.
At the opening of *Nabucco* (then bearing the tongue-twisting title *Nabucodonosor*) on 9 March 1842, the chorus 'Va, pensiero' aroused great enthusiasm, for patriotic as well as musical reasons. It has remained the best-known number from the opera and one of Verdi's most beloved compositions. Toscanini conducted it at Verdi's burial.

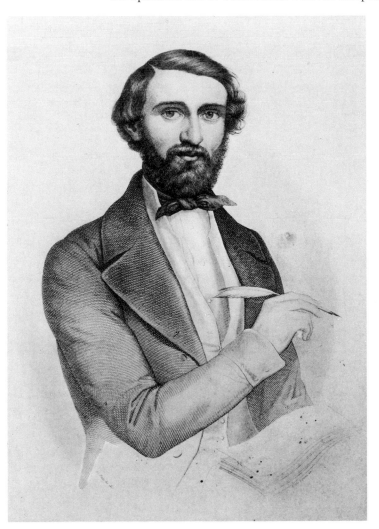

59 Verdi at the time of *Nabucco*. Engraving, 1842. Museo teatrale alla Scala, Milan.
With *Nabucco*, Verdi became immediately, widely known, and the long series of his portraits began. Many of these show him calmly holding pen in hand, though composing for him was a far from serene activity.

60 Temistocle Solera. Photograph. Conservatorio 'G. Verdi', Milan.
Solera (1815–78), librettist of *Nabucco* and of other early Verdi operas, was also a composer, patriot, and – later in life – a secret agent. He and Verdi quarrelled at the time of *Attila* (1846), when Solera failed to provide the verses of the last act in time. Verdi never forgave him.

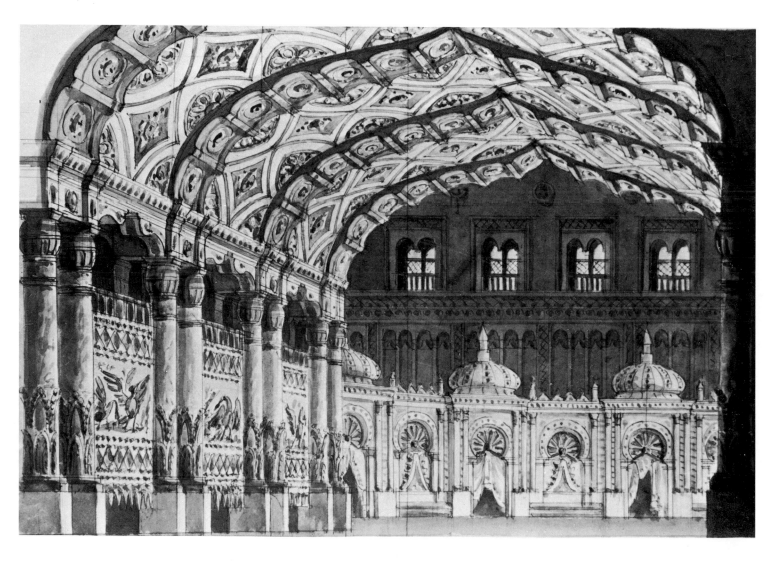

61–63 *I lombardi alla prima crociata*. View of Jerusalem (left, above); Harem scene (left, below); Hermit's cave (above); set designs by Giuseppe Bertoja. Biblioteca Correr, Venice.

Verdi's fourth opera, *I lombardi alla prima crociata*, was first given at La Scala on 11 February 1843, repeating the success of *Nabucco*, which it resembles in many ways. It soon went to other theatres, including the Teatro Regio, Turin, for which production Bertoja designed these sets.

64 Giuseppina Strepponi. Painting. Museo teatrale alla Scala, Milan.

After the success of *I lombardi* at La Scala, Verdi went to Vienna, where *Nabucco* was given, then to Parma, where the same opera was to be performed, again with Strepponi as Abigaille. Verdi remained in Parma about six weeks. This unusually long stay has led biographers to believe that the intimate relationship between the composer and the singer began at this time.

65 Verdi. Painting, c. 1843. Museo teatrale alla Scala, Milan.

Verdi was often described – and described himself – as a 'bear' (*orso*). This early portrait conveys something of the youthful intensity that drove him, in the 1840s, to produce operas at a relentless pace, which he regularly paid for with bouts of ill-health.

66 Sonnet by Luigi Balestra. Autograph, 1843. Monte di credito su pegna, Busseto.

If Milan lionized Verdi, Busseto – or at least his friends there – quickly began the process of idolization. The amateur poet Balestra composed a 'physical and moral portrait of Maestro Giuseppe Verdi', in sonnet form. Balestra says the composer's hair and beard are 'blond', a poetic licence contradicting both Verdi's passport and all paintings of him.

67 Carlo Tenca. Engraving. Museo del Risorgimento, Milan.

68 Countess Emilia Morosini. Painting by Francesco Hayez. Pinacoteca Ambrosiana, Milan.

69 Countess Clarina Maffei. Photograph of painting. Museo del Risorgimento, Milan.

70 Andrea Maffei. Engraving. Raccolta Bertarelli, Milan.

In the mid 1840s the successful young Verdi frequented the famous Milanese salon of Countess Clarina Maffei, who became a life-long, devoted friend. Other Milanese friendships dating from this period were those with Countess Emilia Morosini, with the poet and translator Andrea Maffei, soon to be separated from his wife Clarina, and with her lover, the patriot and writer Carlo Tenca.

71–72 Teatro La Fenice, Venice. Gondola entrance (above) and interior (below). Engravings.

Verdi's first opera written for a theatre other than La Scala was his fifth work, *Ernani*, commissioned by La Fenice in Venice. Apart from some minor modifications, the theatre today is much as Verdi saw it when he arrived in Venice in December 1843. The premiere of *Ernani* took place on 9 March 1844.

73 Francesco Maria Piave. Engraving. Archivio storico Ricordi, Milan.
Piave (1810–76), making his theatre debut, supplied the libretto for *Ernani* (1844), thus initiating a collaboration with the composer which continued, through *La forza del destino*, until the poet was incapacitated by his final illness. Piave eventually moved to Milan, where he acted as stage-director at La Scala.

74 Verdi, *c.* 1844. Photograph. Museo teatrale alla Scala, Milan.
This photograph – dating from the early days of their friendship – was given to Piave by Verdi. Incidentally, Verdi seems to have begun parting his hair on the left by now, a change from his earlier portraits.

75 Sophie Loewe. Portrait.
The German-born soprano Sophie (or Sofia) Loewe (1816–66) was already internationally famous when she created the role of Elvira in *Ernani* in 1844. Her unbridled character equalled her artistic accomplishments (she was blamed, unjustly, for causing Donizetti's insanity). She was the first Odabella in Verdi's *Attila* (1846). In 1848 she married a prince of Liechtenstein and retired from the stage.

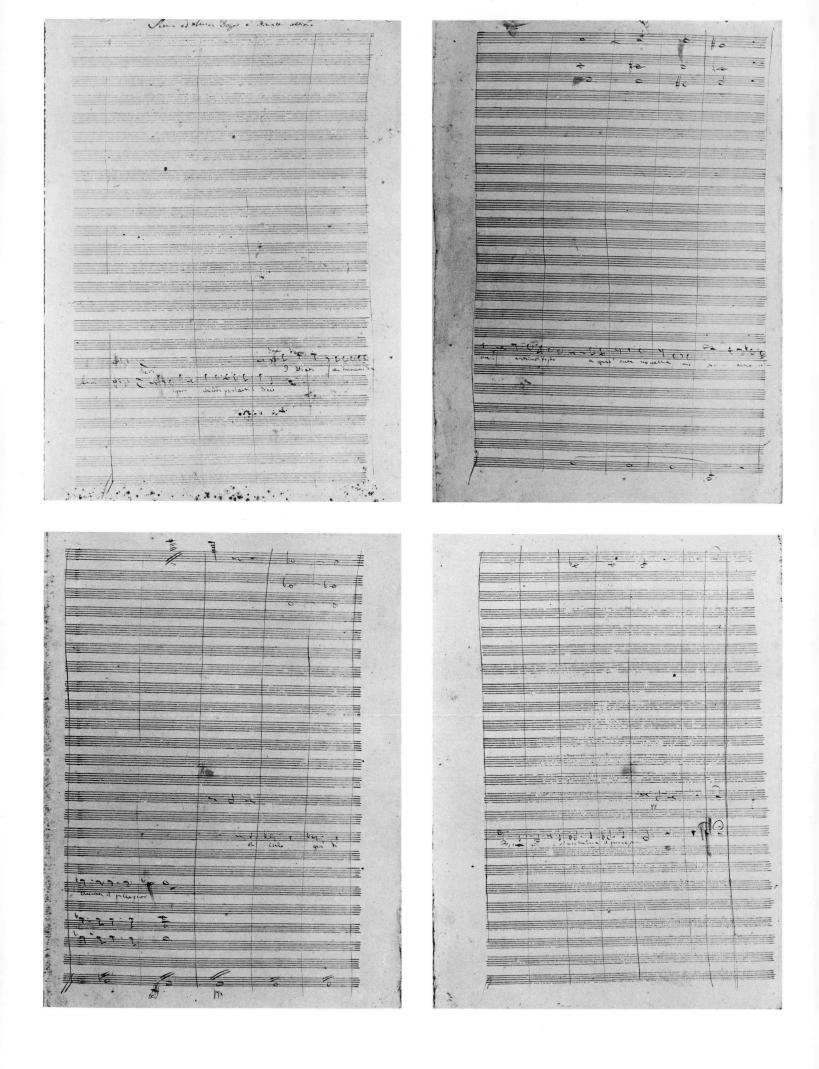

76–79 Verdi, *I due Foscari*. Autograph sketch, 1844. Museo civico, Busseto.
Verdi's sketches for a part of the final scene of the opera. These few pages – as the Italian musicologist Pierluigi Petrobelli, who discussed them for the first time, has indicated – give an insight into Verdi's compositional process at the time. Though the orchestration is incomplete, the musical content of the dramatic situation is present in the vocal line. Verdi's sketches, in other words, were written in a kind of personal shorthand.

80 *The Two Foscari*. Painting by Francesco Hayez, 1844. Galleria d'arte moderna, Florence.
Painted in the year of Verdi's opera, this picture suggests how, in the Risorgimento period, opera, the visual arts, and literature were closely interrelated, often dealing with the same subjects. Hayez (1791–1882) was a leading Italian artist of his time, and Verdi knew him. The painter made several versions of this subject, one (executed in 1842–43) for Andrea Maffei, another for the Emperor Ferdinand of Austria.

81 Verdi with the score of *I due Foscari*. Engraving, 1844. William Weaver Collection, Monte San Savino (AR).
I due Foscari was first performed on 3 November 1844 (Rome, Teatro Argentina). Verdi is seen here holding the score. As Verdi's new operas appeared, new portraits followed. Often the face and figure remained much the same, while the score being held was brought up to date.

GIUSEPPE VERDI

82–83 *Giovanna d'Arco*. Set designs by Giuseppe Bertoja, 1845. Biblioteca Correr, Venice.
After its premiere at La Scala on 15 February 1845, Verdi's *Giovanna d'Arco* was staged at La Fenice in Venice, where Bertoja designed a handsome forest (below) for Act I and a square with the cathedral of Reims for Act II (above).

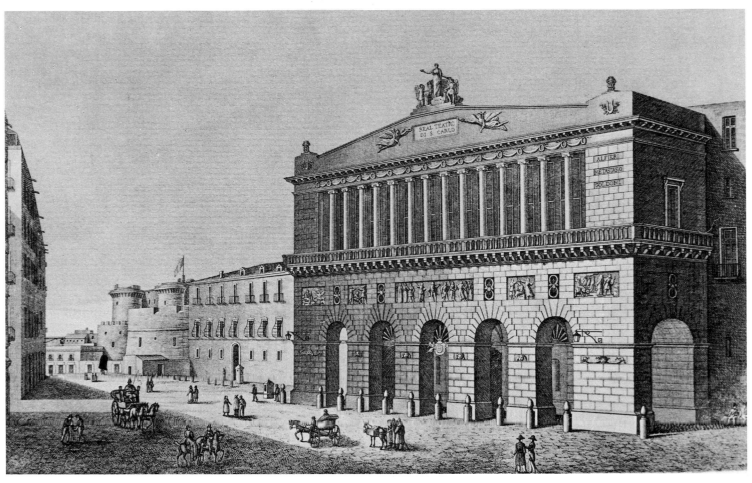

84 Teatro San Carlo, Naples. Engraving.
For the production of his *Alzira* in the summer of 1845, Verdi made the first of numerous journeys to Naples, where the opera was given on 12 August of that year at the San Carlo. During his stay in the city Verdi formed lasting friendships, especially in the lively artistic world.

85 Salvatore Cammarano. Coloured lithograph. Villa Sant'Agata, Busseto.
The librettist Salvatore Cammarano (1801–52) came from a remarkable family of actors, painters, musicians, writers. His first success in the theatre was the libretto for Donizetti's *Lucia di Lammermoor* in 1835. Verdi had great respect for Cammarano's knowledge of the theatre, collaborated with him on several operas, and deeply mourned his premature death.

86 Gaetano Fraschini. Engraving. Raccolta Bertarelli, Milan.
Fraschini (1816–87) sang at the Teatro San Carlo from 1840 to 1848, specializing in the Verdi repertory. He created the role of Zamoro in *Alzira*, 1845, and later took part in the first productions of *Il corsaro*, 1848, *La battaglia di Legnano*, 1849, *Stiffelio*, 1850, and *Un ballo in maschera*, 1859. Verdi wrote of him in 1863: 'I love and respect Fraschini very much.' Fraschini's voice retained its power and quality for a remarkably long time, and Verdi considered him as Radamès for the first *Aida* as late as 1871.

87 Verdi. Engraving by Focosi. Albergo due Foscari, Busseto.
Focosi was one of the most popular illustrators of the time and engraved several portraits of Verdi during the early years of his fame.

88 Verdi, *Attila*, Prologue, scene 1. Autograph sketch, 1846. Bibliothèque Nationale, Paris.
Rediscovered by the English musicologist Julian Budden and discussed in his masterly book on Verdi's operas, this autograph shows that, unusually for his Italian operas, Verdi required four trumpets instead of the customary two for this powerful scene.

89–90 *Attila*. Set designs by Giuseppe Bertoja, 1846. Biblioteca Correr, Venice.
The second Verdi opera commissioned by La Fenice, *Attila* had its premiere there on 17 March 1846. Once again the designer of the sets was Bertoja.

91 Teatro della Pergola, Florence. Istituto di studi verdiani, Parma.
Inaugurated in 1656 and rebuilt on various occasions, the Teatro della Pergola was, throughout the nineteenth century, the major opera house in Florence and a leading Italian theatre. Alessandro Lanari (1790–1862) was its innovative impresario in the 1830s and 1840s, producing new works by Donizetti, Meyerbeer, and – in 1847 – Verdi, with *Macbeth*.

92 *Macbeth*. Frontispiece of first edition, 1847.
Verdi's first encounter with Shakespeare, an author he deeply loved, *Macbeth* was a work to which the composer attached particular importance. He devoted long hours to rehearsing the first production and, nearly two decades later, chose to revise it for a production in Paris.

MARIANNA BARBIERI-NINI

93 Marianna Barbieri-Nini. Engraving. Raccolta Bertarelli, Milan.

Originally the role of Lady Macbeth was to have been sung by Sophie Loewe, but, indisposed, she was replaced by the Florentine Marianna Barbieri-Nini (1820–87), who had already created the role of Lucrezia in Verdi's *I due Foscari*. Remarkably and notoriously ugly, the soprano triumphed over her physical defects thanks to her extraordinary gifts as actress and musician. Later she was the first Gulnara in Verdi's *Il corsaro* (Trieste, 1848). She left lively reminiscences of the composer.

95 Felice Varesi. Bust by Giovanni Dupré, *c*. 1847 (destroyed).

Varesi (1813–89) was the successor of Ronconi in the line of Verdi baritones. He was equally gifted as actor and singer and, after his Macbeth, created the roles of Rigoletto in 1851 and Germont in *La traviata,* 1853. This bust, probably made at the time of *Macbeth* by the sculptor Dupré, who worked in Florence, was destroyed during the second World War. Photograph courtesy of Varesi's great-grand-daughter Contessa Niccolai Gamba.

94 Verdi. Engraving. Raccolta Bertarelli, Milan.

Negli anni tuoi più verdi onor le chiome
D'un lauro che vivrà quanto il tuo nome.

96 Giovanni Dupré in later life. Photograph Mansell-Brogi.

Dupré (1817–82), though born in Siena, worked chiefly in Florence, where he was influenced by the older sculptor Lorenzo Bartolini, his senior by some forty years. In 1879 Dupré published his memoirs, telling briefly of Verdi's stay in Florence.

97 Verdi's right hand. Marble sculpture by Dupré. Villa Sant'Agata, Busseto.

During Verdi's weeks in Florence, Dupré carved his right hand (since Verdi did not have the time – or the desire – to sit for a portrait bust).

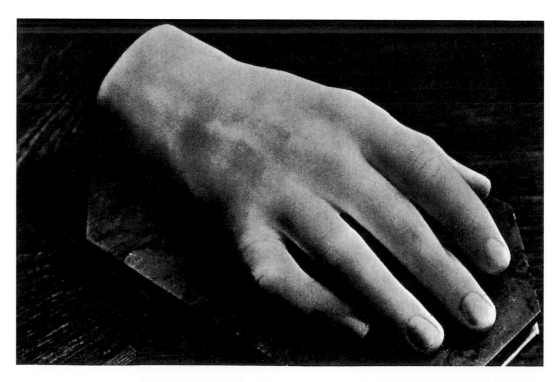

GINO CAPPONI

98 Gino Capponi. Engraving. Raccolta Bertarelli, Milan.
Florence in 1847 was a centre of Italian intellectual life, thanks
also to the easy-going, broad-minded rule of the Grand Duke.
Verdi moved there in artistic and literary circles, meeting such
people as the blind patriot and historian Gino Capponi
(1792–1876), leader of the Tuscan liberals.

99 Giuseppe Giusti. Engraving. Raccolta Bertarelli, Milan.
The poet Giusti (1809–50) was another Florentine friend of
Verdi's. In a famous poem, Sant' Ambrogio, Giusti referred to the
chorus from I lombardi, 'O Signore, dal tetto natio', saying it had
'stirred and intoxicated so many breasts'. After Macbeth, 1847,
the poet wrote to Verdi advising him to abandon such exotic
subjects and return to his patriotic themes.

100 Giuseppe Montanelli. Painting by Ary Scheffer. Galleria
d'arte moderna, Florence.
Montanelli (1813–62) was another Florentine patriot, friend of
Verdi's. They may have met at the time of Macbeth or later, in
Paris, during Montanelli's exile. Early in 1857 he made some
revisions of Piave's libretto for Simon Boccanegra, at the request
of Verdi, who then adopted most of Montanelli's verses. The
Dutch painter Ary Scheffer (1795–1858) worked chiefly in Paris
and probably painted this portrait there.

101 London in the mid 19th c. From Gustave Doré's *London*, 1872.

Verdi's first work to be given its premiere outside Italy was *I masnadieri*, performed in London at Her Majesty's Theatre on 22 July 1847. Verdi made the long journey to England in order to rehearse the work, which enjoyed only a moderate success, despite a cast that included Jenny Lind. London made a deep, if mixed, impression on the composer, who described the city's bustle in graphic letters home.

102 Her Majesty's Theatre, Royal Box, 1847. Mander and Mitchenson Collection, London.

The critical reception of *I masnadieri* was tepid; but its opening was a social triumph. The Queen and the Prince Consort were prominent in the royal box (it seems unlikely that there were Beefeaters actually standing on the stage below them). Also present on the gala occasion were the Duke of Wellington and Louis Napoleon. Verdi himself conducted.

(Opposite)
103–04 Scenes from *I masnadieri*, 1847. Engravings. Mander and Mitchenson Collection, London.

The *Illustrated London News* from which these engravings are taken had special praise for the opera's production and cast: 'such performances as these [...] are indeed calculated to raise the character of the British nation for an enlightened and munificent patronage of the fine arts. [...] The Opera itself is an essentially dramatic work. Of pieces which would make an effect in a drawing-room, there are few [...]; but in return, this professes more nicety of thought and conception, and the immense superiority of the *libretto* over that of any other opera Verdi has written, gives great advantage in its favour.'

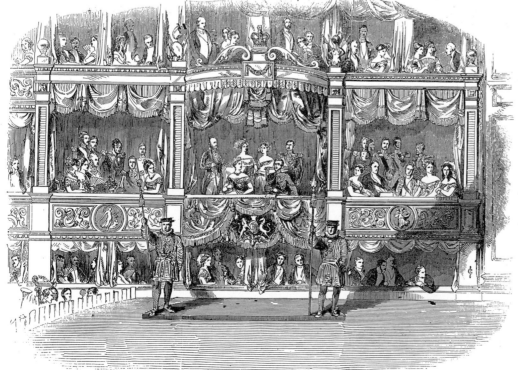

THE ROYAL BOX.

MDLLE. JENNY LIND.   SIG. LABLACHE.

VERDI'S NEW OPERA "I MASNADIERI," AT HER MAJESTY'S THEATRE.—SCENE VI.

IG. GARDONI.   MDLLE. JENNY LIND.   SIG. LABLACHE.

VERDI'S "I MASNADIERI"—SCENE LAST.

105–06 Contract with Paris Opéra for *Jérusalem*, 1847. Soria Collection, New York.

Verdi's contract with Paris for the transformation of *I lombardi* into *Jérusalem* specifies that he will add ballet music as well as a scene and air for the tenor Duprez. Verdi received a payment of 5000 francs for the opera, which – translated back into Italian as *Gerusalemme* – he re-sold to Ricordi for another 8000 francs.

107 Paris Opéra, interior. Engraving. Collection Viollet, Paris.

The Paris Opéra in the decades between 1830 and 1870 was the goal of every composer, French and foreign. After Rossini, Bellini, and Donizetti, it was natural for Verdi to aim at success there. His refashioning of *I lombardi* was thorough and improving, but the work – presented on 26 November 1847 – was not warmly received.

108 Paris Opéra, exterior. Engraving, 1844.

109 *Jérusalem*, Act III finale. Engraving, 1847. Raccolta Bertarelli, Milan.
Though the press gave Verdi's music a perfunctory reception, there was unanimous praise for the sumptuous production.

Théâtre de l'Académie royale de musique. — *Jérusalem*, acte 3e, scène dernière. — Décoration de M. Cambon.
Gaston, M. Duprez ; le légat, M. Brémond ; un écuyer, M. Barbot ; un héraut, M. Molinier.

110 *Le cinque giornate di Milano; Barricades in Borgo delle Fontane, 1848*. Painting by Donghi. Museo del Risorgimento, Florence.

During his prolonged stay in Paris, Verdi followed Italian political developments closely. He was in Paris still during Milan's famous 'five days' of revolution, the popular insurrection against the hated Austrians. Verdi returned to Milan quickly, but his stay there was brief, probably because of his disappointment in the Provisional Government, with its monarchist leanings (Verdi, at this time, was a republican).

111 *Garibaldi's Men at the Tiber, an Episode of the Roman Republic*. Painting by Gerolamo Induno. Museo del Risorgimento, Milan.

On 24 November 1848, the Pope was forced to flee Rome for Gaeta. Verdi arrived in Rome on 20 December, and his vividly patriotic opera *La battaglia di Legnano* was performed there – a frenetic triumph – on 27 January 1849, only three weeks before the proclamation of the Roman Republic. Later, to Verdi's and Italy's dismay, the short-lived Republic was defeated by the combined forces of France, Austria, Spain, and Naples, despite the brave resistance of the Garibaldini. The painter Gerolamo Induno (1827–90) fought for the Roman Republic in 1849 and received twenty-seven wounds.

GIUSEPPE VERDI

Nell'Opera nuova la Battaglia di Legnano

112 *The Battle of Legnano*. Painting by Amos Cassioli, 1860. Galleria d'arte moderna, Florence.

Amos Cassioli (1832–91) was an admired painter of Verdi's time. This *Battle of Legnano* was immensely, immediately popular and launched his successful career.

113 Verdi at the time of *La battaglia di Legnano*. Engraving, 1849. Museo teatrale alla Scala, Milan.

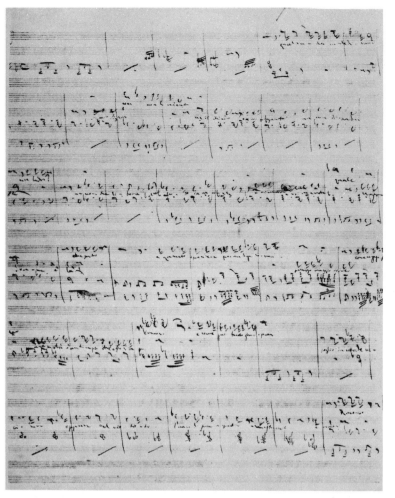

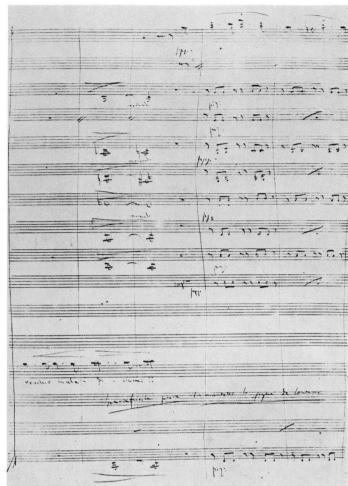

114–15 Verdi, *Rigoletto*, 1851. Autograph sketches of Act 1, scene 2 (beginning). Archivio storico Ricordi, Milan.
These sketches present notable differences – especially in the vocal lines – from the final version, where Verdi also introduced a greater freedom in the accompaniment.

116 Teresa Brambilla. Engraving. Conservatorio 'G. Verdi', Milan.
One of five sisters, all singers, Teresa Brambilla (1813–95) was a leading Verdi soprano, at the height of her career when she created the role of Gilda, in *Rigoletto*, at La Fenice, in Venice, on 11 March 1851. Her other Verdi roles ranged from Abigaille (*Nabucco*) to Elvira (*Ernani*) and the title-role of *Luisa Miller*. Her niece and namesake Teresita Brambilla was also a celebrated singer, wife of the composer Amilcare Ponchielli and creator of his *Gioconda*.

117–19 *Rigoletto*. Set designs for the first production by Giuseppe and Pietro Bertoja, 1851. Biblioteca Correr, Venice.

From 1851 on, Giuseppe Bertoja was assisted by his son Pietro (1828–*c.* 1900), who continued working at the Fenice after his father's death. At left, an early version of the set for Act I, scene 2 (final version above). Below, Act III, Sparafucile's tavern.

120 Teatro Apollo, Rome. Engraving. Istituto di studi verdiani, Parma.
The Teatro Apollo (originally Teatro Tor di Nona) was founded in 1666 – supposedly at the instigation of Queen Christina of Sweden, then living in Rome – and survived, through various metamorphoses, until 1889, when it was demolished to make way for the Tiber embankments. The premiere of *Il trovatore* took place there on 19 January 1853.

121 Vincenzo Jacovacci. Photograph.
Vincenzo 'Cencio' Jacovacci (1811–81), colourful ex-fishmonger, was the impresario of the Apollo from 1840 to the end of his life. In addition to *Il trovatore*, Jacovacci also introduced Verdi's *Un ballo in maschera* (1859) and (in 1863) was responsible for the Italian premiere of *La forza del destino* (under the title *Don Alvaro*). Verdi complained of the impresario's parsimony and his sometimes poor choice of singers, though the *Trovatore* cast was largely excellent.

122 Rosina Penco. Engraving. Raccolta Bertarelli, Milan.
The first Leonora in *Il trovatore* was Rosina Penco (1823–94), whose career had already taken her to Dresden, Berlin, and Constantinople. Verdi's new opera was her greatest success. Verdi spoke of her 'feeling, fire, spontaneity'.

123–24 *Il trovatore*. Set designs by Giuseppe and Pietro Bertoja, 1853. Biblioteca Correr, Venice.
From Rome, *Il trovatore* quickly moved to other Italian theatres. It reached La Fenice in the 1853–4 season (after *La traviata* had been introduced there). The Bertojas, of course, designed the sets: Act I, scene 2 (above) and (below) Act II, scene 1, the gypsies' camp. The latter, following Verdi's instructions, is set in a 'ruined dwelling', not in the open air as it is now usually seen.

125 Verdi in the 1850s. Photograph. Private collection, Venice.

126 Fanny Salvini-Donatelli. Engraving. Raccolta Bertarelli, Milan.
The initial failure of *La traviata* has often been attributed, at least partially, to the soprano Fanny Salvini-Donatelli (*c.* 1815–91), whose plump figure was unsuited to the role of the consumptive Violetta. Actually, the soprano was a good actress (she had appeared in the spoken theatre before turning to opera in 1848); and as contemporary reviews indicate, her performance came close to saving the unsuccessful evening.

127 Autograph of a phrase from *La traviata*, 1853. Album of Fanny Salvini-Donatelli. Archivio, Teatro La Fenice, Venice.
Three days after the opening night of *La traviata*, Verdi wrote a few bars of the score in the soprano's album, the opening of her last-act aria 'Gran Dio morir sì giovine'. Here the passage is in the original key of D flat. The aria is now sung in the lower key of C, according to Verdi's revision of the opera for its second, successful production – also in Venice – the following year.

128 *Souvenirs de Verdi*. Cover of album of piano arrangements. William Weaver Collection, Monte San Savino (AR).
As each of Verdi's operas appeared, it was immediately dismembered – insofar as possible – to provide salon pieces (even arrangements for trumpet, band, and various combinations of instruments). This is a typical collection, published in England, of 'Verdi favourites'. Note that in the *Traviata* illustration (centre) the characters are dressed in a mixture of 19th- and 17th-century costumes.

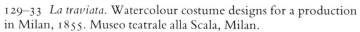

129–33 *La traviata*. Watercolour costume designs for a production in Milan, 1855. Museo teatrale alla Scala, Milan.
Verdi meant *La traviata* to be given in contemporary dress. When the Venetian authorities rejected this revolutionary idea, he suggested the period of Louis XIII. Eventually the work was set in the time of Louis XIV and was not seen in Italy in 1850s costumes until the end of the century, when such costumes were already historical. This set of sketches shows what the characters wore in a Milan production two years after the Venice premiere.

134 *La traviata*. Set design by Giuseppe and Pietro Bertoja for the second Venice production, 1854. Biblioteca Correr, Venice.
Pietro Bertoja's note on this sketch – written some time after the events – dates the revival of *La traviata* 'spring 1853'. Actually the second production opened on 6 May 1854.

Alfredo

Violetta

135 Meyerbeer's *Le Prophète*, Coronation scene. Engraving. Collection Viollet, Paris.
After a promising career in Italy, Jacob – or Giacomo – Meyerbeer (1791–1864) conquered Paris in 1831 with his *Robert le diable*. Its success was repeated with *Les Huguenots* (1836) and *Le Prophète* (1849). His speciality was grandiose spectacle – the bathing scene in *Les Huguenots* and the coronation in *Le Prophète* (above). Verdi disliked and clearly envied Meyerbeer, but was influenced by him, especially in the operas he wrote for France, *Les Vêpres siciliennes* (1855) and *Don Carlos* (1867).

136 Giacomo Meyerbeer. Lithograph.
When Verdi came to Paris in October of 1853, Meyerbeer's *L'Etoile du Nord* was in rehearsal at the Opéra-Comique. Verdi attended the premiere (16 February 1854) and was, expectedly, unimpressed, though audiences and reviewers welcomed the opera enthusiastically.

138 First Paris Exposition, 1855. Lithograph. >
Collection Viollet, Paris.
Napoleon III also wanted to affirm prestige through a grand Exposition. Verdi's commission to write a new opera was in conjunction with this much-heralded international event.

137 Paris scene. Engraving, 1854. Collection Viollet, Paris.
As part of the grand plan for his newly founded Second Empire, Napoleon III encouraged rebuilding on a vast scale. Like the Parisians and foreign visitors to the city at the time, Verdi observed the complicated process with great interest.

CRUVELLI,
dans les Vêpres siciliennes.

(Opposite)

141 *The Sicilian Vespers*. Painting by Francesco Hayez, 1846. Galleria d'arte moderna, Rome.
Between 1821 and 1846, Hayez executed three paintings on this historical theme. This is the last version, depicting the uprising as Verdi showed it in the final scene of his opera.

142–43 *Giovanna de Guzman*. Costume designs by Girolamo Magnani, 1855. Watercolour. Biblioteca civica, Parma.
With a new title, *Giovanna de Guzman*, and with its patriotic content diluted, *Les Vêpres siciliennes* was soon given in Italian translation. The first production was at the Teatro Regio, Parma (26 December 1855). The costumes were designed by Girolamo Magnani, whom Verdi considered Italy's leading scenic artist. Below left, 'Winds' (for the Ballet of the Seasons in Act III); and right, Giovanna (Hélène).

139 Sophia Cruvelli as Hélène in *Les Vêpres siciliennes*, 1855. Raccolta Bertarelli, Milan.
The German soprano Sophia Crüwell (1826–1907), under the Italianized name of Cruvelli, began her career in 1847 in Venice, in Verdi's *Attila*. Her rise was rapid, and by the 1850s she was internationally famous. Her reputation was summed up by Verdi: 'good singer and mad woman'. During the rehearsals of *Les Vêpres siciliennes*, she ran off with Baron Vigier (whom she married only some time later). For a while it seemed that the production would have to be cancelled, but Cruvelli reappeared and created the role of Hélène at the premiere, 13 June 1855.

140 Louis Gueymard as Henri in *Les Vêpres siciliennes*, 1855. Bibliothèque de l'Opéra, Paris.
The first Henri in *Les Vêpres siciliennes* was the tenor Louis Gueymard (1822–80), whose performance was evidently overshadowed by the brilliant singing and impressive acting of Cruvelli. Gueymard was married to the singer Pauline Gueymard, later the first Eboli in *Don Carlos*.

144 Verdi in Paris in the 1850s. Photograph by Disderi. International Museum of Photography at George Eastman House, Rochester, N.Y.
This is one of a series of eight photographs taken by the photographer André Adolphe Disderi of Paris in the 1850s. It is the least flattering of the series and (perhaps for this reason) the least familiar.

145 Verdi. Photograph by Nadar. Museo teatrale alla Scala, Milan.
In Paris, Verdi also posed for Nadar (Félix Tournachon), the leading photographer of the period.

146 Eugène Scribe. Engraving after a photograph by Nadar. Collection Viollet, Paris.
Scribe (1791–1861) was an enormously fertile dramatist and librettist. Alone or in collaboration, he supplied texts to Auber, Donizetti, Offenbach, and – above all – Meyerbeer, whose music was ideally congenial to Scribe's grander conceptions. With his colleague Duveyrier, he supplied the libretto of Les Vêpres siciliennes. Later, his Gustave III (set originally by Auber) became – in an Italian adaptation – Verdi's Un ballo in maschera.

‹147–48 *Simon Boccanegra*. Set designs by Giuseppe and Pietro Bertoja, 1857. Biblioteca Correr, Venice.
Six months after his return from Paris at the end of 1855, Verdi signed a contract with La Fenice for a new opera. It was to be *Simon Boccanegra*, produced there on 12 March 1857. As usual, the new work was designed by the Bertojas.

A
GIUSEPPE VERDI

150 Verdi in Rimini, summer of 1857. Engraving. Mary Jane Phillips Matz Collection, Venice.
Shortly before beginning work on *Simon Boccanegra*, Verdi made an extensive revision of his 1850 opera *Stiffelio*, to a brand-new libretto by Piave entitled *Aroldo*. The work was commissioned to inaugurate the Teatro Nuovo in Rimini. Verdi, Giuseppina and Piave went to Rimini in late July and stayed there until the opening of *Aroldo* on 16 August 1857.

MDCCCLVII.
AD ANGELO MARIANI CAVALIERE

149 Angelo Mariani in Rimini, summer of 1857. Engraving. Raccolta Bertarelli, Milan.
Verdi may have met Mariani (1821–73) in Milan in the 1840s, when the conductor was already well-known. By 1853 they were on *tu* terms. But the Rimini *Aroldo* was their first close musical collaboration and the beginning of a friendship unusually warm for Verdi. The friendship came to a dramatically bitter end some years later.

UN BALLO IN MASCHERA OPERA DI G. VERDI

Oscaro   Riccardo   Renato   Amelia   Tom.   Samuel

E tu ricevi il mio! (ATTO III Scena ultima)

MILANO, Stabilimento Nazionale **TITO DI GIO RICORDI**

Lit. Fr. Tersaghi

151 *Un ballo in maschera.* Frontispiece of Ricordi score. British Library, London.

At the time he was working on *Simon Boccanegra* and the *Aroldo* revisions, in 1856–57, Verdi was again considering a long-cherished project: *Re Lear*. For the librettist he thought of one of his Venice friends, the lawyer-dramatist Antonio Somma. The project had to be abandoned, and Somma prepared instead the text of *Un ballo in maschera*, derived from Scribe. The diversity of costumes in the above engraving of the final scene may be partly explained by the fact that a masked ball is in progress, but brutal censorship of the libretto also created a certain confusion of time and place.

152 Antonio Somma. Engraving. Istituto di studi verdiani, Parma. Born in Udine, Somma (1809–64) lived most of his life – and died – in Venice, where he belonged to the artistic and patriotic circles Verdi knew. The composer's many letters to Somma testify to Verdi's esteem for the poet; they also contain enlightening revelations about Verdi's dramaturgical ideas.

153 Verdi rehearsing *Un ballo in maschera* in Naples with the soprano Fioretti (seated) and the tenor Fraschini (standing). Watercolour caricature by Melchiorre Delfico, 1858. Villa Sant'Agata, Busseto.
Verdi arrived in Naples in January 1858, to prepare his new opera. The cast included his favourite tenor Fraschini. But quarrels with the local censorship became so violent (and their demands so outrageous) that Verdi withdrew his opera and left the city. *Un ballo in maschera* was eventually performed in Rome.

154 Vincenzo Torelli. Watercolour caricature by Melchiorre Delfico, 1858. Villa Sant'Agata, Busseto.
In addition to editing the Neapolitan paper *Omnibus*, Verdi's friend Torelli was also secretary of the Teatro San Carlo management. Here he casts a dubious eye on the libretto of *Gustavo III* (another of *Un ballo in maschera*'s several names).

157 Lulù. Painting by Filippo Palizzi, 1858. Villa Sant'Agata, Busseto.
Verdi's and Giuseppina's beloved Maltese spaniel Lulù (also spelled Loulou, a male despite the name) accompanied them to Naples, where he was painted by Filippo Palizzi (1818–99), another important member of the Neapolitan school, who specialized in painting animals. Lulù died in 1862 and is buried in the garden of the Villa Sant'Agata. Verdi had a stone column erected to mark the pet's grave.

158 Morelli takes Verdi's likeness. Watercolour caricature by Melchiorre Delfico, 1858. Villa Sant'Agata, Busseto.
Delfico shows Morelli achieving a perfect likeness by the obvious expedient: slicing off Verdi's head for the already-prepared frame.

155 Verdi in Naples. Painting by Achille Scalese, 1858. Museo teatrale alla Scala, Milan.
Verdi's frustrating stay in Naples lasted from 14 January to 23 April 1858. While he was in the city, he spent much of his time with his painter friends there, and at least two portraits were made of him then.

156 Verdi in Naples. Painting by Domenico Morelli, 1858–59 (wreath added by Filippo Palizzi). Villa Sant'Agata, Busseto.
Morelli (1826–1901) was a leading figure in the flourishing Neapolitan school. He and Verdi were close friends and corresponded for many years. Verdi bought several Morelli paintings.

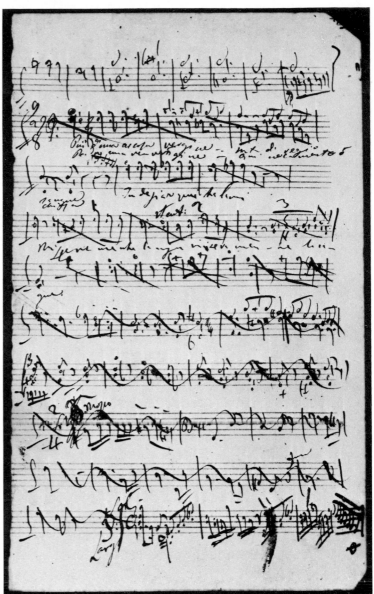

159–60 Verdi, autograph musical sketches. Music Division, New York Public Library, New York. Astor, Lenox and Tilden Foundations.
These rare sketches cannot be firmly dated or explained. Since they are for a father-daughter duet, it is just possible that they are associated with the long-cherished *Re Lear* project, which Verdi considered at length in the mid-1850s.

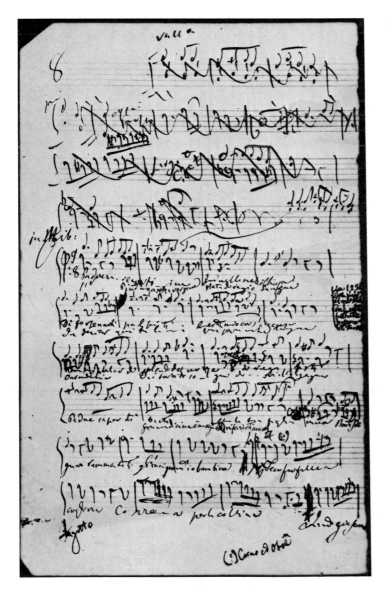

161 Autograph letter by Giuseppina Strepponi Verdi, 5 December 1860. Private Collection.
Strepponi's letters – the few that have been published – are a moving testimony of her devotion to Verdi. This one, written from Sant'Agata to Turin, where Verdi was going to see Cavour, says: 'O my Verdi, I am not worthy of you, and the love you bear me is a charity, a balm to a heart sometimes very sad, beneath the appearances of gaiety. Continue to love me.'

162 Marriage certificate Verdi-Strepponi, 1859. Collonges-sous-Salève (Ain).
On 29 August 1859, Verdi and Giuseppina were very quietly married at Collonges-sous-Salève, on the borders of Savoy, at that time part of Piedmont. The ceremony was performed by Mons. Mermillod of Geneva. The witnesses were the bell-ringer of the church and the driver of the hired carriage that had brought the couple there.

163 'VIVA V.E.R.D.I.' Engraving. Istituto di studi verdiani, Parma.
During the war of 1859, Verdi's name again became a national rallying-cry, also because its letters formed an acronym for *Vittorio Emanuele Re D'Italia*. By this time Verdi had become a monarchist, following the inspiration of his hero Cavour (see ill. 165).

164 *Members of Parliament Arriving at Palazzo Madama, Turin*. Painting by Giganti, 1862. Galleria civica d'arte moderna, Turin.
Verdi was elected Deputy for Borgo San Donnino (now Fidenza) to the first national Italian Parliament in 1861; he attended the opening on 14 February. Later he was a Senator.

165 Camillo Benso di Cavour (1810–61). Painting by Francesco Hayez, 1864. Pinacoteca di Brera, Milan.
Painted after the subject's death. Verdi met Cavour on several occasions and was profoundly affected by his death, which he regarded as a national tragedy. The composer's active participation in politics ceased a few years later.

166 Verdi, autograph musical jottings. Villa Sant'Agata, Busseto.
During boring debates, Verdi amused himself by jotting musical jokes on parliamentary paper. *Trombone* in Italian signifies also 'windbag'. The final 'order of the day' is another pun: *fuga generale* (general flight or general fugue).

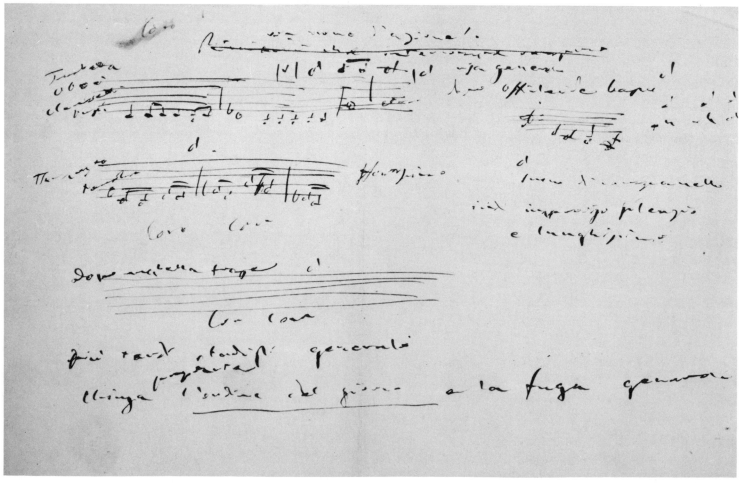

167 Verdi, *Inno delle Nazioni*. Title-page, 1862.
Conservatorio 'G. Verdi', Milan.
In 1862, commissioned to write an occasional piece
for the London Exhibition, Verdi – in Paris at the
time – decided to compose a cantata and asked the
twenty-year-old Arrigo Boito, also in the city, to
furnish a text. The resulting *Inno delle Nazioni* was
thus the first, casual collaboration of the pair who
were much later to create *Otello* and *Falstaff*. The
title-page reproduces an engraving by Focosi,
showing Italy holding hands with her sister-nations,
with the Great Exhibition Hall below them, above
the title.

INNO DELLE NAZIONI

COMPOSTO PER LA GRANDE ESPOSIZIONE DI LONDRA

DA

GIUSEPPE VERDI

Gran Cordone dell'Ordine dei SS. Maurizio e Lazzaro, Ufficiale della Legion d'Onore.

POESIA DI ARRIGO BOITO

MILANO, R. STABILIMENTO NAZ. 🛡 TITO DI GIO. RICORDI

FIRENZE, *Ricordi e Jouhaud*. - NAPOLI, *Ricordi e Clausetti*. - TORINO, *Giudici e Strada*. - MENDRISIO, *Bustelli-Rossi*.
LONDRA, *Cramer, Beale e Wood*. - PARIGI, *Leone Escudier*. - VIENNA, C. A. *Spina*. - SPAGNA, deposito.

168 Great Exhibition Hall, London, 1862.
Photograph. Radio Times Hulton Picture
Library, London.
Verdi was in London in April–May 1862, and
visited the Exhibition. In the event – after some
disagreement with the organizing committee –
the *Inno* was performed away from the
exhibition site, at Her Majesty's Theatre, on 24
May.

169 Tito Ricordi I. Photograph. Archivio storico Ricordi, Milan.
Verdi's relationship with the publisher Ricordi spanned four generations. After the death of Giovanni in 1853, the house was headed by his son Tito (1811–88), whose son Giulio (1840–1912) succeeded him. Giulio's son Tito II (1865–1933) collaborated on the first staging of Verdi's *Falstaff*.

170 Verdi's passport for Russia, 1861. Museo civico, Busseto.
In the winter of 1861–2, Verdi and Giuseppina went to St Petersburg for the first production of *La forza del destino*. The prima donna fell ill, and the Verdis had to return for a delayed premiere on 10 November 1862.

171 Verdi in Russia. Photograph, 1861 or 1862. Istituto di studi verdiani, Parma.
As usual on his foreign visits, Verdi did a certain amount of sightseeing and rode in a characteristic troika, wearing a characteristic fur hat.

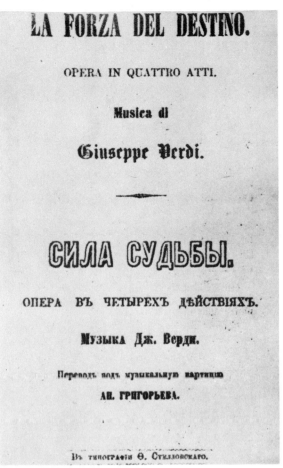

172 First edition of the libretto of *La forza del destino*, St Petersburg, 1862. Istituto di studi verdiani, Parma. *La forza del destino* was performed in Italian, and a bilingual libretto was printed for the premiere.

173 Verdi in Russia. Photograph, 1861 or 1862. Giuseppina complained of the bitter Russian cold, but praised the heating arrangements. Inevitably, Verdi visited a photographer's studio and was portrayed in his Russian outdoor garb.

174 *La forza del destino*. Set design by Carlo Ferrario, 1869. Museo teatrale alla Scala, Milan. *La forza del destino* did not arrive immediately in Italy. On 7 February 1863 – censored and renamed *Don Alvaro* – it was given in Rome. Verdi was not entirely satisfied with the work and eventually revised it. The new version was given at La Scala on 27 February 1869 with Teresa Stolz as Leonora. The sets were by the theatre's house designer, the gifted Carlo Ferrario (1833–1907).

175 Battle of Custoza. Print by C. Penni, 1878.
In June 1866, while Verdi was working on *Don Carlos* for the Paris Opéra, Italy declared war on Austria. The defeat of King Carlo Alberto's troops at Custoza was a crushing humiliation for the Italians, and Verdi was aghast. He wanted to cancel his contract with Paris, but the Opéra held him to his obligation.

176 Palazzo Sauli, Genoa. Engraving, 19th c.
After some searching for a permanent winter home, Verdi and Giuseppina in 1866 found a spacious apartment in Palazzo Sauli on the Carignano hill overlooking Genoa. Their friend the conductor Mariani lived in the same building. Later, in 1874, after the break with Mariani, the Verdis moved to other winter quarters in Palazzo Doria, Genoa.

177 Pauline Gueymard as Eboli in *Don Carlos*. Photograph, 1867. Museo teatrale alla Scala, Milan.
Wife of the tenor Louis Gueymard (first Henri in *Les Vêpres siciliennes*; see ill. 104), Pauline Lauters Gueymard 1834–?) was a remarkable singer, whose range allowed her to interpret both soprano and mezzosoprano roles. She was Azucena in the first French *Trovatore* (her husband was the Manrico), and created the role of Eboli in *Don Carlos* in Paris in 1867.

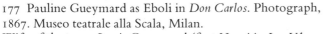

178–79 Marie Sasse as Elisabeth in *Don Carlos*. Watercolour costume designs, 1867. Raccolta Bertarelli, Milan.
Marie Sasse (née Saxe, 1838–1907) sang Elisabeth in the notorious Paris premiere of Wagner's *Tannhäuser* (1861), before creating Verdi's Elisabeth six years later. The rivalry between her and Pauline Gueymard during the preparation of *Don Carlos* became so heated that at one point Verdi refused to attend further rehearsals.

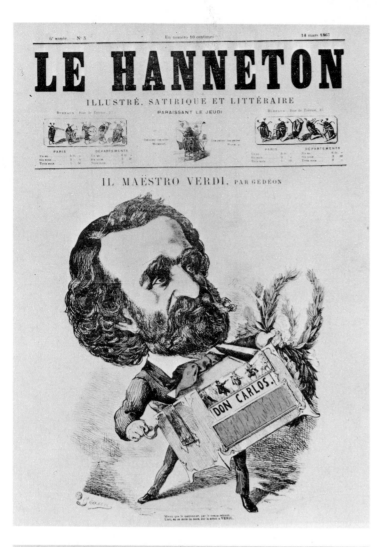

180 Caricature of Verdi at the time of *Don Carlos*. Cover of *Le Hanneton*, Paris, 14 March 1867. Raccolta Bertarelli, Milan.

Don Carlos opened at the Opéra on 11 March 1867, a moderate success. It had forty-three performances during that Exposition year. After various revisions, and a long period of neglect, it has returned to the international repertory.

182 Verdi and Rossini in Paris. Photograph, late 1860s. Museo teatrale alla Scala, Milan.

A clever photomontage. To exploit the popularity of the two Italian composers, a Parisian photographer placed Verdi's head on the shoulders of some other friend of Rossini's.

181 Verdi in Paris with Adelina Patti. Cover of *L'Indépendance Parisienne*, Paris, 12 April 1868. Raccolta Bertarelli, Milan.

Adelina Patti was a singer Verdi much admired at this time. She is seen here wearing her costume for his *Giovanna d'Arco*. This costume is now preserved in the Royal Opera House, Covent Garden, London.

183 The Paris Exposition of 1867. Lithograph. Collection Viollet, Paris.
Paris at the time of *Don Carlos* was quite a different city from the one Verdi had
encountered twenty years earlier, when he created *Jérusalem* there. Though he
was frequently irked or even enraged by the French and, even more, by the
Opéra, he often returned to Paris, also in the later years of his life.

184 Léon Escudier. Photograph. Bibliothèque Nationale, Paris.
With his brother Marie, Léon Escudier (1821–81) was Verdi's French publisher
and a close friend. He became, in 1874, the director of the Théâtre Italien, where
Aida had its French premiere (conducted by the composer). Verdi eventually
became irritated with Escudier – he was not sufficiently prompt in paying
royalties – and their friendship cooled.

185 Teresa Stolz. Pastel by Gariboldi. Museo teatrale alla Scala, Milan.
Verdi's relationship with the Bohemian soprano Teresa Stolz (1834–1902)
is one of the most obscure and debated chapters of his biography. There is
no knowing for certain whether or not they were lovers. Certainly, she was
a devoted friend to Verdi and also to Giuseppina during their old age, and
as long as her career lasted, she was Verdi's preferred soprano. She took part
in the Scala premiere of *Aida* in 1872, in the first performance of the *Messa
da Requiem* in 1874, and in many other important Verdi productions.

186 *Don Carlos* in Bologna, 1867. Souvenir engraving of the performers.
Archivio storico Ricordi, Milan.
For some time Teresa Stolz was the mistress of the conductor Angelo
Mariani (under whose direction she often sang, as in this memorable *Don
Carlos* in Bologna). They separated, perhaps because of her attachment to
Verdi, perhaps for other reasons (Mariani is said to have speculated with her
savings and lost them). At the time of their rupture, Verdi also began to
regard Mariani as an enemy.

Ricordo del D Carlo a Bologna – Autunno 1867

Impresa di Scalaberni

STOLZ TERESINA   CAV. MARIANI ANGELO   FRICCI NERI BARALDI
(Elisabetta)   (M. Concertatore e Direttore)   (Principessa d' Eboli)

STIGELLI GIORGIO MILESI PIETRO CAPPONI GIOVANNI BUSI ALESSANDRO ROSSI LUIGI COTOGNI ANTONIO
(Don Carlo)   (Un Frate)   (Filippo II)   (Sost° al M° Concertatore) (Grande Inquisitore) (Marchese di Posa)

187 Wagner, *Lohengrin*. Italian libretto for the first performance in Italy, 1871. Liceo musicale di Bologna.

The production of Wagner's *Lohengrin* conducted by Mariani at the Teatro Comunale, Bologna, on 1 November 1871, was the first Italian performance of a Wagner opera and, hence, a sensational cultural event, arousing furious controversy. It was arranged by the publisher Lucca, hated rival of Ricordi and a man Verdi intensely disliked. Verdi attended a later performance of the opera, scrawling notes in his copy of the score. At the end he wrote: 'Mediocre impression. Music beautiful when it is clear and there is thought. The action flows slowly like the words. Hence boredom [. . .] Mediocre execution.'

188 *Lohengrin*. Performers at the Bologna premiere, 1871. Raccolta Bertarelli, Milan.

Verdi had already broken with Mariani by the time of the Bologna *Lohengrin*, but the conductor's espousal of the Wagner cause cut off any possibility of reconciliation. Verdi's strictures notwithstanding, Mariani was highly praised for his interpretation. He is seen here surrounded by his cast, which included Italo Campanini (Lohengrin) and Marie Destinn (Ortrud).

189 Giovanni Bottesini and his family in Cairo. Photograph, 1871. Istituto di studi verdiani, Parma.
Bottesini (1821–89) was the leading double-bass player of his time: *il Paganini del contrabbasso*, he was called. He was also a talented composer and conductor. He conducted the premiere of *Aida* in Cairo (24 December 1871). Later, Verdi was instrumental in having him appointed director of the Parma Conservatory. This photograph was dedicated to the Khedive Ismail Pasha.

190 Camille Du Locle. Drawing. Bibliothèque de l'Opéra, Paris.
One of the librettists of *Don Carlos*, Du Locle (1832–1903) was active in persuading Verdi to accept the *Aida* commission from the Khedive. During a stay at Sant'Agata in June 1870, Du Locle – with Verdi – drafted a prose libretto in French, which was translated and versified by Antonio Ghislanzoni. Du Locle was responsible for the French versions of *Aida*, *Simon Boccanegra*, *La forza del destino* (with Charles Nuitter) and *Otello* (with Boito).

191 Auguste Mariette. Bronze bust. Musée Municipal, Boulogne-sur-Mer.
In 1868, during a visit to Egypt, Du Locle became acquainted with the pioneering Egyptologist Auguste Mariette (1821–81), confidant and adviser of the Khedive, who gave him the title of Bey. Mariette was the author of a brief story which was the basis of the *Aida* libretto, and he was also go-between in the negotiations for the *Aida* commission to Verdi. He supervised the designing of the sets for the opera and designed the costumes himself.

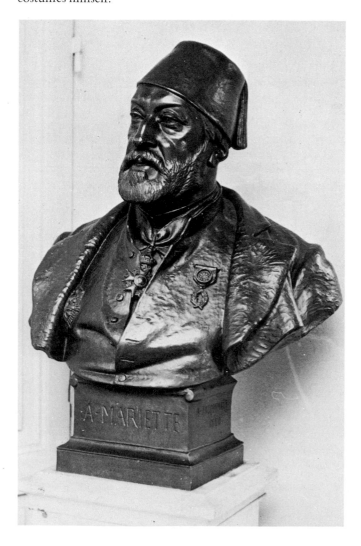

192 Antonietta Pozzoni. Photograph. Museo teatrale, Trieste.

Verdi chose the cast of the first *Aida* carefully. In October 1871, he made a trip from Sant'Agata to Florence and heard the soprano Antonietta Pozzoni (1846–1914) as Violetta in *La traviata*. He decided she could be his first Aida, and her success justified his decision. A few years later she sang the mezzosoprano role of Amneris. Verdi said of her: 'beautiful figure, good actress, with great soul, the true stuff of an artist'.

193 Antonio Ghislanzoni, Photograph. Archivio storico Ricordi, Milan.

Brilliant journalist and inventive librettist, Antonio Ghislanzoni (1824–93), as a young man, had a brief career as a baritone. In addition to preparing the Italian text of *Aida*, he also supplied librettos to Petrella, Catalani, Ponchielli and others. His novel *Gli artisti da teatro* (1856) gives a colourful picture of Italian and French operatic life in the 1840s. He published a valuable description of Verdi at Sant'Agata.

194 Filippo Filippi. Photograph. Museo teatrale alla Scala, Milan.

To ensure international attention for *Aida*, the Khedive invited a number of leading European music critics to be his guests in Cairo for the premiere. Two accepted: Ernest Reyer of *Le Journal des débats* and Filippo Filippi (1830–87) of *La Perseveranza* of Milan. Both published extended accounts of their Egyptian experiences, quoted later in this volume.

195–96 Cairo Opera House, built in 1869, interior and box of the Khedive's harem. Photographs. Istituto di studi verdiani, Parma.

Though constructed in only six months, the Khedive's opera house was sumptuously appointed. Its architects were the Italians Avoscani and Rossi, and for the first years of the theatre's existence its repertory also was exclusively Italian.

197 The Khedive Ismail Pasha. Engraving.
Ismail (1830–95) became Khedive of Egypt in 1863. Paris-educated, he attempted to 'Europeanize' the country, introducing railroads, lighthouses, the telegraph, and political and social reforms. He encouraged Lesseps in the enterprise of the Suez Canal. But Ismail's extravagance led to his downfall and to British domination of the country, after which he was forced to abdicate.

198 Cairo Opera House. Exterior. Photograph.
With a capacity of 850, the Cairo Opera opened – in conjunction with the inauguration of the Suez Canal – on 6 November 1869. The first opera given was *Rigoletto*. The theatre was destroyed by fire in 1971, a few days after this photograph was taken, and shortly before the centenary of *Aida*.

199 *Aida*. Set design by Philippe Chaperon, 1871. Bibliothèque de l'Opéra, Paris.
The premiere of *Aida* was delayed because the sets, costumes, props, and jewellery were all blocked in Paris by the events of the Franco-Prussian war. Du Locle had to send his letters to Verdi by balloon. Verdi, to his annoyance, was unable to answer them.

201 Temple of Amon-Ra, Karnak. Engraving from *Description de l'Egypte*, Paris 1809–22.
Mariette made sure that sets and costumes were as authentic as possible. Chaperon's design above was obviously based on this temple.

< 200 Emanuele Muzio. Painting by Giovanni Boldini. Museo teatrale alla Scala, Milan.
Muzio (1821–90), Verdi's former pupil and old friend, conducted the *Rigoletto* that opened the Cairo Opera in 1869. A regular conductor at the theatre for a while, he was also helpful in directing the Khedive's attention towards Verdi for *Aida*.

202 *Aida*, Radamès. Watercolour costume design by Auguste Mariette, 1871. Bibliothèque de l'Opéra, Paris (upper left).

203 *Aida*, Radamès. Watercolour costume design by Auguste Mariette, 1871. Bibliothèque de l'Opéra, Paris (upper right).

204 *Aida*, an Ethiopian prisoner. Watercolour costume design by Auguste Mariette, 1871. Bibliothèque de l'Opéra (centre).

205 *Aida*, Trumpeter (*musique militaire*). Watercolour costume design by Auguste Mariette, 1871. Bibliothèque de l'Opéra, Paris (lower left).

206 *Aida*, King. Watercolour costume design by Auguste Mariette. Bibliothèque de l'Opéra, Paris (lower right).

208 Teresa Stolz as Aida. Photographs, 1872. Museo teatrale alla Scala, Milan. For Verdi the Scala production was more important than the Cairo premiere. The cast included not only Stolz, but also his favourite mezzosoprano Maria Waldmann (1844–1920) as Amneris, with the tenor Giuseppe Capponi (1832–89), the baritone Francesco Pandolfini (1836–1916), and the bass Ormondo Maini (1835–1906). Stolz, Waldmann, Capponi, and Maini were to be the first interpreters of the *Messa da Requiem*.

◁207 Verdi, *Aida*. Autograph of 'O cieli azzurri', 1872. Archivio storico Ricordi, Milan.
For the premiere of *Aida* at La Scala (8 February 1872, the first performance after Cairo), Verdi composed an additional aria for Aida – sung by Teresa Stolz – the famous 'O cieli azzurri' in the Nile scene.

209 Verdi, *Aida*. Copy of the printed libretto with autograph annotations, 1872. Pierpont Morgan Library, New York.
Verdi supervised the Scala production personally, as well as the Parma production shortly thereafter. On one of these occasions, he made notes in his copy of the libretto, indicating not only the position of chorus and soloists but also certain matters of interpretation.

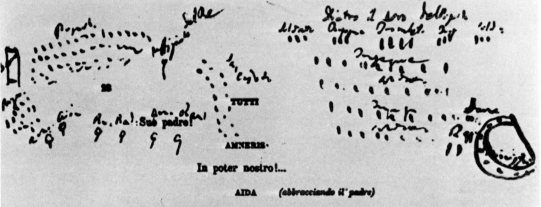

TUTTI

A. Ral: Suo padre!

AMNERIS·

In poter nostro!...

AIDA   (abbracciando il padre)

Tu! Prigionier!

AMONASRO   (piano ad Aida)

Non mi tradir!

IL RE   (ad Amonasro)

Ti appressa...

Dunque... tu sei?...

AMONASRO

Suo padre — Anch'io pugnai...
Vinti noi fummo e morte invan cercai.

(accennando alla divisa che lo veste)

Questa assisa ch'io vesto vi dica
Che il mio Re, la mia patria ho difeso;
Fu la sorte a nostr' armi nemica...
Tornò vano dei forti l'ardir.
Al mio piè nella polve disteso
Giacque il Re da più colpi trafitto;
Se l'amor della patria è delitto
Siam rei tutti, siam pronti a morir!

(volgendosi al Re con accento supplichevole)

Ma tu, o Re, tu signore possente,
A costoro ti volgi clemente...
Oggi noi siam percossi dal fato,
Doman voi potria il fato colpir.

210 Maria Waldmann. Watercolour. Museo teatrale alla Scala, Milan.
Austrian by birth, Maria Waldmann had her first success in Trieste in 1869, in a *Don Carlos* (Stolz, who became a close friend, was the Elisabeth). In March 1871, she made her Scala debut in Mozart's *Don Giovanni*. Her great role was Amneris in *Aida*, which she sang, after La Scala, in other Italian theatres, as well as in Cairo and Paris.

212 Maria Waldmann. Fresco. Villa Massari-Ricasoli, Voghenza.
In 1877, on marrying Duke Galeazzo Massari of Ferrara, Waldmann retired from the stage. On the ceiling of a little private theatre in the park of the Massari villa outside Ferrara, she was frescoed under a laurel crown with a ribbon bearing the name 'Amneris'.

211 Verdi in 1870. Photograph. Private Collection, Ferrara.
In Paris in 1876, where he conducted her both in *Aida* and the *Requiem*, Verdi gave Waldmann this inscribed photograph (misspelling her name). She remained a close friend of his after her retirement.

213 Verdi. Terracotta bust by Vincenzo Gemito, 1872. Villa Sant'Agata, Busseto.

In 1872 Verdi was in Naples to supervise productions of *Don Carlos* and *Aida*. Stolz was to sing, but fell ill, and her indisposition caused the performances to be postponed. Thus Verdi remained in the city five months. During this period of enforced leisure, he composed his string quartet and also sat for the eccentric young Neapolitan sculptor Vincenzo Gemito (1852–1929). The original bust was in terracotta. Two bronze casts were made at the time, one of which is now in the garden at Sant'Agata, the other in the Museo teatrale alla Scala.

215 Filippo Palizzi and Domenico Morelli. Pencil caricature by Melchiorre Delfico, 1872. Collezione Gallini, Milan.

The two Neapolitan painters are seen pondering, as they try to find a way to raise enough money to buy their protégé Gemito's exemption from military service. The Verdi busts were the solution. For them the composer paid 1200 lire – in advance. When Gemito was tardy in delivering them to Sant'Agata, Verdi was severely annoyed and did not accept them in person.

214 Giuseppina Strepponi Verdi. Terracotta bust by Vincenzo Gemito, 1872. Museo teatrale alla Scala, Milan.

Gemito is reported to have done Giuseppina's portrait against his will, since he found her too ugly to inspire him. Verdi did not like the result, which he called cold.

216 Manzoni and Verdi. Engraving. Raccolta Bertarelli, Milan.
The novelist Alessandro Manzoni (1785–1873) was one of Verdi's idols. Through their mutual friend
Countess Maffei, the two men met in June 1868.

218 Verdi with the first performers of the *Messa da Requiem*, 1874. Engraving by Ettore Ximenes. Raccolta Bertarelli, Milan. The soloists of the *Requiem* had all sung in the Scala premiere of *Aida* two years earlier. Verdi was not pleased with the tenor.

<217 Verdi, *Messa da Requiem*. Autograph of 'Libera me', 1869. Archivio storico Ricordi, Milan.
In 1869, Verdi composed this 'Libera me' for a *Requiem* which was to have been written by several composers as a conjoint commemoration of Rossini. The project came to nothing, but on the death of Alessandro Manzoni, in 1873, Verdi decided to compose a *Requiem* all on his own. This first 'Libera me' differs significantly from that which appears in the definitive version of the *Messa da Requiem*.

219 Chiesa di San Marco, Milan. First performance of the *Messa da Requiem*, 1874. Raccolta Bertarelli, Milan.
The first performance of the *Messa da Requiem* took place on 22 May 1874, exactly one year after Manzoni's death. There was, naturally, no applause, but the success was so great and so evident that three days later the performance was repeated at La Scala, where Verdi (who again conducted) and the soloists received a triumphant ovation.

220 Giuseppina Strepponi Verdi. Painting. Villa Sant'Agata, Busseto.
This anonymous portrait of Giuseppina hangs, as it always has, in Verdi's bedroom at Sant'Agata.

221 Verdi. Coloured lithograph by Ape (Carlo Pellegrini). Published in *Vanity Fair*, London, 15 February 1879. William Weaver Collection, Monte San Savino (AR).
This caricature was published in the series 'Men of the Day', no. 193. The accompanying text reads, in part: 'He is held by many to have encouraged a vicious taste, but he has made Italian music popular on all the barrel-organs of Europe. [...] His music is essentially the music of the present, shallow and pleasing, sympathetic and tuneful.'

222 Verdi conducting in Paris. Engraving, *c.* 1876.
Raccolta Bertarelli, Milan.
In the 1870s Verdi travelled considerably, conducting his
works abroad. In 1875 he conducted the *Requiem* in Paris,
London, and Vienna. The following year he conducted
Aida and again the *Requiem* in Paris, and in 1877 he
conducted the *Requiem* in Cologne.

223 Verdi and performers of the *Requiem* in Milan.
Caricature, 1879. Raccolta Bertarelli, Milan.
On 30 June 1879, Verdi conducted a special performance of
the *Requiem* for the benefit of the victims of a recent flood.
Stolz and Waldmann emerged from retirement for the
occasion, which was a triumph. Verdi was serenaded, after
the performance, by the Scala orchestra under the windows
of his hotel. The caption says that if Verdi's Mass does not
save the dead at least it helps the living.

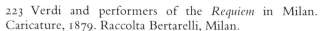

Una Messa di Requiem che, se non suffraga i morti, è molto utile ai vivi !....

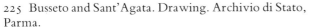

224 Verdi in the late 1870s. Engraving. William Weaver Collection, Monte San Savino (AR).
This portrait was engraved in Paris, probably when Verdi was there to conduct *Aida* in 1876.

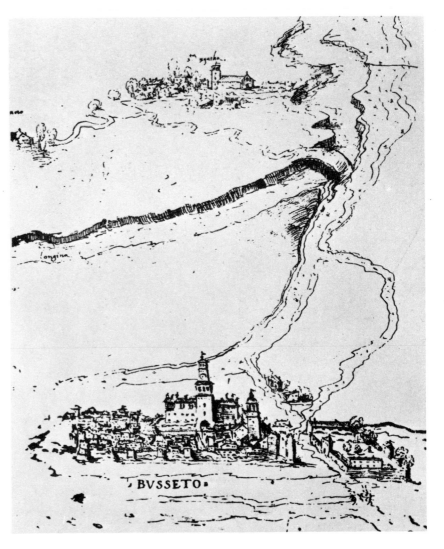

225 Busseto and Sant'Agata. Drawing. Archivio di Stato, Parma.
Verdi's ancestors had been landowners and innkeepers in the Sant'Agata area as early as 1650. It was Verdi's grandfather who, as the family fortunes declined, moved to Roncole in the mid 1780s. Thus Verdi's purchase of the Sant'Agata property in 1848 had a symbolic significance: the family fortunes had been reversed. This drawing, probably dating from the early nineteenth century, shows the relationship of Sant'Agata, on the river Ongina, with Busseto.

226–30 Villa Sant'Agata. Watercolours by Leopoldo Metlicovitz, after 1892. Archivio storico Ricordi, Milan.
The painter and graphic artist Leopoldo Metlicovitz (1868–1944) began working for Ricordi in 1892, designing posters and frontispieces.
He visited Sant'Agata and did this series of watercolours showing the house and estate as they have appeared since the late 1870s. Top left,
the façade of the villa, as seen from the road; left, a part of the vast park; above, Verdi inspecting his horses. Top right, Verdi and his dogs.
Lulù was not Verdi's only pet; dogs were – and still are – very much a part of life at Sant'Agata. In Verdi's bedroom (right) Verdi's piano is
surmounted by the familiar portrait of Antonio Barezzi.

231 Verdi and Boito at Sant'Agata. Engraving by Ettore Ximenes, from *L'illustrazione italiana*, special number 'Verdi e l'*Otello*', 1887.

This engraving, published at the time of *Otello*, represents a fantasy by the artist. If Verdi and Boito are really at Sant'Agata, then Verdi's piano is in the wrong position (as well as having the treble strings on the left). And Boito is seen here as a young man, much younger than he was when he began collaborating with Verdi in the 1880s.

232 Filomena Maria Cristina Verdi. Photograph. Villa Sant'Agata, Busseto.

In 1867 Verdi and Giuseppina took into their home his young cousin Filomena Maria ('Fifao'), born 14 November 1859. She was the grand-daughter of his father's brother Marco. In 1878 she married Alberto Carrara, son of the notary who looked after Verdi's affairs (when Verdi was not looking after them himself). Though the Verdis never formally adopted Fifao, she became the composer's heiress and was left the Sant'Agata property, where her descendants – now legally called Carrara-Verdi – continue to live.

233–34 Palazzo Doria, Genoa. Inland façade and sea-front. Engravings. Raccolta Bertarelli, Milan.
Verdi and Giuseppina moved into Palazzo Doria in the autumn of 1874. He maintained the sumptuous apartment there until his death. In 1837, Joseph Méry, future librettist of *Don Carlos*, had described his view of the palace, from the sea: 'I had opposite me the finest fifth-act set that one could imagine for a drama. It was a palace that stretched all the way down to the sea and whose handsome colonnade of white marble was reflected in the mirror of calm water. This building seemed completely deserted to me; its solitude gave it a touching appearance. [. . .] At that hour, it offered itself to me as a vast tomb where some shade of a king slept to the gentle rustle of orange-trees and waves. ''There is the Palazzo Doria,'' a voyager said at my side.'

235 Verdi. Pencil drawing by Giovanni Boldini, 1886. Museo teatrale alla Scala, Milan.
Giovanni Boldini (1842–1931), the Italian artist living in Paris, met Verdi there in April 1886, when Verdi had gone briefly to the French capital in order to hear the baritone Victor Maurel and engage him to sing Iago in *Otello*. Boldini made two portraits of Verdi, an oil (right) and a pastel (bottom of this page). He was especially fond of the pastel and probably made this drawing from it.

236 Verdi. Pastel by Giovanni Boldini, 1886. Galleria Nazionale d'Arte moderna, Roma.
This portrait was done in a few hours on 9 April 1886. Verdi, who had agreed reluctantly to pose, was so pleased with it that he stayed to lunch with Boldini in his studio, sitting for another two hours after the meal.

237 Verdi. Sketches by Giovanni Boldini, 1886. Collezione E. Piceni, Milan.
Boldini made a number of rapid sketches of Verdi during their Paris encounter.

(*Opposite*)
238 Verdi. Painting by Giovanni Boldini, 1886. Casa di Riposo 'G. Verdi', Milan.
This portrait was executed some days before the pastel. Giuseppina and Muzio were present at the sitting, and their steady stream of talk with Verdi upset the painter, who was then dissatisfied with the result. For this reason he asked Verdi to come back to the studio again, and on that occasion executed the successful pastel (ill. 236). The painting was given to Verdi by Boldini in 1893, at the time of *Falstaff* (the painter attended the premiere).

239 Verdi and Boito at Sant'Agata. Photograph. Archivio storico Ricordi, Milan.
Verdi's long association with Arrigo Boito (1842–1918) began with their brief collaboration on the *Inno delle Nazioni* in 1862. It was resumed in 1879 when they started work on *Otello*, and continued through the revision of *Simon Boccanegra* in 1880–81 and until *Falstaff* was produced in 1893. Throughout the last twenty years of the composer's life the librettist was a frequent and welcome visitor to Sant'Agata.

240 Giulio Ricordi. Archivio storico Ricordi, Milan.
After *Aida*, Verdi seriously considered giving up the writing of operas. It was his canny publisher Ricordi, assisted by Giuseppina, who arranged for Verdi to meet Boito again in 1879. And it was Ricordi who suggested and insisted on the *Otello* project.

241 Verdi with Francesco Tamagno at Montecatini. Photograph by Spezia. William Weaver collection, Monte San Savino (AR).
After singing the role of Gabriele Adorno in the revised *Simon Boccanegra* in 1881 at La Scala, the tenor Tamagno (1850–1905) sang other Verdi roles there, including Radamès and Don Carlos. And he created the role of Otello in 1887. Verdi at first had mixed feelings about the artist, but worked hard with him and obtained a success.

242 Romilda Pantaleoni. Engraving. Raccolta Bertarelli, Milan.
The soprano Romilda Pantaleoni (1847–1917) made her Scala debut in *La gioconda* in 1883 (its composer Ponchielli dedicated his *Marion Delorme* to her, when she created the title role in 1885). Verdi chose her as his first Desdemona in 1887, but was disappointed in her performance. She was the mistress of the conductor Franco Faccio (below) and retired from the stage after his tragic illness and early death.

243 Franco Faccio. Engraving. Raccolta Bertarelli, Milan.
The premiere of *Otello* – 5 February 1887 – was conducted by Franco Faccio (1840–91), who had been Boito's fraternal friend since their days together at the Milan Conservatory. Faccio began his career as a composer (his operas include an *Amleto*, 1865, libretto by Boito), but he soon won fame as the leading conductor of his day. He was chief conductor at La Scala, immensely admired by Verdi. His *Otello* had the composer's total approval (Verdi had closely supervised the long, exhausting rehearsals). Faccio generously encouraged younger artists, including Puccini, and introduced many non-Italian works at La Scala. The last of these was Wagner's *Die Meistersinger*. He died of hereditary syphilis in the same institution where his father was confined, insane.

244 Verdi in Venice. Pastel. Museo teatrale alla Scala, Milan.
This portrait was given by Verdi to Tamagno in 1894, with a
phrase from *Otello* as inscription.

245 Verdi at the time of *Otello*. Painting by Giuseppe Barbaglia,
1887. Conservatorio 'G. Verdi', Milan.
The Milanese society painter Giuseppe Barbaglia (1841–1910)
painted at least two portraits of Verdi. For the last twenty years of
his career, Barbaglia worked only as a copyist, and so the merits of
his earlier pictures have been virtually ignored.

246 *L'illustrazione italiana*, cover of special number, 'Verdi e l'*Otello*', 1887. Raccolta Bertarelli, Milan.
Inevitably, the premiere of *Otello* was an event of national and international importance. Critics, reporters, and celebrities – musical and otherwise – came to Milan from all over the world, and all the Italian papers devoted extra space – or special numbers – to the new opera.

247 *L'illustrazione italiana*, special number, 'Verdi e l'*Otello*'. Scene from Act III, 1887. Raccolta Bertarelli, Milan.
Obviously, the illustrator was allowed to attend rehearsals, since the special number of the magazine appeared before the opening night of the opera.

A terra!... si, nel livido
Fango percossa io giacio,
Piango, m'agghiaccia il brivido
Dell'anima che muor.

248 Verdi, *Falstaff*. Autograph of final scene, 1892. Archivio storico Ricordi, Milan.
While *Otello* took about eight years to write, *Falstaff* – Verdi's last opera – moved with relative speed. Boito produced the libretto in 1889 and the opera was performed four years later. There is every evidence that Verdi enjoyed writing it, to prove to the world that he could create a comic opera and – in the final fugue – that he knew all the rules of academic composition as well as any conservatory-trained composer.

I PRIMI ESECUTORI DELL'OPERA "FALSTAFF" DI GIUSEPPE VERDI.

PRIMA RAPPRESENTAZIONE - TEATRO ALLA SCALA - 9 FEBBRAIO 1893

G. PASQUA (QUICKLY)

G. PAROLI (DR. CAJUS)

VIRGINIA GUERRINI (MEG)

A. PINI CORSI (FORD)

EMMA ZILLI (ALICE)

V. ARIMONDI (PISTOLA)

GIUSEPPE VERDI

ADELINA STEHLE (NANNETTA)

V. MAUREL (FALSTAFF)

EMMA ZILLI - ADELINA STEHLE (ALICE - NANNETTA)

E. GARBIN (FENTON)

PELLEGALLI ROSSETTI (BARDOLFO)

ARRIGO BOITO

249 *Falstaff*. Verdi, Boito and the first cast, 1893. Museo teatrale alla Scala, Milan. The process of casting *Falstaff* was complex, but the title-role was easily assigned. Though Verdi was not personally fond of the vain Victor Maurel (1848–1923), the baritone who had been a superlative first Iago was the obvious choice to sing Sir John. In the end, the selection of artists proved happy, and the triumph was total.

250 Edoardo Mascheroni. Photograph. Istituto di studi verdiani, Parma. After the death of Faccio (ill. 243), Mascheroni (1859–1941) was appointed chief conductor at La Scala, thanks to the intervention (not to say the intrigues) of Boito and Verdi, who wanted him there for *Falstaff*. Verdi called Mascheroni the 'third author of *Falstaff*'. After Milan, he conducted the opera in other Italian theatres, as well as in Germany and Austria.

251 *L'illustrazione italiana*, cover of special number, 'Verdi e il *Falstaff*', 1893. Raccolta Bertarelli, Milan.

252 Verdi and Giuseppina at the Caffè Cova, Milan, in the 1890s. Painting. Courtesy of Fratelli Fabbri, Milan.

This fantasy shows the Verdis in an unlikely assembly of famous musicians and writers (several of whom were not on speaking terms). The time is the 1890s and the place is the Caffè Cova, a favourite artists' rendezvous, just opposite La Scala, at the corner of what is now Via Verdi. Boito is shown between Verdi and Giuseppina, with the bearded Giuseppe Giacosa behind him. Mascagni is at the other end of the table, then, to his left, Puccini, then (behind Puccini) Leoncavallo, who is looking away. Alfredo Catalani is on Giuseppina's right. Giulio Ricordi is also present, standing behind Giacosa, with Luigi Illica standing on his right.

253 Verdi in 1885. Watercolour by Francesco Vinea (1845–1902). Museo teatrale alla Scala, Milan.

Verdi was much more at home in the solitary garden of Sant'Agata than in the crowded Caffè Cova.

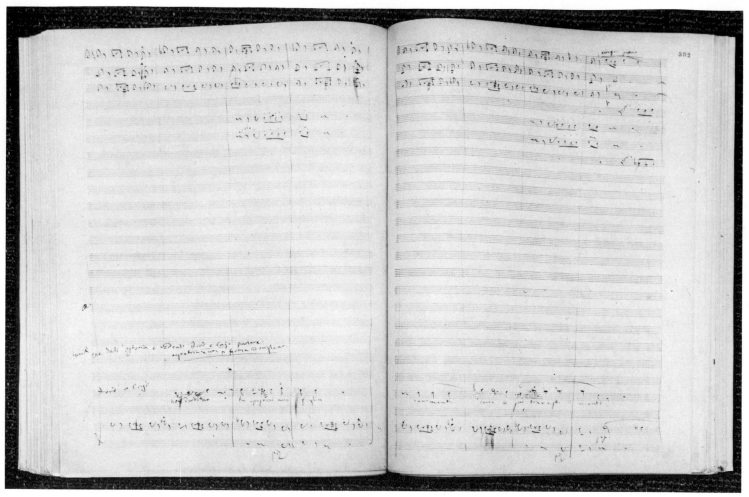

254 Verdi, *Falstaff*. Autograph of Act III, scene 1, 1892–93. Archivio storico Ricordi, Milan.

255 Verdi in the stage-director's room at La Scala. Drawing by Adolfo Hohenstein, 1893. Archivio storico Ricordi, Milan.
From backstage, Verdi keeps an eye on the audience. The drawing is by Adolfo Hohenstein (1854–?), the Russian-born artist who designed the sets and costumes for the premiere of *Falstaff*.

Verdi's Return from Paris.

Although they have tried to prove that the composer of " Falstaff " was born a Frenchman the maestro and his musical laurels are always *Verdi* (green) for the glory of Italy.—*Il Trovatore.*

256 Verdi's return from Paris. Caricature after the periodical *Il trovatore*, 1894. Archivio storico Ricordi, Milan.
In the spring of 1894 Verdi went to Paris, where *Falstaff* was performed in French at the Opéra-Comique on 18 April. The opera, with Maurel now singing in his native language, was a great success. Several numbers had to be repeated, including the aria known in Italian as 'Quand'ero paggio'.

5 minuti e 59 secondi

1

257 Verdi's notes on the ballet music for the French version of *Otello*, 1894. Archivio storico Ricordi, Milan.

After *Falstaff* at the Opéra-Comique, it was the turn of *Otello* at the Opéra (12 October 1894). The inexorable rule of the house required Verdi to compose ballet music, which he did with great effort and many complaints. On the first page of this addition to the score, he wrote instructions for the choreographer: '*5 minutes* and *59 seconds*/ Having before my eyes the splendid Third Act scene with columns, I have decided to write the music in the following way: immediately at the beginning, from the attack of the Trumpets, a group of *Turkish slave-girls* should appear. They dance listlessly and in ill-humour because they are slaves. Towards the end, however, of this 1st movement, hearing the *Arab Song*, they gradually become animated and finally are dancing wildly. [. . .] The Dance to the *Warrior Song* should be performed only by Men. The 1st motive is resumed and all the Venetians can dance: then at the *più mosso*, Venetians, Turks, Greeks, the whole lot can dance – *Amen*.'

(Opposite)
259 Verdi at seventy-four. Painting by Giuseppe Barbaglia, 1887. Grand Hôtel et de Milan, Milan.
Another Barbaglia portrait, painted in the sitting-room of the suite that the composer occupied in the Grand Hôtel (where he died). The picture still hangs in the room where it was painted.

258 Verdi in Maurel's dressing-room during the Paris *Otello*. Photograph, 1894. Though Verdi was angry with Maurel for taking liberties with his music, he posed, somewhat grouchily, for this photograph in the baritone's dressing-room at the Opéra.

260 Giuseppina Strepponi Verdi in old age. Photograph. Villa Sant'Agata, Busseto.

After the Paris journeys, both Verdi and Giuseppina suffered from ill-health. In January 1897, Verdi apparently had a mild stroke, from which he recovered promptly. Giuseppina suffered from lack of appetite and persistent weakness of the legs. The winter was spent in Genoa as usual. In May they were back at Sant'Agata. In July they went to Montecatini for the waters, which did Giuseppina little good. Then they returned to the villa, where she died at 4 p.m. on 14 November 1897.

261 Funeral of Giuseppina Strepponi Verdi in 1897. Painting. Private collection, Milan.

Unlike Verdi, Giuseppina was a devout and practising Catholic, especially in her last years. Following her instructions, her funeral was held at dawn, with only family and servants present. Verdi followed the coffin, bare-headed.

262 Verdi alone at Sant'Agata. Photograph. Archivio storico Ricordi, Milan.
After Giuseppina's death, Boito and Ricordi tried to persuade Verdi to settle permanently in Milan; but he continued to divide his time between Sant'Agata and his winter homes, Genoa and the Grand Hôtel.

263 Verdi on the construction site of the Casa di Riposo. Photograph, 1898–99. Archivio storico Ricordi, Milan.
In 1896, Verdi deposited a large sum with the Banca Popolare, Milan, for the construction of a rest-home for aged and needy musicians. He once called the Casa di Riposo his finest work. The architect was Arrigo Boito's older brother Camillo. Verdi (above) often visited the construction in his last years. He is seen with Camillo Boito (centre) and Signor Noseda, the contractor (right).

(Opposite)
264–65 Verdi on the construction site of the Casa di Riposo, 1898–99. Photographs. Archivio storico Ricordi, Milan.
Above: Verdi (right) again with Noseda and Camillo Boito. Below (left to right): Giulio Ricordi, Verdi, Arrigo Boito, Noseda.

268 Verdi in front of La Scala. Photograph. Conservatorio 'G. Verdi', Milan.
During the last, lonely years, Verdi continued to take an interest in both political and musical affairs. His position as Grand Old Man of Italian music still made him a powerful influence in Italian cultural life.

(Opposite)

266 Casa di Riposo 'G. Verdi', Milan. Photograph.
The Casa di Riposo was completed in 1899, but received its first guests only on 10 October 1902, over a year after the composer's death. Verdi bequeathed the royalties of his operas to the institution.

267 Grand Hôtel et de Milan. Photograph.
The exterior of the hotel has remained much as it was when Verdi lived there. His suite occupied the near corner of the first floor (the sitting-room is under the word MILAN in the photograph).

269 Verdi at his desk in the Grand Hôtel. Photograph, 1900. Archivio storico Ricordi, Milan.
This photograph, dated January 1900, was taken exactly a year before Verdi's death, in his sitting-room in the Grand Hôtel. The desk at which he is seated has been preserved – just as he left it – in the Museo teatrale alla Scala.

270–71 Verdi at Sant'Agata. Photograph, 1900. Accademia chigiana, Siena.

On 21 September 1900, a Captain Enrico Alberto d'Albertis – who had met Verdi casually on two previous occasions – made a tourist excursion to Busseto, Roncole and Sant'Agata. He gave his card to the gate-keeper of the villa, and Verdi, who was alone in the house, came out to welcome the visitor. The Captain had his Kodak with him and, on receiving Verdi's permission, took this photograph. As the Captain wrote on the back of it, it is probably the last one taken of the composer. Verdi is standing in the French window of the living-room of the villa.

14.ª Lascio all'opera Pia Casa di Riposo dei Musicisti eretta in Ente morale con Decreto 31 Dicembre 1899 oltre lo stabile da me fatto costruire in Milano Piazza Michelangelo Buonarroti, e di cui all'istromento 16 Dicembre 1899 a rogito Dott. Stefano Allocchio, —

1.° Lire cinquantamila di Rendita Italiana consolidata 5 % attualment. a me intestata per certificati N.° quattro

2.° Lire venticinquemila di Rendita Italiana al portatore.

3.° Tutti i diritti d'autore sia in Italia che all'Estero di tutte le mie opere comprese tutte le partecipazioni a me spettanti in dipendenza dei relativi contratti di cessione. Di tali proventi il Consiglio d'amministrazione non potrà disporre che della somma di lire cinquemila annue per i primi dieci anni, e ciò allo scopo di formare col residuo un capitale in aumento del patrimonio dell'opera Pia —

4.° Il credito di lire Duecentomila verso la ditta G. Ricordi e C. di Milano sul quale viene ora corrisposto l'interesse del 4 % annuo a tenore della Convenzione ora in corso.

5.° La somma che venisse eventualmente restituita dal Municipio di Milano a termine del contratto di acquisto di terreno nel Cimitero Monumentale di Milano fatto a mezzo del mio avvocato Umberto Campanari.

6.° Lascio alla detta Casa di Riposo pei Musicisti il Piano forte grande formato Erard che trovasi nel mio appartamento a Genova, la mia spinetta che trovasi a S.Agata, le mie decorazioni, i miei ricordi artistici, i quadri indicati con lettera speciale alla mia Erede, e tutto quanto la stessa mia erede crederà opportuno di lasciare per essere conservato in una sala del medesimo Istituto —

Esprimo il vivo desiderio d'essere sepolto in Milano con mia moglie nell'oratorio che verrà costruito nella Casa di Riposo dei musicisti da me fondato —

G. Verdi

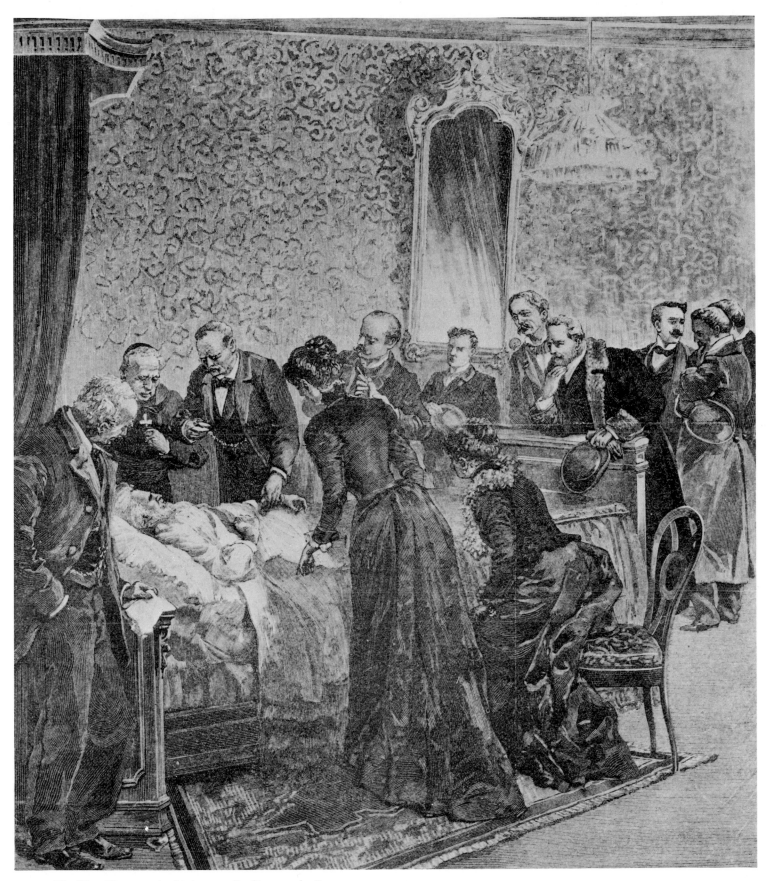

◁ 272 Verdi's will, 1900. Archivio notarile distrettuale, Parma.
Clause 14 of the will – written in Milan on 14 May 1900 – concerns the Casa di Riposo, to which Verdi left not only his royalties but also some bonds, his Erard piano from the Palazzo Doria, and his first spinet (ill. 8). The final sentence reads: 'I express the strong desire to be buried in Milan with my wife in the Chapel that will be built in the Casa di Riposo dei Musicisti founded by me.'

273 Verdi's death. Engraving, 1901. Raccolta Bertarelli, Milan.
On the morning of 21 January 1901, while he was dressing in his hotel bedroom, Verdi had a stroke. Though half-paralyzed and almost always unconscious, he survived until 2.50 a.m., 27 January. During those days of his death-agony, a stream of distinguished visitors came to his room, while a crowd stood silently in the street outside. Straw had been scattered over the cobbles, to muffle the sound of horses' hoofs.

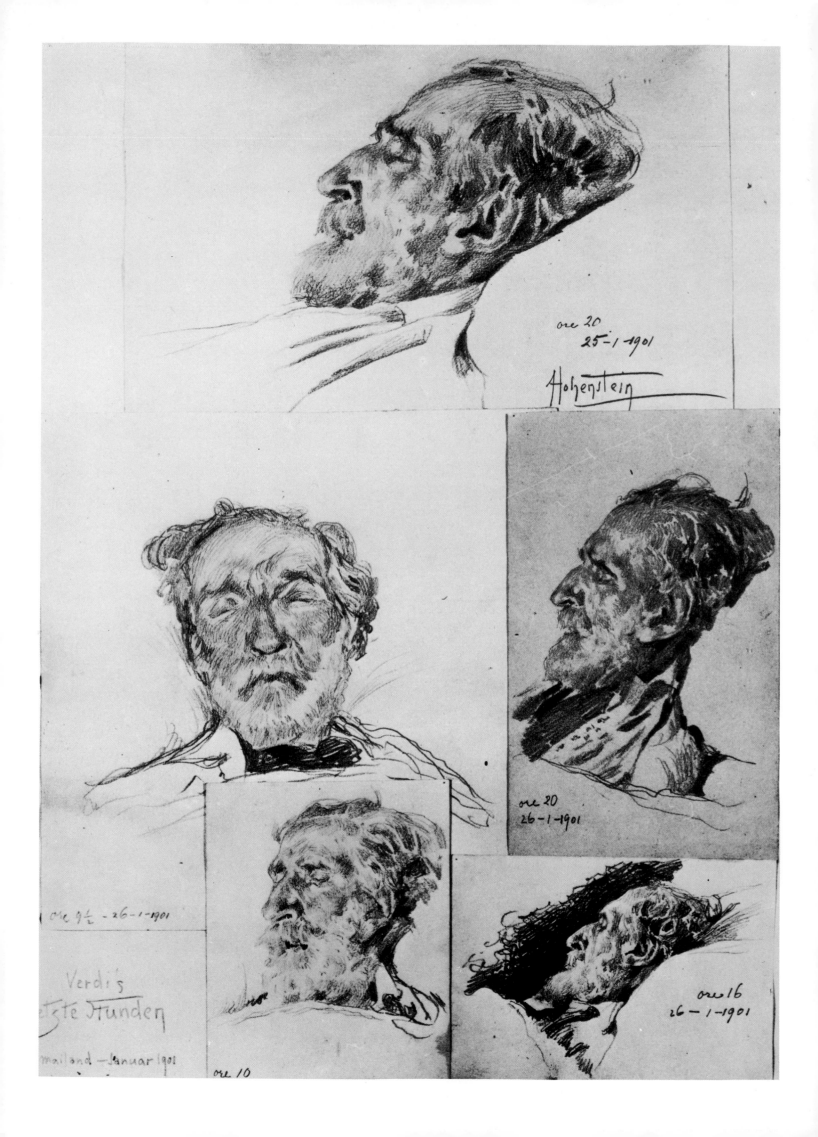

ore 20
25-1-1901

Hohenstein

ore 20
26-1-1901

ore 9½ - 26-1-1901

Verdi's
etzte Stunden

Mailand - Januar 1901

ore 10

ore 16
26-1-1901

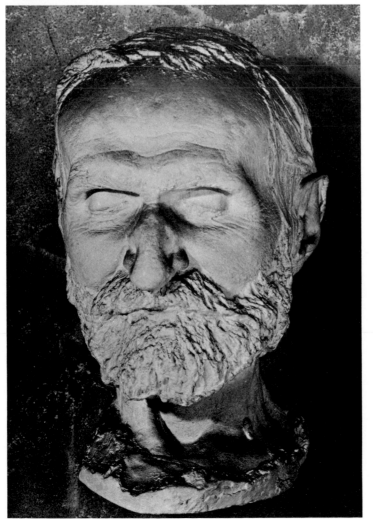

(Opposite)
274 Verdi's last hours. Sketches by Adolfo Hohenstein, 1901. Museo teatrale alla Scala, Milan.
Among the visitors to the dying Verdi's room was Hohenstein, the designer of *Falstaff*. The artist made a graphic – and somewhat macabre – series of drawings, each with the day and hour meticulously indicated.

275 Verdi on his death-bed. Photograph, 1901. Museo teatrale alla Scala, Milan.
The bed and other articles of furniture in Verdi's bedroom were later given by the hotel to his heirs, who placed them in a special little room at Sant'Agata.

276 Verdi's death mask, 1901. Conservatorio 'G. Verdi', Milan.
Two masks were taken immediately after Verdi's death. One is in the Museo teatrale alla Scala, the other in the Milan Conservatory.

277–78 Autograph note by Teresa Stolz, 1901. William Weaver Collection, Monte San Savino (AR). Through the last years of Verdi's life, Teresa Stolz was his frequent companion. She lived only a short walk from the Grand Hôtel and, when he was at Sant'Agata, she often went to stay there. She was overcome with grief at his death (she herself died the following year). In replying to the condolences of some friends, she wrote: 'Our poor beloved Maestro!! I cannot find peace, the whole sad event seems a dream to me!! I comfort myself with the thought that I am not alone in weeping for him, he was loved and venerated by the entire civilized world. [. . .]'

MUNICIPIO DI BUSSETO

CITTADINI!

Il Maestro Giuseppe Verdi

è morto oggi in Milano alle ore 2,50.

L'orribile annunzio pur troppo atteso colla più viva trepidazione, termina sciauratamente la nostra ansia dolorosa e tronca senza conforto ogni nostra speranza.

Il forte colosso è caduto! L'albero meraviglioso dai rami sempre verdi ci è rapito come da folgore!

Il mondo civile lamenta con angoscia la scomparsa dell'Astro più fulgido brillante nel cielo dell'Arte. Tutti immensamente addolora la perdita del venerando *Vegliardo*, circonfuso dalla gloria, sovrano della Musica, principe degli uomini sacri al culto dell'umanità, artefice divino che *tanti petti ha scossi e inebriati*.

Ma fra l'universale compianto, maggiore è il rammarico di tutti noi, perchè *VERDI* è *nostro*, e Busseto, gloriosa di avergli dato i natali, lo venera come suo vanto e suo orgoglio.

Dall'umile casa di Roncole che lo vide sorgere alla luce del sole: dalla villa di Sant'Agata dove si deliziava ne' suoi campi: dai manieri della nostra Busseto plaudente ai primi canti del *Cigno*, voli alla salma del Grande Estinto il saluto reverente del loco natio!

Mentre non è ancor spenta l'eco gioconda dell'entusiasmo con cui abbiamo celebrato l'ultimo compleanno del Maestro, ben lieto dei nostri sensi di affetto e di ammirazione, eccoci piombati nello sbigottimento per la fine improvvisa del Grande Concittadino.

Il dolore nostro è ancora più intenso, chè a si breve intervallo la morte lo abbia colto lontano dal paese che ha nudrito la sua infanzia, gli amori della sua gioventù, gli ideali dell'onore e della gloria, congiunti colla pace di una vecchiezza indomita e benefica.

La Patria che egli ha onorato splendidamente colle più elette rivelazioni del Genio, lo augurava eterno, come eterna ed insigne è l'opera sua.

Mentre *VERDI* è assunto agli onori della immortalità, sia gloria al Suo Nome cui nessun elogio è pari!

Penetrati dalla più profonda commozione ci sentiamo colpiti da un lutto che non si può esprimere a parole, ma che noi non potremo dimenticare giammai!

Il Consiglio Comunale è convocato d'urgenza per deliberare intorno alle solenni onoranze che la Città di Busseto intende tributare al più nobile, al più illustre, al più grande de' suoi figli.

Busseto, 27 Gennaio 1901.

PER LA GIUNTA MUNICIPALE
IL SINDACO
F. CORBELLINI.

279 Announcement to the citizens of Busseto of Verdi's death, 1901. Monte di credito su pegno, Busseto.
The moment news of Verdi's death reached Busseto, the Mayor and the Council issued an announcement which, among other things, laments the fact that the composer had to die far from his home town.

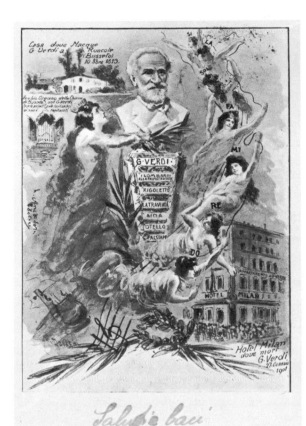

280–81 Commemorative postcards, 1901. William Weaver Collection, Monte San Savino (AR).
Mourning for Verdi was nation-wide, without distinction of class. Throughout the country postcards were printed, to express Italian grief.

282 Temporary graves of Verdi and Giuseppina at the Cimitero Monumentale, Milan. Photograph, 1901. Archivio storico Ricordi, Milan.
Verdi and Giuseppina could not be buried immediately in the crypt at the Casa di Riposo. So they lay temporarily in a plot in the Milan cemetery.

283 Verdi's burial. Photograph, 1901. Museo teatrale alla Scala, Milan.
Following Verdi's written wishes, his funeral was private and simple. But the transferral of his remains from the Milan cemetery to the Casa di Riposo on 26 February 1901, a month after his death, was an impressive, solemn ceremony, with royalty following the catafalque and the Scala orchestra and chorus, under Toscanini, performing 'Va, pensiero' from *Nabucco*.

284 Verdi's funeral cortege in Foro Bonaparte, Milan. Photograph by Guigoni e Bossi, Milan, 1901. Covo verdiano, Parma.

285 Verdi's grave. Casa di Riposo 'G. Verdi', Milan. Photograph.
Verdi is buried next to Giuseppina. A plaque on one wall of the crypt also commemorates Margherita Barezzi and her children Icilio and Virginia.

286 Verdi commemoration in Rome. Gouache by Ismacl Gcntz, 1901. William Weaver Collection, Monte San Savino (AR).
On 12 February 1901 Verdi was commemorated in Rome at the Circolo Artistico Internazionale. Pietro Mascagni gave an address, then accompanied at the piano some singers (including the soprano Celestina Boninsegna) in a group of excerpts from Verdi operas.

287 Verdi monument in Trieste. Bronze model by Alessandro Laforêt, 1906–26. Museo teatrale, Trieste.
Following Verdi's death, streets, squares, theatres were named after him throughout Italy, and many monuments were planned. The first to be erected was in Trieste – not yet part of Italy – in 1906, on the fifth anniversary of his death. The statue became a rallying-point and symbol for Trieste's irredentists, and was severely mutilated in May 1915 by a horde of ruffians, presumably instigated by the Austrian police. Originally in marble, the statue was then recast in bronze, by the sculptor Laforêt himself, and replaced on its pedestal in 1926, when the city was finally Italian.

Documents

There are three important sources of information about Verdi's early life. The best known and probably most reliable are the 'Cenni biografici' (or 'biographical notes') by Giuseppe Demaldè, a kinsman and older contemporary of Verdi's. These were jotted down, in Busseto, sometime in the 1840s or 1850s, while local memories were still fresh. They have been only partially published. Verdi's own recital of the events of his childhood was copied down by his friend Melchiorre Delfico, who illustrated the reminiscences in his characteristic, light-hearted fashion. The third, still less familiar source is another collection of local memories, made shortly after the composer's death by a priest of Roncole, Giovanni Fulcini. They are published in *Roncole Verdi* by Adolfo Rossi.

From Delfico's unfinished biography

The traveller who follows by train the long stretch from Piacenza to Parma, when he has gone a few minutes past the station of Alseno, will come upon a humble stream, the Ongina, which, having descended from the Monte della Ranca, between the hills of Vigoleno and Bacedasco, crosses the Via Emilia, winding tortuously westward, to join the scant waters of the Onginella and the less scant ones of the Arda, offering its tribute to the glorious current of the Po, not without having greeted, on the right, the little city of Busseto and on the left the more humble but today no less famous earth of Sant'Agata. In that direction, but much farther to the east, a good three miles before Busseto there is the town of Roncole, or Le Roncole, hidden from the eye not by its distance but by the sloping of the land itself and by the density of the trees that divide the happy countryside into ample squares, whose symmetrical lines seem to elude the gaze and pursue one another, as the train goes by at the speed of sixty miles an hour.

Roncole is only a village, belonging to the vast radius of the township of Busseto. Its inhabitants are scattered, as is natural and frequently to be observed among the hills of the plain; but it counts about one thousand two hundred souls, mostly farmers. [. . .] The houses are modest, like the modest people, but yet the tall and spacious church does not lack some smile of art. [. . .]

In that serene nest among the green of the fields, during the first decade of this century, there lived a young married couple. Not rich, but not poor either, nor engaged in the labour of the land [. . .].

AB I, 4–5.

From Giovanni Fulcini's memoir

Carlo Verdi and Luigia Uttini, husband and wife, operated in Roncole a rustic tavern, without much custom, and a store, the only one in the place, where they sold flour, lard, bacon, salt meat, coffee, sugar, spices, liquors, wines, salt, and tobacco, from which they derived a bare living from day to day. The Lord granted to this young couple, on 10 October 1813, a boy to whom on the 11th day of the same month were given the baptismal names Giuseppe, Fortunino, and Francesco.

RO, 57

Verdi's baptismal certificate, 11 October 1813

I, Carlo Arcari, Provost of Roncole, baptized this morning a male child born yesterday evening at eight o'clock, son of Carlo Verdi (son of the late Giuseppe) and of Luigia Uttini (daughter of Carlo), a married couple of this parish. The child was given the names of Giuseppe, Fortunino and Francesco. Godparents were Signor Pietro Casali (son of Felice) and Barbara Barsani (daughter of Angelo), both of this parish.

MS., RONCOLE

Because Don Arcari says 'yesterday', Verdi's birthdate is often given as 10 October. He himself always celebrated 9 October, feast of San Donnino, a favourite local saint. Since, in older times, Italians reckoned that a new day began at sunset, it seems likely that Verdi was, in fact, born on 9 October.

From Giovanni Fulcini's memoir

Little Giuseppe grew up a quiet, very reserved boy, sober in word and deed. He avoided unruly swarms and noisy company. He preferred to stay with his mother or alone in the house. He took no part in games, but only watched them as if they were not for him. [. . .] He was, moreover, good, obedient, helpful, nor was he ever scolded or punished. He helped his parents in the store. Only one thing had a strange power over him: music. When some barrel-organ player or fiddler passed by, Giuseppe would run immediately to the door of the shop and enjoy the tunes, all ears. His attention was such that it was obviously something singular and, on noticing it, an old strolling fiddler advised the boy's parents to have him study music. [. . .]

RO, 57–8

From Delfico's unfinished biography

[. . .] But the advice of that strolling player was not so promptly followed. If we had to heed every bit of advice people give us, we would be in a bad way. Giuseppe, for that matter, was only seven years old. As was usual for little boys, he sometimes served Mass in church. [. . .] One day, to his misfortune, as he was kneeling on the altar steps, paying little attention to the requirements of the celebrant

7 and much to the sounds of the organ, he failed to hear the priest ask for the cruets. The request was repeated a couple of times, but in vain; then the celebrant, truly not an example of patience, gave the little assistant a shove and sent him sprawling into a corner. The boy received only a bump on his forehead; but he was at first stunned by the blow and fainted, and water had to be sprinkled on his head, to bring him round. He went home aching, but without tears, and to the tender care, the loving enquiries of his parents, he gave only one answer: they should allow him to study music. [. . .]
AB I, 6–7

Verdi himself often told this story, but with a more dramatic ending. On coming to, he supposedly cursed the priest, in local dialect, saying 'may lightning strike you!' Some years later, in 1828, lightning *did* strike and kill the priest.

From Demaldè's 'Cenni biografici'

Until he reached the age of about ten, he received from his parish priest the first rudiments of reading and writing, but as he listened to music with no small pleasure, his parents procured a teacher for him, a country organist who could paw out a few things as best he was able on the organ, having studied only from memory.

8,9 The need was met by an old and run-down spinet, so that [Verdi] could learn to play, following the pounding of his teacher. During the autumn holidays, later, he would join his friend, the amateur musician Giov. Biazzi, who came there with a supply of music for his entertainment; they amused themselves at the pianoforte, coming to know Music, which his friend and contemporary had some notion of.

From the lessons he took with the pastor in reading and writing, and from those of the organist and from the knowledge of his friend, it did not take long to discover that our Giuseppe in both the former and the latter showed an innate gift.
MS, BIB, BUSSETO

Note inside the lid of Verdi's spinet

By me, Stefano Cavalletti, these new hammers were made and lined with leather, and I adjusted the pedal, which is a gift from me, as I also made the new hammers free of charge, seeing the good aptitude of the boy Giuseppe Verdi for learning and playing this instrument, for this is enough to repay me completely. Anno Domini 1821.
MS, MTS, MILAN

From Delfico's unfinished biography

His father, rightly thinking that his son's musical education should also be accompanied by literary education, had sent
11 him to Busseto, to the school of canon Seletti [the Ginnasio], boarding at the home of a fellow-townsman of Roncole, nicknamed Pugnatta, a cobbler by trade, who housed and fed the boy for the sum of thirty centesimi a day. Mind you, the cost of living then was not so high as it now is; and remember that the boy knew how to make enough a feast; a precocious philosopher, as he was a precocious musician.
AB I, 9

From Demaldè's 'Cenni biografici'

In November 1823, he began lessons at the Ginnasio in Busseto, and at the same time music lessons under the direction of the Maestro di Cappella Sig. Ferdinando Provesi, happily and gratefully remembered for his moral 10 qualities, a true friend, more learned than not, and deeply concerned with the matters of his Profession, having composed abundant and worthy religious works, with the parents' hope that in time [Verdi] would be engaged somewhere as Organist. [. . .] He studied night and day, but he devoted most of the hours of the night to playing, as if heedless and little attentive to the Ginnasio lessons.

From there, however, he derived enough profit to excel among his classmates, not so much through unflagging study as through the alert intelligence with which nature had prodigally endowed him.
MS, BIB, BUSSETO

From Giovanni Fulcini's memoir

On all Sundays and holy days he came back to Roncole on foot, to be ready to play the organ at the holy functions, receiving 40 lire annually from the church council, beyond the proceeds of special occasions. Thus two years of assiduous work passed and Maestro Ferdinando Provesi ingenuously declared that his pupil already knew more than he himself did.
RO, 59

From Delfico's unfinished biography

It was Christmas, and little Verdi had to be at Roncole to play the organ for the dawn Mass. He set out from Busseto in the heart of the night; but the night was dark, so foggy that the road could not be seen and one had to grope one's way. For quite a distance the walker was sustained by his familiarity with the places; but perhaps he had trusted this too much. At a certain point, almost at the end of his journey, either because of a turning not perceived in time or because he had begun inadvertently walking on the edge of the road, he suddenly missed his footing and plunged into the fairly deep ditch that carried the waters of the Roncole canal towards Busseto. The bed was marshy; the boy was trapped there, and the more he struggled with his hands and feet, the deeper he sank into the treacherous mire. Surely he would have been unable to extract himself, if, at his shouts, a peasant woman, also passing by on her way to the village church, had not rushed to him. And thus saved, but in sorry state, the little musician reached his organ.
AB I, 10

From Demaldè's 'Cenni biografici'

The teachers at the Ginnasio, and especially the Professor of Latin grammar and the highly erudite antiquarian and librarian of his city, the abbot and canon Signor Don Pietro Seletti, seeing from [Verdi's] scant application to his studies the immense progress he could make if he applied himself in earnest, never ceased telling him what they thought, urging him to abandon either the Ginnasio or the music lessons since *non potes Duobus dominis servire*, whereupon, out of fear of being expelled from the Ginnasio, he sometimes stayed away from his music lessons. When Gius. was questioned by Maestro Provesi about this alternative to the music lessons and his coldness towards them, he had difficulty answering, but the kindness and sweetness of Provesi gently forced Verdi to tell him the origin of this new system, which did not please the Maestro in the least. [. . .] Provesi, gifted in both [music and letters], added: 'Know, my boy, that if you apply yourself to your lessons as in the past, you will become an excellent Maestro. I could not predict the same for your learned studies, not because you lack talent but because of your overweening love of music.'

MS, BIB, BUSSETO

In the end, Giuseppe divided his time, profitably, between his two masters, though music maintained its dominion.

From Demaldè's 'Cenni biografici'

When he had reached his fourteenth year, he was able to arrange, to compose, and to teach the young. And in fact he wrote marches and Rondòs for band and had them performed. And he was also expert in sight-reading with ease and skill at the piano even the most difficult composition, whether fantasias, capriccios, variations, or concertos for that instrument. [. . .] In 1828, in the Busseto theatre the masterpiece of the immortal Pesarese [Rossini], *Il barbiere di Siviglia*, was being performed, which, as everyone knows, does not have an Overture, and he [Verdi], unbeknownst even to his teacher, composed one which he then offered the orchestra so that it could at least be heard.

It was rehearsed again and again, then considered by the intelligent a not unworthy piece, it was so decided that it could rightly be placed before the opera by the man who had been asked to give it, as the Debut. The ovations he received from the audience for that first creation were many and very tumultuous. This first victory in his native city proved such a strong stimulus to his talent that a short time later he came forth with other overtures, arias, duets, piano concertos, variations on themes of his own or of established composers, for various instruments.

He went still further: using the words of [illegible, but probably Alfieri] he set to music 'the ravings of Saul' for baritone.

MS, BIB, BUSSETO

From Delfico's unfinished biography

Meanwhile the threads of his destiny were being arranged. A leading Busseto merchant, the very one from whom Carlo Verdi purchased supplies for his store, was a great lover of music. Antonio Barezzi, for this was his name, became fond of the good and studious youth; he realized that something could be made of him, certainly something more than a village organist; and meanwhile, to offer him a way of living in the city without being an expense for the family, he took him, aged barely twelve, into his home. [. . .]

Antonio Barezzi plays a great role in Verdi's life, especially in the first period, which was that of the hardest trials. [. . .] Barezzi [. . .] was not only President of the Society [of the Filarmonici, the city's amateur orchestra] but also played the flute, and in the concerts of the city band sometimes the clarinet, sometimes the horn, and perhaps also that complicated and noisy novelty, the ophicleide. In the Barezzi home the Società filarmonica met; in the drawing-room of that house the band rehearsed, and sometimes concerts were also held. I may add, to complete the story, that in the Barezzi home there was a Viennese

piano, made by Fritz: a good instrument on which a dear and pretty girl, Margherita by name, a musician like her father, practised the mastery of notes.

Imagine now how the little organist of Roncole must have found himself in his element. [. . .]

Thus the adolescent lived until his eighteenth year; for music, in the study of music, in an air as impregnated with music as you can conceive. [. . .] The beautiful Margherita was happy for the guest in the house to continue his studies on the same keyboard where she trained her slender, white fingers. At that piano the first strands of a sweet idyll were woven. She, beautiful, full of grace, feeling and intelligence; he, a lively youth, robust of frame, with a deep gaze, a stern face, but already illuminated by that placid smile which still today blooms on the soft, full lips of the glorious old man, tempering the austere majesty of his aspect. The two were born to understand each other.

AB I, 12–16

The time came for young Verdi to continue his studies beyond the limited possibilities of Busseto. The local Monte di pietà, an organization which made its income as a pawnshop but devoted funds to charity, had some scholarships in its gift. Verdi's father applied for one for his son, supporting his application by a petition to the Duchess of Parma, Napoleon's widow, Marie-Louise of Austria.

Carlo Verdi's petition; Roncole, 14 December 1831

Majesty!

To protect and foster the sciences and the arts is among the liveliest concerns of Your Majesty, who equally takes to heart the welfare and the ornament of these most happy States. This encourages the hopes of Carlo Verdi of Roncole of Busseto, Your Majesty's humble servant and most faithful subject, concerning the future, better destiny of his only son Giuseppe, pupil of the music school of the same Busseto under the direction of Maestro Ferdinando Provesi, that Your Majesty may deign to contemplate him among those poor youths who, because of lack of means, are supported by the Sacro Monte di pietà with a stipend for a four-year period, whence to apply themselves abroad to that science, profession, or art in which, having shown talent and special inclination, they leave no doubt as to the most rewarding success.

Modesty forbids your Humble Petitioner to exalt the merits of his own son in the fine art to which he has devoted himself now for four years. With the most sweet swelling of the heart, he hears only public acclamations and applause given him whenever he is heard playing the pianoforte or producing his compositions in every sort of music, whether vocal or instrumental. He is distressed only by his needy state, which prevents him from continuing to assure his son the means by which to develop fully his harmonic knowledge.

The attached certificate will suffice to justify the plea, unless he be asked to demonstrate his talent through an examination: a decision which would be most welcome and desired both by pupil and teacher, as well as by him who sincerely implores the Sovereign's Benevolent Consideration.

MS, MCP, BUSSETO

Provesi's certificate; Busseto, 15 December 1831

I certify out of pure truth that Gius. Verdi, son of Carlo, a

youth of approximately eighteen, has been my pupil in the school of music for the four-year course, during which time he has displayed a singular genius in this art, distinguishing himself especially in performance on the pianoforte as well as in every kind of harmonic composition. [. . .]
MS, MCP, BUSSETO

Antonio Accarini, Mayor of Busseto and President of the Monte di pietà, to Carlo Verdi; Busseto, 13 February 1832

I am pleased to inform you that His Excellency the President of the Interior, with an act of the 9th of this month, forwarded to me by the Chancellery of Borgo San Donnino with a letter of 10 February no. 1860, has approved that your son Giuseppe be provided with an annual sum of 300 lire [. . .] for four consecutive years out of special regard for the extraordinary talent that he has shown. [. . .]

However, he will not be able to benefit from the above stipend until the first vacancy [. . .] which will be on 1 November 1832. [. . .]
MS, MCP, BUSSETO

Barezzi was willing to advance the money, naturally. And so, on 22 May 1832, Verdi's passport was issued. His father and his teacher Provesi accompanied him to Milan, where Professor Giuseppe Seletti (nephew of Don Pietro) lodged him as a paying guest.

Verdi's formal application for admission to the Conservatory; Milan, 22 June 1832

Giuseppe Verdi has already begun the study of Music, but since in his native city of Busseto, Duchy of Parma, there are no means for him to achieve that advancement to which he aspires, he would therefore like to be admitted as a paying, boarding student, in the Imperial and Royal Conservatory of Milan.

Hence he addresses this petition to the Imperial Royal Government, trusting that in any examinations to which he might be put, at the above-mentioned Conservatory of Music, in him there will be found those talents contemplated in article 10 of the regulations of the Institution, so that he will be granted the dispensation required because of his having passed the usual age, being 18. [. . .]
MS, VSA, BUSSETO

Giuseppe Seletti to Antonio Barezzi; Milan, early July 1832

[. . .] The Verdi matter ended badly, as I had foreseen these last few days.

They insist there is no room, and he is the wrong age, and the pianist's opinion I wrote you in my last. Maestro Piantanida [Professor of counterpoint] is of the opinion that *he will prove mediocre.* [. . .]

Now make up your mind what is best for Verdi. Either you decide to support him and to succeed in your determination, or you decide to withdraw him. If you are of the first opinion, then expenses and other inconveniences must be discussed. Not everything can be said in a letter [. . .] considering in detail all a person's necessities, it is unlikely that all Verdi's needs can be met with 600 francs. Through next week, I will keep him in my house, as I have lodged and fed him till now. I would not be averse to keeping him with me afterwards, provided your and my interests are recognized, without giving any cause to alter our friendship in the future. [. . .]
AB I, 110–11

148

Years later, in a letter to the Neapolitan music historian Francesco Florimo, Verdi described his studies under the composer Vincenzo Lavigna.

Verdi to Florimo; 9 January 1871

[. . .] Lavigna was brought (I believe in 1801) to Milan by Paisiello, who was going to Paris, I don't know for what reason. Recommended by Paisiello, he wrote an opera for La Scala, and was engaged as repetiteur in that theatre, where he remained until 1832. In that year I met him and studied counterpoint under his guidance until 1835. Lavigna was very strong in counterpoint, slightly pedantic, and could see no other music but Paisiello's. I remember that in a Sinfonia I wrote for him, he corrected all the orchestration in the manner of Paisiello!! *I'm for it* – I said to myself – and after that I never showed him any free composition; and in the three years spent with him, I did nothing but canons and fugues, fugues and canons, in every possible way. Nobody taught me orchestration and how to handle dramatic music. That's what Lavigna was. [. . .]
MS, BC, NAPLES

Lavigna was pleased with his pupil, and on an early occasion decided to show him off – to Francesco Basily, director of the Conservatory and at least partly responsible for Verdi's rejection. An early biographer tells the story.

From Folchetto's notes to Pougin's biography

One evening the two teachers were conversing together about the deplorable results of a competition for the post of Maestro di cappella and organist of the cathedral of San Giovanni in Monza. None of the twenty-eight young men in competition had been able to develop the theme set by Basily and to make the fugue required by the competition.

Lavigna, surely with a touch of malice, said to Basily: 'That is really an extraordinary thing. Look at Verdi here, who has been studying fugue for about two years. I would bet he could have done better than all those twenty-eight.'

'Truly?' Basily answered, a bit sharply.

'Of course. Do you recall the theme?'

'Yes, I do.'

'Good, write it down.'

Basily agreed, and then Lavigna gave the theme to Verdi, saying: 'Sit at this desk and work on this subject a bit.'

The two teachers went on conversing, and after a while Verdi came over and said simply: 'Here you are!'

Basily took the copybook and examined it, showing signs of amazement as he proceeded. Having reached the end, he could not help but praise it, and at the same time he turned to Verdi and said: 'How does it happen that you have made a double canon of my theme?'

'The fact is,' the young man replied, not forgetting a certain famous rejection, 'the fact is I found it a bit thin, and I wanted to enrich it.'

Basily bit his lip, without a word.
FOL, 15

Verdi's studies, actually, ranged much farther than canons and fugues. Mozart, even more than Paisiello, was Lavigna's idol; and the young student was made to study his works (including *Don Giovanni*) thoroughly. He was also made familiar with the music of Haydn, Beethoven, even early Mendelssohn, as well as that of

the older Italian masters: Corelli, Palestrina, Marcello.
21 In Milan, Verdi was able to attend La Scala, where in
the years 1832–33 there were – among others – operas by
Mercadante and Donizetti. In June 1833 he made a visit
to Busseto.

Giuseppe Seletti to Antonio Barezzi; Milan, August 1833

I have heard of the death of Provesi [26 July]; I am sorry
about it because, except for a few little weaknesses, he was a
man of learning. I imagine you will now arrange for Verdi
to be given his post; Lavigna also believes this. But
somehow or other the nomination must be put off for a
year, with others substituting at religious functions. [. . .]

Lavigna has told me that if Verdi continues to study as he
did at the beginning, he needs only one more year to be
completely trained; but you made a *great mistake* [. . .]
keeping him so long in Busseto. [. . .]
AB I, 126

29 *Vincenzo Lavigna to the Monte di pietà; Milan, 24 February
1834*

I, the undersigned, Maestro di musica and Professor in the
I. R. Conservatory of Music in this city, declare that from
the month of June of the year 1832, until the present, Signor
Giuseppe Verdi, native of Busseto in the state of Parma, has
been taught by me in Counterpoint and Free Composition,
and is also continuing this study at present under my tuition.
I declare further that Signor Verdi has made and continues
in these studies to make praiseworthy, indeed notable
progress, wherefore I am happy to give him this certificate,
the more so because the above-praised Signor Verdi
deserves no less praise for his good moral conduct.
MS, MCP, BUSSETO

Seletti was not a genial landlord, and Verdi was clearly
not an ideal lodger.

Giuseppe Seletti to Antonio Bàrezzi; Milan, 4 May 1834

[. . .] It is no longer convenient for me to have Verdi. He
knows nothing of this decision of mine; had you come, you
could have announced it to him, and I would have told you
in person all those reasons that cannot be written in a letter.
[. . .]
AB I, 127

In April 1834, Verdi had had his first taste of public
acclaim, conducting an amateur performance of
Haydn's *The Creation* (the event is narrated in Verdi's
biographical conversation with Ricordi, see pp. 11–12).
Obviously, Milan – Italy's musical capital – was the place
for him. But duty, Barezzi, and Margherita were all
calling him back to Busseto, to the tedious post of city
music-master and organist.
In June 1834, the question of appointing Provesi's
successor came to a head. Barezzi sent Carlo Verdi to
Milan to bring the candidate home. The next chapter in
Verdi's life is far more complex than it is interesting.
Though the position of Maestro di musica was neither
illustrious nor remunerative, it was sought after. It also
involved clerical-secular conflict. Provesi, obviously a
diplomat as well as a musician, had managed to act both
as organist-director of religious music (Maestro di
cappella) and as director of the Filarmonici, whose ranks

lead). It was for this joint appointment that Verdi
applied to the parish authorities, belatedly, on 20 June
1834, only after his rival Giovanni Ferrari had already
been named organist.
This appointment, made abruptly and without a public
competition, aroused local wrath, and Verdi – no doubt
prodded by Barezzi – wrote directly to Marie-Louise,
petitioning her to set aside the appointment.

Verdi to Marie-Louise; Busseto, 28 June 1834

Majesty,
In November 1833 Giuseppe Verdi of Roncole of Busseto,
Your Majesty's most humble and faithful subject, intended
to present to the parochial council of Busseto an application
to replace his deceased music teacher Ferdinando Provesi,
and he would have done so if the Mayor had not assured
him [. . .] it had been decided to assign the post through a
competition of the candidates, to guarantee a good choice
in the person selected.
The plan was for a long time suspended, and in the
meanwhile the petitioner has, with all his power, worked to
advance in musical instruction, in order to enter and sustain
the struggle of said Competition.
On returning home from Milan on the 18th of the
current month to enter the application, to his greatest
surprise, he was told that Provost Ballarini [. . .] had hastily
summoned the entire Council that same day and had
proceeded to name as Maestro di cappella a certain
Giovanni Ferrari of Guastalla. [. . .]
Thus, Majesty, were disappointed the well-founded
hopes of the Petitioner, who having enjoyed the scholastic
support of the above-mentioned Monte, to complete his
musical studies [. . .] flattered himself that [. . .] he would
be able to demonstrate to his homeland and to the State that
he had fulfilled the purpose for which he was subsidized and
could be useful both to himself and to his poor family, had
he won the Competition. [. . .]
DREI, 5–6.

The issue was a political rather than a musical one.
Verdi's supporters belonged to the faction known as the
coccardisti ('cockade-wearers', revolutionaries, liberals),
and Ferrari's were the *codini* ('pigtail-wearers', re-
actionaries, clericals). The battle raged. Barezzi and his
faction were pilloried in an anonymous poem. The
Bishop of Fidenza feared open violence.

*Luigi Sanvitale, Bishop of Fidenza, to the President (Minister) of
the Interior of Parma; 11 March 1835*

Calumnies, and more calumnies, are those things reported
to Your Most Illustrious Lordship, to which you refer in
your most cordial letter of the 6th of the current month of
March. [. . .] I know well that the local District
Commissioner wrote towards the end of Carnival to the
Mayor of Busseto, saying that the Provost and those Priests
who are part of the parish council and the committee of the
Sacro Monte di Pietà are the chief fomenters of all the
dissent and the turbulence in the city concerning the
Filarmonici, which still continue, indeed increase to such a
degree that it is believed a revolution is at hand. Order the
civil authorities and the military to be vigilant, to suppress
the rebellion at its birth. But it is they, and not the Priests –
absit verbo invidia – who fan the flames. [. . .] Things seemed
settled, but fire lies beneath the ash [. . .].
DREI, 13–14

28 In the end a solution was found. The competition was held, and Verdi won it. Ferrari, who had not competed, was allowed to continue as organist, while Verdi took over all secular musical duties. Negotiations went on for months, during which time Verdi returned to Milan and completed his studies with Lavigna. At his teacher's suggestion, he applied for the better-paid position of organist in Monza; but local pressure from Busseto forced him to withdraw. Understandably vexed, Verdi wrote to Lavigna, appropriately quoting Dante's *Inferno*.

Verdi to Vincenzo Lavigna; Busseto, late 1835

'New torments and new tormented'. Just when I thought I was about to be free of all my problems, and earn my bread honourably and comfortably, I find myself once more plunged into the abyss, where I see only darkness. Last Saturday was the day set for me to go to Milan, and so the day before, I sent an express letter to Parma for my passport, but when in Busseto they learned of my departure there was an uproar you cannot imagine. The faction hostile to the Filarmonici rejoiced and insulted the other. The other became enraged and hurled insults at me and at Signor Barezzi. Finally things reached the point where the Filarmonici party, after telling me of the commitments made and the insults suffered, and the benefits I had received from my homeland, [...] irked by my refusal, came to frighten me with threats even of forcing me to stay in Busseto if I were to leave.

If my benefactor Barezzi had not risked suffering on my account the almost general hatred of the town, I would have left at once. [...] For this reason alone I have remained in Busseto, and now to my great sacrifice there is added another sorrow, that of having involved you and of not being able to respond to all your concern. [...]
GATTI, 99–100

While the outcome of the Maestro di musica controversy was still unknown, Verdi had already begun writing an opera (probably the elusive *Rocester*; see p. 151), evidently with the hope of its being performed by the same amateur group in Milan that had given *The Creation* under his direction. Head of the group was Pietro Massini, with whom Verdi was in correspondence.

Verdi to Pietro Massini; Busseto, 24 January 1836

[...] I am sorry not to have kept my word to you. Before leaving Milan I promised to come back at once to write the opera, but afterwards my freedom was not my own, so I could not maintain what I had promised. If I am named Maestro here, the township grants me two months' holiday, September and October and then (if you consent) I am ready to keep my promises. It will be a great stroke of luck for me, if I can write an opera. Rest assured my gratitude towards you will be eternal. [...]
MS, BQ, BRESCIA

Chancellor of Borgo San Donnino, writing on instructions from the Minister of the Interior, to Mayor Accarini of Busseto; Borgo San Donnino, 12 March 1836

[...] As a result of this nomination (which will be officially communicated by you to the Council of the Monte di pietà,

150

to Verdi, and to the head of the Società filarmonica) proceedings must go forward between the Maestro and the Administrations charged with his stipend, for the regular drafting of the contract. [...] Also through special instructions given me by the above-mentioned Ministry, I further beg you to urge Signor Verdi to avoid all conflict and gossip [...] similar representations will then be made to the influential men of the two factions, warning all to beware of public demonstrations. [...]
GATTI, 108–9

Verdi to the Mayor of Busseto, 14 March 1836

Your esteemed letter of 12 current month No. 4266 leads me to believe that someone, prompted I know not by what motive, mentioned me to the Magistrature in the cited letters as one of the dissenters who caused agitation in Busseto over the nomination of a Maestro di musica.

Your Excellency will surely not be unaware that I was an impassive spectator of this long battle. Immersed in my beloved study of Music, and virtually forgetting the conflict, I expected from Justice what finally arrived, namely a competition, desired by all, and nothing more. [...] All know that I never mixed with the factions, that I have never fomented or vexed any of these, that I have never been so wicked as to take pleasure in these hostilities. [...] I shall never depart from this behaviour, and so neither my competitors nor my adversaries have ever had nor shall ever have cause to suspect that I intrigue with them or against them. [...]
MS, MCP, BUSSETO

Verdi's appointment as Maestro, when it finally came, had one happy result: he could marry Margherita at last.

Verdi's marriage certificate; Busseto, 16 April 1836   30, 34

The year one thousand eight hundred and thirty-six, the sixteenth day of April, before me the undersigned Mayor of the township of Busseto, division of Borgo San Donnino, Duchy of Parma, there have appeared the Signor Verdi Giuseppe, unwed son of the living Signori Carlo and Uttini Luigia, aged twenty-two, Maestro di musica of the township of Busseto, born and resident at Roncole of this same township, and the Signora Barezzi Margherita Francesca Maria Monica, daughter of the living Signori Antonio and Demaldè Maria, aged twenty-one, spinster, born and resident in Busseto, who have declared to me that it is their intention to be united in matrimony, and in compliance with the law they have therefore produced the authentic certificates of their birth, attached to this ledger.

There also appeared Signor Verdi Carlo, innkeeper and landowner, son of the late Giuseppe, aged fifty, resident at Roncole, and Signor Barezzi Antonio, son of the late Giovanni, aged forty-eight with his wife Signora Demaldè Maria [...] all of whom have given their consent to the marriage. The mother of the groom Uttini Luigia did not appear because prevented by poor health. [...]
MS, AS, PARMA

The young couple, accompanied by Carlo Verdi, set off   31, 33
for a brief visit to Milan, where they were the guests of Professor Seletti, Verdi's former landlord. This hospitality had been arranged by Barezzi.

Giuseppe Seletti to Antonio Barezzi; Milan, 25 April 1836

[. . .] As you write to me sincerely and urge me to reply sincerely, I will so write. I cannot like Verdi very much. But you and your daughter and all your family: you can imagine how dear you are to me. Therefore as far as you are concerned, all formality is pointless. And though I said I do not find Verdi likeable, I did not mean that I did not want to see him. You and he and your daughter are masters of my house, and my usual bed will do for the married couple, and there is another for you, procured a few days ago. [. . .]
AB I, 230

During the first months of his married life, Verdi had many things on his mind besides his Busseto duties and the opera he was writing. In Milan, his old teacher Lavigna died (with 'no suspicion of cholera', the official report says). At home there were problems with the Monte di pietà, which owed his father money, owed in turn to Barezzi. After the usual appeals, the sum was granted, and – as a parenthesis – the document of the Monte di pietà, confirming the grant, describes him as 'tireless in his Profession (I am assured he has completed a *dramma serio* which may be heard at the Ducal Theatre)' (GATTI, 116).

38–44

Verdi to Pietro Massini; Busseto, 16 September 1836

For some time I have been eager to have news of you, but the Cholera has interrupted our correspondence till now. I am always the same, and I was awaiting a definite answer about the opera. I foresee there will be obstacles, and for this reason I desire a letter from you all the more. Meanwhile I inform you that I have finished the opera except for those little passages that had to be adjusted by the poet. Help me if you can, for I need it. [. . .]
MS, BQ, BRESCIA

Verdi to Pietro Massini; Busseto, 15 October 1836

From your last letter I have learned what you write about the opera, and though you still encourage me to hope, I foresee clearly that, for this year, nothing will be done. [. . .] In a little town there are no resources for one whose profession is music, there are no hopes of advancement, far from the city, so you see I am spending the finest days of my youth in nothingness. [. . .]
MS, CIMGD, BERGAMO

Verdi to Pietro Massini; Busseto, 21 September 1837

It is not unlikely that I shall be able to stage the opera *Rocester* in this Carnival season at Parma, therefore I beg you to go with the bearer of this letter (who is an intimate friend of mine) to the author of the libretto, Piazza, and tell him the story. If Piazza would like to change some verses we are still in time and, indeed, I would beg him to extend the duet of the two women to make it a more grandiose number. [. . .]

Oh, what a pleasure it would have been for me to stage *Rocester* in Milan, but unfortunately I see for myself that I am too far away from the city to arrange everything that is necessary. [. . .]
MS, CIMGD, BERGAMO

Verdi to Pietro Massini; Busseto, 3 November 1837

I was in Parma for a few days awaiting the new Impresario,

a certain Granci of Lucca. Meanwhile I was securing support from the Theatre Committee, from the Orchestra, in all of which I was successful, because, I will tell you in friendship, not through my own merit, I enjoy some respect in Parma. Day before yesterday the Impresario finally came, and I introduced myself at once in the name of the Committee, and he told me straight out that it was not in his interest to run risks with an opera whose outcome was uncertain. [. . .] I returned home angry and most sad without the least hope. Poor young people, much good it does them to study! Always without recompense!

Tell me: would it not be possible for you to speak to Merelli [impresario at La Scala] to see if it could be performed in some Theatre in Milan? Tell him first of all that I would like the score to be submitted to the examination of worthy composers, and if their judgment were negative, I would not like the opera performed. [. . .]
MS, CIMGD, BERGAMO

49

This mysterious opera of Verdi's, *Rocester*, has a disputed, but brief, history. Early biographers assumed it was simply a primitive version of *Oberto, conte di San Bonifacio*, the first Verdi opera to be performed. Later and more thorough investigation, notably by Frank Walker, has suggested that the two works are distinct. The first, *Rocester*, written at Massini's encouragement, had originally been intended for the Milanese amateurs who had performed *The Creation*. After failure to secure performance in Parma, Verdi himself visited Milan briefly in May 1838, and returned again – with Margherita – during his autumn holidays that year.

Verdi to Antonio Barezzi; Milan, 11 September 1838

We arrived happily in Milan on the evening of the 8th. We found no lodgings for ourselves or for the horse; but luckily we have found apartments with great freedom at Prof. Seletti's. I will not describe the reviews of the troops the Emperor made on horseback or the court ball or the decoration of the Duomo. You can hear the newspapers' descriptions. People are lined up at La Scala and I want to go. I will write you a long letter soon. Greet all the friends. Ghitta [Margherita] is well. A heartfelt kiss.
AB I, 247

The excitement in Milan was due to the presence of Emperor Ferdinand I of Austria, who had come to be crowned King of Lombardy-Venetia in the Duomo.

Verdi to Antonio Barezzi; Milan, 16 September 1838

The Emperor has left and the uproar is over. Milan is always beautiful, but in moments like these! [. . .] Of the important matter I can tell you nothing; but I hope in my next letter you will hear something definite and at length. I send you a copy of my *Romanze* to give to Dr Frignani.[. . .]
AB I, 247–8

46

The *Sei romanze*, six songs, were Verdi's first published work, brought out by the Milanese firm of Canti; Dr Frignani had been a witness at Verdi's wedding. The important matter is, of course, the prospect of an opera's being performed at La Scala. By this time the opera in question seems to be *Oberto, conte di San Bonifacio*.

51

Verdi to friends in Busseto; Milan, 6 October 1838

What the devil gives you people the notion that my opera is to be performed on the 15th of this month? I never said or wrote this. This is one of the usual fine pieces of nonsense. Oh what imaginative minds! I will tell you frankly that I came here to discuss the Opera, but the season was too far advanced and since three operas and a cantata have already been given and three more are to come, already promised to the public (an immense undertaking), there is no time left to stage mine decently.

It might be given next Carnival; but it is a new opera, written by a new composer, to be presented in the first theatre of the world, no less; I want to give it much more thought. [. . .]
AB I, 249

45 *Verdi to the Mayor of Busseto; Busseto, 28 October 1838*

I see clearly that I cannot be as useful as I would have wished to this most unhappy city of mine, and I am sorry that circumstances have prevented me from demonstrating the effects of my wishes, here where I was granted the first means to advance in that art which I profess.

The need to earn enough to nourish my family forces me to seek elsewhere that which I cannot have in my homeland. Therefore in accordance with article 8 of the contract between this Township and myself, made on 20 April 1836, I announce to Your Excellency, before the six months expire, that·I will no longer continue to serve here in the position of Maestro di musica beyond 10 May 1839.

I shall take with me and retain forever all my affection for my native land and the grateful esteem for those who loved me, encouraged me, and assisted me. [. . .[
MS, MCP, BUSSETO

193   Antonio Ghislanzoni (1823–93), baritone, poet, journalist and librettist, describes Milan in the late 1830s.

From Ghislanzoni's 'Storia di Milano del 1836 al 1848'

Nobody breathed a word of politics. The streets were lighted by oil lamps, and the glow of the flames quite blinded the passer-by. The Milanese boasted greatly of their cleanliness, and the side walks, at the same time, were crossed by trickles that did not smell of musk. The cathedral, admired by foreigners, served as urinal for our more civilized citizens, who, to the greater outrage of the building, were numerous. The city would wake up about eleven in the morning; the true *lions* did not appear in public until one in the afternoon. [. . .] Aristocracy and trade glared at each other. The young men of good family got drunk on port or madeira, and later killed themselves with absinthe. This atrocious beverage was introduced in Milan around 1840. The fashion of moustache and full beard encountered furious and persistent opponents. Many fathers of families bore grudges against sons or grandsons for a slight insubordination of hair. [. . .] Three-quarters of the population knew no other world beyond that enclosed within the circuit of the walls. The opening of the railway between Monza and Milan was a colossal event which seemed a miracle. Old men were heard to exclaim: Now that I have seen this wonder, I am happy to die! And several, in fact, died. [. . .] At the tavern of La Foppa, you could dine at the price of one Austrian lira. That dinner was composed of three courses, soup, wine, vegetables. In the taverns and also in the luxury hotels, the table was

152

illuminated by tallow candles. At every change of dish, the *boy* went around with the snuffer – the soot rained into the soup. [. . .] A pound of beef cost seventeen soldi, and half the population tasted meat only on Sunday or the great Church feast days. [. . .] Men who thought of Italy, who fretted beneath foreign servitude, who detested Austria, were very few in number. The majority ignored Italy's existence. And yet, some were acting in secret, some were writing, some assumed the dangerous mission of spreading the papers of Mazzini. Then there were terrible risks in speaking of politics, even with one's most intimate friends.
GHIS, 129–59

This was the Milan to which Verdi came in February 1839, with Margherita and their seven-month son Icilio Romano (a daughter, Virginia, had been born in Busseto on 26 March 1837 and had died on 12 August 1838). His career was about to begin. In April, Canti brought out 47–48 two more songs and a *Notturno* for soprano, tenor, bass, and flute obbligato, which was favourably reviewed. La Scala was thinking of doing *Oberto*, in aid of a theatrical charity, with a cast including Giuseppina Strepponi (the 50 soprano who was to become Verdi's second wife) and the baritone Giorgio Ronconi. Verdi himself told the 56 story years later.

Verdi to Opprandino Arrivabene, 7 March 1874

[. . .] My opera *Oberto* was to have been given in the spring of 1839 for the benefit of the Pio Istituto Filarmonico. It was to have been sung by la Peppina [Strepponi], Ronconi, Moriani . . . the parts had already been distributed when Moriani became seriously ill and sang no more. At the end of the season one fine morning an employee of the Theatre [La Scala] came to tell me that Merelli wished to speak to me. I had never spoken to Merelli and I thought the invitation was a mistake, nevertheless I went. Merelli said these precise words to me: 'I have heard la Strepponi and Ronconi speak well of your opera. If you will adapt it for la Marini, Salvi, etc. . . . . I will have it performed without any expense on your part. If the opera pleases, we will sell it and share the proceeds. If it does not please, so much the worse for you and for me!'
ALB, 170–2

Verdi to Pietro Massini; Milan, 6 October 1839

The affairs of my Opera continue to go well. The singers are all pleased and the women have their parts. The score remains my property, and I am having the parts copied by the firm of Ricordi. [. . .] 53
MS, BQ, BRESCIA

Icilio Romano Verdi died on 22 October 1839.
On 17 November 1839, premiere of *Oberto, conte di San* 52, 54 *Bonifacio* at La Scala, Milan.

La Fama, Milan, November 1839

Milan, Teatro alla Scala. – I would not like *Oberto, conte di San Bonifazio* to be confounded with that wretched array of librettos that outrage the Muses and common sense, through their contempt for proper versification and through those absurdities of plot that are the shame of our operatic Theatre; for two qualities save it from ostracism, its having abstained from ultramontane turpitudes and its having chosen an Italian subject. [. . .]

The music of this Opera, which was specially written by the Maestro Signor Verdi, is very close to Bellini's style, and melody is lavished there generously, perhaps even too much so, for in the places where the words demanded energy and passion, the song is languid and monotonous. Apart from this defect, it well deserved the applause which welcomed it [. . .], thanks to the beautiful orchestration, the sweetness of song, and the purity and novelty of ideas. La Marini's cavatina and that of Salvi in the first act, Marini's aria, Salvi's, and the quartet of the second act are masterly numbers, which reveal great musical knowledge, and which bear the stamp of inspiration. The performance, to tell the truth, did not greatly help us appreciate the beautiful things, since, if you except la Marini, who sang with distinction, the others seemed to be competing at singing off pitch. Salvi, tired after a long series of performances, could not display to its full power the beautiful voice he possesses, and often he did not arrive at the required note. Marini seemed to be playing blind man's buff, lucky when he hit the mark. La Shaw, appearing in the Theatre for the first time, has a voice and a happy enunciation, but, still a novice in both singing and acting, she is not made for a principal Theatre like ours. In the later evenings, if it so happens that the singers gain confidence and are in greater agreement among themselves, this Opera will surely grow in public favour, which was so openly shown from the Introduction on; if the sets and costumes were also better and more suitable, then one's entertainment would be complete.

TAL, 28 NOV. 1839

Allgemeine Musikalische Zeitung, Leipzig, 5 February 1840

[. . .] The season ended with two new operas. The first (29 October), entitled *I ciarlatani* (from a vaudeville by Scribe) by Signor Maestro Giacomo Panizza had already run its course after the second performance. The second (17 November), entitled *Oberto, conte di San Bonifazio*, by Maestro Giuseppe Verdi, pleased in an extraordinary fashion and in a small way was epoch-making; how long it will really last in the repertory time will tell, but a journey for it across the Alps in the near future cannot be lacking, and we will see how it is judged by foreigners. [. . .] This arid subject, supplied by a local journalist [Piazza], was adapted into a libretto with unlikely situations, with some episodes cut and in a fashion as arid as the subject itself by an apprentice in belles lettres, who for a while has also been a composer [Temistocle Solera, future librettist of *Nabucco*]. These two gentlemen are mentioned here because both, through their numerous friends, have powerfully contributed to the opera's good reception. [. . .] As far as the music more specifically is concerned, it must be noted here, out of respect for the truth, that it is generally melodious and hence praiseworthy; still its character often has the hue of the modern school; the melody lacks the fascination of novelty and character; harmony, composition, art in general have scant relief, and there is also in the opera a certain uniformity. Already the Overture shows no mastery. The paradise of today's Italian orchestras is the charming valve trumpet, moving (especially when used in mellifluous cabalettas) to the point of causing the listener to sigh, to languish, and to blink; with this voluptuous instrument Signor Verdi begins his Overture. He has two solo trumpets, that is, perform a cantabile (Adagio, D major, 3/4), which has the flavour of a banal pastoral (what does this have in common with the opera?); the winds repeat it, until the orchestra enters full blast in the traditional manner

and, what do you think?, then there comes an Allegro made of ill-assorted pieces, clumsily patched together: a wretched *non erat hic locus*. [. . .]

This opera, originally commissioned for the Pio Istituto dell'Orchestra alla Scala, has made its author's fortune. It is generally said that Signor Merelli, impresario of the above-mentioned theatre and agent for the management of the Vienna opera, has signed a contract with Signor Verdi for the composition of two more operas. [. . .] Perhaps the Italian composers active at present could be thus classified: Donizetti, Mercadante, Ricci, Verdi, etc. Donizetti is more lyrical than Mercadante and knows composition as well as he. Ricci is more original than Verdi. It remains to be seen if this last can rise higher; it is much to be wished, for he could surpass all his colleagues. [. . .]

CONATI, 83 FF.

From Antonio Barezzi's diary, June 1840

In Milan, at midday on the feast of Corpus Christi [18 June], my beloved daughter Margherita died in my arms of some terrible disease perhaps unknown to medical science; she was in the flower of her years and at the height of her good fortune, for she had become the life-companion of that excellent young man Giuseppe Verdi, composer.

WAL, 33

On 5 September 1840, premiere of *Un giorno di regno* at La Scala, Milan.

La Moda, Milan, September 1840

Un giorno di regno – new Opera buffa by Maestro Verdi (5 September) – Maestro Verdi, author of *Oberto di San Bonifazio*, the young debutant of last year, so fêted, so applauded, received the other evening a stern admonition from the spectators of our great Theatre. His new Opera buffa, *Un giorno di regno*, had quite a different reception from his first opera. The Public either remained silent or condemned the judgment of those who believed applause opportune. The Overture, two duets between two basses in the first and second acts, and the aria of la Abbadia were praised; all the rest failed, and there is little hope that in the following evenings this harsh verdict can be modified, unless the singers decide, with a more strict performance, to underline some of the beautiful passages recognized by the intelligent listeners in the ensembles.

To be sure, this is a misfortune for Verdi, but it must not make him dejected; let him bid farewell to this new path on which he has set out, and let him return to the impassioned inspirations of serious opera; let *Oberto*'s author not deliberately exile himself from that atmosphere of emotions, of love, of sweet and moving song, that won him his first battle, in order to be engulfed in this new labyrinth of outmoded forms, trite phrases, of motives too close to a cold and servile imitation. The future is open before him, the future which does not deceive the man who banishes self-deception.

The performance of this Opera offers us the opportunity of warning some of the present singers of our Theatre that, whatever reception they may be given by the Spectators, whatever spirit of rivalry or envy may corrode their artistic spirit, they must never defy or show contempt for public opinion, that their deportment must always conform to the most severe respect, and to that decorum which should exclude any idea of impropriety, to use the mildest word. We can also add that if the Opera does not please, its

Felice Romani. Engraving. William Weaver Collection, Monte San Savino (AR).
Romani was the author of the libretto of Gyrowetz's opera *Il finto Stanislao*, which Verdi set under the alternative title of *Un giorno di regno* (1840).

Verdi, *Un giorno di regno*, 1840 (*Il finto Stanislao*). Title page of libretto.

performers must nevertheless with equal good will present it to the Public, that to stop singing or merely to move the lips in ensembles shows a culpable ignorance of duty, for the Public does not lavish money on the stage's heroes to have them sing only at their caprice or when they prefer; and finally a singer's indifference or negligence, even in an unsuccessful Opera, can also be considered a chief element in its failure. [. . .]
TAL, 17 SEPT. 1840

Verdi to Tito Ricordi, 4 February 1859

[. . .] Slightly less than a year before that same public maltreated the opera of a poor, ill young man, pressed by time, and with his heart torn by a horrible misfortune! All this was known, but the rudeness was without restraint. Since then I have not seen *Un giorno di regno*, and it may well be a bad opera, and yet who knows how many others, no better, have been tolerated and perhaps even applauded. Oh, if then the public had, not applauded, but borne in silence that opera, I would not have had words enough to thank them! [. . .]
MS, ASR, MILAN

Verdi later (see his autobiographical narrative, p. 13) recalled the period after this fiasco as a time of dejection and idleness, when he had decided to give up any idea of an operatic career. Actually, the month after the single performance of *Un giorno di regno*, the composer conducted a revival of *Oberto* at La Scala, and he was soon composing new music for that opera, which was performed in Genoa, opening on 9 January 1841.

Verdi to Pietro Massini; Genoa, 11 January 1841

Oberto opened on Saturday and was received coldly. There was applause for the Overture, the Introduction (enthusiastically, with a call for Catone and for me), and la Marini's Cavatina was applauded. The Duet for Ferlotti and la Marini, cold (it's a new piece). The Chorus that follows, also new, was also cold (I must point out that in this opera I have added the stage band). Scant applause for the Duet that follows. Trio, cold. Also the Finale. In the second act, all numbers applauded, but very coldly. [. . .] I must tell you, however, that this public is made up half of Genoese and half of soldiers from Turin, and the two halves are always in opposition. [. . .]
CONATI, 92

Shortly after Verdi's return from Genoa to Milan, he was given the libretto of *Nabucco*, his third opera. But there was a slight difficulty before it could be performed. The impresario Merelli wanted to postpone it to the next season (spring 1842).

Giovannino Barezzi to his father Antonio Barezzi, in Busseto; Milan, 26 December 1841

[. . .] And then he [Verdi] decides to write to Merelli in rather harsh terms. Merelli resents that and [to a mutual friend, Pasetti] says: 'See how Verdi has misunderstood this! That is not my intention, but I did it so that I should gain credit with the subscribers when, towards the end of Carnival, I put out a new placard, with the announcement of the opera. Tell Verdi, however, to show la Strepponi her part, and if she wants to sing it I'll gladly put it on.'

Pasetti sends for Verdi and they go to see la Strepponi; they explain the situation and she very willingly agrees to sing in the opera and adds: 'Come here tomorrow at half past one and I'll look through my part.'

Next day – 23rd [December] 1841, that is – Verdi and Pasetti go to see la Strepponi and at the agreed time; she tries over her part at the pianoforte with Verdi and then says to him: 'I like this music very much, and I want to sing it when I make my debut [for the season]', and at once adds: 'Let's go and see Ronconi.' They get in Pasetti's cab, which had been waiting at the door, and go to see Ronconi. La Strepponi *points out to him the beauties of the opera* and Verdi tells him the plot. Ronconi, after hearing all about it, says: 'Very well, this evening I'll speak to the impresario and tell him that I don't want to sing in Nini's opera, but that I want to sing in yours.'

WAL, 166–7

At this point the soprano Giuseppina Strepponi, who was to play a major role in Verdi's life, after creating Abigaille in his *Nabucco*, must be more fully presented. An ideal person to make the introduction is that opera's librettist, Temistocle Solera, who had published a brief biographical article about her.

Temistocle Solera on Giuseppina Strepponi; 1840

Giuseppina Strepponi was born on 8 September 1815, in Lodi, daughter of the composer Feliciano Strepponi. [. . .] When she was barely fifteen she entered the Royal Conservatory of Music in Milan, having been already initiated in the musical art by her father's lessons. Thanks to assiduous study both of music and of literature, she was soon able to emulate the most educated of her companions.

When her father was torn from her by premature death after she had been studying at the Conservatory only two years, she remained another two, until her nineteenth year, the limit set by that establishment. [. . .] As soon as she left it, she went on to make her first appearance in the leading theatres of Trieste along with established artists, and won there flattering palms, heralds of greater successes.

In the mere five years that she has been exercising her art, with rapid and happy acclaim, and at the fresh age of twenty-four years, she has gloriously covered all of twenty-seven theatres. – Vienna, Florence, Venice, Bologna, Rome, Turin, and, last spring, the cultivated Milan, have admired in this young woman the finest gifts of nature, improved by constant study. [. . .]

Endowed with an extremely sensitive spirit, she can win her way, both with singing and expression, into the spectators' hearts. Cultivated and appealing in society, excellent daughter and sister, she has generously taken on the support of her whole family, and her little brothers and sisters are growing up, educated at her expense in the best schools. [. . .]

SOLERA, 170–1

Donizetti, though a friend of Giuseppina's, was not enthusiastic about the state of her voice in 1842, the time of *Nabucco*.

Gaetano Donizetti to his brother-in-law Antonio Vaselli in Rome; Milan, 4 March 1842

[. . .] There remains la Strepponi. Tell him [a Roman

Verdi's letter to Pietro Massini, 11 January 1841. Universitätsbibliothek, Frankfurt am Main.

Giuseppina Strepponi in the 1830s. Engraving. Conservatorio 'G. Verdi', Milan.

impresario] that this singer, in [my] *Belisario* here, made such a furore that she was the only one who never received any applause, that Verdi didn't want her in his opera and the management has forced her on him. [. . .]
ZAVADINI, 580

On 9 March 1842, premiere of *Nabucco* at La Scala, Milan.

Gazzetta di Milano, 13 and 20 March 1842

[. . .] Signor Verdi proved that he well understood the ideas of Solera, and, boldly self-confident, applied himself to interpreting his dramatic ideas. We say boldly, meaning to praise Signor Verdi, for it took this kind of boldness for him to place himself in the small but elect rank of composers who, caring nothing for the bad taste that still clouds the spirit of many, use everything in their power to break down, even partially, the over-worn but still long-used operatic conventions. [. . .] Now we may add that if the new score cannot perhaps be indicated as the perfect type of the true tragic opera, it can still be singled out as a felicitous and clearly determined example of what we would like tragic opera to be, and how we strongly wish it were felt by others. [. . .] From his first operas to this one, Verdi has greatly enriched himself and his ideas have taken on a singular development. So that even if some critic were reluctant to admit that Verdi's new opera marks an obvious progress in operatic art, he still could not deny it a great, indeed extraordinary progress in creative potency. [. . .]

Verdi's melody develops altogether spontaneously, fluent, clear, never forced, never flowery. [. . .] If comparisons are permitted, we might say it was in part generated by that of Bellini: but calmer, less pathetic, [less] impassioned, so that one would say its formation preceded that of the Sicilian composer, and was not derived from it. [. . .] Nor does it appear he handles harmony with any less love: we are led to this opinion by observing how he tends to isolate it in a certain way from the melody. [. . .] A rare display of praise was given Maestro Verdi (after the chorus 58 'Va, pensiero . . .'), and all hands clapped to demand an encore, in spite of the rule that forbids them; and the universal wish was splendidly granted. [. . .]
AB I, 414–15

For political as well as musical reasons, *Nabucco* (and especially 'Va, pensiero' [Go, thought], the oppressed Hebrews' chorus of love for their homeland) had a success unparalleled in the history of La Scala: 57 59 performances in its first year. Verdi was, at once, a composer in demand.

Verdi to Opprandino Arrivabene; 7 March 1874

After *Nabucco* I had all the contracts I wanted, and at its second performance, during the Ballet, Merelli came into Peppina's [Strepponi's] dressing room with a contract signed already by him in which only the figure of the price was missing. I added it myself. The opera was *I lombardi*. [. . .]
ALB, 175–6

According to some biographers, Verdi asked Giuseppina's advice privately and, at her suggestion,

later wrote in the considerable sum of eight thousand Austrian lire, the amount Bellini had received for *Norma*. Success brought social as well as artistic and financial satisfactions. The young Verdi was taken up by the Milanese aristocracy, and began to frequent the salon of Countess Clarina Maffei, who became a lifelong 69 friend. With another noble Milanese lady, Countess Emilia Morosini, Verdi also formed a lasting friendship. 68 Some arch letters to her, in this period, show this social side of the young composer, a still-awkward man of the world.

Verdi to Countess Morosini ; Busseto, summer 1842

[. . .] From a most charming hand I received your most charming letter, nor did that most charming lady know I was being written to by a most charming hand . . .: now a rest and a fermata on all those *charmings* because I don't know how to keep it up.

You will think I'm in a good humour; no, no, I am infuriated, distraught, with a face two feet long, I'm in a hellish mood, I don't know why. It may be because I am far from Milan. Oh Milan! Milan! . . .

I was in Bologna for five or six days. . . . I went to visit Rossini, who received me very politely, and his welcome seemed to be sincere. In any case, I am very pleased. When I think that Rossini is world-wide fame incarnate, I could kill myself and all imbeciles with me. Oh, it's a great thing to be Rossini! . . .

I am always tender, impassioned, ardent, half-dying for you. [. . .]
AB I, 422

Verdi to Countess Morosini; Milan, 21 July 1842

[. . .] I hear that you are enjoying yourself very much, and that the amusements and the waters [at Recoaro] are doing you much good. I am sincerely pleased. Send all domestic cares to the devil and you will be still better. I can tell you little of myself: that I am neither well nor ill, that I have not yet begun to write the new opera because I lack the poem, that I am very displeased with the revival of *Nabucco*. [. . .]
MS, EREDI MAFFEI, MILAN

On 11 February 1843, premiere of *I lombardi alla prima* 61–63 *crociata* at La Scala, Milan.

From Folchetto's notes to Pougin's biography

With *Nabucco* and with *I lombardi alla prima crociata* – that is to say his first great successes – Verdi began, I would almost say instinctively at the beginning, to perform a political action with his music. Foreigners will never be able to realize the influence that was to be exercised for a certain period by the ardent, fiery melodies Verdi found when situations or even individual passages of poetry reminded him of the unhappy condition of Italy, or her memories or her hopes. The audience discovered references everywhere, but Verdi had been aware of them first and had adapted to them his inspired music, which often ended by bringing revolution into the theatre. [. . .] With *I lombardi*, the Austrian censorship, followed by that of the little Italian tyrants, began that patient work of investigation, which it then did forever after, to cleanse the librettos Verdi used, to reduce them *ad usum delphini*, and to render impossible the demonstrations which – the audiences always then found a way of making. Let us see how things went this time. The Archbishop of Milan – to whom the Milanese later made a show of affection since he was more liberal than his masters – Cardinal Gaisruck, heard about the new opera that was being mounted at La Scala. He wrote on this subject a blazing letter to the chief of police, Torresani, in which he said that he knew in *I lombardi* there were processions, churches, the valley of Jehoshaphat, a conversion and a baptism – all things that, according to him could not be put on the stage without sacrilege. He ended by enjoining Torresani to forbid Merelli the production, and he threatened to write directly to the Emperor of Austria (Ferdinand I) about the licence and the lack of respect for religion that reigned in the Imperial and Royal Theatres.

The next day the impresario and the two authors received a communication from the I.R. Police in which it was said that *I lombardi* could not be staged, without serious changes, and it summoned them to the chief's office to define and decide them. Verdi haughtily rejected this summons. 'You two go,' he said to Merelli and Solera; 'as for myself, rehearsals are already well under way, the opera is going well, I will not change a note or a word. *It will be given as it is, or not at all.*'

Merelli and Solera went to the police, and Torresani, to excuse his ukase, showed the Archbishop's letter. Merelli pointed out to him that the costumes were ready, the scenery painted, the rehearsals almost finished; that artists, chorus, and orchestra were enthusiastic about the music of *I lombardi*, and that, Verdi being unwilling to accept cuts of any kind, he, Torresani, would be taking the responsibility for the suppression perhaps of a masterpiece. Solera in his turn defended the libretto. . . . Finally Torresani stood up and said:

'I will never be the one to clip the wings of this youth who promises so much for the art of music. Go ahead. I assume the responsibility.'

He insisted only that the words 'Ave Maria' be changed to 'Salve Maria', a childish concession to the Archbishop's scruples. And so *I lombardi* came to the stage. So much has been said against the Austrian police officials in general, and Torresani in particular, that one good thing might be said. [. . .]

I lombardi was cheered to the skies. The humble people began to besiege the gallery as early as three o'clock, bringing food with them, so that the curtain went up to a strong odour of garlic sausages! That was no obstacle to the success that was immediately proclaimed. The public wanted the quintet repeated, but the police did not allow it, whereas it allowed the repetition of the polonaise 'Non fu sogno' [It was no dream]. The censors had these whims. The famous chorus, 'O Signore dal tetto natio' [O Lord, from our native roof], sparked one of the first political demonstrations that signalled the reawakening of the Lombard-Venetians.
FOL, 47–9

Shortly after the first performances of *I lombardi* (there was a total of twenty-seven that season), Verdi made his first trip outside Italy, to Vienna, where *Nabucco* was given on 4 April 1843 at the Kärntnerthor-Theater, also managed by Merelli. During his short stay in the Austrian capital, Verdi heard from Count Nani Mocenigo, President of the Teatro La Fenice in Venice, where *Nabucco* had triumphed in 1842. The Count wanted a new work for his theatre. Verdi replied from Udine, on his way to Busseto.

Verdi to Count Mocenigo; Udine, 9 April 1843

You will be surprised that I have not answered yours of 20 March, but I had left for Vienna, and your letter reached me from Milan very late.

You will allow me to make some observations on the terms mentioned in your letter. I could not deliver the entirely finished score by 15 December: I could deliver it complete as far as the composition is concerned, and so that all the singers' parts can be copied out, and all the choruses, but as for the orchestration, I am accustomed to do that when the piano rehearsals have begun.

Nor could I commit myself to deliver the libretto by the end of June, because it is quite possible, indeed almost certain, that the poet would let me down. Indeed, in my opinion, the Presidency itself should commission the libretto. [. . .]
MS, ATLF, VENICE

In the latter part of April, Verdi was in Parma, where *Nabucco* was being given at the Teatro Regio with Giuseppina Strepponi.   64, 65

Verdi to Count Mocenigo; Parma, 28 April 1843 (mis-dated 1842)

[. . .] I believe it would not be best for me or for the Theatre to stage the new opera as the second one of the season, especially if the first is to be *I lombardi*. It would be ideal to allow a month's interval between one opera and the other. [. . .]

Now we must speak only of financial matters: for me, to write the new opera and to stage *I lombardi*: twelve thousand Austrian lire. [. . .]
MS, ATLF, VENICE

Count Mocenigo balked at these terms, but finally Verdi was promised his twelve thousand Austrian lire.

Verdi to Count Mocenigo; Milan, 6 June 1843

I return the signed contract. I hope there will be nothing further to be said, for I shall stick to the conditions and will do my duty in all conscience.

I beg you to let me know, as soon as you can, the names of the singers in the company.

As soon as possible I will let the Presidency know the subject of the opera, which will depend on the singers I will have. For example if I were to have an artist of the power of Ronconi, I would choose either *Re Lear* [Shakespeare's *King Lear*] or *Il corsaro* [Byron's *The Corsair*], but since it will probably be best to rely on the prima donna, I could thus perhaps choose either *La fidanzata d'Abido* [Byron's *The Bride of Abydos*] or something else where the prima donna is protagonist. In any case I will choose a subject that will have no relation to the subject of any other score. [. . .]
MS, ATLF, VENICE

In subsequent letters Verdi discussed other possible subjects: a *Caterina Hovvard* ('Catherine Howard'), *Cola da Rienzi*, *La caduta dei Longobardi* ('The Fall of the Longobards'), *I due Foscari* (Byron's *The Two Foscari*). Finally the Fenice produced a young poet eager to write a first libretto, *Cromvello*: Francesco Maria Piave.

Verdi to Count Mocenigo; Senigallia, 26 July 1843

[. . .] *Cromvello*, from what I know of it historically, is certainly a fine subject; but everything depends on how it is handled. I do not know Signor Piave, but if you assure me he is a good poet familiar with theatrical effects and musical forms, I beg you to give him the enclosed letter, after you have kindly read it. [. . .]

MS, ATLF, VENICE

Verdi to Count Mocenigo; Senigallia, 31 July 1843

I have received Signor Piave's scenario. If the Presidency has nothing against it, I am pleased with it.

If you decided to pass on a letter I sent you to Signor Piave dated 20th of this month, I beg you to deliver also the one here enclosed, and so it remains settled that I will set the drama of the above-mentioned Piave. [. . .]

MS, ATLF, VENICE

73, 74 This was the beginning of a long professional association and a deep friendship between Verdi and Piave, who was also to be the composer's favourite whipping-boy. The Verdian whip's first lashes came over *Cromvello*.

Verdi to Count Mocenigo; 5 September 1843

This *Cromvello* is certainly not of great interest, considering the requirements of the theatre. The development is regular, clear, and in short well-made, but it lacks action. The fault perhaps lies more with the subject than with the poet. [. . .]

Oh, if I could do *Hernani*, that would be a wonderful thing! It's true it would be hard work for the poet, but first of all I would try to compensate him, and then we would surely achieve a much greater effect on the public.

Signor Piave also has great facility in versifying, and in *Hernani* he would only have to condense and tighten: the action is ready-made, and the interest is immense.

Tomorrow I will write at length to Signor Piave and will write out all the scenes of *Hernani* that seem to me suitable. I have already seen that the whole first act can be tightened into a magnificent introduction, and end the act where Don Carlos asks Silva for Hernani who is hidden behind his portrait. Make the second act with Act IV of the French drama. And end the third act with the magnificent trio when Hernani dies, etc. . . . [. . .]

MS, ATLF, VENICE

Piave was willing to scrap *Cromvello* and adapt Victor Hugo's drama *Hernani* (1830). The next problem was with the censor. Like Milan, Venice was under Austrian rule, but the Venetian censors were even more strict; and *Hernani* includes a conspiracy against the life of a king. Before beginning the composition of the opera, Verdi wanted reassurance. He was by now corresponding with Guglielmo Brenna, Secretary of La Fenice.

Verdi to Guglielmo Brenna, 29 September 1843

By now you will have spoken with Count Mocenigo, who, I hope, will concern himself with removing all obstacles to the political approval of *Ernani*, since it was he himself who suggested this subject. Ask him then to urge Signor Piave to draft the scenario, so that it can be presented as soon as possible to the proper person.

158

I am of the opinion that *Ernani* will better lend itself to being staged both for the action and for the richness of the costumes etc. . . .[. . .]

MS, ATLF, VENICE

Piave dealt with the authorities himself. The demands included: no drawing of swords, underlining of Charles V's clemency towards the conspirators, and a proper devotion of subject to king in Ernani's dialogue with Charles. The words 'blood' and 'vendetta' had to be eliminated. The authorities also wanted the title changed, but on this point Piave and Verdi won out.

Verdi to Guglielmo Brenna, 15 November 1843

Piave by now will have received my letter together with another I wrote to Count Mocenigo. I am impatiently awaiting [the text of] the fourth act, because I could not come to Venice now. Let him finish the Trio as he wishes; it seems to me, however, that an absolute solo for Ernani would be a bore. What will the other two do? . . . I want to have this trio as soon as possible because I would like to write it here calmly before coming to Venice.

In your letter I find that Piave *would like to come to an agreement with me so as to avoid as far as possible the necessity of changes once the work is finished.* For my part I would never like to bother a poet to change a verse for me; and I have written the music to three librettos by Solera, and if you compared the original, which I have kept, with the printed librettos, you would find only a very few verses changed, and these because of Solera's own conviction. But Solera has already written 5 or 6 librettos and knows the theatre, effect, musical forms. Signor Piave has never written [for the theatre], and therefore it is natural that he is wanting in these things. For example, where will you find a woman who will sing in succession a grand cavatina, a duet that ends in a trio, and a whole finale, as in this first act of *Ernani*? Signor Piave will produce good reasons for me, but I have others, and I reply that the lungs will not bear this effort. Where will you find a composer who can set to music, without boring the hearer, 100 lines of Recitative as in this third act? In all four acts of *Nabucco* or *I lombardi* you will not find surely more than 100 lines of Recitative. And the same can be said of many other little things. You, who have been so kind to me, please make Piave understand these things and convince him. However slight my experience may be, I still go to the theatre all year, and I am very alert: I have seen for myself that many compositions would not have failed if there had been a better distribution in the numbers, better calculated effects, clearer musical forms . . . in short if there had been greater experience both in the poet and in the composer. So many times a recitative that is too long, a phrase, a sentence that would be very beautiful in a book, and even in a spoken drama, is laughable in a sung drama. [. . .]

MS, ATLF, VENICE

Verdi reached Venice in early December 1843 to 71–72 rehearse *I lombardi*, which was performed the day after Christmas. Except for a trip to Verona, to hear a tenor who had been recommended for *Ernani*, he stayed in Venice until the *Ernani* premiere. There were casting problems, and the sets and costumes were late (in fact, when the opera opened, three of the sets were from stock).

Giovannino Barezzi to Antonio Barezzi; Venice, 26 February 1844

Yesterday at ten in the morning I arrived happily in Venice and went at once to Verdi (and am still with him), who is composing at full tilt and will have finished in two days.

I have heard the prima donna's aria, which is very beautiful. I have made the acquaintance of Piave, a young man of high spirits, like Solera. [. . .]

AB I, 497

Giovannino Barezzi to Antonio Barezzi; Venice, 29 February 1844

[. . .] The rehearsals are going well. What I have heard so far is surprising, perhaps more so than *Nabucco* and *I lombardi*.

All the Venetians are eager to hear it. Some people will come from Padua, some from Trieste, some from Verona, some from Bologna, especially to hear *Ernani*, and this I hear at the Caffè Florian from letters they write to the Venetians. [. . .]

AB I, 497

On 9 March 1844, premiere of *Ernani* at the Teatro La Fenice, Venice.

Giovannino Barezzi to Antonio Barezzi; Venice, 9 March 1844

This will be an evening of triumph, the coronation of Verdi as the first composer of the world. Yesterday I heard the rehearsal. All the numbers were applauded. An uproar this evening; what a pleasure to see people coming from all over the place! Oh! here are the gondolas from the railroad, passing beneath my window and bringing more than a hundred young Paduans! Bravi! To *Ernani*! Come swell the triumph of Verdi!

AB I, 497–8

Giovannino Barezzi to Antonio Barezzi; Venice, 10 March 1844

Last night we heard *Ernani* with Guasco without voice and with a frightening hoarseness, and with la Loewe who has never sung so much off pitch as last night. The outcome was very happy. All the numbers were applauded, except Guasco's cavatina.

Four calls at the end of the first act, two at the second, three at the third, and four at the end of the opera. This is the authentic story. If it had had singers, I won't say sublime, but at least capable of singing in tune, *Ernani* would have aroused more enthusiasm than *Nabucco* and *I lombardi* in Milan.

Here is why Guasco had no voice. It was eight o'clock and time to begin and nothing was ready. Guasco continued shouting for an hour, and hence the hoarseness. Two sets were missing, the costumes were missing, and there were some ridiculous ones. Between the second and third acts and then between the third and fourth we had to wait three-quarters of an hour [. . .] because nothing was in order. I swear that if the music hadn't been as I wrote you yesterday, we wouldn't have reached the end. [. . .]

AB I, 498

Giovannino Barezzi to Antonio Barezzi; Venice, 11 March 1844

Last night the singers sang fairly well and it was a real festivity from beginning to end, enthusiasm from the first piece to the last, twenty calls on to the stage, more than forty or fifty between the acts. And so what I wrote came true. [. . .]

AB I, 498

Il Gondoliere, Venice, 10 March 1844

On the walls of our major theatre there waves a banner with, written on it in golden letters, *Ernani*. Populace and Senators cheered this Spanish bandit with a hundred voices. The invention of the drama of Hugo, the Italian version of F. Piave, the harmonies of Verdi, the sweet creator of *I lombardi* and *Nabucco*. His latest strains enraptured, a good four times, even the spirits of grave pedants and severe matrons.

In the foyers, in the streets, in the drawing rooms, in lively gatherings, the new songs are on every lip. On the chariot of well-earned triumphs, the maestro had as his companions the poet and the singers. There were wreaths, flowers, cheers, palms for all.

The music is sown with sweet melodies, choice harmonies, splendid instrumentation. The gem of the bracelet, the most balmy flower of the brimming basket, is the trio in the last part of the drama.

Sofia Loewe, Guasco, Superchi, Selva were the chief interpreters of the new opera. The first through her supreme art, the second through rare grace, the third through mastery, the last – a youth not yet twenty – through the merit of his singing, were well worthy of our audience.

Musicians, chorus, designers, did not make the spectacle less welcome. [. . .]

VELF, 28

For the next few years the story of Verdi's life is largely a chronicle of new productions of old operas and the preparation and presentation of new ones. Even before the premiere of *Ernani* in Venice, the composer had signed a contract to write again for La Scala (this was to be *Giovanna d'Arco*) and another contract with the Teatro Argentina in Rome (which eventually mounted *I due Foscari*). That same month of March, 1844, he agreed to write his first opera for the Teatro San Carlo in Naples: its eventual title was *Alzira*.

Verdi to Vincenzio Flauto, impresario in Naples; Milan, 21 March 1844

It is true, the advantage of writing an opera to the poetry of the distinguished poet Signor Cammarano, and with those performers, and the fame to be won by any worthy composer in the great Theatre [San Carlo] lead me to accept without any hesitation the offer you have made me, on the following conditions:

1. The management will pay me 550 (five hundred and fifty) gold Napoleons of twenty francs, payable in three equal instalments: the first on my arrival in the city, the second at the first orchestra rehearsal, and the third immediately after the day of the first performance.

2. The management must deliver to me in Milan Signor Cammarano's libretto at the end of the present year 1844.

3. I will not be obliged to go on stage before the end of the month of June.

4. I shall have my choice of singers from the list of the company, providing always that this list must include la Tadolini, Fraschini, and Coletti.

COP, 3

In a letter to Piave, Verdi discusses his next opera for La Fenice, which was to be based on the tragedy *Attila* (1803) by the German writer Zacharias Werner. (In the end Solera, not Piave, was to write the libretto.)

Verdi to Piave; Milan, 12 April 1844

Here is the sketch of Verner's tragedy. There are some magnificent things in it, full of effect. Read *De l'Allemagne* by la Staël.

My idea would be to make a prologue and three acts. We must raise the curtain and show Aquileia in flames with chorus of populace and chorus of Huns. The populace prays, the Huns threaten, etc. etc. . . . Then entrance of Ildegonda [Odabella], then of Attila, etc. . . . and the prologue ends.

I would open the first act in Rome, and instead of having the festivity on stage, have it off, with Azzio [Ezio] pensive on stage, meditating on events etc. etc. . . . I would end the first act when Ildegonda reveals to Attila the poisoned draught, whence Attila believes that Ildegonda makes this revelation out of love, when instead it is only in order to keep for herself the pleasure of avenging the death of her father and brothers etc. etc.

It would be magnificent, in the third act, to have the whole scene of [Pope] Leo on the Aventine, while they are fighting below; perhaps it will not be allowed, but you must take care to disguise it so that they will allow it; but the scene must be exactly as it is.

I don't like the finale of the fourth act, but if we think about it we can find something beautiful. – You ponder, and I'll do the same.

Meanwhile there are three stupendous characters: Attila, who suffers no alterations of any kind; Ildegonda, also a beautiful character, who seeks vengeance for her father, brothers, and lover; Azzio is splendid and I like him in the duet with Attila when he suggests sharing the world, etc. . . . It would be necessary to invent a fourth, effective character, and it seems to me that Gualtiero [Foresto], who believes Ildegonda dead, if he were to survive you could have him appear either among the Huns or among the Romans and thus create a place for some fine scenes with Ildegonda, perhaps have him take part in the poisoning scene, but especially in the fourth act, in agreement with Ildegonda to have Attila die. [. . .]

It seems to me a fine work can be created, and if you reflect seriously you will make your finest libretto. [. . .]
COP, 437

At this time, a new and important figure appears in Verdi's life. Emanuele Muzio (1821–90) was eight years Verdi's junior and, like him, a young musician from Busseto. Of a very poor family, Muzio received assistance from the Monte di pietà and, more importantly, from Barezzi, who sent the young man to Milan to be Verdi's pupil. Muzio soon became a discreet, devoted friend, who literally adored 'il Signor Maestro Verdi' to the end of his days. Fortunately for posterity, he acted for some years as a kind of secretary, writing to Barezzi regularly to keep him informed of Verdi's activities.

Muzio to Antonio Barezzi; Milan, 22 April 1844

[. . .] For several days now Signor Maestro Verdi has been giving me lessons in counterpoint. [. . .] He will also be so

kind as to give me the certificate, which I will send you as soon as I have it; many music students would pay even two or three thalers for lessons if Signor Maestro Verdi wanted to give them; but he gives them to no one except a poor devil to whom he has done a thousand favours, and still, to make them complete, also that of giving him lessons not two or three times a week but every morning. . . . I am amazed, and what's more, sometimes when he has me do something for him, he also gives me dinner. He, my Maestro, has a greatness of spirit, a generosity, a wisdom, a heart that, to make a pair, would have to have yours set beside it: namely the two most generous hearts in the world.

My respects [. . .] to Signor Don Balestra, and tell him to send me those two songs because the Maestro also gives me verses to set to music, to practise free composition. [. . .]
GAR, 157–8

In Vienna Donizetti, the leading Italian opera composer since Rossini's retirement, was Court Composer. He paid *Ernani* a signal compliment.

Verdi to Gaetano Donizetti; Milan, 18 May 1844

Most esteemed Signor Maestro,
It was a welcome surprise to read your letter to Pedroni, in which you kindly offer to supervise the rehearsals of *Ernani*.

I do not hesitate a moment in accepting the kind offer with the greatest gratitude, certain that my notes can only derive great benefit, when *Donizetti* devotes his thoughts to them. Thus I can hope that the musical spirit of that composition will be interpreted truly.

I beg you to take care of the general direction and make as many minor adjustments as may be needed, especially in Ferretti's part.

To you, Signor Cavaliere, I will pay no compliments. You belong to the small number of men who have sovereign genius and need no individual praise.

The favour you show me is too great for you to be able to doubt my gratitude.
MS, CIMGD, BERGAMO

Muzio to Antonio Barezzi; Milan, 20 May 1844

[. . .] *Ernani*, given at the Teatro San Benedetto in Venice, has aroused an enthusiasm greater than the other time.

In Rome they have forbidden the libretto *Lorenzino*; and instead they will give *I due Foscari* in that theatre. I have copied out the outline to send to Rome, to submit to the censorship of those Prelates. [. . .]

I hope your health is excellent. I have a headache at times. The Signor Maestro tells me it is the study of counterpoint [. . .].
GAR, 158–60

Muzio to Antonio Barezzi; Milan, 29 May 1844

[. . .] Now I go to school at eleven; because he is rising early now to write *I due Foscari*. The introductory chorus, which is the Council of Ten, is magnificent and awesome, and in the music you feel that mystery which reigned in those terrible meetings that decided life or death; and you can well imagine that the *Papà of choruses*, as the Milanese call him, has set it well!! [. . .]
GAR, 162

Certificate written by Verdi for the Monte di pietà, Busseto, 13 September 1844. Monte di credito su pegno, Busseto.
'I certify that Signor Emanuele Muzio is pursuing with profit, under my direction, the study of counterpoint and ideal composition.'

Muzio to Antonio Barezzi; Milan, 11 June 1844

[. . .] In Milan all say that the outcome of *Ernani* in Vienna is a double triumph, because of the dislike there of all that is not written by Donizetti; the other day at Ricordi's they were reading some German papers, which overflowed with praise.

If you, Sir, had been in Signor Maestro Verdi's house that day when the news arrived of the most happy outcome, to see, for a good hour, first someone coming to whom Donizetti had written, then another who had received the news from a Count, I don't remember the last name, then another, who had a letter from Merelli, and so many more there was no end, and to hear the beautiful things they wrote of the Signor Maestro and of his *Ernani*, you would surely have wept, Sir, because you are so sensitive, and then to see them all sitting there, now one reading his letter, now another, and with these writings in their hands they seemed so many schoolboys reciting their lesson; and the Signor Maestro there in the middle, at his desk, seemed the teacher, and I, in a corner, wide-eyed, seemed the school door-keeper. It was something that gave pleasure and delight. [. . .]

The Signor Maestro is composing at full speed, and doesn't leave the house until towards evening, at the dinner hour, and every morning, when the lesson is over, I go to bring him his lunch, then I go to the Post; the Signor Maestro always guesses when there is a letter from you, Sir, and it is the first to be opened. [. . .]

GAR, 164–5

Not everyone in Vienna was overjoyed by *Ernani*. Otto Nicolai (who composed several Italian operas as well as *The Merry Wives of Windsor*, 1849) expressed a long-sustained German disapproval of Verdi – as well as a trace of pique.

From Otto Nicolai's diary; Vienna, 13 September 1844

And so I have gone on conducting these three years past – and, especially in the last year, have been constantly active; for, if I am not very much mistaken, good German operatic music is beginning to drive the Italian from the field. And how low Italy has sunk in the last five years?! Donizetti lives in Paris or Vienna almost all the time – and in the latter city he has been appointed Imperial and Royal Kapellmeister and Court Composer with a salary of 4000 florins for life – and does no more work for Italy. Rossini is totally silent. In Italy now, only Verdi is writing operas. He set the libretto, which I had rejected, of *Nabucodonosor*, and had a great success with it. His operas are truly abominable, and bring Italy to the depths of degradation. I do not think Italy has any lower to sink than these works – and I should not now like to write any operas there.

NICOLAI, 129–30

On 3 November 1844, premiere of *I due Foscari* at the Teatro Argentina, Rome. 80–81

From Prince Agostino Chigi's diary; Rome, 2–3 November 1844

Saturday, 2 November 1844: [. . .] Rained all day and continued all evening. [. . .] This evening the theatres were dark.

Sunday, 3 November 1844: Rain with strong wind in the night but without thunder. Rainy almost all day. This evening then at the Ave Maria a downpour, preceded by some lightning and rather strong thunder. The river threatens to flood. [. . .] This evening at the Argentina a new opera was performed entitled *I due Foscari* music specially written by Maestro Verdi with Signora Barbieri prima donna, tenor Roppa, and for bass De Bassini. The outcome was apparently below the very great expectations. Torlonia, owner of the theatre, gave a dinner in the rooms of the theatre itself with numerous guests. 93

MS, BIB. VATICANA

Muzio to Antonio Barezzi; Milan, 16 November 1844

[. . .] The Signor Maestro is well; but when he first arrived [from Rome] he was worn out, he was overcome with fatigue. His friends were awaiting him at the stage-coach office; these were Maffei, Toccagni, Pasetti, Ricordi, Pedroni, etc. All of whom, the next day, went to dinner with the Signor Maestro and toasted him with Bordeaux and Champagne.

You will already have heard that the opera (*I due Foscari*) was a great furore. On opening night the singers, chorus, and orchestra had so distorted and disfigured it that, on the second night, the Romans said he had changed everything. I transcribe below the article from the gazette *La Rivista di Roma*:

'Evening of the 4th: One of the most marked triumphs was had by Maestro Verdi last night, the 4th, at the second performance of his most meritorious opera, *I due Foscari*. The performers, having recovered from their stage fright,

having abandoned the screeching that so displeased the night before, and having better penetrated the characters they were playing, sang vigorously, with mastery. The audience, also in a better humour, and in the absence of a faction that is accustomed to intervene on all opening nights of operas with the firm intention of creating an uproar, applauded each number loudly, and the Maestro came on stage at least thirty times amid the enthusiastic cheers of a very crowded audience.' [. . .]
GAR, 173–4

Muzio to Antonio Barezzi; Milan, 9 December 1844

[. . .] I have made the acquaintance of that fever known as *quartana* and I could only just manage to write those little notes that the Signor Maestro kindly enclosed in his own [. . .] I tell you this now because I am cured and, Heaven be thanked, I am very well. But let us come to *Giovanna [d'Arco]*.

If with her exploits she had not made her memory eternal, the Signor Maestro's music would make her immortal; no Joan has ever had music more philosophical and beautiful. The awesome introduction (an inspiration which came, as you know, along the cliffs), [and] the magnificent number 'Maledetti cui spinse rea voglia' [Cursed ones, driven by evil desire], are two things that will startle any poor man. The choruses of the devils are original, popular, truly Italian; the first ('Tu sei bella' [You are beautiful]) a very pretty waltz, full of seductive tunes, which when heard twice can immediately be sung; the second ('Vittoria vittoria s'applauda a Satàna' [Victory, Victory, let Satan be extolled]) is a music of diabolical exultation, a music that makes you shiver and tremble; in short they are divine things; in that opera there will be every kind of music: theatrical, religious, martial, etc. I like everything I have heard, very, very much. [. . .]
GAR, 175

82–83 On 15 February 1845, premiere of *Giovanna d'Arco* at La Scala, Milan. Barezzi was present. At about this time, Verdi had a violent quarrel with Merelli, La Scala's impresario, who – in producing *I due Foscari* – had blithely placed the third (last) act before the second. Verdi stated in public that he would never write for that theatre again. He kept his vow for almost a quarter-century.

Muzio to Antonio Barezzi; Milan, 27 February 1845

[. . .] On Wednesday, Thursday, Saturday and Sunday there is still *Giovanna*; and in these days the theatre is packed as on the first evenings and they count a thousand and more tickets in the stalls (besides the subscribers), 500 and even 600 in the gallery; if it weren't for this opera, the management's affairs would have gone badly. Merelli wanted to sign up the Signor Maestro again for the final year of his management, that is in five years' time, at the price of his own choice; but he will not write any more for La Scala, or stage or conduct any opera of his there; and he says he will never set foot on that stage again. [. . .]
GAR, 184

Marie-Louise, Archduchess of Parma, to her daughter Countess Albertina Montenuovo Sanvitale; Parma, April 1845

[. . .] I have heard again, with pleasure, *Beatrice di Tenda*.

Verdi, 'Brindisi', one of the *Sei canzoni* written in March–April 1845, title page. Istituto di studi verdiani, Parma.

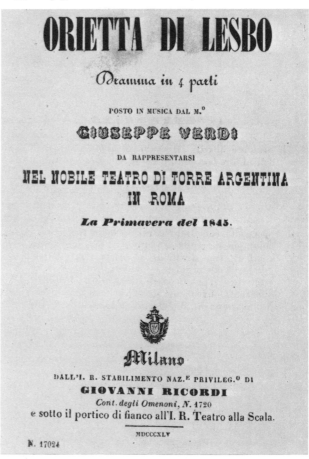

Verdi, *Giovanna d'Arco*, 1845 (*Orietta di Lesbo*). Libretto. Papal censors had Verdi's nationalist Joan moved to Lesbos, as a Genoese heroine rousing the Lesbians to repel the Turks.

Bellini is always good, whereas Verdi will not last. Do not be amazed, as a daughter of Parma, at my feeling about Verdi. I write that he will not last, because he has great talent but little schooling and a new genius may be born, who will lead music in a different, more learned direction. I hope, meanwhile, that Verdi will gradually find in the spirit of his homeland the sublime inspirations that have eternal life. [. . .]
MARC, 35

85   In Naples Salvatore Cammarano (librettist of Donizetti's *Lucia di Lammermoor*) was working on a libretto based on Voltaire's tragedy *Alzire* (1736).

Verdi to Salvatore Cammarano; Milan, 18 April 1845

I have been in bed for two days with stomach-ache. They have bled me, and God willing there will be an end of it. I am, however, better, but for the present it would be best to suspend work.

Two days ago I received the finale which is stupendous. I am awaiting, as you promised, some clarifications and at least the outline of the last act.

You must perforce try to make the management postpone the opening of the opera for a month at least, because even when I become able to work on it, I will have to go slowly. [. . .]
MS, BLP, NAPLES

Verdi to Flauto in Naples; Milan, 25 April 1845

I have not answered your first letter, which I received quite late, forwarded from Milan to Venice and from Venice back to Milan, because I was ill at the time. Now I receive your second and I am sorry to have to tell you that I cannot present the opera [*Alzira*] at the fixed date, because the doctors force me to rest at least a month, and thus we could open only at the end of July or the beginning of August. In a few days I will present the [medical] certificate, to do things properly.

I repeat that I deeply regret this misfortune, and I assure you that as soon as I can work, I shall do so with all zeal.

Cammarano is perfectly in order and I have received the whole Prologue and the entire first act, and he assures me I will have the second in a few days. I am very pleased with this work, which is very well written and of an ever-mounting interest.
COP, 9

Flauto to Verdi; Naples, May 1845

We are supremely sorry to learn from your esteemed two letters of the 23 and 26 of this past April that you are indisposed. The illness that troubles you is of slight consideration and requires no remedies other than tincture of absinthe and your immediate journey to Naples, as I assure you the air here and the excitability of our Vesuvius will set all your functions working again, especially that of the appetite. Resolve then to come quickly, and leave the host of doctors who, with the indisposition that ails you, can only make things worse. You must count on your cure from the Naples air and the advice I will give you when you are here, since I was once a doctor myself and have abandoned impostures. [. . .]
COP, 10

Marie-Louise, Archduchess of Austria, Duchess of Parma. The dedicatee of *I lombardi nella prima crociata*, 1843.

Verdi to Flauto; Milan, 14 May 1845

I am very sorry to have to inform you that my illness is not of slight consideration, as you believe, and *tincture of absinthe* is not indicated.

As to the excitability of your Vesuvius, I assure you that is not what is required to set my functions working again; instead I need calm and rest.

I cannot leave quickly for Naples, as you suggest, because, if I could, I would not have sent a medical certificate. I inform you of all this, so that you may take the steps you think opportune, while I devote myself seriously to recovering my health.
COP, 11

Verdi to Cammarano; Milan, 14 May 1845

I received today a letter from Signor Flauto which is truly curious. Without answering my request, supported by a medical certificate, to postpone the production of the opera for a month, he actually urges me to come to Naples. Moreover, this letter is written in a certain tone which I do not like at all. I have answered almost in his own words, and I will add that for the present I cannot come to Naples. [. . .]
MS, BLP, NAPLES

Flauto insisted, only making Verdi still angrier.

Verdi to Flauto; Milan, 29 May 1845

The medical certificate was written in good faith, nor were any illnesses imagined or supposed. For what reason? For almost two months I have been unable to work and even now I can write only at intervals, and very brief ones.

Therefore it is impossible for the opera to be finished before the end of July.

I have never quarrelled with anyone in the world, nor do I wish to do so with you. Let us then agree, and do me, as you say, the *little service* of postponing the opera for a month, and even more, if you like. – You mention your obligations towards the Government; but if prisoners when ill are treated with care, why cannot I be? [. . .]
COP, 12

Verdi to Cammarano; Milan, 2 June 1845

We artists are not allowed to fall ill. Having always been an honest man is not enough! . . . Impresarios believe or do not believe, according to their financial interests. I cannot be pleased with the way Signor Flauto has written to me. Also what he said to you casts doubt on my illness and my certificate. [. . .]

Dear Cammarano, in thanking you for the trouble you have taken, I beg you to forgive the nuisance I have given you, and assure the Management that the sooner they grant me the extension the sooner I will leave for Naples. [. . .]
COP, 13

Muzio to Barezzi; Milan, 26 May 1845

184   Signor Escudier, editor of the *Gazette musicale de France*, visited the Signor Maestro and wanted a statuette of him, to put in his Paris office between Rossini and Bellini.

The Signor Maestro, after he has given the opera in Naples, is going straight to Paris with this Signor Escudier, who will come from Paris to meet him in Naples. This is secret. [. . .]
GAR, 203

Muzio to Barezzi; Milan, 9 June 1845

The day before yesterday the Signor Maestro gave permission to print his biography and to have his portrait made; and in fact today Signor Focosi is beginning to draw it and engrave it on the stone at the same time, because he says it comes out better. It will all be printed within the month, before he goes to Naples. I have read it; and there are many, many praises of you, well-earned and deserved. [. . .]

Signor Flauto promised Ca[m]marano and [the tenor] Fraschini that he will grant the requested month and la Tadolini; but the Maestro doesn't want words, he wants it in writing; and Cam[m]arano having asked this of Signor Flauto, he wouldn't do it. What a rogue! [. . .]
GAR, 203

Muzio to Barezzi; Milan, 30 June 1845

[. . .] The Signor Maestro left Milan, having written everything but the last act finale, because he didn't have the poetry.

He hadn't orchestrated anything, but he hoped to do it all in six days. [. . .]
GAR, 205

Muzio to Barezzi; Milan, 9 July 1845

Yesterday I had a letter from the Signor Maestro in which he informed me of the welcome, full of enthusiasm, that he received from the Neapolitans; in no city has he been received better than there, not even Rome and Venice. In

the evening they found out he was in the theatre (they were doing *I due Foscari*) and though they are by nature very loath to call composers on to the stage, especially for old operas, they still called him out several times. And the cheers and bravos never ended.

Mercadante, Pacini, Battista will be chewing their fingers with anger. [. . .]
GAR, 207

Verdi to Andrea Maffei; Naples, 30 July 1845   70

[. . .] Don't worry, it won't be a fiasco. The singers like singing it, and there must be something tolerable in it. I will write immediately after the opening night. [. . .] The Neapolitans are odd: some are so crude, so uncivilized, that they have to be beaten into showing respect, the others overwhelm you with a storm of politeness enough to kill you through asphyxiation. I, to tell the truth, can only be content, because even the Managers are kind to me (which is to say everything). [. . .]
MS, BNB, MILAN

On 12 August 1845, premiere of *Alzira* at the Teatro San Carlo, Naples.

Verdi to his Milanese friend Luigi Toccagni; Naples, 13 August 1845:

The outcome of *Alzira* last night was like that of *Ernani* the first evenings in Venice. You, who were present at *Ernani*, can form a perfect idea of the evening yesterday. The same old story: the public expects too much, and the performance is always unsure, precisely because of these demands on the public's part.
COP, 432

Verdi to Léon Escudier; Milan, 12 September 1845

[. . .] In a few days I will begin *Attila* for Venice, which is a   88 stupendous subject! The poem is by Solera, and I am pleased with it. . . . How beautiful *Attila* would be for the Grand Opéra of Paris! Only a few things would have to be added, and all the rest would go well. You, who previously wrote me about having either *I lombardi* or *Ernani* translated this year; tell me now if *Attila* could not be given in two years' time. By then I will be free, and if there were a chance of arranging something for that theatre, I would not accept other engagements in Italy.
AB I, 581

While Verdi was working to supply Italian theatres with   87 new operas, his old ones were making their way abroad. In the autumn of 1845 *Nabucco* had a great success in Paris, arousing the interest of foreign impresarios, including Benjamin Lumley of London.

Muzio to Barezzi; Milan, 27 October 1845

[. . .] As soon as Lumley heard about the outcome of *Nabucco* he came from London along with Escudier, to sign up the Signor Maestro for next spring. Not finding him in Milan, they went to Clusone, where he was [visiting Countess Maffei]; but as they were on their way there, he was coming back, so they keep running after him till they

find him. They thought he was in Busseto, and wanted to go there directly. It is very likely they will sign him up for London, with a third more than the fee he would receive in Italy, plus lodging, because there two little rooms cost twenty francs a day. [. . .]
GAR, 227

Muzio to Barezzi; Milan, 19 November 1845

Now thanks to the goodness of the Signor Maestro I am covered, and what is more important, without having spent anything. He himself on Monday bought me clothes, and so I won't feel the severity of the cold. You can't imagine how much love he bears me and how close I am to him. [. . .]

From Paris they have written asking him to compose an opera buffa for Carnival 1846–47; but he has answered that he is engaged in Rome.

Benelli, agent of the Opéra, has had a commission from the impresario M. Pillet Léon to engage the Signor Maestro for a grand opera to be written in French, when all his commitments are fulfilled. [. . .] I believe it likely that for Carnival 1846–47 at the Opéra of Paris they will do *I lombardi* in French; however, the Signor Maestro will make some additions, ballet, and other things. This is a suitable opera for the theatres there. [. . .]

Escudier, while he was in Milan, bought the rights of all the Signor Maestro's operas, beginning with *Oberto*, *Un giorno di regno*, etc., including all those he will write in Italy, and he paid 500 francs each for them. These are the rights for France only. [. . .]
GAR, 232–4

Verdi left for Venice without the last act of the libretto for *Attila*. Solera had gone off to Spain with his wife, a singer. So the loyal Piave had to be called on. Then Verdi sent Solera the completed text.

Solera to Verdi, January 1846

My Verdi, your letter was a thunderbolt for me; I cannot conceal from you my unspeakable sorrow in seeing a work, with which I dared to feel satisfied, now end in parody. In the ending you send me I find only a parody. Attila who pursues Odabella, Odabella who flees a nuptial bed in which she had placed her hopes of vengeance, etc., seem to me things that ruin everything I thought I had infused into my characters.

Fiat voluntas tua. The cup you make me drink is too painful. Only you could convince me that being a librettist is no longer the job for me. . . .

I hope you will promptly give me news of yourself and of the opera once it is staged. Meanwhile I beg you to change at least some of the verses that are not mine, so that the pill will be less bitter for me.
VELF, 32

Verdi to his friend the sculptor Vincenzo Luccardi in Rome; Venice, 11 February 1846

[. . .] I need a great favour! I know that in the Vatican, either in the tapestries or the frescoes of Raphael, there must be the meeting of Attila with St Leo. I would need the figure of Attila: so make me a few strokes with your pen, then explain to me with words and numbers the colours of the costume: I particularly need the headgear. If you do me

this favour I will give you my holy blessing. Nothing new here. [. . .] I am weary of staying in Venice: this grim and melancholy calm now puts me in a sometimes unbearable humour. [. . .]
COP, 441

On 17 March 1846, premiere of *Attila* at the Teatro La Fenice, Venice. 89–90

Verdi to Clarina Maffei; Venice, 18 March 1846

Generally speaking the outcome of *Attila* was quite happy. Applause and calls were even too many for a poor sick man. Perhaps not all was understood, but will be understood this evening. My friends say this is the best of my operas; the public cavils. I say it is not inferior to any of my other ones: time will decide.

My health is improving daily. Maffei, who is fine, will write you tomorrow about the outcome of this evening, and we will leave for Milan together as soon as possible. [. . .]
MS, EREDI MAFFEI, MILAN.

Gazzetta previlegiata di Venezia, 18 March 1846

Maestro Verdi's opera began last night with the most splendid auguries. The Prologue not only moved, but roused the spirits, kindled them with the liveliest enthusiasm. There is in it a lovely cavatina, sung also with great mastery and expression by la Loewe, a grand duet 76 between the two bases, Marini and Constantini, a chorus of hermits, followed by a magnificent instrumental number, in which with admirable craft of sounds the waking of nature at morning is imitated; nor could words express the profound impression produced especially by this highly ingenious harmony, worthy of the great composer. [. . .]

In the rest of the opera the omens were less resplendent. A sweetly melodious romanza of la Loewe was justly applauded, in the first part of a duet between her and Guasco; a largo, beautifully and learnedly made, in the first act pleased, as did the rich and various work of the finale of the second; but the effect of the music was less lively; though no less lively, if perhaps not so universal, were the applause and calls for the Maestro.

Justice demands, however, that we say that all the arias were not enjoyed to their perfection; in the grand finale, for example, some artists entered too soon, and the ensemble and the beauty were marred; Costantini had a fever, and Guasco did not seem in good voice, so there is more hope for the future performances. For this reason, the third act was virtually unheard, and to tell the truth it ended in the most desolate silence. [. . .]

And now we address a request to Attila. Let him dress, and dress his men, however he likes; let him take no thought for the pomp and magnificence of his house: that may or may not distress, but it does no harm. But may he have compassion on us, and have the hundred flames of his banquet, which takes place in the dark anyway, burn of some less odorous material, so that people are not made ill when, at an evil moment, the flames are extinguished. Let the scourge of God not be the scourge of noses. [. . .]
VELF, 33–4

Verdi to Lumley; Milan, 9 April 1846

I know that the news I am going to give you will not be

Verdi in the 1840s. Engraving from the *Illustrated London News*, 30 May 1846. Mander and Mitchenson Collection, London.

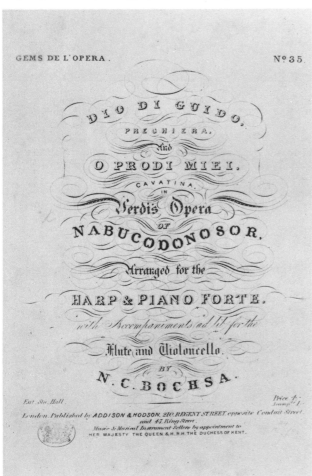

Verdi, *Nabucco*, 1842. Title page of salon arrangement of the aria 'Dio di Giuda' [God of Judah], London 1846. British Library, London.

unexpected, namely that because of the illness suffered in Venice, I am not able to come to London, and still less to write the opera there. This same day Signor Lucca [the publisher who was to bring out Verdi's London opera] will send you two medical certificates given him, which will authenticate things. You cannot imagine how distressed I am to have to renounce the honour of writing for London. My health is improving so slowly that it makes me incapable of even the slightest occupation, and I am forced to remain here idle, scrupulously following a medical cure until it is time to go to Recoaro to drink the waters, etc. [. . .]
COP, 20

Probably in view of Verdi's projected trip to London (which was to take place a year later), and probably inspired by the impresario Lumley, a biographical article about the composer appeared in a London weekly.

Illustrated London News, 30 May 1846

We offer to our readers, in the present number, a portrait of the great star of the musical world at this day – Guiseppe [*sic*] Verdi – on whose productions the fate of lyrical art would now seem to depend, as the great *maestri* whose works for the past thirty years have had possession of the Italian lyrical stage, Rossini, Bellini, Donizetti, are precluded from any longer wielding the pen for our profit – one by advance of years and exhaustion of mind, the other by premature death, and the third, alas! by a still more terrible fate – loss of reason. And amongst the young composers whose works are being daily produced in Italy, there is not one as yet that gives promise of future fame.

The works of Verdi are now well known and duly appreciated in England; for, though we have as yet heard but three operas of this great composer, fragments of most of his other works have found their way hither, and have been admired in the drawing-room or the concert room. Yet is his music eminently dramatic.

Never was a career so plainly marked out for any child of genius as that of Verdi; had he been any other than a lyrical composer, he would indeed have mistaken his vocation. [. . .]

The last work of the great *maestro* is 'Attila', a highly dramatic and most original composition, with a degree of local colouring and effectiveness quite new to the lyrical stage. This opera, brought out at Venice with Loewe Guasco Marini and Costantini, enjoys that favour which the works of this master always command amongst his countrymen. The enthusiastic appeciation in Italy of a composer of Verdi's stamp would appear strange to those who have imagined Italian musical taste to be represented by the sickly, sentimental compositions until lately classed as 'Italian music', *par excellence*; but Verdi's works show that the 'fatherland of song' has newer and more vigorous resources, and may give brilliant promise for the future.

We have only to add that our composer is thirty [actually thirty-two] years of age, though looking much older. The traces of care and illness, as well as of deep thought, are visible on his countenance. He lives quiet and retired; his active mind, however, is always employed, and he devotes a large portion of his time to his musical and literary studies.

Verdi went to Recoaro to take the waters, with Maffei, at the beginning of July 1846.

Muzio to Barezzi; Milan, 22 July 1846

[. . .] Cav. Maffei [. . .] had to come back for some business matter. At first I was frightened, seeing him come to my house alone, and I thought something bad had happened to the Signor Maestro; but he immediately reassured me to the contrary; and he told me that the Signor Maestro will not be back until Monday (27th) because he has to finish the cure completely; he assured me that he [Verdi] has almost changed appearance, and has become fat and is very well, and that the waters have done him much good and have strengthened his stomach, that he has a bit of sore throat, but the causes were the long walks he took in the mountains, and the sun was what did him a bit of harm. [. . .]
GAR, 254–5

The big event in Italy that summer was the election of Pope Pius IX on June 16. A month later, he declared a general political amnesty, which won him – for a time – the hearts of all liberals and nationalists.

Muzio to Barezzi; Milan, 13 August 1846

[. . .] The Signor Maestro is concerning himself with the libretto for Florence; the subjects are three: *L'avola* [Grillparzer's *Die Ahnfrau*], *I masnadieri* [Schiller's *Die Raüber*] and *Macbeth*. – If he has Fraschini he will do *L'avola*, if instead of Fraschini, they give him Moriani, as it appears, then he will do *Macbeth* and he will no longer need a tenor of great power. If Moriani were still in voice he could be given a protagonist's part, but it is said he is burnt out. The Signor Maestro, however, will hear him in Bergamo and then decide. In Bologna, on the occasion of the proclamation of the amnesty, they performed in the theatre the finale of *Ernani* ('O sommo Carlo!' [O supreme Charles!]) – and they changed the name of Carlo to Pio and the enthusiasm was so great they repeated it three times; and when there were the words 'Perdono a tutti' [pardon for all], cheers burst out on all sides. [. . .]
GAR, 258–9

While Verdi was trying to decide on a subject for Florence, Piave wrote to ask him if he could have back the rights to *Il corsaro*, a libretto which he had already completed but which Verdi had not set. Piave could have used it to fulfil an obligation to another composer.

Verdi to Piave; Milan, 27 August 1846

What? You've either gone mad or are going mad! You want me to give you *Il corsaro*? . . . That *Corsaro* which I have so cherished, which costs me so much thought, and which you yourself have versified with more care than usual? . . . And I should cede it to you? . . . And you don't even tell me for where or for whom? . . . It's true that this was set for London, but though the London business has fallen through, I must still write the opera for [the publisher] Lucca. And, almost without being aware of it, I was doing little by little this *Corsaro* of which I have sketched out some of the things I like best, the prison duet and the final trio . . . And you want me to cede it to you? . . . Away with you, off to the hospital and have your head examined. – You beg me in the name of *friendship to save you from a serious commitment*: Listen to me. If you had been any

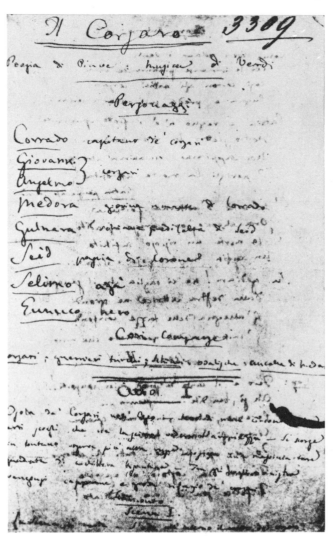

Verdi, *Il corsaro*, 1848. First page of libretto by Francesco Maria Piave. Civico museo teatrale, Trieste.

other person I wouldn't even have bothered to answer: I would have refused the poet, in other words; but the friend, *Francesco Maria Piave*, whose care, lavished on me with more than fraternal heart, during the period of my illness, I shall never forget, to him I cannot deny this wish. [. . .] So do as you think best, and if you want this *Corsaro* I yield it to you on condition, however, that you must make me another libretto with the same love with which you made this one. [. . .]
MS, ADC, ROVIGO

Muzio to Barezzi; Milan, 27 August 1846

[. . .] Perhaps in the Signor Maestro's opera in Florence neither Moriani nor Ferri will sing. Now all depends on a reply from [the baritone Felice] Varesi; if Varesi agrees to sing during Lent in Florence, then he writes *Macbeth*, where there are only two principal parts: Cordelia [*sic*] and Macbeth: la Loewe and Varesi; the others are secondary parts. No actor, at present, can do *Macbeth* better than Varesi, both for his way of singing and for his intelligence, and even for his short, ugly physique. Perhaps you will say he sings off pitch, but this doesn't matter because the part would be almost all declaimed, and he is very good at that. [. . .]
GAR, 261–2

95

Verdi to Piave; Milan, 4 September 1846

Here is the scenario of *Macbet*. This tragedy is one of the greatest human creations! . . . If we cannot make something great from it, let's try at least to make something out of the ordinary. The scenario is clear: without convention, without forcing, and brief. I beg you to make the verses also brief; the briefer they are the more effect you will achieve. Only the first act is a bit long, but it will be up to us to keep the numbers short. In the verses there must be no superfluous words: everything must say something, and you must use a sublime language except for the choruses of the witches: those must be common, but bizarre and original.

When you have done the introduction, please send it to me; it is made up of four little scenes and can be contained in few verses. Once this introduction is done, I will leave you all the time you want, because I know the general character and the hues as if the libretto were written. Oh I beg you, do not neglect this *Macbet*, I beg you on my knees; take care with it for me, if for no other reason, and for my health, which is now good but becomes immediately bad if you upset me . . . Brevity and sublimity. . . .

AB I, 643

Verdi to Piave; Milan, 22 September 1846

I have received the cavatina, which is better than the Introduction. All the same, how prolix you always are!! For example the letter that Lady reads is really just words in verse: scant energy in the rest of the recitative – and very little in the first quatrain of the Adagio – the line 'Vieni su questo core' ['come to this heart'] is so commonplace that it drains all the force from the strophe: the cabaletta is all right; so correct in this part the letter, which can be abbreviated without omitting anything [. . .]

As for the Introduction, many things must be done. The first strophes of the witches, to have character, must be more strange: I don't know how to tell you the way, but I know they are not good as they stand [. . .] BEAR ALWAYS IN MIND TO SAY FEW WORDS . . . FEW WORDS . . . VERY FEW BUT SIGNIFICANT [. . .].

AB I, 644

91 *Verdi to Alessandro Lanari, impresario of the Teatro La Pergola, Florence; Milan, 15 October 1846*

Here is the outline of *Macbet*, and you will understand what it's about. You see that I need an excellent chorus: especially the female chorus must be good because there will be two witch choruses of the greatest importance. Pay attention also to the stage-machinery. In short, the things that require the greatest care in this opera are: *Chorus and Machinery*.

I am sure you will mount all the rest with that splendour that so distinguishes you and that you will pay no heed to economy. Remark also that I need ballerinas to do a pretty little dance at the end of the third act. Do not (I repeat) count the cost, for you will have recompense, I hope, and then I will bless you a thousand times a day, and mind you my benedictions are worth almost, almost, those of a Pope.

All joking aside, I really urge you to see that all goes well [. . .].

AB I, 650

Verdi's vast correspondence about *Macbeth* – with Piave, Lanari and others – confirms his particular interest in this

opera. He virtually wrote much of the libretto himself, speech by speech. He also enlisted the help of Maffei. In December 1846 he learned that Sofia Loewe, who was to have sung Lady (as Verdi calls her), would be replaced by Marianna Barbieri-Nini.

Verdi to Lanari; Milan, 22 December 1846

[. . .] My health is good: but as I told you in my last, I am a bit tired. – La Barbieri must be a bit patient, for if she likes this genre, she is treated very well. Addio Addio.
P.S. Mind you, the ghost of Banco must rise from underground: he must be the same performer who played Banco in Act I. He must have an ashen veil, but very loose and fine that can hardly be seen, and Banco must have disheveled hair and various wounds visible on the neck. –

I have received all these ideas from London, where this Tragedy has been performed constantly for 200 years and more.

MS, BNC, FLORENCE

Verdi to Lanari; Milan, 21 January 1847

[. . .] I must also inform you that, speaking with [the Scala designer] Sanquirico a few days ago about *Macbet* and expressing to him my desire to stage very well the Third Act with the apparitions, he suggested various things to me, but the most beautiful is surely the *phantasmagoria*. He assured me it would be extremely beautiful and highly suited; and he himself has offered to speak with the optician Duroni, to have him prepare the machine.

You know what the *phantasmagoria* is, and it's pointless for me to describe it to you. My God, if the thing works out well, as Sanquirico described it to me, it will be something amazing, and will make a host of people come running for it alone. As to expense, he assures me it will be little more than another machine. . . . What do you say?

Within the week you will have the whole third act, the beginning of the fourth, the libretto concluded, and I hope also the costume designs. I want the designs made well: you may be sure they will be well done, because I have sent for several from London. I have had first-rate literary men consulted about the period and the costumes, and then they will be examined by Hayez and by the others of the [Scala's artistic] Committee etc. etc.

When you receive the music, you will see that there are two Choruses of very great importance: do not economize on the number of the chorus members and you will be pleased: mind you, the witches must always be divided into three groups and it would be excellent that they were 6,6,6, in all 18, etc. . . . Take care about the tenor who must do Macduff, and see that all the secondary parts are good, because the concerted numbers need good people. And these concerted numbers mean a great deal to me – [. . .]

I'm sorry the man who is to play the part of Banco didn't want to do the Ghost! And why not? . . . Singers must be engaged to sing and act: moreover it is time these usages were abandoned. It would be monstrous for another person to be the Ghost, since Banco must retain his appearance precisely also when he is a ghost.

MS, BNC, FLORENCE

The baritone Felice Varesi, who was to play Macbeth (and later create the roles of Rigoletto and Germont), was a singer of unusual intelligence, and Verdi consulted him also about the opera.

Verdi to Varesi; Milan, 7 January 1847

I have been a bit tardy in sending you the music, because I needed some rest. Now here you have a Duettino, a big Duet, and a finale. I will never stop urging you to study the situation and the words: the music will take care of itself.

In short, I want you to serve the *poet* better than the *composer*. From the first Duettino you can derive great advantage (better than if it were a cavatina). Bear the situation well in mind, for it is when he meets the witches who predict a throne for him. At such an announcement you remain amazed and aghast; but at the same time the ambition to gain the throne is born in you. Therefore at the beginning of the Duettino you will say sotto voce, and mind you give the verses their full importance: 'Ma perché sento rizzarsi il crine?' [But why do I feel my hair stand on end?] [. . .]

In the grand Duet the first verses of the recitative must be said without emphasis, as he gives orders to the servant. But after he remains alone, he is gradually aroused, and he seems to see a dagger in his hands, which points out to him the road to killing Duncan. This is a very beautiful moment, dramatic and poetic, and you must work hard on it!

Mind you, it is night, all are asleep: the whole Duet must be said sotto voce, but with a grim voice such as to inspire terror. [. . .] That you may understand my ideas clearly, I will tell you also that in all this recitative and Duet the instrumentation consists of muted strings, two bassoons, two horns, and a kettledrum. You see the orchestra will play extremely softly, and you singers must also sing with mutes. [. . .]

MS, AMC, SIENA

Verdi to Varesi; Milan, January 1847

Here is the third act, which, as you will see, has come out less taxing than I thought. The scene is a cavern where the witches do their witchcraft in a chorus. Then you enter to question them in a short recitative, after which come the apparitions, where you have only a few words, but, as actor, you will accompany everything with mime. Then you have the Cantabile, when the eight Kings appear to you: at first the singing is broken, to accompany the apparitions, but then there is a Cantabile (*sui generis*) in which you should produce great effect. I do not have to tell you there is an effect on the words 'Muori fatal progenie' [Die! fatal progeny] and then another at the end, on the words 'Ah che non hai tu vita' [Ah! you have no life]. This passage is written in two ways: do it as it comes best for you and write to tell me which one I must orchestrate. [. . .]

I hope you have also received the first act. When you have received this, write at once. I am convinced the tessitura suits you well, but perhaps there might be some note, some passage that is awkward for you, so write to me before I do the orchestration.

Now only the last scene is missing, which consists for you in a calm Adagio cantabile, and in a very brief death; but it will not be one of those usual, sentimental deaths, etc. . . . You realize that Macbetto must not die the way Edgardo [in Donizetti's *Lucia*] and such die –

In short, mind the words, and the subject: that's all I ask. The subject is beautiful, and so are the words. [. . .]

MS, AMC, SIENA

Muzio to Barezzi; Florence, 25 February 1847

Yesterday evening la Barbieri arrived. Today there are the rehearsals of *Attila*, which will open on Sunday. The Maestro does not want to attend any rehearsals and has given this assignment to me. Saturday, then, the first piano rehearsals of *Macbeth* will begin. Next week perhaps I will be able to write and tell you the exact day of the premiere. Remember, we expect you with Giovannino, who is desired by some of his acquaintances. We are staying at the Pensione Svizzera, where we have a magnificent apartment, with paradisiacal air, and a *table fit for a king*; and the Maestro takes care of paying . . . that is, the impresario does.

To tell you that the Maestro is idolized, sought out again and again by all, is something you will already have imagined. The most famous men have wanted to make his acquaintance: Niccolini, Giusti, Bartolini, Dupré, etc.; and even the Grand Duke has sent word to invite him to come and see him, and yesterday evening he went, a bit against his will. The Grand Duke could tell him all about his [Verdi's] life. Even the fact that they didn't want him in Busseto. In short, he knew everything. [. . .]

GAR, 311

From the memoirs of the sculptor Giovanni Dupré   96–97

At that time Giuseppe Verdi came to Florence to stage *Macbeth*. If I am not mistaken, it was the first time he came amongst us. His fame had preceded him; of enemies, as is natural, he had many; I was a partisan of his works then known there: *Nabucco, I lombardi, Ernani* and *Giovanna d'Arco*. His enemies said that as an artist he was very vulgar and a corruptor of Italian bel canto, and as a man they said he was a downright bear, full of pride and haughtiness, who disdained intimacy with anyone. I wanted to find out at once: I wrote a note in these terms: 'Giovanni Dupré would like to ask the illustrious Maestro G. Verdi to deign, at his own convenience, to come to his studio, where he is finishing in marble his *Cain*, which he would like to show him before shipping it.'

But to see to what extent he was a bear, I decided to take the letter myself and present myself as an apprentice in the Professor's studio. He received me with great urbanity, read the letter, and then, with a face neither smiling nor grave, said to me:

'Tell the Professor that I thank him very much and as soon as it is possible for me, I will call on him, since I intended to meet personally a young sculptor who . . . etc. –'

I answered: 'If, Signor Maestro, you want to meet that young sculptor as soon as possible, then you can be contented at once, for I am he.'

He smiled pleasantly and, shaking my hand, said: 'Ah, this is a real artist's trick.'

We talked at length, and he showed me some letters of introduction he had for Capponi, Giusti and Niccolini. The one for Giusti was from Manzoni.

The whole time he remained in Florence we saw each other almost every day; we made some excursions into the environs, such as to the Ginori [porcelain] factory, to Fiesole, and the Torre del Gallo. We were a little band of four or five: Andrea Maffei, Manara, who later died in Rome, Giulio Piatti, Verdi and I. In the evening he allowed one or the other of us to attend the rehearsals of *Macbeth*; in the morning he and Maffei often came to my studio.

He liked painting and sculpture very much, and spoke of them with extraordinary acumen. His particular favourite was Michelangiolo, and I remember that in the Chapel of Canon Sacchi, which is under Fiesole on the old road, where a fine collection of works of art can be admired, he remained almost a quarter-hour on his knees to admire an altarpiece said to be the work of Michelangiolo.

I wanted to do his portrait, but then, for reasons beyond his control or mine, this plan could not be carried out, and I contented myself with doing his hand, which I then carved [. . .]. Verdi's hand is in the act of writing. In removing the form, the pen remained stuck there, and now it serves as a stake in a sketch for my *St Antoninus*. . . .
DUPRÉ, 145 FF.

On 3 March 1847, premiere of *Macbeth* at the Teatro alla Pergola, Florence. The soprano Marianna Barbieri-Nini, Verdi's first Lady Macbeth, has left her own memoirs of this period. Though surely somewhat exaggerated, they give an idea of what Verdi was like when preparing the production of a new opera.

From the reminiscences of Marianna Barbieri-Nini

The rehearsals of *Macbeth*, at the piano and with orchestra, amounted to more than a hundred, because Verdi never seemed satisfied with the performance and demanded a better interpretation from the artists, who, partly because of his exaggerated demands and partly because of his closed and taciturn character, did not particularly like him. Morning and evening, in the foyer and on stage, as soon as the Maestro entered for rehearsals, all eyes turned to him, trying to guess from his expression if there was something new. If he came in smiling, it was almost certain that, on that day, there would be some addition to the rehearsal. I remember that for Verdi there were two culminating points in the opera: the sleepwalking scene and my duet with the baritone. It will be hard to believe, but it is a fact that the single sleepwalking scene took three months of study. For three months, I tried to imitate those who speak while sleeping, who articulate words, as the Maestro said to me, almost without moving their lips, leaving the other parts of the face immobile, including the eyes. . . . It was enough to drive one mad! And the duet with the baritone which begins 'Fatal mia donna, un murmure' [My fatal wife, a murmuring], it will seem incredible to you, but it was rehearsed more than one hundred and fifty times, to achieve, Verdi said, that it be *more spoken than sung*. Now listen to this: the evening of the dress rehearsal, with the theatre full, Verdi also made the artists put on their costumes, and when he was determined about something, woe if you contradicted him! So we were then all dressed and ready, the orchestra in place, the chorus on the stage, when Verdi, motioning to me and Varesi, called us into the wings and said that, to please him, we were to go with him into the foyer, to rehearse once more at the piano that accursed duet.

'Maestro,' I said, horrified, 'We're already in Scotch costume. How can it be done?'

'You will put on a cloak.'

And Varesi, irked at such a request, tried raising his voice, saying: 'But we've already rehearsed a hundred and fifty times, by God!'

'You won't be saying that in half an hour, because it'll be one hundred and fifty-one!'

We had perforce to obey the tyrant. I still remember the grim looks Varesi hurled at him, heading for the foyer, with his fist on the hilt of his sword, as if planning to slaughter Verdi, as he was later to slaughter King Duncano.

For the rest, resigned, he also gave in; and the one hundred and fifty-first rehearsal took place, while the impatient audience was making an uproar in the stalls. Now then, if someone were to say that duet aroused enthusiasm,

he would be saying nothing: it was something incredible, new, never seen before. I have sung *Macbeth* everywhere, and every evening during the Pergola season, that duo regularly had to be repeated two, three, even four times. One evening we had to submit to a fifth encore.

On opening night, I shall never forget the sleepwalking scene, which is one of the last in the opera. Verdi circled around me uneasily, saying nothing: it was very clear that the success, already great, would not appear definitive to him until after that scene. So I made the Sign of the Cross (it's a custom maintained still today on stage in the most difficult moments) and I went ahead. The newspapers of that time will tell you if I interpreted rightly the dramatic and musical thought of the great Maestro. I know this: that as soon as the fury of applause calmed down, when I re-entered my dressing room, all trembling and exhausted, I saw the door flung open – I was already half-undressed – and Verdi entered, waving his hands and moving his lips as if he wanted to say something, but he was unable to utter a single word. I was laughing, weeping, and I could say nothing either; but looking at the Maestro, I saw that his eyes were also red. . . . We clasped hands, very hard; then he rushed out. That scene of sincere emotion repaid me generously for the many months of constant work and constant fears.
MONALDI, 84FF.

Verdi to Barezzi; Milan, 25 March 1847

For some time it has been my intention to dedicate an opera to you, who have been to me father and benefactor and friend. It was a duty I should have performed before now, and I would have done so, if imperious circumstances had not prevented me.

Now here, for you, is this *Macbeth*, which I love more than my other operas and which therefore I consider worthier of being presented to you. The heart offers it, may your heart accept it, and may it be witness to you of the eternal memory, the gratitude and love borne you by your most affectionate [Giuseppe Verdi].
AB I, 687

During the composition of *Macbeth*, Verdi had resumed negotiations with Lumley in London, which was to be his next stop.

Verdi to Lumley; Milan, 4 December 1846

The opera I was to write for Naples in the spring of 1847 has been postponed for another season, so I would be free to write in June for London unless there is some important obstacle.

Last year I had chosen *Il corsaro* as the subject, but after it was versified, I found it cold and of scant theatrical effect, so I changed my mind and decided, though it doubled my expense, to make another libretto from Schiller's *I masnadieri*. My illness had cancelled our contract of last year, so I had every right now to select another subject, especially since this was known to Signor Lucca, who further knew that I had composed almost one half of *I masnadieri*, because it is more effective, more suited to the company. [. . .]

I repeat I am under no obligation to anyone to set one subject rather than another, and if I am to compose for London I have time to finish *I masnadieri* but not to write the whole of *Il corsaro*.

If *I masnadieri* suits you, I commit myself now to compose it for London, provided you write me a letter committing yourself to allow me to choose the singers from the list of the company, in which list there must be the names of la Lind and Fraschini, as we agreed in Milan. [. . .]

86
103–4   COP, 33

Lumley accepted the conditions, and immediately after the success of *Macbeth*, Verdi returned to Milan to work on the opera.

Verdi to Escudier; Milan, 23 May 1847

[. . .] I have received your letter in which you so thoughtfully give me news of the results of la Lind. I am glad (since I am obliged to compose) that she has had such a success, and in two or three days' time I will set out for London. It is probable that I will go straight there, because time is too pressing. We will meet, nevertheless, on my return, and then I will stop in Paris for some months, to see your city and also to rest from the constant labours of four continuous years, and I really want to see for once in my life how fine it is to live like a gentleman.

My health, while not perfect, is no worse than usual.

AB I, 700

Muzio to Barezzi; Paris, 1 June 1847

This morning at 7 we arrived in Paris, after having covered more than 1000 miles. We had a delightful journey, nor were there any accidents.

Wednesday we left Milan in a stifling heat; when we reached Como we no longer felt it so much, because we followed the Lake, and being among the mountains, we always had a bit of wind. At 4 on Thursday we reached Fiora in Switzerland, and went on the lake in a steamer, which took us to Lucerne.

From Lucerne we went by stage-coach to Basle. From Basle by rail we went to Strasbourg. When we reached Strasbourg we found no stage-coach leaving at once for Paris; and the Maestro, not wanting to wait, got the sudden whim of going to Paris via Brussels; and instead of continuing through France, we crossed the river Rhine, and entered the Grand Duchy of Baden-Baden. Beyond the river an omnibus took us to Kehl; from Kehl we travelled by train to Karlsruhe; from Karlsruhe to Mannheim, from Mannheim to Mainz, from Mainz to Koblenz, from Koblenz to Bonn, from Bonn to Cologne, from Cologne to Brussels, from Brussels to Paris. [. . .] I can tell you nothing about Paris, because I haven't left the house; we have Escudier who acts as our cicerone; Guasco is here, and many others; but Verdi wants to see no one. [. . .]

GAR, 321–2

Verdi, however, made another sudden change of plan and stayed a bit longer in Paris, perhaps also to see Giuseppina Strepponi, who had now retired from the stage and settled in the French capital, giving voice lessons.

Muzio to Barezzi; London, 4 June 1847

I have been in London since yesterday, and I am here alone, without the Maestro, who is still in Paris and will come tomorrow evening. He sent me on ahead, because in Paris

they had told him la Lind did not want to sing new operas. If all this was true, since he had it in his contract that la Lind had to sing in his operas, he would make formal protest to the management and not come to London, and I would go back to Paris in 10 hours' time, as I had come.

As soon as I reached London I went to Lumley with a letter from Verdi, and he insisted the gossip was not true and la Lind could hardly wait to have her part and learn it, and he was deeply distressed not to see Verdi in London. Then I immediately wrote a letter to the Maestro at Boulogne-sur-Mer to let him know, and so tomorrow he will resume his journey and at 6 in the evening he will be in London. I came from Paris to London in 10 hours.

Steam by land and by sea. The steam-train flew over the ground; the steamer flew over the sea. What chaos London   101
is! What confusion! Paris is nothing in comparison. People shouting, the poor crying, steam-cars flying, men on horseback, in carriages, on foot, and all yelling like the damned! My dear Signor Antonio, you can have no idea!

Milan is nothing! Paris is something compared to London, but London is a city virtually unique in the world; just imagine almost two million inhabitants; then you can imagine what an immense city it is. To go from one end of the city to another, you have to pass three posting stations, and change horses three times.

I have engaged the apartment for the Maestro and me, on condition that he likes it, because if he can't work in peace, then we'll go to the country. [. . .]

Here business is not done in francs, all in sterling; the money I have spent here in one day would last me 10 in Milan, and I'm not exaggerating. As soon as Verdi is here we'll work hard and quickly flee this Babylon. It isn't so much the noise, but the *denabro* [*denaro*: money], as the Canon says, that counts. For the three rooms I wanted to take they asked 5 pounds sterling a week, and half a pound for the maid. So I took only two; and in the living-room I had them put a bed for me, which in the daytime turns into a very handsome sofa. [. . .]

GAR, 325–7

Verdi to Clarina Maffei; London, 8 June 1847

I have been in London barely two days. [. . .] In Paris I went to the Opéra. I have never heard worse singers and more mediocre choristers. The orchestra itself (with due respect to all our *lions*) is little more than mediocre. What I saw of Paris I like very much, and above all I like the free life that can be led in that country. On my return I will stop there, and then I will tell you frankly what I think of it. Of London I can say nothing, because yesterday was Sunday and I didn't see a soul. I am annoyed, however, by this smoke and this smell of coal: it's like being on a steamboat. Any moment I will go to the theatre to see about my business. Emanuele (whom I sent ahead) has found me a lodging so homeopathic that I can't move: still it is very clean, like all the houses in London.

La Lind arouses an indescribable fanaticism: at this hour they are already selling boxes and seats for tomorrow evening. I can't wait to hear her. [. . .]

MS, EREDI MAFFEI, MILAN

Verdi to Giuseppina Appiani; London, 27 June 1847

Evviva per sempre our sun, which I loved so much, but which I now adore, since I have been among these fogs and this smoke that suffocates me and blinds my spirit! For the rest, though, what a magnificent city! There are things that dumbfound you . . ., but this climate paralyses all beauty. Oh, if here there were the sky of Naples, I believe it would be futile to desire Paradise. I haven't yet begun the rehearsals of my new opera because I lack the will to do anything. Mind you: *not anything*. Which is saying a lot! For that matter, la Lind has not erased other impressions; I am the faithful type. . . . [. . .]

COP, 457

Muzio to Barezzi; London, 29 June 1847

[. . .] Everything has been arranged for the piano rehearsals to begin tomorrow with all the singers, who are: (Amalia) la Lind, (Carlo) Gardoni, (Francesco) Coletti, (Massimiliano) Lablache; – I have already been to them all, to go over their parts. I have spent more time with la Lind than with the others, not because of the difficulty of the music, but because of the words, since her Italian isn't too good. I have found la Lind very good, kind, and polite and considerate. She is a perfect, thorough musician; she can read any vocal piece at sight. Her face is ugly, grave, and there is something Nordic about it that makes it unpleasant to my eyes; she has a thick nose [. . .], Nordic complexion, very thick hands and feet; I wanted to have a good look at her, as they say, and so one must with all celebrities. [. . .] She leads a very withdrawn life, receives no one [. . .] she hates, she told me, the theatre and the stage. [. . .] On this point she is very much in agreement with the Maestro, who also hates the theatre and can't wait to retire. [. . .]

GAR, 334–5

Verdi to Clarina Maffei; London, 17 July 1847

You will be amazed to hear I am still in London and the opera not yet performed! But it is the fault of the smoke and the fog and this devilish climate that robbed me of any desire to work. Now at last, all or almost all is finished, and we will surely open on Thursday the 22nd. I have held two orchestra rehearsals, and if I were in Italy I could express a detached opinion of the opera, but here I understand nothing. . . . Blame the climate, blame the climate!! . . .

MS, EREDI MAFFEI, MILAN

Muzio to Barezzi; London, 17 July 1847

[. . .] If you could see that little old man Lablache with that belly that seems a mountain, you would be amazed; he still has the most beautiful voice imaginable. The other day he went to the Queen, who gave him many messages for the

Maestro, wishing to meet him in person; but he doesn't want to go. The Queen herself has given orders that the opera open on the same day Parliament closes, which will be one of the greatest diplomatic solemnities in England; it is something that happens only every 7 years; she will attend the gala performance, and all the posters are already up, saying so; with the Queen coming to the theatre in gala, Lumley will make an extra 50 thousand francs. The day will be the 22nd, that is Thursday [. . .]. Gardoni was very late in learning the part, and this was the cause of the delay. [. . .]

GAR, 338–9

On 22 July 1847, premiere of *I masnadieri* at Her Majesty's Theatre, London.   103–4

From Queen Victoria's journal; London, 22 July 1847   102

[. . .] Went to the Opera, where we saw the production of Verdi's 'I Masnadieri' in 4 acts, which is the same subject as 'I Briganti' by Mercadante. In this new Opera by Verdi based on Schiller's 'Die Räuber' the music is very inferior and commonplace. Lablache acted the part of Maximilian Moor, in which he looked fine, but too fat for the starved old man. Gardoni acted the part of Carlo Moor & was beautifully dressed. Lind sang & acted most exquisitely as Amelia & looked very well & attractive in her several dresses. She was immensely applauded.

GODEFROY, 164

From Lumley's reminiscences

On Thursday, July 2nd [*sic*], 'I Masnadieri' (after wearying rehearsals, conducted by the composer himself), was brought out, with a cast that included Lablache, Gardoni, Coletti, Bouché, and, above all, Jenny Lind, who was to appear for the second time only in her career, in a thoroughly original part composed expressly for her.

The house was filled to overflowing on the night of the first representation. The opera was given with every appearance of a triumphant success: the composer and the singers receiving the highest honours. Indeed, all the artists distinguished themselves in their several parts. Jenny Lind acted admirably, and sang the airs allotted to her exquisitely. But yet the 'Masnadieri' could not be considered a success. That by its production I had adopted the right course, was unquestionable. I had induced an Italian composer, whose reputation stood on the highest

Queen Victoria arriving at Her Majesty's Theatre, London. Engraving from the *Illustrated London News*, 19 June 1847. Mander and Mitchenson Collection, London.

ARRIVAL OF HER MAJESTY.

pinnacle of continental fame, to compose an opera expressly for my theatre, as well as to superintend the production. More I could not have done to gratify the patrons of Italian music, who desired to hear new works.

It may be stated, in confirmation of the judgment of the London audience, that 'I Masnadieri' was never successful on any Italian stage. The *libretto* was even worse constructed than is usually the case with adaptations of foreign dramas to the purpose of Italian opera. To Her Majesty's Theatre the work was singularly ill-suited. The interest which ought to have been centered in Mademoiselle Lind was centered in Gardoni; whilst Lablache, as the imprisoned father, had to do the only thing he could not do to perfection – having to represent a man nearly starved to death.
LUMLEY, 192–3

Muzio to Barezzi; London, 23 July 1847

[. . .] The theatre took in a sum of 6000 pounds, which surpassed anything it had earned even when the Queen went there in grand gala. The Maestro was fêted, called on the stage, alone and with the singers, flowers were thrown to him, and you could hear nothing but: viva Verdi, *bietifol* [beautiful].
GAR, 344–5

Verdi conducted the first two performances, then handed over the baton to Michael Balfe. On 27 July he was back in Paris.

Verdi to Emilia Morosini; Paris, 30 July 1847

[. . .] Though I found London's climate horrible, I still liked the city immensely; it is not a city, it is a world: nothing is comparable to its greatness, richness, the beauty of the streets, the neatness of the houses, and you are amazed and depressed when, among the many magnificent things, you examine the *Bank* and the *Docks*. Who can resist that nation? The environs and towns near London are stupendous! I do not like many English habits, or rather, they are not suited to us Italians. How ridiculous certain imitations of the English are in Italy! . . .

I masnadieri, without creating a furore, pleased the audience, and I would have come back to London next year to write another opera if the publisher Lucca had accepted ten thousand francs to release me from the contract I have with him [for *Il corsaro*].
MS, MTS, MILAN

Muzio to Barezzi; Paris, 8 August 1847

I have been in Paris for almost two weeks and I haven't yet written to you: now I shall fulfil my obligation. [. . .]

105–8   Verdi has been contracted by the Grand Opéra of Paris to adapt to a new libretto the music of *I lombardi*, making some additions. The opera will open at the beginning of November. They give him all rights as if it were a new opera.

The performers will be la Julian, Duprez, Alizard; for the dances la Rosati-Galetti.

The impresarios have placed the whole theatre at his disposal. They have ordered the costumes. The libretto is shifted to the period [*sic*] of Gascony, retaining the same plot; so instead of being Italians who go to the Crusade, they will be French.

Authors of the libretto are: Scribe, Rogier [Royer] and Vaëz. All the big newspapers have already announced it. [. . .]

Today I leave for Milan; Verdi remains in Paris. [. . .]
GAR, 349–50

Verdi to Giuseppina Appiani; Paris, 22 August 1847

More operas for London? Hardly! Imagine: finding oneself all day surrounded by two poets, two impresarios, two publishers (here everything is done in pairs), engaging a prima donna, arranging a subject of a libretto, etc. etc. Now tell me if it isn't enough to drive one mad. . . . But I do not wish to go mad, and I defy all theatrical affairs, all Parisians, all newspapers both *pro* and *contro* and the comic articles of the *Charivary* and *L'Entr'Acte* . . . I will be here till around 20 November, and at the end of that month I will see again the cupola of the Duomo.

My health is better than in London. I don't like Paris as I do London, and I have an extreme dislike for the *Boulevards* (hush, let no one hear me utter such blasphemy). . . .
AB I, 728

Verdi to Giuseppina Appiani; Paris, 22 September 1847

I have begun rehearsals of my opera, which is *I lombardi*, but so revised it is beyond recognition. – All seem pleased, and so am I. We will surely open in November, for I shall make them hurry.

The *mise en scène* will be absolutely stupendous, for here money is no object; also the new managers are very eager, not because the opera is mine, but because, since it's the first opera under their management, it is very much in their interest to inform the public of their desire to raise the Opéra from its state of decline.
COP, 464

On 26 November 1847, premiere of *Jérusalem* at the   109
Opéra, Paris. The reception was mixed.

Le Coureur des spectacles, Paris, 27 November 1847

[. . .] The understanding of the stage manifest in this work, which entailed great difficulties, reveals the practised talent of the authors of the poem. Obliged to accept as a point of departure [. . .] the unfortunate *Lombardi*, the music of which was ill received almost everywhere, these writers have freed themselves at a stroke from the embarrassment which this unhappy stumbling-block must have caused them. In their hands the subject has acquired as dramatic a form as can ever be attained when one groans beneath the yoke of a musical score. This thing which in theatrical parlance is known as A TRANSLATION – far more because the ideas of the composer have to be translated than those of the librettist, who normally has none – this thing has many pitfalls. These would have been compounded in this case by the poor opinion generally left behind it by the late unlamented music of M. Verdi, had not the latter conceived the happy idea of composing some pieces on our inspiring soil. From that moment the prospects began to appear brighter; and from a downright bad Italian programme, swamped in notes no better than it deserved, there emerged a French piece adequate for the occasion. There are five of these new passages: one in the first act, for Duprez; two in the second (trio of basses with chorus and March of the Crusaders); some dance music, and the so-called Degradation scene, in the third act. This last, which has been over-praised, and which Duprez, who had lost his voice, merely declaimed, is not in fact the best thing among the additions; and it owed something to the importance with which the singer endowed it by making himself as solemn as he could. It is, moreover, most clumsily staged. The rest is as it was before: that is to say, heavy, clogged, cumbersome, full of the muddles, the reminiscences, the *longueurs*, the inexpressiveness and the claptrap of Italian music when it is not at its best. Had it not been for the pomp of the spectacle with which this unprepossessing work was surrounded, the Signor Maestro would have been in great danger of repeating the fiasco which it has encountered in a number of its performances abroad. [. . .] This is not true drama, as we understood the term in France. This is *made* music, and we want music that is *inspired*. To sum up: *Jérusalem*, which cannot be called new, as Racine said, since it springs from the ashes of *I lombardi*, and four numbers do not make a new score – this *Jérusalem* will earn its author, M. Verdi, some esteem among us; but it will maintain him at an immeasurable distance from the great artists whom we possess. When one has *Robert le diable*, *Les Huguenots*, *La Muette de Portici* and *La Juive*, *Guillaume Tell*, etc., one may smile at the efforts, be they always honourable and sometimes happy, of the foreigner in pursuit of success who craves our hospitality; one applauds him; but one does not compromise one's judgment by an admiration which would serve only to discourage true genius; for this admiration is to be awarded only to those who are *chosen*, and M. Verdi is only one of those who are *called*. [. . .]

This was the effect upon us of a first hearing, always a fleeting thing (particularly when boredom presses with all its weight, as it did last night, upon the unfortunate hearers). Nevertheless, it is incumbent upon us to return to certain parts which may have been too quickly assessed or perhaps the occasion of error. The artist devotes a year to the gestation of his work; and in less than four hours the journalist gives his verdict.

QISV, II, 102–4

Jérusalem was soon given at La Scala (26 December 1847) as *Gerusalemme*. For some years both it and *I lombardi* were performed in Italy, though the earlier version of the score was the more popular, because of its stronger patriotic content.

Despite his avowed dislike of the Boulevards, Verdi stayed on in Paris, where his relationship with Giuseppina Strepponi deepened. Barezzi visited him there briefly. During that winter the composer finally completed *Il corsaro* and sent it off to the publisher Lucca. Meanwhile he took an active interest in French politics and in the revolution which overthrew King Louis-Philippe and established the Second Republic.

Verdi to Giuseppina Appiani; Paris, 9 March 1848

[. . .] You will know all about events in Paris; after 24 February nothing happened. The procession that accompanied the dead to the memorial column of the Bastille was impressive, magnificent, and though there were no soldiers or police to maintain order, there was not the least disturbance. The grand National Assembly which will decide the government will be held on 20 April. I still cannot understand why it was not called earlier: I am too obstinate, or perhaps too malicious. There is no talk of

Thiers at all; who knows? He may show his talons all of a sudden!! . . .

I cannot hide from you the fact that I am greatly entertained and nothing so far has disturbed my sleep. I do nothing, I enjoy myself, I hear lots of nonsense and nothing more; I buy about twenty newspapers a day (naturally without reading them) to avoid the persecution of the vendors; because when they see you with a bundle of papers in your hand, nobody offers you any, and I laugh, and laugh, and laugh. If nothing important calls me to Italy, I shall stay here through April to see the National Assembly. I have seen everything that has happened so far, serious and comic (I beg you to believe that *seen* means *with my own eyes*) and I want also to see the 20th of April.

COP, 465

If Verdi could laugh at French political events, he could not help being deeply concerned and excited by developments in Italy. On 18 March Austrian troops fired on a Milanese crowd and the glorious 'Five Days' of revolution began. A few days later the Venetians rose up against their oppressors and declared a republic.

110

Verdi to Piave in Venice; Milan, 21 April 1848

You can imagine whether I wanted to remain in Paris, after hearing there was a revolution in Milan. I left the moment I heard the news, but I could see nothing but these stupendous barricades. Honour to these heroes! Honour to all Italy, which in this moment is truly great!

The hour of her liberation has sounded, you may be convinced of that. It is the people who want it: and when the people want something there is no absolute power that can resist them.

They can agitate, intrigue as much as they like, those who want to be necessary perforce; but they won't succeed in defrauding the people of their rights. Yes, another few months and Italy will be free, united, republican. What else should it be?

You speak to me of music!! What's got into you? . . . Do you believe I want to concern myself now with notes, with sounds? . . . There is and must be only one music welcome to the ears of the Italians in 1848. The music of the cannon! . . . I would not write a note for all the gold in the world: I would feel immense remorse in using music paper, which is good for making cartridges. Bravo, my Piave! Bravi all Venetians! Banish all parochial thoughts, let us extend a fraternal hand, and Italy will become the first nation of the world!

You're a national guard? I like your being only a plain soldier. What a fine soldier! Poor Piave! How do you sleep? How do you eat? . . . I, too, if I could have enlisted, would want to be a simple soldier, but now I can be only a tribune, and a wretched tribune because I am eloquent only in fits and starts.

I must return to France for commitments and business. Imagine: beyond the nuisance of having to write two operas, I have various sums to collect there, and others in bank-drafts to cash.

I have abandoned everything there, but I cannot neglect an amount which for me is large, and my presence is necessary to save at least a part of it in the present crisis. For that matter, whatever happens, I will not be upset by it. If you could see me now, you wouldn't recognize me any more. I no longer have that glum look that frightened you!

I am drunk with joy! Imagine: no more Germans!! You know how much I liked them! [. . .]
AB I, 745

From Milan, in early May, Verdi went to Busseto, and while he was there he took the first step towards the purchase of the farm property at Sant'Agata, which was eventually to become his home. He jotted down the conditions of the contract in his *Copialettere*, the notebook in which he drafted his correspondence.

Verdi's memorandum; Busseto, 1 May 1848

For the possessions (including houses, etc. . . .) of the Merlis in Sant'Agata, guaranteed to be approximately 350 biolchi, to take possession at Martinmas 1848 – with all the grain, winter stores, stakes for the vines, plus the four large hogsheads of about 50 brente each, three of the best and largest vats and the water wheel or machine in the Ongina, for irrigating the vegetable garden. I will cede my property at Roncole with crops, winter stores, stakes; I will assume the following mortgages on said properties: [. . .].
COP, 48

At the end of May Verdi returned to Paris. Despite his protests to Piave, he *was* thinking about music. He had an opera to write for Naples: *La battaglia di Legnano. Il corsaro* was to be performed (exceptionally, without the composer's presence) in Trieste, on 25 October 1848. Instead of settling in Paris, Verdi went to live at Passy for the summer, with Giuseppina. By now their union was established, and they continued to live together openly. Not incidentally, *Jérusalem*, Verdi's first French opera, is dedicated 'à Joséphine Strepponi'.

Verdi to Piave; Paris, 22 July 1848

I don't know if you are aware that I have been in Paris for over a month, and I'm not sure how much longer I will stay in this chaos. Have you heard about this latest revolution? How many horrors, my dear Piave! Heaven grant that it be all over! And Italy? Poor country!!! I read and reread the papers, always hoping for some good news, but . . . why do you never write to me? It seems to me that these should be the very moments when friends remember their friends!

In the midst of these world upheavals I have neither the head nor the will to concern myself with my affairs (it seems to me even ridiculous to busy myself with . . . music) and yet I am obliged to think of them and to think seriously. Tell me then, if I asked you to write me a libretto, would you do it? [. . .]
AB I, 751

In August the Austrians re-occupied Milan. The exiled Italian patriot Giuseppe Mazzini, whom Verdi had met in London the previous summer, asked the composer to set to music a patriotic poem by a young Genoese, Goffredo Mameli. Though Verdi disliked writing occasional pieces (and wrote very few), he could not refuse.

Verdi, *Il corsaro*, 1848. Poster for the premiere in Trieste. Civico museo teatrale, Trieste.

Verdi to Giuseppe Mazzini; Paris, 18 October 1848

I send you the hymn, and though it is a little late, I hope it will reach you in time. I have tried to be as popular and easy as it possible for me. Make whatever use of it you like; burn it even, if you do not believe it worthy. If, however, you make it public, have the poet change some words at the beginning of the second and third strophes, where it would be well to have a phrase of five syllables with a meaning of its own, like all the other strophes: *We swear it . . . Sound the trumpet*, etc., etc., then, obviously finish the verse with the word accented on the third last syllable. In the fourth verse of the second strophe the interrogative must also be removed, and the meaning must end with the verse. I could have set them as they stand, but then the music would have become difficult, hence less popular, and we would not have achieved our aim. –

May this Hymn amid the music of the Cannon soon be sung in the Lombard plains! – [. . .]
MS, MTS, MILAN

Verdi to Cammarano in Naples; Paris, 15 September 1848

I am surprised and mortified not to receive letters from you, or more poetry with which to continue the drama [*La battaglia di Legnano*]. What is the reason for this? The change of Management? It seems to me this should not prevent you from continuing your work. [. . .]
COP, 52

Verdi's dealings with the San Carlo were always complicated. In addition to the change of management, there was now the problem of censorship, which would surely have forbidden an inflammatory, patriotic subject like *La battaglia di Legnano*. Finally the composer agreed to write a different opera for Naples (it was to be *Luisa Miller*), while urging Cammarano to send him verses to complete *La battaglia*, now well begun.

Verdi to Cammarano; Paris, 23 November 1848

[. . .] Since the woman's part doesn't seem to me to have the importance of the other two, I would therefore like you to add, after the death chorus, a grand, very agitated recitative in which she shows her love, her despair in learning that Arrigo is consecrated to Death; her fear of being discovered, etc. etc. . . . .; after a beautiful Rec[itative] have the husband arrive to sing a fine pathetic little Duet; have the father bless his son, or something else. . . . etc. . . . etc. . . . [. . .]

Tell me another thing (don't take fright!): I would need in the concertato of the Introduction to have another voice, a tenor; could you put in for example a *Squire* of Arrigo? This Squire, it seems to me, could also be put in the last Finale! . . . he could support Arrigo when wounded. [. . .]

I know that you are rehearsing *Macbeth*, and since this is an Opera in which I take more interest than in the others, allow me then to say a few words to you about it. The part of Lady Macbeth has been given to la Tadolini, and I am surprised that she has agreed to do this part. You know how greatly I admire la Tadolini, and she herself knows it; but in our common interest I believe it necessary to make some remarks. La Tadolini has too great qualities to do that part! This will perhaps seem absurd to you!! . . . La Tadolini has a good and beautiful figure, and I would like Lady Macbeth ugly and bad. La Tadolini sings to perfection; and I would like Lady not to sing. La Tadolini has a stupendous voice, clear, limpid, powerful; and in Lady I would like a harsh, stifled, grim voice. La Tadolini's voice is angelic; I would like Lady's voice to be diabolical. [. . .]

COP, 61–2

Actually, la Tadolini, at this time, was in poor vocal condition, at the end of her career, and Verdi knew it. He also knew that, in the small and gossipy world of the San Carlo, his letter to Cammarano would become known to others, including the soprano. Tadolini *did* sing Lady, however; and in more recent times, Verdi's letter has been used by other inadequate sopranos as an excuse to sing the role badly.

Work was still continuing on the libretto of *La battaglia di Legnano* when Verdi arrived in Rome early in January 1849. It was a strange, excited Rome. Pius IX had been forced to flee the city by the liberal opposition; the Roman Republic was about to begin its brief existence. The atmosphere was perfect for the reception of Verdi's most explicitly, blazingly patriotic, nationalistic opera.

Muzio to Barezzi; Mendrisio, 4 February 1849

[. . .] Yesterday I received news of the dress rehearsal of the opera; I am awaiting that of the premiere. At the dress rehearsal, the people wanted at all costs to attend the performance, and they burst into the theatre until it was full *as an egg*, as we say. The Maestro was called on the stage 20 times. The next morning not a box, not a ticket, not a

libretto of the Opera was to be found: all was sold! [. . .]
GAR, 362

On 27 January 1849, premiere of *La battaglia di Legnano*   112
at the Teatro Argentina, Rome.

La Pallade, Rome, 5 February 1849

Verdi in this work has soared to sublimity. Far from obeying the antiquated conventional rules, he has felt that his spirit needed freedom, as Italy needed independence. . . . His melodies are not mechanical combinations of notes, but a happy grafting of phrases that correspond to the poetic expression and the dramatic interest. . . . This Italy, which not long ago was charmed by the sweet melodies of this Lombard genius, today must draw from the severity of this latest patriotic work that ardent spark which serves to reawaken and carry far and wide the intrepid spirit of the nation.
VER, 15

Verdi to Piave; Paris, 1 February 1849   113

I left Rome with sorrow, but I hope to return there very soon. I am trying somehow to put in order the tangled affairs I have here, then I shall fly to Italy. God bless you, my good Venetians! Whatever the outcome may be, you will certainly have the blessing and the gratitude of every good Italian. I am happy about Rome and Romagna, and also in Tuscany things are not going altogether badly. We have cause for great hopes. [. . .] There is nothing to be hoped for from France, and now less than ever.
WAL, 194

The Venetians were soon defeated. In March there was another battle between the Piedmontese and the Austrians, who won. King Carlo Alberto of Piedmont abdicated. In Busseto, meanwhile, Verdi's parents had moved into the farmhouse at Sant'Agata.

Carlo Verdi to Verdi; Busseto, 15 May 1849

On the 12th of this month we moved into the little house at Sant'Agata. The Merlis left it free on the 10th, having first given me the three vats I selected and the four hogsheads. . . . Now I'll send you the accounts. . . .

Almost all the cows calved happily; there is still one that will calve in the next few days, and then I will organize the stables. . . .

Your mother is very pleased to be in the country and would want never to return to Busseto; she has also had your bed moved to Sant'Agata, so if you want to come, I hope you will stay with us and enjoy yourself in your beautiful property. [. . .]
AB II, 9

Early in May, Cammarano had sent Verdi an extended outline of a libretto for Naples: *Eloisa* (later *Luisa*) *Miller*, based on Schiller's *Kabale und Liebe* (1784).

Verdi to Cammarano; Paris, 17 May 1849

I have just received the outline and I confess to you that I would have liked two prima donnas, and I would have liked to have the Prince's favourite in the full dimension of her character, exactly as Schiller made her. Then there would have been conflict between her and Eloisa, and Rodolfo's love for Eloisa would have been more beautiful; but, after all, I know we can't have what we want, and it's all right as it is. It seems to me, however, that all that infernal intrigue between Walter and Wurm, which dominates the whole drama like fate, does not have here all the colour and all the power as in Schiller. Perhaps it will become something else, when it is versified, but in any event see for yourself whether or not I am right. [. . .]

In the second act, I recommend to you the duet between Wurm and Eloisa. There will be a fine contrast between the terror and desperation of Eloisa and the infernal coldness of Wurm. It seems to me, indeed, that if you give Wurm's character a certain comic element, the situation will become even more terrifying. [. . .]

The third act is very beautiful. Develop well the duet between father and daughter: make it a duet that wrings tears. The duet that follows is also very beautiful and tremendous, and I believe also it is necessary to end with a trio including the father. [. . .]

MS, BLP, NAPLES

Cammarano to Verdi; Naples, 4 June 1849

Here is the finale of Act I. [. . .] I will give all your other observations sober consideration; now I can't, so as not to delay these verses, an essential part of the drama. – The idea that Miller in his youth served in the army is not bad, it ennobles his character, and it gives him some energetic impetus, and forms a dramatic antithesis with the pathetic element which is beautiful in his character. [. . .] However you choose to weave the concerted passage, I would be of the opinion that, towards the end, the tempo should accelerate, and should have a very lively conclusion. Otherwise, it seems to me that (since there is no stretta), the number could sink into languor. [. . .]

COP, 472

Cammarano to Verdi; Naples, 17 June 1849

If I were not afraid of being called an Utopian, I would be tempted to say that, to achieve the possible perfection of an opera, a single mind should be author of both verses and notes; from this idea clearly comes my opinion that, since the authors are two, they must at least fraternize, and if the Poetry must not be servant to the Music, it must not be its tyrant either. Convinced of this maxim, I have always followed it in my work; and the composers with whom I have collaborated have always been consulted whenever necessary. I have therefore carefully examined your letter of 17 May, and I answer it.

Schiller's dramatic concept in the part of Milady is sublime: I could defend its suppression only weakly, but we must bow to the inexorable necessity. For that matter, even if the Favourite had remained and the number of her arias had been increased, no prima donna (of music) would have taken the part; because no effort could counterpoise, on the operatic scale, the part's effect against the powerful effect of the part of Luisa. [. . .]

COP, 473

While Verdi in Paris and Cammarano in Naples were hammering out the story of *Luisa Miller*, political events in Rome had taken a disastrous turn. The French laid siege to the city, which was defended by Garibaldi. Mameli, the young poet of Verdi's *Hymn*, was mortally wounded; so was Lucio Manara, another patriot friend of Verdi's. The city was occupied by the French, the Triumvirate which included Mazzini fell, and the Pope was restored.

Verdi to Vincenzo Luccardi; Paris, 14 July 1849

For three days I have impatiently awaited your letters. You can well imagine that the catastrophe of Rome has plunged me into grave thoughts, and it is wrong of you not to write me promptly. Let us not speak of Rome!! What would be the use!! Force still rules the world! Justice? . . . What good is it against bayonets!! We can only weep over our misfortunes, and curse the authors of such woes!

Tell me about yourself! Tell me of your events. What are you doing now? Tell me, in short, everything our new masters allow you to tell. Tell me also about my friends! Write me at once, at once: don't delay a minute, because I am in hell.

COP, 474–5

At the end of July Verdi left Paris for Busseto, where he settled in his town house, the Palazzo Orlandi. In August Giuseppina was in Florence on private matters, probably to settle there her illegitimate son, little Camillino, as apprentice to the famous sculptor Bartolini (who died a short time later). The letter below contains one of Giuseppina's rare references to the boy, who apparently did not survive to manhood.

Giuseppina Strepponi to Verdi; Florence, 3 September 1849

I shall have finished my business by Wednesday and shall perhaps leave for Parma that same evening. Don't come to fetch me, however, until Friday evening or Saturday morning, because I should be sorry if you had to wait for me in vain in Parma. When I tell you who has charged himself with Camillino's artistic education, you will be astonished! It must suffice for now that I kissed the hands of the famous man, who said to me: 'Will you entrust him to me?' I have seen only a few people in Florence, but they have worked with zeal and, be it noted, mere acquaintances. No aristocrats, of course. In truth, one sometimes finds a heart where one expects only indifference, and *vice versa*.

Farewell, my joy! Now that I have almost finished my business, business too important to be neglected, I should like to be able to fly to your side. You speak of the unattractive country, the bad service, and furthermore you tell me: 'If you don't like it, I'll have you accompanied (N.B. I'll *have you* accompanied!) wherever you like.' But what the devil! Does one forget how to love, at Busseto, and to write with a little bit of affection?

I'm not there yet, so can still write what I feel, which is that the country, the service, and everything else will suit me very well, as long as you are there, you ugly, unworthy monster!

Farewell. Farewell. I have scarcely time to tell you that I detest you and embrace you.

P.S. Don't send anybody else, but come yourself to fetch me from Parma, for I should be very embarrassed to be presented at your house by anyone other than yourself.

WAL, 195

Verdi completed *Luisa Miller* during the late summer and early autumn of 1849. On 3 October, with Antonio Barezzi, the composer left for Naples, while Giuseppina apparently went to Pavia. The two men were held up in Rome, en route, by a cholera scare, so reached Naples only on 27 October.

Verdi to Marie Escudier, Léon's brother and sometime partner; Naples, 3 November 1849

The affairs of our country are desolating! Italy is no longer anything but a vast and beautiful prison! If only you could see this sky, so pure, this climate so mild, this sea, these mountains, this city, so beautiful!! To the eyes – a paradise; to the heart – an inferno!! The rule of your countrymen in Rome is no better than that of the rest of Italy. The French do their best to win the favour of the Romans, but so far the latter are most dignified and firm. One sees Frenchmen everywhere – parades, reviews, military bands that torment the ears in every part of the city, all the time, but one never sees a Roman taking part. Whatever your newspapers may say, the demeanour of the Romans is most praiseworthy, but . . . the French are in the right . . . they are the strongest!!!

Theatrical affairs are desolating: the management is about to go bankrupt! For my part I'm not at all happy about that, for I desire nothing more than to retire to some corner of the earth, to blaspheme and to curse!
WAL, 198

From Antonio Barezzi's diary; Naples, October–November 1849

27 evening, 5 o'clock, arrived in Naples.
28, saw with Arata the Cemetery, the Teatro San Carlo, and heard *Saffo* by Pacini.
29, with Tesorone saw the Royal Palace, Capo di Monte, the Park, the Hermitage, San Gennaro, the Gesù nuovo, Santa Chiara, Campo di Marte, two big obelisks, San Severo with surprising marble *Veiled Christ* and *Deposition from the Cross*, and at evening with Verdi in Chiaja [the seafront] to see sunset.
30, [. . .] in the evening with Verdi and Signora Gazzaniga to the Teatro Fiorentini.
31, saw Churches and in the evening to the Teatro nuovo del Fondo and heard *Il barbiere di Siviglia* with la Tadolini, De Bassini, etc.
GAR, 378–9

Barezzi had to leave Naples on 14 November, before the opening of *Luisa Miller*, which was delayed because of the composer's enforced stay in Rome. Verdi's own weeks in Naples were spent not only in sightseeing, but also in composing and quarrelling with the egregious impresario Flauto, who was having some difficulty paying the composer. At one point Verdi contemplated withdrawing his music and seeking refuge from the Neapolitan authorities on a French warship at anchor in the harbour. At last matters were settled, not very amicably.
On 8 December 1849, premiere of *Luisa Miller* at the Teatro San Carlo, Naples. It was a great success.
Verdi had originally agreed to write another opera for the next season at the San Carlo, but after his unhappy experiences there, he decided to compose the work for himself and worry later about where to stage it (he had

followed this course with *La battaglia di Legnano*). The librettist of the new opera was again to be Cammarano.

I do not cast the slightest doubt upon what you say in yours of the 26th. I know very well the times are critical, that you have enormous expenses to bear, that you have lawyers all over the place (though not for my scores alone) [. . .].

As for the other opera I was to write for Naples, I luckily found a way to free myself, disgusted by the infamous behaviour of that Management and Direction; nevertheless, since the subject has already been settled with Cammarano, I will write it all the same and, I hope, it will be finished in four or five months. I will give this score willingly to you, leaving you the charge of having it staged by the end of the month of November of this year of 1850, in one of the major theatres of Italy (except La Scala) with a first-class company, and with the commitment that I myself will supervise all rehearsals. In compensation you will pay me (16,000) sixteen thousand francs. [. . .]
MS, ASR, MILAN

To Flauto, before their quarrel, Verdi had suggested that Victor Hugo's *Le Roi s'amuse* would be 'a fine subject' (it was later to become *Rigoletto*). Now, he turned to another favourite project: *King Lear*.

Verdi to Cammarano; Busseto, 28 February 1850

At first sight *Re Lear* seems so vast, so complex that it would appear impossible to extract an opera from it; however, after close examination, I feel that the difficulties, undoubtedly great, are not insuperable. You know that *Re Lear* must not be made into a drama with the forms more or less used in the past, but must be handled in a completely new way, vast, without regard for any sort of convention. It seems to me the characters can be reduced to five principal roles: Lear, Cordelia, Fool, Edmondo, Edgardo. Two comprimarie: Regana and Gonerilla (perhaps the latter would have to be made another prima donna). Two bassi comprimari (as in *Luisa*), Kent and Glocester; the rest minor parts.

You rightly say that the pretext for disinheriting Cordelia is a bit infantile (in our present day, certain scenes will absolutely have to be omitted, such as the one where Glocester is blinded, those in which the two sisters are carried on stage, etc. etc., and many, many others which you will know better than I). The scenes can be reduced to 8 or 9, and I will remind you that in *I lombardi* there are 11, nor was this ever an obstacle to its production. [. . .]
AB II, 51

A lengthy synopsis follows, divided into four acts and eleven scenes, with the musical moments clearly indicated: the first scene ends with an 'Addio di Cordelia', the next scene opens with 'Edmondo's soliloquy', in Act II, scene 2, a 'Grand Chorus' tells of Glocester's disobedience and his being sentenced to blinding, in Act IV there is a 'little pathetic Duettino' between Edgardo and Glocester.

Verdi to Piave; Busseto, 28 February 1850

I have heard nothing from the Presidency of La Fenice. If

that contract should work out, you can count on me: I fear only that the proposals will reach me too late. [. . .] I will read your *Elisabetta* [*di Valois*] this evening.

AB II, 56

From London, Lumley suggested an opera on *The Tempest*. Verdi refused, for lack of time. He was offered yet another Shakespearean subject by his friend Giulio Carcano, translator of Shakespeare.

Verdi to Giulio Carcano; Busseto, 17 June 1850

[. . .] It would have been very dear to me to link my name with yours, and I am convinced that if you suggest I set *Amleto*, it must be an adaptation worthy of you. Inevitably these great subjects require too much time, and I have had also to renounce *Re Lear* for the present, leaving Cammarano the assignment of adapting the drama for another, more convenient moment. Now, if *Re Lear* is difficult, *Amleto* is even more so; and pressed as I am by two commitments, I have had to select shorter and easier stories to fulfil my obligations. [. . .]

COP, 482

Verdi and Piave were meanwhile discussing possible subjects for the Venice opera. Verdi proposed *Gusmano il buono* (which Royer and Vaëz had adapted from a Spanish drama, *Guzmán el bueno*, by Nicolás Fernández de Moratín, 1777). Brenna, of the Fenice, suggested Dumas's *Kean*. Piave also submitted a list.

Verdi to Piave; Busseto, 28 April 1850

[. . .] Brenna writes to me about *Kean*: it is still a good subject, and you will see this when, in time, I do it. But we will talk about it no more.

Stradella is impassioned, but trivial, and all the situations are old and banal. A poor artist who falls in love with a patrician's daughter and is persecuted by the father: these are things that offer nothing great, nothing new.

I don't know *Stifelius*. Send me an outline.

I know *Le comte Herman* of Dumas; it can't be done.

As for the genre, whether it is grandiose, impassioned, fantastic, it doesn't matter to me, provided it is beautiful. But the impassioned is the safest. The characters must be as many as the subject demands. If an artist concerns himself with these trivial questions, he will never do anything beautiful, original. [. . .] There would be another subject that, if the police would allow it, would be one of the greatest creations of the modern theatre. Who knows! They allowed *Ernani*, the police might allow this one also, and here there would be no conspiracy scenes.

Try! The subject is great, immense, and there is a character who is one of the greatest creations that the theatre of all countries and all ages can boast. The subject is *Le Roi s'amuse*, and the character I speak of would be Tribolet, and if Varesi is under contract, nothing better for him and for us.

P.S. As soon as you receive this letter, start moving: run throughout the city, and find an influential person who can obtain permission to do *Le Roi s'amuse*. Don't sleep. Stir yourself. Hurry. I expect you in Busseto, but not now, after the subject has been chosen.

AB II, 59–60

Verdi to Piave; Busseto, 8 May 1850

[. . .] *Stiffelius* is good and interesting. It wouldn't be difficult to place the Chorus in it, but the customs [. . .]. Shift the action where you like, but he must remain a Lutheran and a sect-leader. By the way, is this Stiffelius a historical figure? In the history I know, I don't recall the name.

Oh, *Le Roi s'amuse* is the greatest subject and perhaps the greatest drama of modern times. Tribolet is a character worthy of Shakespeare!! *Ernani* can't be compared!! This is a subject that cannot fail. You know that 6 years ago when Mocenigo suggested *Ernani* to me, I cried: 'Yes, by God . . . that one can't go wrong.' Now, in reflecting on various subjects, when *Le Roi* returned to my mind, it was a thunderbolt, an inspiration, and I said the same thing: 'Yes, by God, that one can't go wrong.' So then, arouse the interest of the Presidenza, turn Venice upside down, and make the Censorship allow this subject. What does it matter if [the singer] la Sanchioli isn't right? If we were to heed this, no more operas would be written. For that matter, with no offence to anyone, who is reliable among today's singers? What happened the first night of *Ernani*, with the leading tenor of the time? What happened the first night of the *Foscari*, with one of the outstanding companies of the period? Singers who can make successes by themselves . . . la Malibran, Rubini, Lablache, etc. etc., no longer exist. . . . [. . .]

AB II, 62–3

Through the spring and early summer of 1850, Verdi worked on two projects: the composition of *Stiffelio* (after a French play by Souvestre and Bourgeois, 1849) for Trieste and the drafting of the libretto for Venice from *Le Roi s'amuse*. The latter was, obviously, foremost in his mind.

Verdi to Piave; Cremona, 3 June 1850

There is no problem about the division of the stage [for the last scene] nor for the sack. Just follow the French and you can't go wrong.

As for the title, if we cannot keep *Le Roi s'amuse*, which would be beautiful . . . the title must necessarily be *La maledizione di Vallier*, or to be shorter *La maledizione*. The whole subject lives in that curse, which also becomes moral. An unhappy father who bemoans his daughter's stolen honour, mocked by a court jester whom the father curses, and this curse affects the jester in a frightful way, seems to me moral and great to the highest degree. Mind you, Le Vallier must only appear twice (as in the French) and say very few, emphatic, prophetic words.

I repeat: the whole subject lies in that curse. I haven't time to say more to you. [. . .] Submit the subject to the Presidenza [of La Fenice], to the Police. Hurry, really hurry.

AB II, 63–4

In late summer Piave came to Busseto. On 5 August 1850 the subject of *Rigoletto* was sent to the Presidenza, though the title was still left blank. Verdi was uneasy about censorship problems.

114–15

Verdi to President Marzari of La Fenice; Busseto, 24 August 1850

I have myself urged Piave to return to Venice for the sole

purpose of personally bringing you this letter, to tell you at length what I can only indicate in writing.

The suspicion that *Le Roi s'amuse* may be forbidden creates serious embarrassment for me. I was assured by Piave that there was no obstacle to this subject, and trusting his word, I set myself to study it and ponder it profoundly, and the idea, the musical colour had been found in my mind. I could say that the main, most toilsome part of the job was done. If I were now obliged to think about another subject, I would lack the time for such study, and I could not write an opera that would satisfy my conscience. Moreover, as Piave wrote you, I am not convinced by la Sanchioli, and if I had imagined that the Presidenza was going to make such an engagement, I would not have accepted the contract. – My interest, and I believe that of the theatre, is to guarantee insofar as possible the outcome of the opera, so then, Signor Presidente, you must concern yourself with overcoming two obstacles: obtaining permission for *Le Roi s'amuse* and finding a singer [. . .] who can suit me. If these obstacles should be impossible to overcome, I believe it is in our common interest to cancel the contract. [. . .]

MS, ATLF, VENICE

On 16 November 1850, premiere of *Stiffelio* at the Teatro Grande, Trieste. This premiere had been preceded by last-minute problems with the censor, distressed by the unusual story of a Protestant pastor who, using actual words from the Bible, forgives an adulterous wife.

La Favilla, Trieste, 17 November 1850

[. . .] The tragicomic events of the previous few days, which had aroused doubt that the opera would even be given, had increased the expectancy of the public, prepared to hear this new offspring of the happy muse of Verdi. So, on the one hand, some people went to the theatre full of that favourable attitude with which well-bred spirits are always ready to welcome the fruit of an extraordinary talent such as Verdi's surely is. Some others, however, arrived there with the wicked anticipation of seeing ruined, to a great extent if not wholly, a work that was born of toil, a work on which a profane hand had been laid with shocking irreverence. Others still – and these made up the majority – crowded into the stalls, torn between the lively desire to greet a new triumph of Italian art and the fear of seeing it lost through the effect of the puerile caprices and obscurantist intrigues of a faction opposed to all light, to all forward movement along the untried ways of human progress. Their representatives are too well known for us to have to single them out. – Unquestionably these various attitudes in the audience had a great influence on the outcome of the opera, even if we leave out of consideration many other elements, more or less contrary. [. . .]

But despite all this, the outcome of *Stiffelio* was very happy, such as to add lustre to the name of its most distinguished author; and the causes of this outcome must be sought in the intrinsic values of the spirit, so abundant that they virtually forced the public, already confused by divergent impressions, to listen with constant attention, broken only by repeated applause. [. . .] Verdi's decision to interpret in music a dramatic subject so removed from the universally accepted conventions of serious opera must be considered very daring. [. . .]

QISV II, 104

Il Diavoletto, Trieste, 19 November 1850

[. . .] Expectation was great, especially after the impression made by *Luisa Miller*, but, alas, the public did not find what it had hoped for. Among the main causes of this opera's scant success one must surely list the choice of subject, which can with every reason be called antidramatic, and the deficiency of the poetry.

In the midst of a host of clamorous events, touching scenes, and heroic stories that history offers us, how did Signor Piave get the idea of choosing a subject which presents no action, no dramatic plot, and, being almost contemporary with us, having the actors appear on the stage in ridiculous clothes like our own? [. . .]

QISV, II, 104

Elsewhere in Italy, *Stiffelio* suffered even more from censorship, though Verdi himself held the work in high consideration. He followed its fortunes, and – years later – made an attempt to salvage it, adapting the music to a new libretto, *Aroldo* (1857). The second version of the opera was no more fortunate than the first.

From Trieste, Verdi hurried to Venice with Piave, but he did not, as he had hoped, receive the censor's permission at once.

Verdi to Piave; Busseto, November 1850

I have awaited in vain the letter from the Presidenza, bringing me the political authorization for *Le Roi s'amuse*. I am not wasting time, I continue writing, but I am uneasy. [. . .]

Mind you: do not let yourself be induced to make modifications that would lead to alterations of the characters, the subject, the situations. If it's a matter of words, you can agree. If it's a matter also of changing the scene where Francesco [the Duke in the final version] uses the key to enter the bedroom of Bianca [Gilda], you can also do it. In fact (as I wrote to you in my last) I believe we would be well-advised to find something better on our own. But be sure you leave intact the scene where Francesco goes to the house of Saltabadil [Sparafucile]. Without this, the drama no longer exists. You must also leave in the business of the sack [with Gilda's dead body]. This cannot matter to the Police, for it's not their job to think about the dramatic effect. [. . .]

AB II, 84

Chief of Police to the Presidenza of La Fenice; Venice, 21 November 1850 (delivered 1 December)

His Excellency the Military Governor Cavalier de Gorzkowski, by his esteemed despatch of the 26th of this month no. 731, has ordered me to inform this Noble Presidenza that he deplores the fact that the poet Piave and the celebrated Maestro Verdi were unable to choose a field wherein to display their talents other than that, repulsively immoral and obscenely vulgar, of the argument of the libretto entitled *La maledizione*, submitted by this Presidenza for production on the stage of La Fenice.

The above-mentioned Excellency has therefore determined to prohibit absolutely the performance and, at the same time, enjoins the Presidenza to refrain from any further insistence on the subject. [. . .]

VELF, 41

Verdi to President Marzari of La Fenice; Busseto, 5 December 1850

The letter which has arrived with the decree absolutely prohibiting *La maledizione* was so unexpected that I nearly went out of my mind. In this, Piave has a serious responsibility: all the responsibility! He assured me in several letters, written as long ago as last May, that he had obtained approval. Therefore I composed a good part of the drama and worked hard to complete it by the fixed date. The decree refusing it plunges me into despair, because now it is too late to choose another libretto, which it would be impossible, *quite impossible* for me to set for the winter. [. . .]

AB II, 85

To resolve the impasse, Verdi's first offer was to come to Venice and put on a production of *Stiffelio*, for which – anticipating more censorship trouble – he was willing to write a new ending. But Piave, with the help of Marzari and even of the Chief of Police, tried to salvage the Hugo project, recasting the libretto with a new title, *Il Duca di Vendôme*. The revised text involved changes that had nothing to do with politics: the protagonist was no longer a hunchback, Gilda was not allowed to die in a sack. Verdi was sent the libretto early in December.

Verdi to Marzari; Busseto, 14 December 1850

In replying to your esteemed letter of the 11th of this month, I have had very little time to examine the new libretto: I have seen enough, however, to understand that, reduced in this way, it lacks character and importance, and the situations, finally, have become very cold. If it was necessary to change the names, then the locality should also have been changed, and he should have been made a Prince, Duke of some other nation, for example a Pier Luigi Farnese or someone else, or else shift the action back in time, before Louis XI, when France was not a united kingdom, and make him a Duke of Burgundy or of Normandy etc. etc., in any case an absolute ruler. – In scene 5 of Act I, the courtiers' wrath against Triboletto has no meaning. – The old man's curse, so awesome and sublime in the original, here becomes ridiculous because the motive that drives him to curse no longer has the same importance, and because it is no longer the subject who speaks so boldly to the king. Without this curse, what purpose, what meaning does the drama have? The Duke becomes a nonentity: the Duke must absolutely be a libertine; without that there can be no justification for Triboletto's fear of his daughter's leaving her refuge. Without that this drama is impossible. Why does the Duke, in the last act, go to a remote tavern alone, without an invitation, without an amorous rendezvous? – I don't understand why the sack was removed: what did the sack matter to the police? Are they worried about the dramatic effect? But, allow me to say, why do they think they know more about this than I? Who is the composer here? Who can say this will have an effect, and that not? There was a difficulty of this sort about the horn in *Ernani*: well, who laughed at that horn? – With that sack removed, it is not likely that Triboletto would speak for half an hour to the corpse without a flash of lightning's revealing it as his daughter's. Finally I note that they have avoided making Triboletto ugly and hunchbacked!! For what reason? A hunchback who sings, some will say! And why not? . . . Will it be effective? . . . I don't know, but if I don't know, then I repeat, he who proposed this change does not know. I

Verdi, *Stiffelio*, 1850. Poster for the premiere in Trieste. Civico museo teatrale, Trieste.

Verdi, *Rigoletto*, 1851 (*Il duca di Vendôme*). Revised libretto by Francesco Maria Piave. Archivio Teatro La Fenice, Venice.

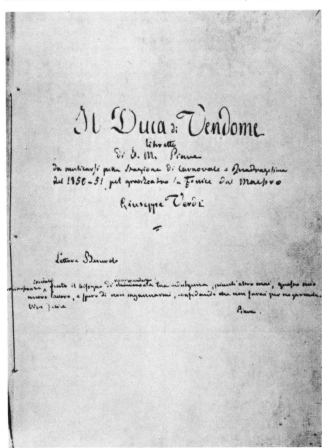

find it, in fact, very beautiful to portray this character externally deformed and ridiculous, and internally passionate and full of love. I chose this subject precisely for all these qualities and if all these original features are removed, I cannot set it to music any longer. If I am told that my music can stand just the same, with this drama, I answer that I do not understand such reasoning; and I say frankly that I do not write my notes at random, ugly or beautiful as they may be, and I try always to give them a character. In short, from an original, powerful drama, something very common and cold has been made. –

I am deeply grieved that the Presidenza has not answered my last letter. I can only repeat, and beg you to do what I said in that; for, as a conscientious artist, I cannot set this libretto to music.

MS, ATLF, VENICE

On the same day Verdi wrote sharply to the culpable Piave.

Verdi to Piave; Busseto, 14 December 1850

I thank you for the powder and the *baicoli* [a kind of Venetian sweet biscuit] for which you will debit me. – Save yourself the trouble of procuring the fish, because I cannot send to Cremona for it.

I am writing to the Presidenza about the new libretto.

I am not sending you the 200 Austrian lire, since I will not write the opera for Venice and since I commissioned you to write *Le Roi s'amuse* on condition you obtain Police permission. Since it is not allowed (to my grave detriment) our contract is naturally dissolved. [. . .]

COP, 111

To save the situation (and perhaps the 200 lire), Piave decided to come, with Brenna, to Busseto. Verdi was still in a bad humour.

Verdi to Piave; Busseto, 29 December 1850

I will send my little conveyance for you, to bring you to Busseto with Brenna. The servant (Giacomo) will be on this side of the Po because he has no passport. Have the kindness then to walk those few steps and cross the Po towards La Croce, where Giacomo will be on the shore. He will wait for you from ten o'clock on tomorrow morning (Monday), so arrange to leave Cremona around eight.

You know my house, and now that my mother is living in your room, I no longer have two rooms free. If the two of you can make do with two beds in one room, they will be prepared. Otherwise a few steps from here there is the hotel that you know.

AB II, 90–1

Agreement, drawn up 'in the residence of Maestro Giuseppe Verdi'; Busseto, 30 December 1850

In accordance with the assignment received, by order dated 27 December, from the Presidenza of the association of owners of the Teatro La Fenice of Venice, the undersigned Secretary of the Presidenza invites Signor Maestro Verdi to determine the changes to which he consents in the libretto presented under the title *La maledizione*, to be composed for the current Carnival-Lent season of 1850–51 [. . .] so as to remove the obstacles created by the Authority of Public Order to permission of the production.

Therefore, also with the poet Francesco Maria Piave, it is agreed as follows:

1. The action will be moved from the Court of France to that of one of the independent Duchies of Burgundy, Normandy, or one of the little absolute Princes of the Italian states, and probably to the court of Pier Luigi Farnese, and in the period most suitable for the decorum and success of the staging.

2. The original aspects of the characters of Victor Hugo in the drama *Le Roi s'amuse* will be retained, changing the names of the people according to the situation and period that will be chosen.

3. The scene will be absolutely avoided in which Francesco declares himself determined to use the key in his possession to introduce himself into the room of the abducted Bianca. This will be replaced by another scene which preserves the necessary decency, without detracting from the interest of the drama.

4. The King or Duke will be invited to the amorous rendezvous at the tavern of Magellona by a deceit of the character who will replace Triboletto.

5. At the appearance of the sack containing the body of Triboletto's daughter, Maestro Verdi agrees to make such changes as will be considered necessary in practice. [. . .]

COP, 489–90

On 11 March 1851, premiere of *Rigoletto* at the Teatro La Fenice, Venice.

Gazzetta di Venezia, 12 March 1851

An opera like this is not judged in a single evening. Yesterday we were as if overwhelmed by the novelty: novelty, or rather oddities, in the subject; novelty in the music, in the style, in the very form of the numbers; and we could not form a general idea of it. Nevertheless, the opera had the most complete success, and the Maestro was fêted after almost every number, called out, acclaimed; and two had to be repeated. And what is true, admirable, stupendous is the work of instrumentation: the orchestra speaks for you, weeps, conveys passion to you. Never was eloquence of sounds more powerful.

Less splendid, or so it seemed to us at a first hearing, is the vocal part. It is removed from the style used until now, because it lacks great ensembles, and you barely notice a quartet and a trio in the last part, of which all the musical thought was not perfectly grasped.

VELF, 44

A few days after the premiere of *Rigoletto* (whose success increased at each performance), Verdi left Venice for Busseto. He was already in correspondence with Cammarano about a new libretto, based on the Spanish play *El Trovador* by Antonio García Gutiérrez. But Cammarano was slow – actually he was in ill-health – and Verdi complained to their mutual friend in Naples, Cesarino De Sanctis:

Verdi to Cesarino De Sanctis; Busseto, 29 March 1851

[. . .] I am furiously angry with Cammarano. He has no consideration for time, which is something extremely precious for me. He has not written me one word about this *Trovatore*: does he like it or not? I don't understand what you mean about the difficulties both for *common sense* and for the theatre!! For that matter, the more Cammarano furnishes me with novelty, freedom of forms, the better I will do. Let him do whatever he likes: the bolder he is, the more pleased I shall be. He must only aim at the demands of the public, which wants brevity. You, then, who are his friend, urge him not to waste a moment's time.

Though I am angry, give Cammarano a kiss from me. . . . [. . .]

MS, ANL, ROME

Cammarano was prompted to write to Verdi, but his letter was unsatisfactory. He raised some objections, especially about the scene of Leonora's taking vows as a nun. Obviously, the librettist feared censorship restrictions.

Verdi to Cammarano; Busseto, 4 April 1851

[. . .] The scene of [Leonora's] taking the veil must stay (it is too original a thing for me to give it up); and it must indeed be exploited to the full, with all possible effects. If you don't want the Nun to flee voluntarily, have the Trovatore (with many followers) abduct her, in a faint. [. . .]

You don't say a word to me about whether or not you like this drama. I proposed it to you because it seemed to me to offer beautiful dramatic moments, and above all, something singular and original in general. If you were not of my opinion, why didn't you suggest another story? For this sort of thing it is well for poet and composer to be in unison!

As for the arrangement of the numbers, I will tell you that, for my part, when I am given some poetry to be set to music, any form, any arrangement is good; in fact, the more new and bizarre they are, the happier I am. If in operas there were no Cavatinas, or Duets, or Trios, or Choruses, or Finales, etc. etc., and the whole opera were only (I would almost say) a single number, I would find this more reasonable and right. Therefore I say that if we can avoid beginning this opera with the Chorus (all operas begin with a Chorus) and the Cavatina of Leonora, and actually begin with the Trovatore's song and make a single act out of the first two, it would be well; because these numbers, so detached from one another, with change of scene at each number, give me rather the impression of concert pieces rather than opera pieces. If you *can*, do it. I too am not over-pleased with Manrique's being wounded in the duel. But do as you feel best. When one has a Cammarano, only good can be done.

P.S. I have no noose about my neck to write this opera, though I want to begin. So I am waiting for the outline, then the poetry, gradually. I have been invited to write for the San Carlo but I have answered, refusing.

AB II, 122–3

Verdi to Cammarano; Busseto, 9 April 1851

I have read your outline, and you, a man of talent and such superior character, will not be offended if I, most humbly, take the liberty of saying to you that if this story cannot be handled for our theatres with all the novelty and bizarre quality of the Spanish drama, it's better to give up the idea.

It seems to me, unless I'm mistaken, that various situations do not have the power, the originality they had before [in the play], and that especially Azucena does not retain her strange and novel character. It seems to me that this woman's two great passions, *filial love* and *maternal love*,

are not present in all their force. – For example, I wouldn't want the Trovatore to be wounded in the duel. This poor Trovatore has so little to him that if we take away his valour, what does he have left? How could he interest Leonora, a lady of such high degree? [Verdi then goes through the opera, almost scene by scene, with his observations.]

12. Do not make Azucena insane. Overcome with fatigue, grief, terror, lack of sleep, she cannot speak logically. Her senses are oppressed, but she is not mad. To the very end we must retain this woman's two great passions: her love for Manrique, and her fierce thirst to avenge her mother. When Manrico is dead, the feeling of vengeance becomes gigantic and she says with exaltation . . . 'Sì Luci luci egli è tuo fratello! . . . Stolto! . . . Sei vendicata, o madre!!' [Yes, lights, lights, he is your brother! . . . Fool! You are avenged, O mother!!]

Please forgive my boldness: I am surely mistaken, but I couldn't help telling you everything I felt. Moreover, my first suspicion that this drama did not appeal to you is perhaps true. If this is so, we are still in time to remedy matters, rather than do something you don't like. [. . .]

MS, BLP, NAPLES

A few weeks after writing this letter, Verdi moved with Giuseppina from Palazzo Orlandi in Busseto out to the farm at Sant'Agata. The Villa Sant'Agata today is the picture of comfort and mid-nineteenth-century elegance. But, at first, life there was not so easy. Years later, Giuseppina described the evolution of the house.

225–30

Giuseppina Strepponi Verdi to Clarina Maffei, 4 June 1867

Many years ago (I daren't say how many), since I loved the country very much, I asked Verdi with some insistence to leave Paris and to take, beneath the pavilion of the open sky, those salutary baths of air and light that give as much vigour to the body as calm and serenity to the mind. Verdi, who, like Auber, felt a kind of horror of staying in the country, after many pleas agreed to taking a little house not far from Paris. In the order of pleasures this new life was for Verdi, I would dare say, a revelation. He took to loving it so much, with such passion, that I found myself defeated and overwhelmed in this cult for the sylvan Gods. He bought the property of Sant'Agata, and I, who had already furnished a house in Milan and another in Paris, had to organize a *pied-à-terre* in the new possessions of the illustrious Professore of Roncole. We began, to our infinite pleasure, planting a garden which, at the beginning, was called *Peppina's garden*. Then it was extended and called *his* garden; and I can tell you that he acts as Czar over this garden of *his* so much that I am now confined to a few palms of terrain, where he, by established convention, must not stick his nose. In all conscience, I couldn't say he always respects this convention, but I have found a way of calling him to order, by threatening to plant cabbages instead of flowers. This garden, as it was extended and beautified, demanded a house a bit less *rustic*; Verdi transformed himself into an architect; and during the construction I cannot tell you how the beds, dressers, all the furniture, strolled and danced. Suffice it to say that, except the kitchen, the wine cellar and the stable, we have slept and eaten in every hole in the house. When the fate of Italy was in turmoil [in 1859], and Verdi and some other gentlemen carried the States to King Vittorio in their pockets, Guerrieri, Fioruzzi, etc. came to Sant'Agata and had the *honour* of dining in a kind of vestibule, or entry, in the presence of various nests of swallows, who calmly came and went through a grille, to bring food to their little ones. When God willed, the house was finished [in the 1860s], and I assure you Verdi directed the work well and perhaps better than a real architect. This then was the fourth apartment I had to furnish. But the sun, the trees, the flowers, the immense and various family of birds, who make the country so beautiful and animated for a good part of the year, leave it sad, mute, and bare in winter. Then I do not love it. When the snow covers those immense plains, and the trees with their naked branches seem desolate skeletons, I cannot raise my eyes to look outside: I cover the windows with flowered curtains as high as a person, and I feel an infinite sadness, a desire to flee the country, and to feel that I live among the living and not among the ghosts and silence of a vast cemetery. [. . .]

COP, 498

Muzio to Giovanni Ricordi; Busseto, 29 June 1851

I have some very sad and painful news to communicate to you: at 3 yesterday afternoon, Verdi lost his mother, after a long and painful illness. I cannot tell you his grief, it is immensely great, and Peppina suffers at seeing him weep, and I have the sad duty of arranging the funeral, priests, etc. I had persuaded him to come there [Milan], then he changed his mind and now he doesn't want to leave the house.

AB II, 137

Verdi to Cammarano; Busseto, 9 September 1851

An accumulation of misfortunes, and grave ones! has prevented me thinking seriously about *Il trovatore* till now. Now that I am beginning to recover my energy, I must also concern myself with my art and my business affairs. Rome and Venice have asked me for an opera. Rome offers me as singers la De Giuli, Fraschini and Colini. Venice la Frezzolini and Coletti. The Rome company is more suited to *Il trovatore*, but they lack the singer for Azucena, that Azucena that means so much to me! [. . .]

AB II, 142

Verdi and Giuseppina left Busseto in December 1851 for Paris, where they stayed for the better part of the winter. During that period, the composer signed a contract with the Opéra for a new work (it was to be *Les Vêpres siciliennes*) and, as usual, went to the theatre. The great hit play of the season was *La Dame aux camélias* by Alexandre Dumas *fils*, a tale set in the present. This was to form the subject of Verdi's next opera for Venice, *La traviata*.

Verdi and Giuseppina both liked Paris, and they were no doubt glad to get away from provincial Busseto, where their irregular union was the source of much gossip and embitterment. The situation threatened to affect even Verdi's filial relationship with Antonio Barezzi, as can be seen from a well-known letter the composer wrote to the older man that winter.

Verdi to Barezzi; Paris, 21 January 1852

My dearest father-in-law,
After waiting so long, I did not believe I would receive from you such a cold letter, in which, unless I am mistaken,

there are some quite pointed remarks also. If this letter were not signed *Antonio Barezzi*, which is to say my benefactor, I would have answered very sharply or not at all; but since it bears such a name, which I will always hold it my duty to respect, I will try to persuade you as far as possible that I deserve no reproach of any kind. To do this, I have to go back to past things, speak of others, of our town, and the letter may become somewhat prolix and boring; but I will try to be as brief as I can.

I do not think that you would have written me, on your own inspiration, a letter you know can only grieve me; but you live in a town that has the bad habit of concerning itself often with other people's affairs, and of disapproving everything that does not conform to its own ideas. By habit, I never involved myself, unless asked, in the affairs of others, precisely because I demand that no one involve himself in mine. From this stems the gossip, the murmuring, the disapproval. This liberty of action which is respected even in the least civilized countries is something I have a right to demand also in my own. Judge for yourself, and be a severe but dispassionate and detached judge: what wrong is there in my living for myself? If I choose not to make visits to those who bear titles? If I do not take part in the festivities and joys of others? If I manage my property myself, because I like to and it amuses me? I repeat: what wrong is there? In any event, nobody could suffer any harm from it.

After this premiss, I come to the sentence of your letter: 'I realize very well that I am not a man for serious tasks, because my time has already gone by, but would I still be capable for little things? . . .' If by this you mean that once I gave you serious tasks and now I make use of you for little things, alluding to the letter I enclosed in yours, I cannot find any excuse for this, and although I would do the same for you in similar circumstances, I can only say this will serve me as a lesson for the future. If the sentence signifies a reproach, because I have not charged you with my affairs in my absence, allow me to ask you: Why should I have been so indiscreet as to charge you with such great responsibility, you who never set foot on your own farms, because your duties at the shop are already too heavy? Should I have entrusted Giovannino with them? But is it not true that last year, during the time I was in Venice, I gave him an ample power-of-attorney in writing, and he never set foot once at Sant'Agata? Nor am I reproaching him with this. He was perfectly right. He had his own affairs, which are important enough, so he could not take care of mine.

This has revealed to you my opinions, my actions, my will, what I might call my public life; and since we are making revelations I have nothing against raising the curtain that veils the mysteries enclosed within four walls and telling you of my home life. I have nothing to hide. In my house there lives a Lady, free, independent, who, like me, is fond of solitary life, with sufficient means to protect her from all need. Neither she nor I owes anyone an account of our actions. But, furthermore, who knows what relationship exists between us? What business matters? What ties? What rights I have over her, and she over me? Who knows whether or not she is my wife? And in this case, who knows the special reasons, motives for keeping its publication secret? Who knows whether that is good or bad? Why could it not also be a good thing? And even if it were bad, who has the right to cry scandal? To you, however, I will say that in my house she is owed the same, indeed greater respect than is owed to me, and no one is allowed to fail in his duty towards her in any way; and finally she is fully entitled to it, both by her demeanour and her spirit, and by the special regard she never fails to show others.

With all this long talk I have meant only to say that I insist on my freedom of action, because all men are entitled to it, and because my nature rebels against acting according to others' fashions; and that you, who are so fundamentally good, so just, and have so much heart, must not let yourself be influenced and must not absorb the ideas of a town that, towards me – this must really be said! – some time ago would not deign to have me as its organist, and now mumbles on all sides about my actions and my affairs. That cannot last; but if it should, I am a man who knows what steps to take. The world is so large, and the loss of 20, 30 thousand francs will never prevent me from finding a home elsewhere. There cannot be anything offensive in this letter; but if by chance something should distress you, let it be as not written, because I swear to you on my honour that I do not mean to offend you in any way. I have always considered you and still consider you my benefactor, and I hold this as an honour, and I boast of it. Farewell, farewell, with the same friendship as always.

AB II, 150–2

Barezzi's reply to this letter is not known, but all misunderstandings were cleared up. His – reciprocated – love for Verdi never wavered, and was extended to include the devoted Peppina.

Muzio to Giovanni Ricordi; Sant' Agata, 19 March 1852

A few words to tell you that Verdi finally arrived last night, and today, his and Peppina's name-day, we spent in the private joy of the family, not disturbed by any vexations. [. . .]

AB II, 159

For *Il trovatore*, now nearing completion, Verdi was negotiating with the colourful Roman impresario Vincenzo 'Cencio' Jacovacci, of the Teatro Apollo.

Verdi to Vincenzo Jacovacci; Busseto, June 1852

I will come to write an opera in Rome during the next Carnival season, to open about 15 January 1853, on the following conditions:

1. That I receive satisfactory news about the worth of la Penco.

2. That you find another dramatic prima donna to play the role of a gypsy in the drama I have in mind.

3. That the censorship approve Cammarano's libretto *Il trovatore*.

All rights to libretto and score remain mine. You have the right only to present it at the Apollo only during the Carnival season of 1852–53. I shall be in Rome on 20 December 1852 to attend all rehearsals of said opera. In recompense you will pay me six thousand francs. [. . .]

AB II, 167

On 17 July 1852, Salvatore Cammarano died, after a lingering illness, with the libretto of *Il trovatore* not quite finished.

Verdi to De Sanctis; Busseto, 5 August 1852

I was struck as if by a thunderbolt at the sad news of our Cammarano's death. It's impossible for me to describe to you my profound grief! I read of this death not in a friend's letter, but in a stupid theatrical newspaper!! You, who loved him as I did, will understand everything I cannot tell you. Poor Cammarano!! What a loss!!

How is it you did not receive my letter written you on the 19th of last month? How is it that there was not found at the post a draft sent by Ricordi, in my name, to our poor friend? [. . .]

As you know, if the Censorship allows it, *Il trovatore* will be done in Rome. My head is so confused that I cannot speak to you about it at length, but, as you will see in my last letter, this *Trovatore* seems to me a bit long, and tell me: What if some judicious cuts had to be made? What if the Censorship required some little change? Or if I myself needed some little thing adjusted or changed? Mind you, all these things must not alter in the least the work of our poor friend, whose memory I am the first to want respected. In this case to whom should I turn? Did this Bardare enjoy Cammarano's trust? Is he skilled? Write at once because there is no time to lose. [. . .]

MS, ANL, ROME

In August of 1852 Verdi was named Chevalier of the Legion of Honour, and Louis-Napoléon (now Emperor Napoleon III) sent Léon Escudier to Italy, to present the decoration to the composer. Escudier's description of his journey begins with a misstatement of the facts, but the account is otherwise convincing.

From Léon Escudier's memoirs

After his art and his country, what Verdi loves most in the world is his native village – the heart of his fatherland, if one may use the expression – the little town of Busseto, so small that you would seek it in vain on the ordinary maps of the Peninsula. And yet it is already famous today! Just outside Busseto Verdi owns an immense property, where he has had a villa built, which the country folk designate with the name of *La Villa del professore Verdi*. [. . .]

It is in this beautiful property, extending about ten leagues, that Verdi goes to rest from his labours and the annoyances of the big cities, – from his triumphs most often (which he calls his nuisances). There, rifle on his shoulder or book in hand, he strolls about and visits his numerous farms, chats with his *contadini* about crops, ploughing, sowing, reaping, etc. Verdi has studied agriculture no less seriously than counterpoint, so between Busseto and Parma there is no better-maintained property than his. The peasants [. . .] adore him and demonstrate their adoration to him in a thousand ways and on many occasions. [. . .]

It is, however, within these walls that he has written the majority of his masterpieces. So that one can say that, if the villa is due to a part of his works, it has shown its gratitude in hatching the others. It is there that Verdi withdraws. He summons there his favourite poet, Piave, with whom, after having chosen the subject, he tailors the situations; and it is beneath his eyes that Piave seeks the metres and aligns the verses. [. . .]

I found Verdi about to go to table. There was also present a man with a frank, open, likeable face, a magnificent presence, his age about twice Verdi's; his simple manners, his sweet and affectionate language, his broad shoulders, struck me; he had on me the effect of a patriarch. It was Verdi's father-in-law. His name is Antonio. We soon made acquaintance, and a quarter-hour later, I was calling him familiarly Papa Antonio.

Now, to Papa Antonio, Verdi is a demigod; and in saying demi, I am speaking a half-truth. He cannot mention him or his works without tears' coming to his eyes. He lives in Busseto, and is its natural custodian and archivist. With a pride that makes the composer smile and shrug his shoulders, he shows you the room where Verdi wrote *I due Foscari*. Then, if you have been able to win his trust, if he recognizes in you a very great admiration for Verdi, he shows you a pile of manuscripts, which he guards jealously. These are the composer's first attempts. [. . .]

How many times would Verdi have liked to stuff his fireplace with those old papers! Only a heartrending look from Papa Antonio has prevented the *auto da fé*. I saw there a number of pieces of religious music, and I recalled that the first studies of the author of *Rigoletto* and *La traviata* were made on the organ of the neighbouring church. These are the archives, or rather the *sancta sanctorum* of Papa Antonio; he has the key to that room and entrusts it to no one.

We sat down at the table; I need hardly add that it was Papa Antonio who led the conversation and that Verdi was its subject, to the great despair of the Maestro, who gave up, battle-weary, trying to silence him.

At the dessert, I stood up a moment and came back with a little box in my hand.

'Dear Maestro,' I said to Verdi, setting the box before him, 'here is a token of the affection of the French government, and I should add, of the French public.'

Verdi frowned, opened the box, and found the Chevalier's cross, with two or three metres of red ribbon which I had taken care to add to it.

He tried to dissimulate his emotion; at heart, he felt a lively satisfaction, and firmly clasped my hand.

But it was Papa Antonio who remained stunned. He wanted to speak, and it was impossible for him to articulate a word. He waved his arms, stood up, flung himself on Verdi's neck, clasped him to his bosom, embraced me in turn, then his eyes flooded and he wept like a baby. [. . .]
ESC, 84FF.

After this emotional interlude, Verdi resumed work on *Il trovatore*. With Cesarino De Sanctis acting as intermediary, the composer had some revisions made by a young poet friend of Cammarano's, Leone Emanuele Bardare.

De Sanctis to Verdi; Naples, 29 October 1852

The young poet is beside himself with joy at having worked for Verdi: you will find his feelings expressed in a letter which I enclose. To me the verses seem sufficiently good. I, who know your heart and the poet's need, will reveal his hope to you. He expects, I believe, a token for the time spent on this work, having for a while neglected other operatic tasks . . . [. . .]

La Penco, under your direction, will be able to satisfy you: she has some defects, but many merits. I believe she is mistaken to sing always in the upper range. She is not a perfect soprano. I will tell you that she is very pretty. Watch out, Maestro! I warn you, however, that she is a demon! She will certainly bludgeon the other prima donna. . . . They tell me la Goggi is an old artist; you will rejuvenate her with the magic of your music.

Maestro, we are all awaiting a masterpiece in *Il trovatore*. With his music, Verdi must immortalize the last work of

Cammarano. Remember that the last number, written a week before he died, was the aria of the Tenor! [. . .]
AB II, 172

Verdi to Luccardi; Piacenza, 5 November 1852

[. . .] I will be in Rome towards 20 December; in fact I will write you again to ask you to find me an apartment of two or three rooms at the Europa. It doesn't matter if it's high, but I would like sun: for two or three years I have been accustomed to the country, and walls stifle me. Sun sun sun!

[. . .] Piave is still here, finishing the libretto for Venice [*La traviata*]. [. . .]
AB II, 176

Verdi to Jacovacci, late 1852

[. . .] I warn you that for the part of Ferrando you need a somewhat baritonal bass. He certainly doesn't have to be a *primo assoluto*, but not one of the usual minor parts. Think about this in advance, because I attach great importance to the Introduction, which all rests on this Ferrando.

For this same Introduction there is needed a big Bell that can toll *Midnight*. . . .
AB II, 177

Verdi to De Sanctis; Sant'Agata, 14 December 1852

Il trovatore is finished, and on the 25th of this month I shall be in Rome. I must disturb you again, to consult the poet Bardare. In the finale of the second act, which is the first Cammarano wrote, almost without realizing it I have made the first tempo not an Adagio, which is the usual thing, but a *mosso*, lively, etc.

I thought (if I'm not mistaken) I did well, at least I did as I felt: a Largo would have been impossible for me. After this I thought to omit the stretta, especially since it doesn't seem to me necessary to the drama, and perhaps Cammarano only wrote it to follow convention. This, then, is what I have done, and I beg you to submit it to the judgment of Signor Bardare, and if he does not approve, we will print the libretto with the stretta between inverted commas; but I would not like to do this. [. . .]
MS, ANL, ROME

Verdi virtually wrote the definitive words of Act II, scene 2, of the opera. Bardare apparently did not feel any changes were necessary.

Verdi to Luccardi; Sant'Agata, 14 December 1852

I shall be in Rome on the 25th! Coming from Civitavecchia. You, who have always been so good to me, please be so still, and fix my apartment for that day. *Price and all!* Further, go to Jacovacci, who will give you a piano, and have it put in my study so that, as soon as I have arrived, I can write the Venice opera without losing a minute's time. *Il trovatore* is completely finished: not one note is missing, and (*inter nos*) I am pleased with it. So long as the Romans are! In short, I beg you to have everything in order, so that, on arriving, I can start writing, if I feel like it. [. . .]
MS, ANL, ROME

But *Il trovatore* was not quite finished. At least the libretto was not definitive, and Verdi wrote to De

Sanctis, on New Year's Day, 1853, to settle a few matters of wording. Apparently De Sanctis had suggested that Verdi read some friend's libretto (Bardare's perhaps).

Verdi to De Sanctis; Rome, 1 January 1853

[. . .] I would like nothing better than to find a good libretto and therefore a good poet. We have such need of them. I will tell you frankly, however, that I am reluctant to read librettos that are sent to me. It is impossible, or almost impossible for another person to sense what I want: I want subjects that are *new, great, beautiful, varied, bold* . . . and bold to extremes, with *new forms* etc. etc. and, at the same time, suitable to be set to music [. . .]

For Venice I am doing *La Dame aux camélias*, which will be entitled, perhaps, *Traviata*. A subject of our time. Another perhaps would not have done it, because of the costumes, the times, and for a thousand other awkward scruples. I am doing it with great pleasure. Everyone made an outcry when I suggested putting a hunchback on stage. Well: I was happy to write *Rigoletto*. [. . .]

MS, ANL, ROME

Escudier, who had occasion to observe Verdi at work, has left a description of the composer's habits at the time.

From Léon Escudier's memoirs

And now do you want to know how Verdi writes his scores? He begins by grasping the subject, mastering it. He reads and rereads the poem, to whose creation [. . .] he is not a stranger in the choice and disposition of scenes and numbers. He engraves it in his mind, so that he becomes, so to speak, identified with the drama and the characters of the action. He studies the characters, the passions, and spends whole months seeking the proper way to clothe them. Hence the unity of the whole and the great variety in details, qualities that characterize his works; hence that special colour of each score, in which one number is in admirable accord with all the rest. [. . .] What he seeks with the greatest care and finds with the greatest joy is the effect of contrasts. The greater the difficulty, the more completely he triumphs over it; and he enjoys creating these difficulties for himself, where another would try to evade or dismiss them. To cite only one example from a hundred: look at the quartet in *Rigoletto*. On the one hand, there is the outburst of the courtesan's laughter; on the other, the racking sobs of the betrayed mistress; here, the insouciance of the libertine; there, the poignant grief of the father. [. . .]

On seeing the rapidity with which – materially speaking – Verdi writes his scores, on seeing above all the absence of erasures in his manuscripts, one must not believe he improvises his scores. As in nature, gestation is long, birth is prompt. He carries the works for whole months in his head and in his heart; then the hour arrives, he brings them into the world in the shortest time possible.

Immediately on getting out of a carriage, Verdi wrote on a hotel desk the masterpiece known as the 'Miserere' from *Il trovatore*. Who can say how long that page grew in his mind?

ESC, 78FF.

Giuseppina had accompanied Verdi as far as Leghorn, where he had taken ship for Civitavecchia. They did not yet travel together as man and wife. Giuseppina stayed

on in Leghorn a few days, before continuing her journey to Florence.

Giuseppina Strepponi to Verdi; Leghorn, 2 January 1853

[. . .] I can't tell you how impatiently I await your return! . . . I have given myself over to reading, and I read and read and read, until my eyes are inflamed; but I fear that sadness and ennui will assail me during these days in which you have sentenced me to *cellular* life. You will say: spend money and amuse yourself. First of all I don't like you to say 'amuse yourself' to me, and besides I have no use for amusements! If I could see you a quarter of an hour out of every twenty-four, my spirit would be happy, I would work, read, write, and time would pass for me all too swiftly. [. . .]

AB II, 203

Giuseppina Strepponi to Verdi; Leghorn, 3 January 1853

[. . .] I am very happy that you find yourself lost without me, and I wish you such boredom that it will make you give up the barbarous idea of leaving me in isolation, like a saint in the Thebaid! My dear Mage, your heart is the *heart of an angel*, but your head, when it comes to gossip and certain ideas, has the bony part of such an *épaisseur*, that if Gall were alive, he could add some curious observations to his treatise on *Craniology*. [. . .]

AB II, 203

Giuseppina Strepponi to Verdi; Leghorn, 3 January 1853

[. . .] Sometimes I fear that love of money may waken in you and condemn you to many more years of work! My dear Mage, you would be very wrong! You see? We have spent a great part of our lives, and you would be quite mad, if, instead of enjoying the fruit of your glorious and honoured labours in peace, you sweated to accumulate money and give joy to those who in the sad word *Death*! see the moment of their infamous wishes come true, in the wicked word *Inheritance*!

We will not have children (since God perhaps punishes me for my sins, decreeing that before I die I shall not experience any legitimate joy!). Well, having no children by me, you will not, I hope, give me the sorrow of having any by another woman; now, without children, you have a fortune more than sufficient to provide for your needs and even for a bit of luxury. We adore the country and in the country one spends little – and there is great pleasure. [. . .]

Don't you agree with me? Now I will suspend my chatter, which I realize is a little too long. But you will have compassion on me . . . if you knew the sad life I am leading in these days! . . .

AB II, 205–6

On 19 January 1853, premiere of *Il trovatore* at the Teatro Apollo, Rome. The American journalist Blanche Roosevelt collected some contemporary accounts.

120–24

From Blanche Roosevelt's life of Verdi

Those who have seen Rome will remember the Apollo Theatre, which overlooks the Tiber, and is just a stone's throw from the bridge and castle of St Angelo. *Trovatore's* success had been so great, that the morning after the first performance the streets were filled with an immense affluence of people: not only surging to and from the theatre doors, but the crowd was so great that it covered the bridge from one end to the other, whilst the shoutings and echoes were heard across the water even to the very door of the castle. The whole day long the Roman streets, which had once resounded to the cries of tribunes and triumvirs, reëchoed to the name of this Cæsar in art, Verdi. 'Long live Verdi, the greatest composer Italy has ever known!' The excitement was kept up until nightfall. People even went to the theatre to look at the bare walls – and Heaven knows they are bare enough to look at from the outside – they stared and stared at the dull columns and plaster, as if they could coax new enthusiasm from out the gray stone pillars and porticoes of L'Apollo.

122

Madame Penco, a fine dramatic soprano, was the Leonora; Grossi [actually Carlo Baucardé], the tenor, was Manrico, and several celebrities were intrusted to the creation of the chief rôles. If I pay so much attention to *Trovatore*, it is because the airs of this favourite score are as well known throughout the length and breadth of the land as the legendary cradle or nursery song with which we were rocked to sleep in our babyhood.

ROOS, 46

Verdi to Clarina Maffei; Sant'Agata, 29 January 1853

Here I am again in my desert, and unfortunately for only a few days. I am very tired from the journey and I have to work again.

You will have heard about *Il trovatore*: it would have been better if the company had been complete. They say that this opera is too sad and there are too many deaths. But finally, in life all is death! What else exists? . . . [. . .]

MS, BNB, MILAN

Verdi to President Marzari of the Fenice; Cremona, 30 January 1853

The news I receive from Venice, especially after the [revival of] *Ernani*, is so depressing that I am obliged to declare to you that I will surely not give the part of the Traviata to Signora Salvini! I believe it is in both my interest and the theatre's to engage a prima donna immediately. I know it is very difficult to find an artist who can satisfy the requirements of the theatre, but circumstances demand that some attempt be made.

The only women who would seem suitable to me are: (1) Signora Penco, who is singing in Rome; (2) Signora Boccabadati, who is singing *Rigoletto* in Bologna; and finally Signora Piccolomini, who is now singing in Pisa. La Penco (*the only one of these I know*) would be best, I believe. She has a fine figure, spirit, and she is at ease on stage: excellent qualities for *La traviata*. [. . .]

My arm is still giving me trouble: I desire and hope it is a passing ailment. I will keep the Presidenza informed, and if unfortunately I cannot fulfil my commitments, I will send the necessary medical certificates. [. . .]

MS, ATLF, VENICE

126

Piave came to Sant'Agata, and the final work on *La traviata* was done there. The direction of the Fenice had also hoped he could persuade Verdi to accept the soprano Fanny Salvini-Donatelli, who formed part of the theatre's company for the season.

Piave to Marzari; Sant'Agata, 4 February 1853

After using all my insistence through a long conversation yesterday evening, I succeeded in making our friend Verdi arrive at the following decision, which I repeat to you word for word.

'The Presidenza,' he said, 'is legally right, I confess, but artistically it is wrong, because not only la Salvini but the whole company is unworthy of the great Teatro La Fenice. I don't know if my illness will allow me to finish the opera, and in this uncertainty it is pointless for the management to engage other artists, so let it be la Salvini and companions. But I declare that, in the event that the opera is given, I have no hopes for the outcome, which indeed will be a total fiasco, and so the interests of the management will be sacrificed (and they will finally be able to say *mea culpa*), and so will my reputation be sacrificed, as well as a large sum of the owner of the opera's rights. Amen.' [. . .]
P.S. I wrote all the above in the name of Verdi, but now I must add on my own that he is truly in an infernal mood because of his illness, but more because of his total lack of faith in the company. I myself have read the letters sent him from Rome, which analyse and pulverize not only la Salvini, but also the *exhaustion* of Varesi, and the *marmoreal, monotonous* singing of Graziani (these are the epithets I read!). I also received my share of reproaches for not having spoken to him of this *chronic condition* (he says) of the company. [. . .] You can easily imagine how much handling and re-handling I've had to do; but I am pleased, because if his health, as I hope, assists him, the opera will be finished, since it is already well along. I have indeed heard the first act, and I believe it wonderful for effect and novelty. Today I feel like a new man because I have saved the good and talented Salvini. [. . .]

MS, ATLF, VENICE

Verdi to Piave; Sant'Agata, 16 February 1853

You will receive two more numbers, *tenor aria* and *bass aria*, and so the second act is finished. [. . .] In the scene where Giuseppe comes in to say Violetta has left, Annina cannot have returned, so Violetta and Annina could not leave together. I have fixed it up, in order to write the notes, but you will write other, better verses.

I have received today the tenor's cabaletta. It says nothing.

I will be in Venice Monday evening. Have the usual apartment prepared for me at the Europa with a good piano, well-tuned; moreover I would like you to find from a carpenter or on loan a music-stand so that I can write standing up. Be sure all is ready because I plan to start orchestrating immediately, the night I arrive.

I have received an anonymous letter from Venice which says that if I don't make them change prima donna and bass [i.e. baritone], it will be a complete fiasco. I know, I know. I'll show it to you. [. . .]

AB II, 217

Again Giuseppina was left alone, in the wintry gloom of Sant'Agata. She wrote to Verdi frequently and at length, about her health, local gossip, theatrical news (as she received it), and the work on the farm.

Giuseppina Strepponi to Verdi; Sant'Agata, 23 February 1853

[. . .] As I promised, I am writing you to tell you I am no better or worse than Sunday; but Frignani assures me that

Verdi, *La traviata*, 1853. Poster for the premiere in Venice. Archivio Teatro La Fenice, Venice. The poster shows that the opera was followed by a five-act ballet, 'The Magic Lantern'.

with today's little powders I will have a notable and prompt improvement. Separations seem to cause much bile. He has forbidden me meat and vegetables, prescribing a diet of soup and eggs to be eaten tepid. Provided it's tepid, he also allows me black coffee, and you know this is my only sin of *gluttony*. All I ask and hope is to be completely recovered by your return. How upset I was these past days, seeing you, my poor Mage, working like a black and having, on top of that, the sight of my illness, you can't imagine! . . . But I will be healthy again, and with my good humour I will try to make you forget past annoyances. You are so good to your Livello [a pet-name she and Verdi used for each other] . . . and I am desolate not to be able to repay in any way what you do for me! . . . I dare not even speak to you of your generous and delicate . . . but you see, it isn't ingratitude, you know that, you feel it, you understand it! More than once I have swallowed, cleared my throat, etc. to begin my speech . . . but my emotion chokes the words in my throat, I want to weep, blood rushes to my head, etc., and I have to renounce those sincere expressions I would like to say to you and that you have the right to expect.

[. . .] Write me when you can: hurry up the rehearsals and return to your den. Our youth is past, still for each other we are the whole world, and we see with lofty compassion all the human puppets who bustle, run, climb, crawl, fight, hide, reappear, all in order to mask themselves on the first step or steps of the social masquerade. [. . .]

Our affection and our characters, which are so attuned, will not give way to those frequent and bitter quarrels which diminish love and end by destroying all illusions. [. . .]
AB II, 220–1

On 6 March 1853, premiere of *La traviata* at the Teatro la Fenice, Venice. Verdi's reactions are well known.

Verdi to Muzio; Venice, 7 March 1853

La traviata last night, fiasco. My fault? Or the singers'? . . . Time will judge.
COP, 533

Verdi to Ricordi; Venice, 8 March 1853

I am sorry to have to give you sad news, but I cannot conceal the truth from you. *La traviata* was a fiasco. Let us not enquire as to the causes. That is the story. [. . .]
COP, 533

Verdi to Luccardi; Venice, 9 March 1853

I didn't write you after the first performance of *La traviata*; I am writing after the second. The outcome was *fiasco*!

Verdi, *La traviata*, 1853. Postcard showing the last scene, with the Doctor in seventeenth-century costume, Bologna 1905. Raccolta Bertarelli, Milan.

Decided fiasco! I don't know whose fault it is: better not to speak of it. [. . .]

COP, 533

Unusually, the opera was more of a success with the press than with the audience.

Gazzetta previlegiata di Venezia, 7 March 1853

[. . .] La Salvini-Donatelli sang those agility passages, of which the Maestro wrote many for her, with an indescribable skill and perfection: she enchanted the theatre, which literally engulfed her with applause. This [first] act brought the Maestro the greatest success; they began calling him out even before the curtain went up, because of a very sweet harmony of violins that is the Prelude to the score. Then at the Brindisi, then at the duet, then I don't know how many other times, both alone and with the prima donna at the end of the act.

In the second act, alas, fortune took on another aspect. Three things are required in the art of music: voice, voice, voice. And, to tell the truth, it is no use the Maestro inventing if he does not have those who are able or know how to perform what he creates. Verdi had the misfortune last night of not finding the above-mentioned three things except in one case; so all the numbers not sung by la Salvini-Donatelli went for nought. [. . .]

VELF, 50

One of the incriminated singers was the baritone Felice Varesi, successful creator of *Macbeth* and – at the same Fenice – of *Rigoletto*. Stung by the criticisms, he unburdened himself to his friend, the publisher Lucca. 95

Varesi to Lucca; Venice, 10 March 1853

I am taking advantage of the kindness you showed me during your brief stay in Venice, and I beg you, in giving information about Verdi's opera *La Traviata*, to defend me against the impudent article in the *Gazzetta di Venezia* which has outraged even Verdi's idolaters.

I will cite for you as witnesses true Milanese including Ariolo, Giulini, and Vittadini here present, with whom you can speak in Milan in a few days. They will tell you how I sang in *La traviata*, and whether I was in voice; and the most powerful proof is that, since the third performance was suspended because of the illness of [the tenor] Graziani and they put on *Il corsaro*, I made such an effect and won such applause that the public declared I was unrecognizable from one opera to the other. I do not mean to set myself up as judge of the musical merit of *La traviata*, but I certainly insist that Verdi did not know how to exploit the gifts of the artists at his disposal. Of la Salvini's whole part only the cavatina lies well for her. For Graziani, little or nothing. For me an Adagio of an aria, and this disgusted the Venetian public, which expected instead that I would be treated well, since Verdi had already created for me the colossal parts of *Macbeth* and *Rigoletto* with such success, and also because, before the opening, it was known that the Maestro was very pleased with me.

Here is the story of last night, third performance. Benefit performance for the poor: very sparse house. Some applause at the Brindisi and much at the cavatina of la [Salvini-]Donatelli, with two calls. The big duet between la Salvini and me: some applause at the Adagio and at the cabaletta. Applause at the second finale and two calls for the Maestro and the artists. Third act, no applause, and one call to say goodbye to the Maestro, who, it was known, was leaving the next morning. [. . .]

AB II, 229

From Blanche Roosevelt's life of Verdi

There are plenty of memoirs which tell of this first *Traviata* performance, but I prefer a personal reminiscence, and recall to mind a conversation once held with Randegger, the eminent London singing-master and composer. Maestro Randegger was present at that first performance in Venice, and remembers it as if but yesterday. I readily recall the occasion of his mentioning it. We were at Covent Garden listening to the divine Patti, and saying how lucky even she was in having such an opera to sing.

'O, you think so?' said Prof. Randegger; 'but what would you say to hear that once *La Traviata* was a dead failure? I was present in Venice at La Fenice on its first representation, and must say it was a curious experience. The first act was received almost in silence, the finale alone provoking a storm of alternate applause and hisses. This was because of Madame Donatelli's bravura singing, which was simply superb. The second act was almost a greater failure than the first, and the last part of it, which is now the third act of the opera in its present state, was such a total collapse that Verdi was perfectly disheartened.

'It is true that Madame Donatelli, who sang the music of 127 Violetta, was the exact antithesis in personal appearance of the beautifully fascinating but painfully consumptive

Marguerite Gautier. Graziani the tenor was very hoarse, and it was almost impossible for him to sing his part; whilst Varesi, a very eminent baritone of that time, was so displeased with the part of the Father Germont, that he wouldn't give himself the trouble either to act or to sing.'
ROOS, 54–5

Despite his reputation as a recluse, Verdi actually enjoyed cities and, more and more, a certain kind of society. In Naples, he made many friends – musicians, artists, writers – and, even more, in Venice, where he went not only for his operas, but also for pleasure. Those friends included the psychiatrist Cesare Vigna, the music-publisher and impresario Antonio Gallo (who was to present the second, successful *Traviata* in Venice in 1854), Piave of course, and the lawyer-dramatist Antonio Somma. It was shortly after the first *Traviata* that Verdi began a long correspondence with Somma, reviving his old project of a *Re Lear*. The correspondence continued for several years, as the libretto was drafted; and in his letters to Somma, the composer expressed – more fully and coherently than in his exchanges with Piave and Cammarano – his ideas (in the 1850s) concerning the ideal libretto for him.

152 *Verdi to Antonio Somma; Sant'Agata, 22 April 1853*

[. . .] Nothing would be better or dearer for me than to join my name to your great name: but for me to set worthily, or the best I can, the very lofty poetry that you will surely not fail to create, allow me to indicate some opinions of mine, for what they are worth. Long experience has confirmed the ideas I always held about theatrical effectiveness, even though in my early days I had the courage to show them only in part. (Ten years ago, for example, I would not have risked doing *Rigoletto*.) I believe our [Italian] opera suffers from too much monotony, and so I would refuse today to write subjects of the genre of *Nabucco*, *Foscari*, etc. etc. They offer interesting scenes, but without variety. It is a single note, elevated if you like, but still always the same. And to make myself more clear; Tasso's poem may be superior, but I prefer Ariosto a thousand times. For the same reason I prefer Shakespeare to all dramatic authors, not excepting the Greeks. [. . .] When poor Cammarano was alive, I had suggested *Re Lear* to him. Take a look at it, if you don't mind. I'll do the same, since it is some time since I read it. And tell me your view. [. . .]
MS, BU, PISA

Somma to Verdi; Venice, 30 April 1853

[. . .] Your ideas on Italian opera are mine: and since you mention *Re Lear* to me, I can say plainly that the choice suits me, both because of what the great drama is in itself and because it doesn't resemble any of the subjects you have set so far. So I would gladly take on, if you so decide, the writing of a libretto on such a subject.

[. . .] I will begin by speaking to you, generally, of the plan of the libretto; and how I would handle it, how I would like it, if instead of the poetry I were to write the music. [. . .]
CV II, 65

Somma then went on to outline the opera, dividing it into five acts and a number of scenes.

Verdi to Somma; Busseto, 22 May 1853

I have re-read *Re Lear*, which is marvellously beautiful; but it is frightening to have to reduce such a vast canvas to narrow dimensions, retaining the originality and grandeur of the characters and of the drama. But take heart. Who knows but that we may manage to produce something out of the ordinary?

It would be my opinion to reduce the libretto to three acts or, at most, four. [. . .]

The outstanding pieces of this work, as I believe I can already understand, will be: The introduction with Cordelia's aria; the scene of the storm; the [mock] trial scene; the duet between Lear and Cordelia; and the final scene.   159–60

This is my view, but in your wisdom do as you consider best. Bear in mind only the necessary brevity. The public is easily bored!

It has always seemed to me, and it seems to me still that, in the first scene, Lear's reason for disinheriting Cordelia is puerile, and for our day perhaps ridiculous. Couldn't something more important be found? Perhaps then the character of Cordelia would be spoiled: in any case that scene must be handled with great prudence. [. . .]

I recommend to your attention the part of the Fool which I love very much; it is so original and so profound. Take care that the part of Lear does not prove too wearing.
PASC, 48

A first outline of the *Re Lear* libretto was finished in June 1853.

Verdi to Somma; Busseto, 29 June 1853

[. . .] Two things in this plan have caused me much thought. The first is that it seems to me the opera will become excessively long, especially the first two acts, so if you find something to cut or condense, do so, and the effect will not be lost. And if this cannot be done, at least take care in the less important scenes to say things as briefly as possible. The other is that there are too many scene-changes. The one thing that has always kept me from using Shakespearean subjects more frequently has been precisely this necessity of changing scenes all the time. When I went to the theatre it was something that made me suffer immensely, it was like watching a magic lantern. In this the French are right: they arrange their dramas so that they need only one scene for each act. [. . .]
PASC, 51

That summer of 1853 Somma began sending Verdi the libretto, scene by scene. And Verdi immediately began making suggestions, offering criticisms.

Verdi to Somma, 30 August 1853

[. . .] I have received the rest of the first act: I will say nothing to you about the verses, which are always beautiful and worthy of you, but, with all the respect I owe your talent, I will tell you that the form does not lend itself too well to music. No one loves novelty of forms more than I, but such novelties as can still be set to music. Everything can be set to music, true, but not everything can prove effective. To make music one needs strophes for composing Cantabiles, strophes for combining the voices, strophes for making Largos, Allegros, etc. etc. and all this alternating, so that nothing proves cold and monotonous. Allow me to examine this poetry of yours. I will not speak to you of Edmondo's aria, which, though it shifts too brusquely from Adagio to Allegro, can still stand. In the following Duettino there is no place to make a melody and not even a melodic phrase, but since it is brief, it could stand, adding at the end of the Duettino a strophe of four verses of the same metre for Edmondo, and another four for Edgardo. [. . .]

What causes great trouble is the rest, which would become, musically speaking, the finale of the act. The Fool's strophes are fine, but from the moment when Nerilla [Goneril] enters there is no doing anything. You perhaps meant to make a concerted number in the six strophes of six verses each, but in those strophes there is dialogue, so the characters must respond to one another, and thus the voices could not be joined. Then one would for the same reason have to make another concerted number of the eight-verse strophes when Regana enters. In the end you have Nerilla and Regana leave, and Lear ends the act alone. This is all right in a tragedy, in a spoken drama, but in music it would be, at the least, cold. If you would take a look at the best librettos of Romani (from whom surely you have nothing to learn) you would perhaps say I am right. [. . .]
PASC, 54

Verdi to Somma; Sant'Agata, 9 September 1853

[. . .] As for the recitatives, if the moment is interesting, they can run a bit long. I have made some very long ones, for example the soliloquy in the duet of the first act of *Macbeth*: and the other soliloquy in the duet of the first act of *Rigoletto*.
PASC, 56

Verdi to Somma; Sant'Agata, 15 October 1853

I had decided to spend the winter in Naples; but instead I am going to Paris, and am leaving this very day. I have read and reread *Re Lear* and wanted to write to you especially about the second act, which more than the others needs changes, but now I couldn't say what. I will write from Paris. [. . .]
PASC, 56

146
Verdi had signed a contract with Roqueplan in February 1852 for a new work which was to be given at the Opéra by December 1854. Scribe, the librettist specified in the contract, still had not furnished a text, or even the scenario, which was to have been submitted by 30 June. In the end Scribe supplied the libretto of *Les Vêpres siciliennes* (*I vespri siciliani*) by the date set in the contract, 31 December; he persuaded Verdi, in fact, to accept a revision of a libretto written in 1840 for Donizetti, *Le Duc d'Albe*, never performed (until the 1880s) because Donizetti had gone mad before completing the opera. The libretto had been written in collaboration with Charles Duveyrier, whom Scribe naturally had to inform of the proceedings and call in to work on the revision.

Scribe to Duveyrier; Paris, 3 December 1853

My ally and always my friend, I have not at all forgotten our old offspring, who has long been sleeping in the dust of the folders; but I believe he will have lost nothing by waiting, and I have just found for him a position worthy of his age and his merit.

Verdi is in Paris. I have been asked for an opera for him. He has a contract with the management, a contract according to which the manager guarantees to give this opera next year, in 1854, and to put on forty performances of it. Verdi, for his part (and modesty should prevent me from informing you about this clause), asked as first condition that the poem to be given him should be by your ally. That is why the management turned to me.

I had, as always, several subjects in my head alone; but I had the good idea of resuscitating that poor *Duc d'Albe* that everyone believed dead. [. . .]

I suggested it to Verdi, telling him all about the adventures of the deceased. Several situations suited him; there were many things he did not like.

[. . .] It was necessary to change the title. I consented without any difficulty.

Change the chief character. This was more difficult, almost impossible. I believe, however, that I have solved it. It was necessary to change the place of the action, to situate it in a climate less cold than that of the Low Countries, a warm and musical climate, like Naples or Sicily. This was less difficult: I have done it.

It was finally necessary to change entirely the second act, for there are no beer-halls in those countries; to change totally the fourth, which represents the embarkation and departure of the Duke of Alba, and finally to add a fifth, for he wants a big, grand work in five acts, of dimensions as broad as *Les Huguenots* or *Le Prophète*. Moreover (and I will be as good as my word) I have promised and signed that all this would be finished within this month of December 1853, so that the maestro can immediately set to work. [. . .]

135

I know, my dear friend, that you no longer concern yourself with the theatre, that you have other tasks than those of the stage: do not worry about anything. The outline is more or less in my head, and before executing it, I would like only to converse with you, to have your always excellent ideas [. . .]
RDM, 887

The libretto was on time, but the composition did not proceed easily.

Verdi to Giuseppina Appiani; Paris, 25 February 1854

[. . .] I am writing quite slowly, indeed I may not write at all. I do not know what is the cause, but I know that the libretto is there, always in the same place.
COP, 538

Verdi to Clarina Maffei; Paris, 2 March 1854

[. . .] Will I write for La Scala? No. If I were asked the reason, I would have trouble answering: I could say my scant desire to write, or even more my repugnance in signing a contract. It is not, as has been said, because of commitments made already until after '56, for I have no other commitment beyond the opera I am writing; it is not because of the desire (as has also been said) to *put down roots* here!! *Put down roots*? It is impossible! . . . And for that matter why? For what reason? For glory? I don't believe in it. For money? I earn as much and perhaps more in Italy. Besides, even if I wanted to, it is impossible. I love too much my desert and my sky. I do not tip my hat to counts or marquesses, to no one. Finally I do not have millions and I will never spend my few thousand hard-earned francs on réclame, on claque and such filth. And that seems necessary for success! A few days ago even Dumas in his paper said, of the new opera by Meyerbeer: 'What a pity that Rossini did not present his masterpieces in 1854! It is true to say that Rossini has never had that Germanic vigour which brings a success to the boil in the press six months in advance and thus makes ready for the explosion of publicity on the first night.' This is quite true: I attended the first performance of *Etoile du Nord* and I understood little or nothing, whereas this good public understood everything, and found everything beautiful, sublime, divine! . . . And this same public, after 25 or 30 years, has still not understood *Guglielmo Tell*, and so it is performed distorted, mutilated, with three acts instead of five and with an unworthy *mise en scène*! And this is the first theatre in the world . . . But, without realizing, I am speaking to you of these things that cannot interest you. So I will close by saying that I have a fierce longing to come home. I say it to you in a whisper, because I am sure you will believe me. Others would believe it an affectation on my part. And I have no interest in saying what I do not feel. But our Milanese *lions* have such an exaggerated opinion of everything that is done and exists in Paris! . . . So much the better, for that matter. May they enjoy themselves! The weather has been very beautiful in the three days of Carnival, hence great crowds on the boulevards.

COP, 539–40

Verdi continued his correspondence with Venice, where Somma was still revising *Re Lear* and where Verdi's friend Antonio Gallo, music-publisher and impresario, was planning a revival of *La traviata* at the Teatro San Benedetto.

Verdi to Somma; Paris, 31 March 1854

[. . .] If there are some verses of recitative that you can shorten or cut, it will be that much gained for the opera as a whole. In the theatre *long* is synonymous with boring, and the boring is the worst of all genres.

Farewell, my dear Somma, I can hardly wait to apply myself to *Re Lear*, which I like very much, and I hope to do something less bad than my other compositions.

Greet Vigna and Gallo. Tell the latter to think carefully about *La traviata*, and to make sure that he doesn't have to repent later. [. . .]

PASC, 65

Piave was, of course, also in Venice and deeply involved in staging the second *Traviata*.

Piave to Tito Ricordi; Venice, 5 May 1854

I have already taken four rehearsals of *La traviata*, and tonight we will have the dress rehearsal more as a formality than because it is needed, and I am pleased to tell you that la Spezia is made for this opera, and this opera seems made for la Spezia, and that if nothing else happens and if the lungs of this excellent young girl hold out, she will perform our opera as nobody in the world will ever dream of doing. Believe me, because you know I am sincere. [. . .]

I wish he [Verdi] were here instead of breaking his balls, combatting that rich Jew of a Meyerbeer. He renounces the throne offered him by Italy, to sit on a bench in France! [. . .]

AB II, 271

Tito Ricordi to Verdi; Milan, 12 May 1854

[. . .] I must repeat to you that there was never in Venice a success equal to that of *La traviata*, not even in the days of your *Ernani*. Gallo writes to me that, the third evening, there was an indescribable storm of applause, and that the third act in particular produced an effect, if anything, superior to the other two evenings, and that he also had to bow amid the applause. [. . .]

AB II, 272

Verdi to Vigna; Paris, 17 May 1854

So then this poor sinner of ours did not deserve to be stoned, as she was last year at La Fenice? Good for me, for Gallo, for Ricordi, and also for you, since I know what interest you take in my affairs in general, and in particular what you thought, said, and wrote of this *Traviata*, cursed then by all. [. . .]

Last year, the morning after the first performance of *La traviata*, Gallo came to me and, also in the name of our mutual friend, expressed some opinions to me especially about the third act. I answered simply: 'I believe you are mistaken: it seems to me the best.' Now he writes me with nothing but praise for that act. So I was right then and afterwards when I wrote to you. [. . .] You must remember that an opera executed not only badly but in a way counter to its meaning makes the effect of a painting seen at the evening Ave Maria: you can just discern the figures but can see nothing of the colour, the drawing, the perspective and, especially, of the expression of the figures. Everything seems dark and monotonous. [. . .]

BONG, 36

Verdi to Somma; Paris, 17 May 1854

[...] You can take your time, because the winter cold and illness have prevented me from completing the [Paris] opera by the proper date: so the period of la Cruvelli's leave has come. The rehearsals will not begin until September, and the opera cannot be given till winter, so I must deprive myself of the pleasure of having you in my hovel, as you led me to hope. Another year, and then if you do not have a *Re Lear* to bring me, you will bring me your self which will be very dear to me.

I thank you for the news of *La traviata* and I am very pleased. I can imagine the racket Gallo will make, and the position of his hat, to which he will have attached a string behind, to make it stand quite high. I hear *mirabilia* about la Spezia. Could she be a good Cordelia? Let me know. Would the voice be sufficient for a large theatre? No matter whether it is big or small, it must be heard. [. . .]

PASC, 66–7

Verdi to De Sanctis; Mandres, 26 May 1854

[. . .] By now you will have heard that *La traviata* was given in Venice and went well! But who told you that *La traviata* needed to be revised? Who told the *Gazzetta musicale* of Naples that I had made changes?

Know then that *La traviata* being performed now at the San Benedetto is the same, the very same, that was performed last year at the Fenice, except for some changes in key, and some touches that I made myself to adapt it better to these singers: which changes and adaptations will remain in the score because I consider the opera as if written for the present cast. For the rest not one number has been changed, not one number has been added, or cut, not one musical *idea* has been altered. Everything that existed for the Fenice exists now for the San Benedetto. Then it was a fiasco: now it is a furore. Draw your own conclusions!!

[. . .] I am in the country and am writing, but very slowly because I have little desire, I'm cold, in a bad humour, etc. . . . The opera cannot go on before winter.

AB II, 273

Verdi and Giuseppina, now openly living together, had spent the summer months of 1854 – exceptionally cold – at Mandres (Seine-et-Oise). By 1 October he was back in Paris, to begin rehearsals of *Les Vêpres siciliennes* at the Opéra. To his Paris address came a letter from his old Milanese friend Countess Appiani, who had addressed the letter to 'Giuseppina Strepponi'. Obviously, this caused some embarrassment since Giuseppina was living as Madame Verdi. She charged Verdi with replying to the imprudent Contessa. His letter ended their sixteen-year friendship, as his relationship with Giuseppina had, in fact, cut him off from many Milanese acquaintances, except the loyal Clarina Maffei.

Verdi to Countess Appiani; Paris, 21 October 1854

Chance, pure chance caused your letter to Peppina to arrive here. Since the address that you put on it is unknown at the door of this house, that charming letter thus risked being lost if, I repeat, chance had not had me encounter the postman, and if he, seeing a name ending in *i*, had not asked me. I collected it and delivered it. Peppina said to me that, having renounced letters and arts, and maintaining correspondence only with her family and with a few very intimate friends, she would be grateful if I would express her apologies and answer such a *spirituelle* letter. – And here am I, who cannot write like you or like Peppina, in the greatest embarrassment, to answer a letter so well written, so sensitive, and I also repeat, so *spirituelle*. But I, with my headlong style, cannot make a show of pride or of wit: so in brief I will tell you that we are packing our trunks in great haste; that the flight of la Cruvelli from the Opéra has required me to ask for the dissolution of my contract which I hope to obtain; that I will go at once to Busseto, but I will stay there only a few days. Where will I go? I couldn't say! Now that the bag of news is emptied, I press your hands.

COP, 540

After just a week of rehearsals, the eccentric soprano Sophie Cruvelli had disappeared from Paris. Rehearsals were interrupted. Verdi thought at once of returning to Italy and, naturally, of a next opera. He had asked Bardare (the Neapolitan poet who had completed *Il trovatore*) for a new libretto, to be fitted to the old music of *La battaglia di Legnano*. But the poet's efforts had not satisfied him. Similarly Piave had been asked to find a new libretto for *Stiffelio*, but Piave, busy with staging *La traviata*, had been in no hurry to think about the project.

Verdi to Piave; Paris, end October 1854

I hope by now you will be well informed of the musical matters that take place here. La Cruvelli has fled! Where? the devil knows! At first this news gave me a pain in the a . . . but now, secretly, I laugh at it. It's true I lose a lot of money, but that doesn't matter: if I were greedy, I would

have twice as much as I do. This desertion gives me the right to dissolve my contract and I haven't let the opportunity slip, and I have formally asked for it.

It's true the Minister of State has made me a heap of offers, to engage whomever I like, to translate for the moment either *Trovatore* or *Rigoletto*, to write immediately another opera in three acts while they are fixing things to give the grand opera in five acts, but I, with all the *grâce* you have been able to teach me, said no to everything. I have shown that it is not wise to make translations, nor to give a little opera, and I cannot give the five-act opera because it was written for la Cruvelli.

[. . .] Coming to Italy, I cannot write an opera by Carnival season, but I could adapt one of my old ones as I have had in mind to do for some time. Rascal, if you had thought of me by now I could devote myself to *Stiffelio*! Why have you never thought of finding me another subject for this music? Answer me at once if you are prepared and if you have time to concern yourself with it. It is a matter that I consider very important. Answer me immediately here!

AB II, 279

Cruvelli, as it happened, had run off to the Riviera with Baron Vigier, later to become her husband. She returned to Paris in mid-November and to her role as Hélène.

Verdi to De Sanctis; Paris, 29 November 1854

The rehearsals have begun, that is to say re-begun. The title is *I vespri siciliani*: very harsh subject for our Censorships. If la Cruvelli doesn't run off a second time, I hope to be able to open at the beginning of February. [. . .] I would not want them to give in Naples either *Rigoletto* or *Traviata*. There is not the company suited to either opera. Both will surely fail . . . [. . .].

MS, ANL, ROME

Verdi to François Louis Crosnier, director of the Opéra; Paris, 3 January 1855

I believe it my duty not to allow any more time to go by without making some observations to you about *Les Vêpres siciliennes*.

It is both discouraging and humiliating for me that M. Scribe does not bother to amend the fifth act, which everyone agrees in finding without interest. I am well aware that M. Scribe has a thousand other things to do, which perhaps mean more to him than my opera! . . . but had I suspected in him this supreme indifference, I would have remained in my country where, to tell the truth, I was not too badly off!

I was hoping that M. Scribe (since the situation, in my opinion, lends itself to such a thing) would have found, to end the drama, one of those numbers that wring tears and whose effect is always sure. Mind you, Monsieur, that this would have helped the whole work, which is completely lacking in pathos, except for the fourth act aria.

I was hoping that M. Scribe would have condescended to appear now and then at rehearsals, to repair certain awkwardnesses in the words, verses difficult to sing: to see if there was something to touch up in the numbers, the acts, etc. etc. For example: the 2nd, 3rd, 4th act are all cast in the same mould: an aria, a duet, a finale.

Finally, I took it that M. Scribe, as he had promised from the beginning, would have changed everything that attacks the honour of the Italians. – The more I think about this subject, the more I am convinced it is dangerous. He offends the French because they are massacred; he offends the Italians, because, altering the historical character of Procida, M. Scribe (in his favourite system) has made him a common conspirator, putting the inevitable dagger into his hand. Mon Dieu! in the history of every nation there are virtues and crimes, and we are no worse than the others. In any case, I am first of all an Italian, and at any cost, I would never be a party to an insult offered my country.

I have something still to say about the rehearsals in the foyer. I overhear here and there some words, some remarks, which if they are not entirely offensive, are at the least out of place. I am not accustomed to them and I could not tolerate them. There is perhaps someone who does not find my music up to the stature of the Grand Opéra; others perhaps do not consider their roles worthy of their talent; it is possible that I, for my part, find the performance and the kind of singing different from what I would like! . . . Finally it seems to me (or else I am strangely mistaken) that we are not in unison on the way of feeling and interpreting the music, and without perfect agreement there is *no possibility* of success.

You see, Monsieur, that everything I have just said is quite serious, so that one must take thought to avert the mischief that threatens us. For myself, I see only one solution, which I do not hesitate to suggest to you. That is the *cancellation of the contract*.

I well know that you will say to me: That the Opéra has already lost time, and has had some expenses! . . . but that is not much compared to a year which I have wasted here, and in which I could have earned a hundred thousand francs or so in Italy.

You will also say; that when there is a debit, cancelling a contract is quickly done. To that I answer: that I would already have paid, if my losses and my expenses here were not excessive for me!

I know that you are too fair and too reasonable not to choose, between two evils, the lesser. Believe, Monsieur, in my musical experience: in our present conditions, *a success is very difficult!* A semi-success profits no one. The best thing is to make an end of it. Each of us will try to make up for wasted time. Let us try, Monsieur, to settle things without noise, and perhaps we will both gain. [. . .]
COP, 157–9

Verdi to Somma; Paris, 5 April 1855

A few days ago I received the last two acts of *Lear*. I think that you did not do well in cutting the Andante in the aria of Delia [Cordelia]. This way only an incomplete piece remains. I believe it had to be changed, not cut. I liked very much that strophe of distant voices after the battle: it had character and colour. The *coup d'état* that Albania makes does not seem natural to me. How can this Duke, who has been an imbecile up to this point, become so strong as to have the true Queen imprisoned along with her lover, to whom she had given full powers? The death of Nerilla and the duel were more natural! . . . [. . .]
PASC, 76

Hector Berlioz to Auguste Morel; Paris, 2 June 1855

[. . .] Verdi is at loggerheads with all the people at the Opéra. He made a terrible scene at the dress rehearsal yesterday. I feel sorry for the poor man; I put myself in his place. Verdi is a worthy and honourable artist. [. . .]
BERLIOZ, 229

On 13 June 1855, premiere of *Les Vêpres siciliennes* (*I vespri siciliani*) at the Opéra, Paris. The English singer Charles Santley was in the audience. — 139–41

From Santley's reminiscences

[. . .] I filled up my time with a visit to the Exhibition, which had the same depressing effect upon me as that of 1851 and all others I have visited since. I noticed Verdi's opera, the 'Vêpres Siciliennes' was announced for Wednesday, with Sophie Cruvelli in the cast, and I could not resist the temptation of staying one day more in order to have another opportunity of hearing the goddess who had enchanted me a couple of years before. I knew nothing about the distribution of places, and took what was offered me in exchange for my money, in consequence found myself with the crown of my head almost touching the ceiling, planted behind a row of people who, with that French politeness of which I have often heard, but seldom experienced, would insist upon standing, and entirely obstructing any view of the stage. Spite of the discomfort, I enjoyed the performance. Obin, the bass, especially pleased me; I was somewhat disenchanted by my goddess; the tenor I did not like; and the baritone, Bonnehée, I liked very much, only, as he did not go down to F, or anywhere near it, I did not take the interest in him I would have done a few years later, when I learned to distinguish between bass and baritone. — 138
SANTLEY, 53

Verdi to Clarina Maffei; Paris, 28 June 1855

[. . .] It seems to me that *I vespri siciliani* is not going too badly. That you share in the evil and the good (assuming that a mere opera can be evil or good) that concerns me, I am more than persuaded: I know you too well and therefore I am grateful to you for it, I love you and always will.

The journalism here has been either adequate or favourable, if we except the only three who are Italian: Fiorentini, Montazio and Scudo. My friends say: what injustice! what an infamous world! But no: the world is too stupid to be infamous.

La Ristori is making a furore and I am very pleased. She has annihilated la Rachel, and in fact she is quite superior to la Rachel and the French themselves – something unheard of – agree. The difference is that la Ristori has a heart and la Rachel, in that place, has a piece of cork or of marble.

I still have not seen the Exposition thoroughly. I have glanced through the rooms where there are Italian things. I say this with sorrow: I would have wished for better. Still, there is one beautiful, sublime thing, the *Spartacus* of Vela. Glory to him!

Farewell, my dear Clarina, I hope to be in Italy in a fortnight's time.
COP, 542

Verdi actually stayed in Paris – with a side-trip to London, to conduct *Il trovatore* at Covent Garden – until just before Christmas. He was busy supervising the French translation of *Il trovatore* by Emilien Pacini. He arrived in Busseto on 23 December, just as *Les Vêpres siciliennes*, under the title *Giovanna de Guzman*, was being performed in Parma and Turin. — 137, 144–5; 142–3

Verdi to De Sanctis; Busseto, 7 February 1856

[. . .] If time permitted I would like to tell you of my affairs:

Verdi, *I vespri siciliani*, 1855 (*Giovanna de Guzman*). Title page of libretto as played in Turin, 26 December 1855. William Weaver Collection, Monte San Savino (AR).

for that matter they are not very important and are reduced to almost nothing. Total abandonment of music: a bit of reading: some slight occupation with agriculture and with horses: *voilà tout*.

I won't say I'm coming to Naples because you wouldn't believe it and you would be right.

CV I, 32

Verdi to De Sanctis, Busseto, 28 March 1856

[. . .] Yesterday Piave arrived here to change for me the subject of *Stiffelio* (which, with all the respect due the Neapolitan public, I plan to have circulate like other operas of mine) and this *Stiffelio* will be finished towards 20 April, because I will only have to do some different recitatives and two or three new numbers. [. . .]

CV I, 33

The *Stiffelio* revision was not completed until late May. Verdi had signed a contract with La Fenice for a new opera to be given there the following season. Negotiations also began, painfully as usual, with the San Carlo, for a new opera to be given within the year 1857. Meanwhile Verdi and Giuseppina decided to take a brief trip to Venice, to enjoy the sea-bathing at the Lido. There Verdi was surrounded by his friends: Piave, Vigna, and even Peppina's doctor from Paris, Franco.

Verdi to Piave; Busseto, 31 July 1856

I am leaving today for Paris. Send your letters there. I have

received the poem of *Stiffelio*, and it would be all right if there were not here and there some half-verses and some whole verses that are useless, some padding, some ah's, ih's, oh's to make the metre. . . . I believe I have found the subject for Venice, and I will send you the outline from Paris.

AB II, 368.

The subject was *Simon Boccanegra*. Verdi's trip to Paris was devoted to protecting the rights of his works, which the impresario Calzado threatened to perform from pirated Spanish editions. Verdi had to bring suit; he also urged the Parma government to sign an international copyright agreement. Piave was pressing him to settle the details of the final (verse) draft of *Simon Boccanegra* by letter, so that it could go to the Censorship.

Verdi to Piave; Enghien, 3 September 1856

What is the use of finishing the story of *Simon Boccanegra* within the month? Don't the police and the Presidenza have a sufficiently extended draft? Or rather, it is not the draft but the completely finished drama. In the libretto there will not be an idea or a word changed. What does it matter whether it is in prose or in verse? And as you have observed very well, this *Simone* has something original. Thus the layout of the libretto, of the numbers, etc. etc. must be as original as possible. This cannot be done unless we are together; so now it would be time wasted.

AB II, 371

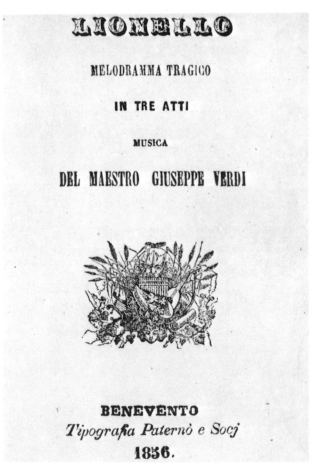

Verdi, *Rigoletto*, 1851 (*Lionello*, 1856). Title page of libretto as played in Naples. William Weaver Collection, Monte San Savino. The censors in the Kingdom of the Two Sicilies had bowdlerized Rigoletto into a non-hunchback Venetian noble.

Piave's verses eventually reached Verdi in Paris, but did not completely satisfy him. So he turned for revisions to an exiled Tuscan patriot, Giuseppe Montanelli.

100

Giuseppe Montanelli to Verdi; Paris, late January 1857

I send your requested modifications by return of post. When you have need, don't hesitate to make use of me. I have already twice heard your magnificent *Rigoletto*. I will not tell you what I felt in hearing this magnificent music of yours. Nor perhaps could I, if I wished. You speak to the soul a mysterious language whose sweetness not even the word of poetry can render. I do not know how content you would be with the tempos, but the artists sing marvellously, and Erminia [Frezzolini] is a miracle, an enchantment. I have no doubts about the triumph of *Boccanera* [sic].
BSV III, 1772–3.

Montanelli's letter enclosed extensive passages, revised. Verdi had him revise others, and accepted many of his suggestions. He then sent the text back to poor Piave.

Verdi to Piave; Paris, early 1857

Here is the libretto shortened and reduced to just about what it should be. As I told you in my other letter, you may put your name to it or not. If what has happened upsets you, it has also upset me, and perhaps more than you, but I can say nothing to you except 'it was a necessity'!!
BSV III, 1785

On 12 March 1857, premiere of *Simon Boccanegra* at the Teatro La Fenice, Venice.

Verdi to Vincenzo Torelli; Venice, 13 March 1857

147–8

[. . .] The Carnival of Venice was splendid; the theatre season good so far, but last night the troubles began. There was the first performance of *Boccanegra*, which had a *fiasco* almost as great as that of *Traviata*. I thought I had done something passable, but apparently I was mistaken. We'll see later who was wrong.
AB II, 393

Gazzetta previlegiata di Venezia, 15 March 1857

The music of *Boccanegra* is of the sort that does not make an immediate impression. It is very elaborate, conducted with the most exquisite artifice, and it must be studied in detail. Hence on the first night it was not understood, and some rushed to a hasty judgment: a severe, hostile judgment in the form in which it was displayed towards a man whose name is Verdi, one of the few who represents abroad the glories of Italian art. [. . .]

What can in part explain that first, sinister impression is the genre of the music, perhaps too grave and severe, that lugubrious hue that dominates the score, and the prologue in particular. [. . .]
VELF, 54–5

Cesare Vigna to Verdi; Venice, 23 March 1857

[. . .] By now it is clear that there exists a well-organized hostile faction, not just with the usual chatter and malicious insinuations [. . .] but with gold, a logical argument of prime strength. [. . .]

Some see here the hand of Meyerbeer himself. [. . .]

Though I attach no importance to it, accustomed as I am to the witty inventions of these fine people, still for your information I will tell you that a rumour has spread saying the libretto is your own composition. [. . .]
AB II, 395–6

In Verdi's answer, note that he says 'bears the name of Piave', not 'is by Piave'; the lines he quotes are *not* among those revised by Montanelli.

Verdi to Vigna; Sant'Agata, 11 April 1857

I will be sincere with you (as I always am, for that matter, with you and with everyone) and tell you I haven't written before because from morning till evening I am always among the fields, the woods, in the midst of the peasants, animals . . . the best kind, though, the quadrupeds. Arriving home tired, I have not yet found time and courage to pick up the pen. A serious fault, true, but in your friendship you will forgive it me.

Are the Venetians calm again? Who would ever have said that this poor *Boccanegra*, good or bad opera that it may be, should have raised such a racket. [. . .] All we needed was the invention that the libretto is of my writing! ! ! A libretto that bears the name of Piave is judged in advance as the worst poetry; and I frankly would be content if I were capable of writing verses like:
'Vieni a mirar la cerula . . . [Come and behold the azure]'.
'Delle faci festanti al barlume [At the glow of the festive torches]'
and others, many others, along with many other verses here and there. I confess my ignorance. I am not up to it. [. . .]
AB II, 398

Verdi did not spend all his time in the fields. *Boccanegra* was to be performed in Reggio Emilia, and he – with Piave at Sant'Agata – made some revisions for this production, which he also supervised.

Verdi to De Sanctis; Reggio Emilia, 14 May 1857

[. . .] I am not quite sure that I will write *Re Lear* for Naples. The Company would not be too suited: I am looking for another subject but so far have found nothing. [. . .]
AB II, 416

Giuseppina Strepponi to Léon Escudier; Sant'Agata, 4 July 1857

[. . .] He seems quite determined not to accept any engagements with fixed dates after Naples. He says he has been chained too long and that now he is rich enough to free himself. [. . .]

In about a week we leave for Rimini, where they will give *Stiffelio* under the name of *Aroldo*, the religious censorship not permitting it to be given as it was created. . . . [. . .]
AB II, 420

The conductor of the *Aroldo* in Rimini was the forty-five-year-old Angelo Mariani, Italy's first real conductor in the modern sense, already at the height of his fame. He and Verdi had met before, but this summer period in Rimini was to seal a deep friendship. On 16 August 1857, premiere of *Aroldo* at the Teatro Nuovo, Rimini.

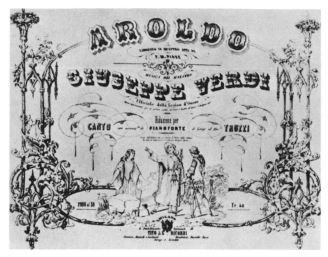

Verdi, *Stiffelio*, 1850 (*Aroldo*, 1857). Title page of score published by Ricordi, Milan.

Angelo Mariani to Tito Ricordi; Rimini, 1 a.m., 17 August 1857

[. . .] I have just come from the Theatre, or rather from Verdi's house, where I left a crowd of people with a band, wax torches, cheering and the most frenzied ovations.

Aroldo created a furore, there was no number that was not applauded; the Maestro was called out an infinity of times on stage. He is very pleased, the performance was good. [. . .]

Also called on stage was our dear Checchino Maria Piave, and he was so content he could hardly contain himself.

AB II, 425

Mariani to Tito Ricordi; Rimini, 26 August 1857.

The members of this stupendous orchestra determined to honour me by having my portrait lithographed. I will send you a copy as soon as I am in Genoa. They also had lithographed the portrait of the Illustrious Verdi. [. . .] The portraits are very handsome and good likenesses. I may add that we were the only ones who had this honour . . .

AB II, 427

Though Verdi's operas, throughout his career, were widely reviewed, the critics were more often journalists than scholars. The first serious musicological study of Verdi's works was by the Florentine Abramo Basevi, whose *Studio sulle opere di Giuseppe Verdi* appeared in 1859. The last opera to be considered is *Aroldo*.

From Abramo Basevi's study of Verdi's operas

The difficulties created by censorship and the cold reception given *Stiffelio* by the public were the causes which equally moved the Maestro to change the story and also to introduce notable changes in the music.

The chief change in the story was this: that Stiffelio the priest became Aroldo the warrior. This change eliminated some inconsistencies that existed in the first libretto, but it created some new ones. The librettist changed only the clothing of the character, who otherwise remained identical. Now it is clear that many situations which are fitting for a priest are unfitting, or at least odd, for a warrior. And so it happened in the second act finale, when

198

Aroldo faints, overcome with emotion at an off-stage sacred chorus; and in the finale of the opera when, quite abruptly, he pardons his wife with those words of the Gospel, about the repentant adulteress, which are heard uttered by a hermit-companion of his. Everyone can see that what was natural in a priest, who preaches and who has devoted all his thought to holy scripture, becomes forced in a warrior, even in one who has become a hermit. [. . .]

BASEVI, 281–2

Verdi's next commission was the opera for Naples. The *Re Lear* project had been, once again, abandoned. He had thought of Victor Hugo's *Ruy Blas*, but had had to give that up for the same reason: the unsuitability of the Neapolitan singers.

Verdi to Vincenzo Torelli, Busseto, 19 September 1857 154

I am in despair! These last months I have gone through an infinite number of dramas (including some very beautiful ones), but none suited to my needs! My attention had rested on a very beautiful and interesting drama: *Il Tesoriere del Re D. Pedro* [García Gutiérrez's *El tesorero del Rey, 1850*], which I had translated at once; but in making the sketch to reduce it to proportions for music, I found so many difficulties that I had to give up the idea. Now I am condensing a French drama, *Gustavo III di Svezia*, libretto by Scribe, given at the Opéra [with music by Auber] about twenty years ago [1833]. It is grand and vast; it is beautiful; but this too has the conventional forms of all works for music, something which I have never liked and I now find unbearable. I repeat, I am in despair, because it is too late to find other subjects. Therefore I will make you a suggestion that can settle everything and can be of interest both for the theatre and for my reputation. Let us set aside the thought of writing for this year a completely new opera, and replace it with *La battaglia di Legnano*, adapting another subject to it, and adding the necessary numbers, as I did for *Aroldo*. [. . .] Accepting this arrangement, as of this moment (if you like) I will commit myself to write *Re Lear* for the coming year, but putting together a suitable company, indispensable, as you know. [. . .] If this does not suit you, I would be forced to do *Gustavo*, with which I am only half-satisfied.

COP, 561

Though Verdi was willing also to make a financial sacrifice, the San Carlo did not accept the offer. So the composer had to proceed with *Gustavo* (which eventually became *Un ballo in maschera*). The librettist was to be Antonio Somma.

Somma to Verdi; Venice, 13 October 1857 152

[. . .] I agree to versify *Gustavo III di Svezia* from the version that you will hasten to send me. In addition to the scenario you will provide, it would be best for the musical rhythm if you make a note in the margin of the form of the stanzas, the verse and the metre for each stanza, so that I can more easily offer you the poetry that suits. So I beg you to be generous with suggestions. [. . .]

I must ask only one thing of you. I would like, if you do not mind, to remain anonymous for this work, or use a pseudonym. Thus I would write with greater freedom. [. . .]

CV I, 219

Somma had already had troubles with the authorities for his patriotic ideas, and apparently he foresaw trouble with the censors over the subject of *Gustavo III*, which involves a regicide. In Naples, Verdi's friend Torelli, secretary to the San Carlo management, was also concerned; and, before Somma had even finished the first draft, the Neapolitan was thinking about toning down the situations.

154

Verdi to Torelli; Busseto, 14 October 1857

I have sent the poet your letter, and I believe it will not be difficult to shift the setting elsewhere and change the names, but now that the poet is hard at work, it is best to finish the drama, then afterwards he will attend to changing the subject.

A pity! To have to renounce the pomp of a court like that of *Gustavo III*, and it will be quite difficult to find a Duke of the sort of that *Gustavo*!! Poor poets and poor composers!
COP, 563

Verdi sent the prose draft of the libretto to Torelli at the end of October, so that it could be submitted to the censors. Meanwhile both he and Somma worked at top speed, and the opera was virtually composed by the end of 1857, by which time the censor had informed the Naples impresario Alberti that the subject was forbidden. Aghast, Alberti kept this news a secret from Verdi. The composer arrived in Naples – with Giuseppina and their beloved Maltese spaniel Lulù – on 14 January 1858, having already made, with Somma, some revisions of the libretto, now entitled *Una vendetta in domino*.

Verdi arrived as the San Carlo was performing *I vespri siciliani* (rebaptized *Batilde di Turenna*).

155–8
157

Omnibus, Naples, January 1858

[. . .] The very evening of his arrival, the famous Maestro, begged by his friends, came to the theatre. As he arrived in his box, there was a general murmur in the vast San Carlo, and all eyes and opera-glasses were turned on him. [. . .] After the magnificent duet between Fraschini and Coletti, the applause grew out of all proportion, and Maestro Verdi was dragged by his friends and by his feeling of gratitude to descend and appear on the stage, where several times with the others, then alone, he was called out. The orchestra chose to pay him homage by repeating the Overture, and after this the Celebrated Maestro was called out twice more, amid warm, unanimous, resounding applause. Thus the Italian genius was hailed, great and sublime, here in the seat of harmony and of song [. . .].
AB II, 467

86

Verdi to Alberti; Naples, 23 January 1858

As you know, I have been in Naples for eight or ten days, and ready to fulfil the obligations of my contract. I have therefore the honour to inform you that, in accord with clause 3, I have chosen to perform the parts in my new opera *Una vendetta in domino* the following artists: *Amelia*, Signora Penco; *Oscar*, Signora Fioretti; *Fortune-teller*, Signora Ganducci; *Duke*, Signor Fraschini; *Count*, Signor Coletti. The other parts of no importance I will choose later. Be so kind as to answer me in writing whether the above artists are free and at my disposal, so that I may begin the rehearsals as soon as possible.
COP, 565

153

BATILDE DI TURENNA

MELODRAMMA IN CINQUE ATTI

MUSICA DEL

CAV. GIUSEPPE VERDI

DA RAPPRESENTARSI

NEL REAL TEATRO S. CARLO

Nell' autunno del 1857.

NAPOLI
DALLA TIPOGRAFIA FLAUTINA
1857

Verdi, *I vespri siciliani*, 1855 (*Batilde di Turenna*, 1857). Title page of libretto as played in Naples, 1857–58.

Finally Verdi learned that the libretto was forbidden, and that its veto dated back almost three months.

Verdi to Somma; Naples, 7 February 1858

I am in a sea of troubles! The Censorship will almost certainly prohibit our libretto. Why? I do not know. I was quite right to tell you to avoid any phrase, any word that might be suspect. They began by objecting to some expressions, some words, from words they went on to scenes, from scenes to the whole subject.

They have suggested to me these modifications (and this as a favour):

1) change the protagonist to a gentleman, removing completely the idea of a sovereign;
2) change his wife to a sister;
3) modify the scene of the Witch, shifting it to a period when they were believed in;
4) no ball;
5) the assassination off-stage;
6) eliminate the scene of the names drawn by lot;
And on, and on, and on!!...

As you will imagine, these changes cannot be accepted; therefore no more opera; therefore the subscribers will not pay two instalments; therefore the government withdraws the subvention; therefore the Management is suing everyone and threatens me with damages of 50 000 ducats!! ... what an inferno! ... Write at once and tell me your opinion.
AB II, 469

Somma to Verdi; Venice, 13 February 1858

I reply to yours of the 7th, without missing the post, which is leaving. For the two hours I have had it in my hands, I have been thinking of a reply that could satisfy you. You ask me for 'an opinion and at once' on the unpleasant situation you are in, and which I had heard of from other sources two days ago. But what sort of opinion, I ask, and on what, is wanted of me? A legal opinion on the suit that the Management threatens you with? But the matter is very simple and the defence is obvious. If the Censorship, you know as well as I, allowed the scenario on condition of modifications, which the libretto then carried out, and if later it then forbids the libretto without giving a reason, you can have no responsibility towards anyone at all; and otherwise, is it possible that you are asking of me an opinion on how to reshape the text, when you say the opera will not be given, since the changes asked for by the Censor are impossible?

So I am forced to the conclusion that your letter asks me something else which is not an opinion. Well, my friend: I will sacrifice all my vanity as an author, if this is enough to reconcile you with the S. Carlo and with the Censorship.

Of the poetry that belongs to me make the use you like best. Cut and revise as the Censorship chooses if there is time, retaining what is permitted and making new scenes and dialogue when the Censor demands it; do whatever those Gentlemen like: *but I demand two things*, one, that instead of my name on the frontispiece there appear *that of someone else*, anonymity no longer being enough for me after everyone has announced I am the author of the poetry; the other, that the opera no longer be called *La vendetta in domino* but something else, as you like.

AB II, 470–1

Verdi to Torelli; Naples, 14 February 1858

[. . .] They propose more, and more, and more (it seems to be a joke, if not an insolence) changes in the libretto, which do nothing but remove all its character and effect .

Shift the action back five or six centuries?! What anachronism! Remove the scene where the name of the assassin is chosen by lot?! . . . But this is the most powerful and most original situation of the drama, and they want me to give it up?! I have already told you, I cannot commit the monstrosities that were committed here with *Rigoletto*. They are done because I cannot prevent them. Nor is it any use talking to me of the success: if here and there some numbers, two, three, etc. etc. are applauded, that is not enough to form the musical drama. On artistic matters I have my own ideas, my precise, clear convictions, which I cannot and must not renounce.

AB II, 471

The theatre authorities had provided meanwhile their own, anonymous libretto, *Adelia degli Adimari*, which was given to Verdi. As ammunition for his lawyers – the lawsuit was imminent – he carefully annotated, scene by scene, the new monstrosity, which ran to ninety pages.

Verdi's notes on 'Adelia degli Adimari'

[. . .] There would be many, many other things to say; but even these few observations are enough to prove that my drama has been totally mutilated, and it is therefore impossible that the music can achieve the effect imagined by me.

La Vendetta in domino consists of 884 verses: in *Adelia* 297 have been changed, many have been added, very many cut. I ask further if, in the drama by the Management, there exists, as in mine:

The title?	No.
The poet?	No.
The period?	No.
The place?	No.
Characters?	No.
Situations?	No.
The drawing of lots?	No.
Ball?	No.

A Maestro who respects his art and himself could not and should not dishonour himself accepting as subject for music, written to quite another plan, these oddities which distort the most obvious principles of dramaturgy and outrage the artist's conscience. [. . .]

CV I, 269

Verdi then points out, at some length, the steps he and Somma had already taken to satisfy the censors, changing the scene from Sweden to Pomerania, the King into a Duke, the revolver into a dagger, and so on. The lawsuit took place, the judge agreed that the libretto could 'damage the music', and the score became Verdi's property. The only condition for Verdi was that he return to Naples in the autumn to stage *Simon Boccanegra* at the San Carlo.

Giuseppina Strepponi to Caterina De Sanctis; Naples, 20 April 1858

Forgive me, forgive me, forgive me a thousand times for the thousand bothers I have given you . . . but you are so good that I use and perhaps abuse your goodness. Now the end is in sight and this will be the final nuisance.

I would like to have the hat made I spoke to you about, and if the modiste can do it for me in a few hours. Send it to me with 5 or 6 straw hats, light and not *dear*. I will be home until noon. Love me. . . .

[Postscript by Verdi, to Cesarino:]

If you were a gentleman you would come with your wife to us for dinner. It is the eve of our departure and you will not deny me this favour. Tell me the hour that suits you. [. . .]

CV I, 40–1

At that dinner Verdi gave Cesarino, with a suitable inscription, the monstrous libretto of *Adelia degli Adimari* with his autograph rebuttal.

Verdi to Clarina Maffei; Busseto, 12 May 1858

I have been back from Naples ten or twelve days and I would have written you at once, if I had not been forced to make some trips to Parma and to Piacenza. Now I am here and, after the upheavals of Naples, this profound peace is more dear to me than ever. It is impossible to find an uglier place than this, but on the other hand it is impossible for me to find for myself a place where I can live with greater freedom; and then, this silence which leaves time for thinking, and this never seeing uniforms of any colour is also a good thing! I had intended to go to Venice for the bathing season, but since they have invited me to write an opera there, to avoid annoyance I will stay here. I will return to Naples perhaps in the autumn, and to Rome at Carnival, if the Censorship there will allow the opera that

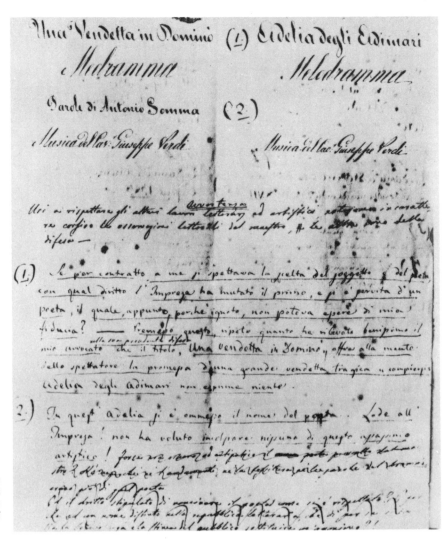

Verdi, *Un ballo in maschera*, 1859 (*Una vendetta in domino*, 1858). Parallel text of Somma's original libretto and the San Carlo management's mangled version, *Adelia degli Adimari*, with Verdi's notes. CV II, 240.

was written for Naples; if not, so much the better, for thus I will not write even next Carnival. From *Nabucco* on I have not had, you could say, an hour's peace. Sixteen years of the galleys!

Give me, dear Clarina, your news at length, and of your health: tell me about things in Milan, and what life is like there now. It has been ten years since I saw that city, which I loved so much, and where I spent my youth and began my career! How many memories, dear and sad!! Who knows when I shall see it!
COP, 572

Even before leaving Naples, Verdi had been in touch with his Roman friend the sculptor Luccardi and, through him, with the impresario of the Teatro Apollo, Jacovacci. Curiously, the Rome Censor had allowed a play called *Gustavo III* to be performed, so Verdi – and Jacovacci – had hopes that, under some title or other, *Una vendetta in domino* would be permitted.

Telegram from Vincenzo Jacovacci to Verdi in Parma, and by post to Busseto; Rome, 8 June 1858

Am negotiating to obtain title Duca di Stettino protagonist your opera will write soon conclusion which hope favourable to signing our contract.
COP, 572

Verdi to Somma; Busseto, 8 July 1858

I am planning to make a trip to Venice to talk once again about the libretto. The Rome Censorship has made new concessions, and I would like to see this opera performed and, as I wrote you before, after everything that has happened, Rome is preferable to anywhere else. [. . .]
P.S. The Censorship would allow the subject and situations, etc. etc., but would like the setting shifted outside of Europe. What would you say to North America at the time of the English domination? If not America, another place. The Caucasus perhaps?
PASC, 92

Vigna to Verdi; Venice, late July 1858

[. . .] Somma is working tirelessly. Every now and then, however, he becomes angry with that damned Censorship. He is wrong: I shout him down and say it must be forgiven all, and we cannot honestly speak ill of it after the benefit it has procured us. Without it and its logic we would not have enjoyed three delightful days. [. . .]
AB II, 505

Somma to Verdi; Venice, 11 August 1858

[. . .] It is all right to take away from Riccardo the title of Duca di Surrey; I have nothing against that, but you must grant me at least that he be a Count. The Censorship itself had converted the protagonist into a Conte di Göthemburg: so I believe such a title will find no opposition: so if you do not mind we will call him Riccardo Conte di Warwick....

AB II, 506

On his way to Naples to stage *Simon Boccanegra*, Verdi found time to write to Escudier.

Verdi to Léon Escudier; Genoa, 20 October 1858

You speak to me of the theatre?... and of writing for the Opéra?!!... You?!!... Let us speak open-heartedly, and allow me to say everything I feel.

1. I am not sufficiently rich or sufficiently poor to write for your major theatre. Not sufficiently poor to need those scant earnings; not sufficiently rich to lead a comfortable life in a country where the expenses are very great.

2. For the Opéra I wrote *Vespri* and translated two operas, with an outcome neither too hostile nor favourable. If they hope for or demand any better of me they are deceiving themselves. Now as then (I say this to you in confidence, into your ear) I have some facility in inventing *tunes*, but these do not seem the right merchandise for the Opéra. Later perhaps I will not invent them any more, and then I too will write some *brum brums* for orchestra. You'll see! In *Vespri* there are two or three real *tunes*, whether beautiful or ugly, Perhaps for this reason the score is lying on the shelf. [. . .]

AB II, 512–13

Boccanegra in Naples was an immense success, on 30 November 1858. Verdi and Giuseppina stayed in the city through the month of December.

Verdi to De Sanctis; Civitavecchia, 12 January 1859

We spent an infernal night and we reached port this morning at half-past ten, which means almost nineteen hours at sea! Peppina was very ill; the great Lulù also suffered; only I gave nothing to the sea, but that *illness*, and then sixteen hours lying down, unable to move!... Furious, cold wind, and water everywhere. Now it's two o'clock and too late to go to Rome. I'll leave tomorrow morning at seven with a post coach. [. . .]

AB II, 515

151 On 17 February 1859, premiere of *Un ballo in maschera* – now set in Boston – at the Teatro Apollo, Rome. The opera was a success with the first-night audience, less so with the press. But trouble was ahead. The husband of the soprano Eugénie Julienne-Dejean (the Amelia of the opera) wrote to his friend Escudier.

J. Dejean to Léon Escudier; Rome, 22 February 1859

The 3rd performance did not take place, but instead I must tell you what did happen, and I urge you to stigmatize in your paper the behaviour of Roman authority.

Already at the 2nd performance [the baritone] Giraldoni had a bad cold and expressed his fear of not being able to sing the following day, Sunday, and asked them not to post *Un ballo in maschera* without consulting him. At 9 in the morning the Impresario asked news of him. Giraldoni

answered that he could not sing. The poster was kept up, and the authorities sent a doctor, who, having no other medical opinion but the needs of the manager (who gives him boxes for his family), declared that he could sing.

At 4 o'clock the manager sends word to Giraldoni that, the doctor having declared he could sing, he must sing. Giraldoni, *without a single note*, refuses again. At 5 o'clock the representative of the Deputation comes to insist that he had to sing. Another refusal, based on total lack of voice. Complete aphony.

At 6 o'clock they send a carriage for him. Another refusal. At 7 o'clock the police come. Forward march! He dresses, he goes on stage, and after some vain efforts to utter a sound, he bows to the public, saying 'I was forced.' He takes off his costume and goes home, where from that moment a policeman has established residence, and only after much begging, in the antechamber and not in the bedroom, as he had been ordered.

Giraldoni is French. He has committed no crime, and his domicile has been violated, despite my objections to the French Ambassador, the French Prefect of Police, Giraldoni is still under guard at his house, and our French authorities allow it. [. . .]

The house was full. Verdi was to be crowned, and the work's success was launched at full steam. [. . .] The new work was replaced by *Norma* – which began at 9 o'clock and ended with *4* people in the stalls.

The money had to be returned and the whole house emptied, except for the subscribers in the boxes, who didn't yet have their carriages. [. . .]

MS, OPÉRA, PARIS

On 26 April 1859 war broke out between Piedmont and Austria. Napoleon III involved himself on the Piedmontese (i.e. the Italian) side. The Duchy of Parma was still in the Austrian sphere of influence.

Giuseppina Strepponi to De Sanctis; Busseto, 21 May 1859

We are at Sant'Agata. Verdi has received several letters from you and says he answered them regularly: so one must have been lost, nor I am surprised these days, when communications are interrupted, and hardships, as far as letters and papers are concerned, immense.

We thank you; and thank our friends in our name for their affectionate interest. We are in good health, without fear, but worried about the grave things that are happening. This morning at eight the drawbridges were raised, and the gates closed at Piacenza, which is about 18 miles from us. Part of the Franco-Piedmontese Army is coming down to attack that fortress and we will hear tomorrow, perhaps this evening, the thunder of cannon. Everything is being prepared to make this a war of giants. Verdi is serious, grave, but calm and trusting in the future. I am surely more uneasy, more anxious, but I am a woman and of a more lively temperament. I send you half a dozen kisses for Caterina and half a dozen for Peppino. Teach him to say Peppina Verdi for this coming autumn. [. . .]

CV I, 61

This last sentence is an oblique reference to the fact that Giuseppina and Verdi were finally about to be married. Secretly, they went to the Piedmontese village of Collonges-sous-Salève on 29 August 1859, and were 162 married by a distinguished priest of their acquaintance,

Abbé Mermillod of nearby Geneva. In 1860 Collonges, with all Savoy, was to become part of France. Years later, after the unification of Italy, Verdi, concerned to know whether his marriage was also valid by Italian law, wrote to his friend, the parliamentarian Piroli, about it, as usual spelling proper names incorrectly.

Verdi to Piroli, 27 October 1868

Collange is in Savoy, perhaps two miles from Geneva.

And if Savoy, in August 1859, was still part of Piedmont, the marriage (as you say) should be quite valid. It was registered in the ledgers of that parish with two witnesses, but not by the village pastor. That priest *Mermillot* Rector of Notre-Dame de Genève, who dealt with everything that had to be dealt with completely, wanted to celebrate the marriage (sending the village pastor out for a stroll) perhaps to receive the profits all alone. [. . .]

CV III, 57

Subscription initiated by Verdi; Sant'Agata, 20 June 1859

The victories so far achieved by our brave Brothers have not been without bloodshed, and therefore without supreme sorrow for thousands of Families! At times like these, anyone who has an Italian heart must assist, according to his own powers, the cause that is being fought.

I propose a subscription in favour of the wounded; and of the poor families of those who are dying for the fatherland.

G. Verdi.

Giuseppe Verdi for 25 Nap. gold –	fr. 550
Giuseppina Verdi for four Nap. gold –	fr. 83
Carlo Verdi –	fr. 22
[. . .]	
Antonio Barezzi for 4 Nap. gold –	83

COP, 577

Verdi to Clarina Maffei; Busseto, 23 June 1859

For ten or twelve days I have wanted to write to you, but after those Illustrious ones blew up the forts of Piacenza, so many things have happened and are happening in this shell, so many alarms, so much news both true and false, that there is never a moment's peace. Finally they have left! Or at least they have gone off, and may our good star send them even farther off, until, driven beyond the Alps, they go and enjoy their climate, their sky, which I hope will be beautiful, clear, resplendent even more than ours. How many wonders in a few days! It doesn't seem true. And who would have believed in such generosity from our allies? For myself, I confess and say: *mea grandissima culpa*, that I did not believe the French would come into Italy, and that, in any case, they would have shed, without thought of conquest, their blood for us. On the first count I was mistaken; I hope and wish to be mistaken on the second, that Napoleon may not contradict the Milan proclamation. Then I will worship him as I worshipped Washington, and even more; and, blessing the great nation, I will gladly tolerate all their *blague*, the insolent *politesse*, and the contempt they have for everything that is not French.

Day before yesterday a poor priest (the only right-minded person in all this countryside) brought me the greetings of Montanelli, whom he had met in Piacenza, a plain soldier among the volunteers. The former professor of national law who sets such a noble example! That is beautiful, sublime!

COP, 577–8

Verdi's admiration for Napoleon III was short-lived. On 12 July 1859, the French Emperor signed the treaty of Villafranca, which gave the Austrians continued domination over Venice and favoured an Italian Confederation with the Pope as President. Victor Emanuel signed the treaty. Verdi's political idol, Count Camillo Cavour, resigned as chief minister of Piedmont. Verdi – like many other Italians – was outraged.

Verdi to Clarina Maffei; Busseto, 14 July 1859

Instead of singing a hymn to glory, it would seem to me more suitable to raise a lament on the eternal misfortunes of our country.

Along with your letter I received a Bulletin of the 12th which says . . . [. . .] Peace is made . . . Venice remains Austrian!!

So where is the long-hoped-for and promised independence of Italy? What does the proclamation of Milan mean? Or is Venice not Italy? After so many victories what a result! So much blood for nothing! so many poor young people disappointed! And Garibaldi who has even sacrificed his long-standing, constant opinions in favour of a King without achieving the desired goal. It's enough to drive one mad! I write in the grip of the deepest dismay and don't know what I'm saying. It is then quite true that we will never be able to hope for anything from foreigners, of whatever country! [. . .]

COP, 579

In accordance with the treaty, all the municipalities of the Duchy of Parma voted to confer the government on the patriot and statesman Luigi Carlo Farini and to hold an election for delegates to the Assembly of the Provinces of Parma. The election took place on 4 September and Verdi was chosen, by the citizens of Busseto, to represent them.

Verdi to the Mayor of Busseto; Sant'Agata, 5 September 1859

The honour that my fellow-citizens have chosen to confer on me, nominating me as their representative at the Assembly of the Provinces of Parma, flatters me and makes me very grateful. If my scant talents, my studies, the art I profess make me little suited to this sort of task, may at least the great love I have borne and bear our noble and unhappy Italy be of value. [...]

COP, 580

The Assembly met in Parma on 7 September and five days later voted unanimously in favour of Parma's annexation to Piedmont. A delegation – including Verdi – was chosen to go to Turin and present to the King the decision of the inhabitants of the Duchy. On this occasion, through the British Minister, Sir James Hudson, Verdi met Cavour, then in temporary retirement.

Camillo Cavour to his agent Corio; Leri, 16 September 1859

Hudson writes to me that the famous composer Verdi, author of *Il trovatore, Traviata*, etc., will come tomorrow by the first train to Leghorn, with the intention of paying me a visit. He is a European celebrity, I believe you will be pleased to accompany him, and so I will not send my

carriage. If this creates difficulties for you, send me an express letter and I will send my horses in time tomorrow.
COP, 582

Verdi to Cavour; Busseto, 21 September 1859

May Your Excellency forgive the boldness and the tedium that I perhaps cause you with these few lines. For a long time I had wished to know personally the Prometheus of our nation; nor did I despair of finding the opportunity to satisfy this fervent desire of mine.

What, however, I would not have dared hope for is the straightforward and kindly welcome with which Your Excellency deigned to honour me.

I left, moved! I shall never forget that Leri of yours, where I had the honour of shaking the hand of the great man of State, the supreme citizen, he whom every Italian will have to call father of the country. Receive kindly, Excellency, these sincere words of the poor artist who has no other merit save that of loving and having always loved his own fatherland.
COP, 582

Things were still not peaceful in the Parma region. In the city itself a reactionary colonel had been put to death by the mob. Napoleon III wanted the Bourbon Duchess Regent, Louise de Berry, to be reinstated. The communities were arming local militia.

Verdi to Mariani; Busseto, 25 October 1859

I have received your very dear letter and *Il Movimento*, and though your letter is dismaying, I refuse to plunge into despair as yet. We shall see! Meanwhile let us talk of other things. You know that in Turin Sir Hudson gave me a letter for Signor Clemente Corte, officer under Garibaldi, to direct me where to buy rifles. Signor Corte accepted the task with a very kindly letter of 28 September and at the same time sent me a telegraphic despatch he had received in the matter from the firm of Danovaro of Genoa: 'Ready perhaps 6000 different kinds, mostly English, price 23 to 30 francs [. . .]'.

After this letter and despatch I wrote to Corti on 2 October to order for the present 100 rifles. With another letter on 18 October I ordered another 72, all to be shipped to Castel San Giovanni, where I would send someone to collect them [. . .].

I have received no answer. [. . .]
COP, 584

So Mariani was charged with tracking down the missing rifles.

Verdi to De Sanctis; Sant'Agata, 17 December 1859

[. . .] We are still here amid a yard of snow and 10 degrees of cold.

What do you say to that, you inhabitant of a mild climate? So it is, but any moment we will go to Genoa, where one lives as well, perhaps, as in Naples.

After returning from Rome I have written no more music, seen no more music, thought no more of music. I don't even know what colour my last opera is and I hardly remember it. So tell [the impresario] Zarlatti that I wouldn't know how to pick up a pen to manufacture notes, and let him think of other things. [. . .]
CV I, 66

Verdi to Leon Escudier; Genoa, 10 February 1860

Peppina has received *Le Bon Domestique* and *Le Journal des demoiselles*, but has not received the bill, as she asked you. But now you will repair this oversight by adding that bill to another you will make for me, of which I will now speak to you. Open your ears then, hold your breath, and listen. Since I no longer manufacture notes I plant cabbages and beans, etc. etc., but, this occupation no longer sufficing for me, I have taken to shooting!!!!!! that is to say, when I see a bird, *Bang!* I shoot; if I hit, good; if I don't, good night. I am supplied with good Saint-Etienne guns, but now I have got the whim of having a double-barrelled *Le Faucheux*, Double System: that is to say, *old system* loading with powder and shot, along with *the so-called Le Faucheux system*, with cartridges. [. . .] Good hunters shoot straight even with mediocre guns, but a Music Master needs a weapon that shoots straight by itself. [. . .]
AB II, 568

The year 1860 was crucial to Italian unification. Cavour returned to office on 21 January. On 12 March the people of Parma voted once again for annexation to Piedmont. The town councillors of Busseto voted to show their devotion to their new king by presenting him with a cannon.

Verdi to the town councillors; Sant'Agata, 28 April 1860

The Township of Busseto did a most praiseworthy thing in voting and donating a cannon to the King, who will surely prefer it to any other gift. I wish every Italian town would imitate your example, for, not with celebrations and illuminations, but with arms, and with soldiers will we be able to become strong, respected, masters in our own house. And it must not be forgotten that the foreigner, powerful and threatening, is still in Italy.

If I do not accede to the request to set to music the poem sent me it is because, besides feeling little suited to composing occasional Hymns (and what use would a Hymn be?), I could not do so without deeply offending the city governments of Turin and Milan to whom I gave a negative answer, though I was asked repeatedly. [. . .]
MARV, 265

Verdi to Tito Ricordi; Busseto, 4 May 1860

For several years I have lived in the country in a hut, in such bad condition, so modest, so indecent, I would almost say, that I am ashamed to show it even to my most intimate friends; and you, who have seen it, know that I am telling the truth. For three years I have wanted to have it fixed up, not that I meant to make it a palace or a villa, but simply a decently habitable house.

Various circumstances have prevented me from carrying out so far this project of mine, but several days ago the work began (modest work on which I will not spend more than a few thousand francs of the more than 10 thousand you owe me) and now I would not like to and could not suspend it, also because of the commitment already made to the workmen. You see that I cannot do without this 10 thousand francs. All I can do is have you pay the sum to me not all at once, but in four equal instalments the first of every month beginning 1 June [. . .].
AB II, 578

Verdi to Mariani; Cremona, 23 June 1860

[. . .] Let me know the possible price of a grille of wrought or cast iron, to be put at the windows of the ground floor. They must be 3.0 metres high; 1.20 metres wide. I would need four, or perhaps seven: we will put them at the three big windows of the façade, and on our rooms. They must rest on the ground, be in two leaves, to be set in the wall on a wheel, so that when we want to open them they will not be seen and will disappear into the walls. [. . .]

COP, 545

Verdi to Mariani; Busseto, 28 June 1860

I don't know that I will buy the iron grilles in Genoa, because I am assured that they can be had at Cremona for a better price, and all of Bergamo iron. [. . .]

COP, 545

Verdi to Piave; early November 1860

I was unable to answer your very dear letter because I had rheumatism in my right arm. Now, if not well, I am better and I thank you very, very much for the birthday wishes of 9 October, and a bit less for your congratulations on the success of *Ballo* [in Bologna]. You know, I have never been greatly moved at this sort of business, and now I am so indifferent it is incredible. If some people knew it, they would cry for my crucifixion, would accuse me of being an ingrate and of not loving my art.

Oh no! I worshipped and do worship this art, and when I am by myself, concerned with my notes, then my heart pounds, tears stream from my eyes, and the emotion and the pleasures are unspeakable, but when I think that these poor notes of mine must then be flung before beings without intelligence, before a publisher who sells them to serve then as an object of amusement or scorn to the masses, oh then I no longer love anything! . . . Let us not speak of it.

You haven't said a word to me about Clarina, or about Venturi and his wife! Don't you see them any more? Well, go in my name to visit them and clasp their hands and tell them to remember this peasant who loves them very much. As for you, write to me often, love me. [. . .]

AB II, 591

At the end of 1860 Cavour decided it was time for elections to Italy's first national parliament. Rumour already insisted that Verdi – as an outstanding Italian – would be obliged to stand for the Chamber of Deputies. In an attempt to avoid this assignment, Verdi went, via Genoa, to Turin to see Cavour. He left Giuseppina at home at Sant'Agata.

Giuseppina to Verdi; Sant'Agata, early December 1860

Wretched town! You will not receive the letter written this morning until Thursday perhaps. Cristoforetti today did not make the usual trip for the second post. I am grieved but it is not my fault.

Here it is raining in torrents, uninterruptedly, and I fear in Genoa it will be the same. Poor Verdi, what amusement!

[. . .] Today my stomach left me a bit of peace, but to exercise my patience my tooth waged a great war with me; add the sadness of the weather and you will understand my mood! Today I dined in the dining-room spending about ten minutes on it; this evening I had supper in my

room. The living-room without you is too deserted and that empty place at table saddens me.

As you fall asleep think of me: think of the companion who has lived with you so many years and would like to live with you for as many centuries. Don't make a face. . . I would seek and perhaps find in my heart a way of never being a nuisance or a burden for you, and so as not to be that even at this moment, I say farewell and go to bed. I wish you a peaceful night, and a blue sky tomorrow morning!

AB II, 594

Giuseppina to Verdi; Sant'Agata, early December 1860

[. . .] Here is Luigi with two letters . . . Thank you, my dear Verdi, for your affectionate words, thank you a thousand times! What can I say then about your thoughtfulness in sending me the Hoffmann elixir?! I appreciated it with tears in my eyes, a thousand times more than if you had sent me the most beautiful diamonds in the world. What a heart of gold yours is!!

Loulou greets you and I embrace you tight, as in the *active* period of our life . . . Farewell, my joy.

AB II, 595

Giuseppina to Verdi; Sant'Agata, 5 December 1860

Perhaps when this letter arrives, you will be in Turin, if, as you planned, you definitely intend to see Cavour and Sir James. What it means *to have genius!* . . . One visits Ministers of State and Ambassadors, just as I go to Giovanna's.

And yet the quality that obliges the world to take off its hat to you is the one I never think of, or almost. I swear to you, and it will not be hard for you to believe me, that many times I am almost surprised that you know music! Though this art is divine and your genius worthy of the art you profess, still the talisman that fascinates me and that I worship in you, is your character, your heart, your indulgence for the errors of others, while you are so severe with yourself. Your charity, filled with modesty and mystery – your proud independence and your boyish simplicity, qualities proper to that nature of yours which has been able to retain a fierce virginity of ideas and feelings in the midst of the human cloaca!

O my Verdi, I am not worthy of you, and the love you bear me is a charity, a balm to a heart at times quite sad, beneath the appearances of gaiety. Continue to love me, love me even after I am dead, so that I may present myself to Divine Justice enriched by your love and your prayers, o my Redeemer!

I reread this rambling scrawl, which perhaps I should not send you, but I haven't the heart to recopy it. Though it is the pure expression of my feelings, still I should have written you in another style, and with much more serene thoughts. Forgive this *spleen* which has persecuted me for some time and which is not the predominant fault of my character, but of yours. Oh, at last a fault of yours, a sin of yours. *Enchantée* that you have at least one, or some. I will take care to make a memorandum of it and humiliate you at the first opportunity. [. . .]

Good night, my Pasticcio, amuse yourself but remember that I am at Sant'Agata.

AB II, 595–6

The Verdis' friend Mauro Corticelli, travelling in Russia as secretary to the great Italian actress Adelina Ristori, had met there the famous tenor Enrico Tamberlick, an influential figure in the St Petersburg Italian opera.

161

Enrico Tamberlick (1820–89) in the title role of Rossini's *Otello*, in which he made his Paris debut in 1858. Raccolta Bertarelli, Milan.

Enrico Tamberlick to Verdi; St Petersburg, 11/23 December 1860

The good fortune that so frequently offers me the opportunity of interpreting your stupendous operas has not been equally generous with the pleasure of meeting you. Still I take the liberty of writing to you, and allow me to do so with that unabashed frankness that best corresponds to the long admiration and sincere esteem which I profess towards you. I will leave out therefore the useless formalities that are too far beneath the loftiness of your merit, and renouncing even the use of the very cold *Lei* I address *Voi* with the familiarity of one accustomed to living amid your thoughts and nourishing himself on your harmonies.

I have heard from Corticelli, who has arrived here with Signora Ristori, that it would perhaps not be impossible to persuade you to add another jewel to the splendid crown of your works whose series you threaten to close. As soon as this ray of hope flashed before me I immediately spoke of it with the Director of the Imperial theatres here, Signor Sabouroff, who immediately authorized me to invite you as warmly as I could to reserve one spark of your genius for the theatre of Petersburg. To Signor Sabouroff's invitation and to the hopes of the whole population, I cannot help but mingle a sense of noble selfishness in adding my insistence to the others . . .

The Management of the Opéra of Paris is in fact suggesting to me a three-year contract, and assuming the obligation of offering me the creation of an opera written by a celebrated composer, and I was inclined to accept; but I am suspending all negotiations, nor will it be difficult for you to believe how joyfully I would renounce any other offer to be able, at least once, to be the immediate interpreter of your sublime inspirations. Here the Management offers you all the advantages that you can wish if you agree to write a work for the coming season. You are free to

choose the subject, the poet, you may decide the conditions, the opera remains your property. The public, which adores you without having seen you, will be overjoyed to possess you. I cannot tell you how festively the artists will receive you. . . .

The climate, whatever people say, is not at all to be feared. The delightfully heated apartments make domestic life incomparably more comfortable and pleasant than in any southern land. The carriages and the furs afford stupendous protection against the rigours of the outside atmosphere. [. . .]
AB II, 625

The widower Barezzi, to the dismay of his feckless sons, had recently married his housekeeper, Maddalena.

Giuseppina to Barezzi; Sant'Agata, 31 December 1860

Farewell, tempestuous 1860! Go to join the many years already past while we greet your successor 1861, about to begin. I want to be able to write you another hundred (is that enough?) of these notes of best wishes, and this out of love for you, dear Signor Antonio, and a bit also out of love for me. Though they are spreading the charitable rumour that I have a scirrhus of the pylorus, so far I eat well and digest better. . . . Instead of inventing so many tales, why don't they come and ask directly about my health? . . . They would write my history with a bit more truth and justice. [. . .]

We love you always despite your grave sins towards us, some of which are no longer coming to dinner in the summer because it's hot, in the winter because it's cold, sighing when you are with us the moment the sun sets, to make sure that cursed shop of yours hasn't run off from Busseto. . . . Wish every happiness to your Maddalena. She deserves it for her constant and *sincere* goodness.
AB II, 598–9

After some difficulties with another local candidate, an acquaintance of his and Giuseppina's, Verdi felt obliged to announce his candidacy for the first Italian Parliament. He was elected on 3 February 1861. One of his fellow-parliamentarians was his old friend Count Opprandino Arrivabene. 164, 166

Verdi to Arrivabene; Busseto, 11 February 1861

On Thursday 14th I shall be in Turin, and if I am not being too bold, I would ask you to tell [the hotel-keeper] Trombetta that I would need a little sitting-room, a bedroom and a little adjoining room because I will come with my wife and her maid. I would plan to stay in the Hotel, if the prices are artistic, all the time I remain in Turin [. . .]
ALB, 3

Meanwhile discussions of the possibility of an opera for Russia were going forward. Whether for financial reasons, or for reasons of national prestige, Verdi was interested. He suggested Hugo's *Ruy Blas* as a possible subject, but this was refused. For a moment, negotiations seemed to end.

Verdi to Tamberlick; Turin, early March 1861

I am in Turin, as perhaps you know. I received your

telegram a bit late, because it was forwarded from Parma. I hope you have already received the reply, and I will make myself clearer by letter.

Since *Ruy Blas* is impossible in St Petersburg I find myself in the greatest difficulty. I have rummaged through many, many dramas without finding one that suits me completely. I cannot and will not sign a contract before finding a subject adapted to the artists I would have in St Petersburg, and approved by the Authorities. Unable therefore to settle anything for the moment, time will perhaps be too short to write for next winter. I realize the Management will want to be free of the uncertainty, and in this case they are free to do as they please. [. . .]

After St Petersburg are you coming to Italy, and if so where are you going? If we could meet we would understand each other much better. [. . .]
AB II, 628–9

Giuseppina to Mauro Corticelli; Turin, 17 April 1861

[. . .] We have met Signor Achille Tamberlick [son of Enrico], an educated young man, likeable, distinguished, and of a patience! . . . oh what patience! For that matter this patience shows that he knows the human heart and knows how true is the word of the Gospel which says *knock and it shall be opened unto you*. He came, he saw the terrain not too favourable and he swore to conquer despite the fact that Verdi, after the veto on the subject imposed through that famous telegram, was much more concerned with the Chamber than with the Theatre.

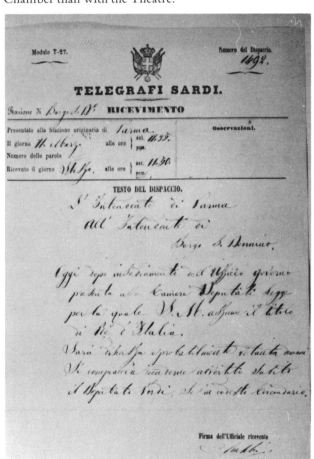

Telegram from Parma instructing the local authorities at Borgo San Donnino to inform Verdi, as a Deputy, of the law by which Victor Emanuel of Piedmont assumed the title of King of Italy, 11 March 1861. Private collection.

Then he gently began his mission, rectifying the error of the telegram and declaring with the greatest calm that [Verdi] could compose *Ruy Blas* or whatever he liked, since he [Tamberlick] had instructions to grant him all possible conditions he might ask, except that of obliging the Emperor Alexander to proclaim a Republic in Russia.

Verdi scratched his head, pointing out to him that for *Ruy Blas* there was such-and-such a difficulty; that for the other dramas leafed-through there was such-and-such another; that a certain drama, read in the past, which had pleased him, was impossible to find. . . . Enough! . . . Once the title was said, there we were, all of us, making the rounds of the booksellers, to *bouquiner* throughout Turin, leaving no alley unexplored. Nothing! It cannot be found! [. . .]

Now, then, the chances are ninety per cent that Verdi will write for St Petersburg. In this probability I have already begun having lined, altered, be-furred dresses, petticoats, bodices and chemises . . . [. . .]
AB II, 630

The drama that could not be found in Turin was almost certainly *Don Alvaro o la fuerza del sino* (1835) by Angel Pérez de Saavedra, Duque de Rivas. Eventually it was found, and on 3 June 1861, from Paris, Verdi was sent the contract.

Contract with the Russian Imperial Theatre; Paris, 3 June 1861

The General Direction of the Imperial Theatres of Russia engages Maestro Chevalier Verdi to write an opera for the Imperial Theatre of St Petersburg on the following conditions:

1. Monsieur Verdi must be in St Petersburg to rehearse his opera in time so that the first performance may take place early in January 1862 new style.

2. The Management accepts the poem *D. Alvaro ou la Forza del Destino* or others that Monsieur Verdi will deem suitable.

3. Monsieur Verdi will have his choice among the artists engaged in St Petersburg to cast the roles in his opera.

4. Costumes and sets will be completely new and as usual there will be a dress rehearsal equivalent to a first performance.

5. The Imperial Management of St Petersburg will have the right to make a copy of the score whose rights will be granted to it for all the Russian Empire.

6. It is understood that the rights remain to Monsieur Verdi for all the other parts of the world.

7. Monsieur Verdi will be paid sixty thousand francs in gold in three equal instalments, the first on his arrival in St Petersburg, the second at the first rehearsal, the third at the dress rehearsal.

The Management commits itself to paying Monsieur Piave for the libretto between two and three thousand francs. [. . .]
BSV IV, 307

Gazzetta del Popolo, Turin, 7 June 1861

The death of Count Cavour took place yesterday at 7 a.m. The King and the Prince of Carignano had been long at his bedside during the same night. Already the day before all hope of recovery was lost: still the announcement of the death had the effect of an unexpected thunderbolt. 165

Grief and consternation were general. In the batting of an eye most of the shops were closed. The people of all classes without exception felt stricken by an irreparable calamity.

Throughout the course of his illness Cavour maintained a steady calm. He spoke sensibly and clear-sightedly. He himself asked for Padre Giacomo to confide to him that his conscience was secure. And when all his affairs were in order, he began speaking again with the political men of Italy.

And repeatedly he ended his discussion with these words: Oh! but the thing is working! Rest assured the thing is working!

ALB, 8

Verdi to Tamberlick; Turin, 12 June 1861

I have arrived at this moment in Turin and I find here your letter and the contracts, waiting several days.

The misfortune which strikes us is so great that I cannot get over it. I have no head for reading or speaking of business. I will write to you in a few days' time; for that matter you may consider the thing settled; I will add the clause that you ask for in the case of illness.

As for the two Spanish dramas you suggest I read, please send them to me by registered mail because I would not find them here. Send them to me in Turin and very quickly. [. . .]

MARTIN, 324

Verdi to Arrivabene; Busseto, 14 June 1861

Cavour's obsequies were celebrated on Thursday with all the pomp that could be expected of this little town.

The clergy officiated gratis, which is no small thing.

I attended the gloomy ceremony in full mourning, but the lacerating mourning was in my heart.

Inter nos I could not restrain my tears and I wept like a child. . . .

Poor Cavour! and poor us. [. . .]

ALB, 9

Giuseppina to Corticelli; Busseto, 17 July 1861

The St Petersburg affair was almost settled, as I told you in my letter of 17 April, when Tamberlick came to Turin; now it is finally signed and I am surprised you have heard no more about it.

Well then, if the Devil doesn't come and get us first, we will all meet in the perpetual *sorbets* of St Petersburg. Verdi says he was an an idiot to sign that contract, because it obliges him to work, and therefore, to sweat too much in the summer, to go then and cool off too much in the winter. It will require quite perfect *tagliatelle* and *maccheroni* to keep him in a good humour amid the ice and the furs.

I, meanwhile, to avoid all squalls, have decided to agree with him always from mid-October till the end of January, foreseeing that during the toil of writing and the rehearsals there will be no way of convincing him he is wrong even once! When the weather seems too dark, however, I'll go out for air. Wait! . . . I was forgetting that the air of Russia freezes the nose! I'll go to bed, the only locality where I believe you can be comfortable in those boreal regions.

By the way, before I forget: if la Ristori expects *to surpass, to predominate* with her *tagliatelle*, Verdi plans to outshine her with the risotto which truly he knows how to prepare divinely. Inasmuch as, despite your wanderings and the *entourage* of so many grand thespians, you remain what you

were, an excellent friend, we gladly take advantage of your offers and beg you to purchase some provisions also for us.

We will stay in Russia about three months, that is from 1 November through January 1862, and there will be four of us eating, Master, Mistress and two servants. If the Interpreter is indispensable and if it is the custom to feed him, instead of four we will be five. Could you, in proportion to this number, supply us with the provisions you arrange for la Ristori in the following items: *Rice, Maccheroni, Cheese, Salumi* and those objects you know cannot be found in Russia or are found at an exorbitant price. As for the wine, here are the number of bottles and the types Verdi would like: 100 small bottles *Bordeaux* for meals; 20 bottles fine *Bordeaux*; 20 bottles *Champagne*.

Perhaps it will be less bother for you to make more abundant provisions for La Ristori and cede to us the superfluous part, necessary for us. I will settle the accounts with you then on arrival in St Petersburg, since I have risen from the rank of singer to that of housewife, a station far more dear to me, nor will you, who know me, have trouble believing it, knowing how little I loved the boards of the stage.

Don't accuse me of being prosaic! Mind you, there can be as much poetry in the modest, and so to speak solitary, domestic occupations as in that sort of delirium that one feels and at times communicates from the stage to the crowded audience.

AB II, 643

Piave came to Busseto in July and began work on the libretto of *Forza*. Summoned back to Milan, he continued to work on the libretto there, exchanging letters with Verdi, who, as usual, was demanding modifications and condensations.

Piave to Verdi; Milan, 9 August 1861

I accept with joy your variations on the duet. I have made, and I hope with effect, all those you asked me in your previous letter, indicated here and there throughout the first act, except the verse

'Soffrire, luce ed anima'
[To suffer, light and soul]

which, I confess, I wouldn't know how to improve on; but I will think about it.

If you want me to send you this whole first act corrected, write me and I'll send it. Meanwhile I have worked on the second act in which I am, *I believe*, at a good point, but I proceed slowly because I would like to avoid, if I could, your inexorable pincers.

What I will not attempt to begin far from you is the camp scene, where, though I am an old warrior (see the Regidora's [Giuseppina's] special opinions on my martial valour) . . . [illegible] without having you as Fellow-soldier.

I conclude; I spend time only at my desk and in the theatre, and I burn like a Mongibello [Etna] with the desire not to try your patience to which I do not cease to recommend myself. In short this is a genre à la Tacitus, in which one does not advance so easily. However, I wish, wish, wish to succeed.

AB II, 648

Verdi to Piroli; Sant'Agata, 12 October 1861

My estate agent will tell you about an action, whether

illegal or cowardly I don't know, taken against me. While my peasants in the courtyard of my house in Busseto were pressing the grapes, to pass the time, they were singing. The National Guard called the Carabinieri and, together, they imposed silence on those poor devils. Is there a law that prohibits you from singing in your own house? And if this law does exist, shouldn't one be warned with a bit of civility before its being imposed by armed force? Tell me what can be done, after you have carefully questioned my agent. I am disgusted, and reluctant to swallow this insult (and it is not the first) from my amiable fellow-citizens. Write to me at once.

How are you getting on? I am writing day and night to finish the opera for St Petersburg. [. . .]

CV III, 18

Piave to Verdi; Milan, 11 November 1861

My dear Bear, All goes very well. I await with impatience the divine Regidora with whom I will arrive at Sant'Agata to give you a kiss and complete any little changes if you need them.

My Angel, you've also finished Act III!!! It's useless; you were born to command even inspirations; you are a true tyrant. . . .

AB II, 665

Verdi to Escudier; Busseto, 22 November 1861

The 28 or 29 of this month I will be with Peppina in Paris, where I will stay only two days, before continuing my journey to Berlin and St Petersburg. Book me a couple of rooms at the Hôtel des Italiens, or in some other hotel in the vicinity.

Do me the favour also of taking the enclosed letter to *Laurent Richard* and ask him also to cut out at once a black evening suit for me, *pantalon, gilet, frach*, so that I can have a fitting as soon as I arrive, and he will finish it at once because I want to leave the evening of the 30.

MS, OPÉRA, PARIS

From the diary of Count Oldoini, Chargé d'affaires for Piedmont at St Petersburg

[. . .] Winter is the season of high society, many parties and balls, theatres very well-attended and very good, splendid receptions at Court with 3000 guests, with all seated for supper, superb service, one frequently gives dinner, and excellent dinners with French chefs of the first rank. The society is very cordial and very hospitable towards foreigners, especially Diplomats.

I have spoken of the Theatres. There is a taste for the Theatre in Russia, and there are the Italians, the French, the Germans, the Russians, all Imperial Theatres and very good. The Italian Opera in winter, like Covent Garden in summer, becomes the foremost theatre in the world. The leading Artists are engaged at exorbitant fees, and about twenty Operas are sung every year by a double and triple troupe of the first rank. The *mise en scène* of Operas and Ballets costs at times even hundreds of thousands of francs. The Theatre is very dear in St Petersburg, eight roubles (thirty-two francs) for the parterre, the boxes in proportion. The Emperor attends performances every evening with the Court, the Ministers, and many important persons are in the parterre in uniform, bedecked and bemedalled. The Ladies in the boxes, very elegant. [. . .]

BSV IV, 17

Giuseppina to Arrivabene; St Petersburg, 20 January/1 February 1862

I would have liked to initiate correspondence with you in quite a different way. Surely the news I am about to give you will make you open, all at once, eyes, mouth and ears! But though you may exclaim in every key with basso profondo voice, oh! ih! and ah!, the news is none the less true – Verdi will not give his new opera in St Petersburg . . . this year!

Alas! singers' voices are fragile as . . . (I leave you to finish the sentence) and the voice of Signora La Grua is, to her misfortune and Verdi's, a depressing example of this fragility. Now then, lacking the prima donna for whom it was written, and there being here no other singer suited for the part, Verdi asked that the contract be dissolved. This request was answered with a broad, long *no*, though preceded, followed, and spiced with the most beautiful phrases in the world. Then they agreed to give the opera next winter, on condition that etc., etc. etc.

Here then is Verdi condemned to facing 24, 26, 28 and more degrees of cold, Réaumur thermometer! And yet this frightful cold hasn't inconvenienced us in the least, thanks to the apartments: *the cold is seen, but not felt*. Mind you, however: this strange contradiction is a boon reserved for the rich, who can actually exclaim: Long live the cold, ice, sled, and other terrestrial joys! But the poor in general, and coachmen in particular, are the unhappiest creatures in the universe! Think, Count, that many coachmen sometimes spend whole days and a part of the night, motionless on their box, exposed to a mortal cold, awaiting their masters who are revelling in warm and splendid apartments, while some of those wretches are perhaps killed by the cold! These atrocious cases happen every year! I can never accustom myself to the sight of such suffering! . . . [. . .]

ALB 13–14

Verdi to Escudier; St Petersburg, 29 January 1862

On receiving this letter of mine you will burst into loud laughter at my fruitless journey to St Petersburg. So it is [. . .] Rather than give the opera with a woman in poor health like la Lagrua, or with another unsuited to the part, I prefer to swallow these four thousand miles and I will come back next September to St Petersburg to open about the middle of November. Then I will be able to leave again before the great cold arrives and be back in Paris at the end of November or early December.

Within the week I will go to see Moscow and then I will leave at once for Italy. Towards the middle of February or perhaps earlier, I will be in Paris.

BSV V, 716

At about the time of his arrival in Paris, Verdi was commissioned to write an occasional piece for the 1862 London International Exhibition, to represent Italy, along with Giacomo Meyerbeer (Germany), Daniel Auber (France) and William Sterndale Bennett (England). Also in Paris in that period were the young composers Franco Faccio and Arrigo Boito, fresh from the Milan conservatory and armed with letters of introduction to Verdi from Clarina Maffei. Both were later to become important in Verdi's life, Faccio as a conductor, and Boito as the librettist of *Otello* and *Falstaff*. Verdi asked Boito to provide him with a text for a cantata, which became the *Inno delle nazioni*.

1862

Verdi to Arrigo Boito; Paris, 29 March 1862

In thanking you for the excellent job done for me, I take the liberty of offering you, as a sign of esteem, this humble watch. Accept it cordially, as it is cordially offered. May it remind you of my name, and of the value of time.

Greet Faccio and glory and fortune to you both!

NARDI, 91

Verdi to the editor of The Times; London, 23 April 1862

Just arrived in London, I hear that in one of your articles of the 19th inst. it is stated that of the four composers who were to write each a piece of music for the opening of the International Exhibition I am the only one who has not yet sent in mine. I beg to say that this is not the fact. On the 5th inst. a gentleman appointed by me wrote to the secretary, Mr Sandford, that my composition was in his hands completely finished, and at the disposal of Her Majesty's Commissioners. I have not composed a march, as was first arranged, because Auber told me in Paris that he was composing one. I composed instead a vocal solo with choruses which Tamberlik kindly offered himself to sing. I thought that this change would not have distressed the Royal Commissioners but instead they intimated that 25 days (sufficient time to learn a new opera) was not enough time to learn this small piece, and refused to accept it. I wish to state this fact not to give any importance to a transaction itself of no consequence, but only to rectify the mistake that I have not sent in my composition.

I should be very much obliged if you will make this public, by inserting this in your most valuable paper.

TIMES 24 APR 1862

Verdi to Arrivabene; London, 2 May 1862

I expected you to congratulate me, since my Cantata was not given at the Exhibition, but instead you attach to this affair an importance which, in my view, it does not have. I have always thought, and think, that these occasional pieces are, artistically speaking, detestable things; and, believe me, in these vast halls, attention is too distracted, and nothing can, and, let me say, nothing did have any effect. [. . .]

As for Italy, her music does not need to be represented at the Exhibition. It is represented here every evening in two Theatres, and not only here, but everywhere; because despite the present decadence discovered by the *Savants!* never in any period have there been so many Italian Theatres as in this, never have the Publishers in whatever country printed and sold so much Italian music, and there is no corner of the earth, where there is a theatre and a couple of instruments, where Italian opera is not sung. When you go to the Indies and the interior of Africa you will hear *Il trovatore.* [. . .]

I have been once to the Exhibition but everything is in too great disorder for me to be able to say anything about it.

So far the most interesting things are shattered packing cases, rolls of paper, heaps of straw, porters you have to steer clear of if you don't want your ribs broken, and drops of water that fall from the glass roof to cool the noses of the curious. [. . .]

ALB, 15

Finally, the *Inno delle nazioni* was performed at Her Majesty's Theatre on 24 May 1862.

Verdi to Arrivabene; London, 30 May 1862

I didn't write to you about the *Cantata* because it would have seemed to me to be giving it an importance it does not have. It was performed for two evenings and repeated both times. Now as I write it is being performed at a matinee; and tomorrow evening it will be given again in the Theatre. The newspapers large and small have all spoken well of it. That's all.

ALB, 19

Verdi to Mariani; Sant' Agata, 1 August 1862

A very grave misfortune for me has struck us and made us suffer atrociously. Loulou, poor Loulou is dead! Poor creature! The true friend, the faithful, inseparable companion of almost six years of life! so affectionate! so beautiful! Poor Loulou! It is difficult to describe the sorrow of Peppina, but you can imagine it. Fraschini, who was here for five or six days, during the illness of that poor animal must have been very bored and saddened. And you want to come with the Minister [Hudson]?

Heaven knows how happy and honoured I would feel to receive in my house that Man I love and revere so, and you know my words are sincere. But, my dear Mariani, in my house now there is desolation. [. . .]

CV II, 205

Giuseppina to Corticelli; Sant' Agata, August 1862

First and most serious of the things that distress us, and distress me in particular, is the illness of my sister, who has been declared *poitrinaire*. . . . The second affliction (and some perhaps may laugh but I weep still in writing of it) is the loss of my dear Loulou! Four days of atrocious suffering have taken him to rest eternally under a willow in our garden, where you too will come to bid a farewell to the memory of that faithful and charming friend. [. . .] I count, *we* count on seeing you before our departure for St Petersburg. [. . .]

Verdi's health is good and he is orchestrating the opera for Russia.

BSV IV, 737

Verdi to Tito Ricordi; St Petersburg, 28 October/9 November 1862

Last night, Saturday, we had the dress rehearsal. Theatre full. Good performance. Let us hope it remains so tomorrow evening Monday.

ASR, MILAN

On 29 October/10 November 1862, premiere of *La forza del destino* at the Imperial Italian Theatre, St Petersburg.

Journal de Saint-Pétersbourg, 30 October/11 November 1862

[. . .] It is midnight. We have just come from the first performance of the new opera that Maestro Verdi has written especially for the Théâtre italien of St Petersburg. We do not want this number of the paper to go to press without declaring in it the brilliant success obtained by this beautiful work.

We will speak further, at leisure, of this magnificent score and of this evening's performance; but we can declare today the triumph of the Maestro and the ovations given the artists, who – to satisfy the vociferous demands of the whole house – on several occasions drew the famous composer out on the stage, to the sound of enthusiastic cheers and prolonged applause.

We believe that *La forza del destino* is, of all Verdi's works, the most complete, both as to inspiration and the richness of melodies and as to development and orchestration. [. . .]

BSV V, 835

Three days later the same paper, after a detailed and favourable examination of the opera, scene by scene, printed its mature conclusions.

Journal de Saint-Pétersbourg, 2/14 November 1862

[. . .] One cannot but love the music of Verdi, but it would be impossible for one to deny that his latest work is superior to those which preceded it, and opens, as we said in the beginning, thanks to the innovations it comprises, a new era in the composer's fame.

One hears, however, against *La forza del destino*, one reproach which has some importance, if one considers only the question of the work's future vogue; it is said: this is too sad a drama, too grim and too long.

This defect does not disturb us at all, and we do not believe that the vogue of *La forza del destino* will suffer by it. *Les Huguenots, Le Prophète, Il trovatore, Lucrezia Borgia, Otello, Norma, Il giuramento*, etc. . . . are not exactly vaudevilles of a mad gaiety, and their sombre and dramatic cast has not greatly harmed, so far as we know, their glorious career.

We feel certain that *La forza del destino* is destined to have a lasting success, which will increase as more numerous hearings allow the public better to appreciate its various merits and beauties.

The artists were all worthy, and almost equally successful. Our preference goes to Graziani and Mme Barbot as, at the premiere, they, of the first rank, were also preferred by the audience. Tamberlick is quite capable of placing himself soon at their side; but, as we said, the emotion caused him by the responsibility of his role gave him visible trouble on the first night.

He sang with all the maestria of his magnificent talent; but when he was not in the vigorous passages of his role, his voice betrayed an inner trembling in the phrases of tender song, in the sweetly melodic parts where vigour is out of place. [. . .]

BSV V, 855–6

Giuseppina to De Sanctis; St Petersburg, 14/26 November 1862

I was silent, you were silent, he was silent. We have been silent, etc. . . .

It is true I haven't written. Verdi did not write, and you have lost pen, paper, and inkpot. In this reciprocal silence, there are no reproaches to be made, because, if it is a sin, we have all committed it. Since, however, silence of the pen does not mean silence of the heart, so I hope that you and la comariella [Caterina] will love us always, as we love you and have always loved you. You will admire, I hope, the ease of the conjugations and the abundance of verbs.

But let us come to our affairs. The proverb that says: 'no news is good news' is not always exact. This time I give you news, and good!!! *La forza del destino* opened with excellent outcome. Good performance in general by Singers, Chorus, and Orchestra. The Emperor, afflicted

with bronchitis, could come only to the fourth performance.

Your *Compare* [Verdi], however, in the waiting lost nothing, because the Emperor, after having applauded him and called him out himself by name, wanted his Minister to introduce him into his box, and there, so to speak, buried under an *avalanche* of compliments specially from the Empress, who was very cordial and acute in everything she said. You will perhaps believe that all was at an end, with this presentation in the temple? *Niett* (as the Russians say), Saturday Verdi received the Imperial and Royal Order of St Stanislas (Commander's Cross to be worn around the neck) and this without the proposal or intervention of anyone, but through *moto proprio* of the Emperor of all the Russias!!! Doff your hat and bow to the Emperor, to the cultivated public, to the Illustrious Garrison, and good night!

We will leave soon for Spain, where Verdi, after insistent invitations, has agreed to stage the new St Petersburg opera.

He is tired, however, of these colossal perambulations and wants to return to his cavern at Sant'Agata to establish calm and long residence. [. . .]

CV I, 86

Meanwhile preparations were being made for the Roman premiere of *Forza* at Jacovacci's Teatro Apollo.

Report of censor; Rome, 14 November 1862

I have marked with a pencil the proposed corrections, which I have thought advisable for the wretched subject of the opera. If they are not liked, they can easily be erased with sandarac.

All the scenes of begging, since they are simple episodes, outside, indeed detached from the ugly subject, can be removed. The whole, then, is immoral, impolitic, and a sordid compound of modern corruption. [Signature illegible]

MS, AS, ROME

The title of the opera was changed to *Don Alvaro*. Verdi, from Madrid, expressed his concern about the results.

Verdi to Luccardi; Madrid, 13 January 1863

[. . .] I have been in Madrid only two days, and here I will stage *La forza del destino*. I can tell you nothing of this city, but I will write you about the works of art I will see here, and about my opera. You must also write me frequently about this opera, and about the rehearsals and the performance. For the rest I fear greatly, not so much for the musical performance as for the changes that will be made to the libretto. It is an opera of vast dimensions and needs much care. Well, we shall see. Write me in any case, and the very frank truth. [. . .]

COP, 611

Verdi to Luccardi; Madrid, 17 February 1863

I thank you very much both for the telegram sent me and for the letter I have received at this moment. If the opera in Rome went fairly well, it could have gone a thousand times better if Jacovacci could once get it into his head that, to have successes, you need *both operas suited to the artists and artists suited to the operas*. It is certain that in *La forza del*

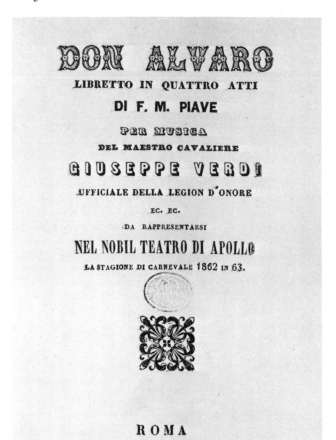

DON ALVARO

LIBRETTO IN QUATTRO ATTI

DI F. M. PIAVE

PER MUSICA

DEL MAESTRO CAVALIERE

GIUSEPPE VERDI

UFFICIALE DELLA LEGION D'ONORE

EC. EC.

DA RAPPRESENTARSI

NEL NOBIL TEATRO DI APOLLO

LA STAGIONE DI CARNEVALE 1862 IN 63.

ROMA

Tip. di G. Olivieri al Corso 336

con permesso

Verdi, *La forza del destino*, 1862 (*Don Alvaro*, 1863). Title page of the libretto as played in Rome. William Weaver Collection, Monte San Savino (AR).

destino it is not necessary to know how to do solfeggi, but you must have spirit and understand the *word* and express it. It is certain that, with a lively soprano, the duet of the 1st act and the aria of the second would also have had success, as well as the Romanza of the fourth and especially the duet with the *Guardiano* of the second act. These are four pieces that failed because of the performance. And four pieces are many and can make the fortune of an opera! The part of *Melitone* is effective from the first word to the last. If Jacovacci has now seen the need of changing the artist who sang that part, he, an old impresario, should have seen it earlier. [. . .]
COP, 612

Verdi to Arrivabene; Paris, 22 March 1863

As soon as I arrived here I found your welcome letter of 5 March and yesterday I received the other of the 20th. I didn't write you at once because I was so tired from the journey that I had to go to bed to rest and to treat also a heavy cough caught during my journey in Andalusia, an extremely uncomfortable, long, and tiring journey. The Alhambra, *in primis et ante omnia*, the cathedrals of Toledo, Cordoba, Seville deserve their reputation. The Escorial (forgive me this blasphemy) I do not like. It is a mass of marble, there are very rich things in the interior, and some very beautiful, including a fresco by Luca Giordano marvellously beautiful, but on the whole good taste is

lacking. It is severe, terrible, like the fierce sovereign who built it. [. . .]
ALB, 24

Verdi to Clarina Maffei; Turin, 31 July 1863

I received your very dear letter just as I was leaving for Italy. I stopped off for two days in Turin, went home, and now I am back in Turin, where I will stay only a few hours. [. . .]

Last year in Paris I saw Boito and Faccio often, and they are surely two young men of great intelligence, but I can say nothing of their musical talent, because of Boito I have never heard anything, and of Faccio only a few things that he came and played for me one day. For that matter, since Faccio will be presenting an opera, the public will pronounce its sentence. These two young men are accused of being very warm admirers of Vagner. Nothing wrong with that, provided admiration does not degenerate into imitation. Vagner is made and it is useless to remake him.

Vagner is not a fierce beast as the purists would have him, nor is he a prophet as his apostles wish. He is a man of great intelligence who takes delight in the difficult ways, because he cannot find the easier and straighter ones. The young must not deceive themselves, there are very many who believe they have wings, because really they lack the legs to stand on their own feet.

Let Faccio put his hand on his heart and paying heed to nothing else, write as it dictates; let him have the boldness to attempt new ways and the *courage* to face opposition. [. . .]
AB II, 755

Clarina Maffei to Verdi; Clusone, 3 September 1863

[. . .] For some time I have owed you an answer to the dear and very beautiful letter you wrote me the last day of July, of which I communicated the conclusion to the young Maestro, and he answered me, moved, 'I will treasure the sincere advice of your illustrious Friend, especially the last counsel which is absolutely sacrosanct. And I will put my hand on my heart and pay heed to nothing else and write what my heart will dictate, and in fact it is because music comes from the heart that it appeals to the masses.'
AB II, 756

Verdi to Tito Ricordi; Sant'Agata, 3 October 1863

I have delayed somewhat in answering you because I find myself involved in fairly serious matters. My estate agent has run off, and you can imagine how troubled I am by all these affairs that must be looked out, attended to, settled, etc.

It is true: I haven't yet sent you the score of *La forza del destino* because I planned to revise the denouement and modify some things at the end of the third act, but so far I have found no solution. I am writing today to Escudier to send me the Romanza composed recently for *Vespri* [a new aria for the tenor in a recent revival of the opera] and to which you will have the rights in the same way and for the same countries as *Vespri*; and you will credit me with the amount you consider just.

Write more operas? And why? To see them performed always, always, in the most barbarous fashion? Do you believe that *Ballo in maschera* has been, I won't say executed, but a bit interpreted, a bit understood? Never. And you saw it in Milan. We must go back to Cavatinas, to duets in thirds, to elaborate Rondòs, or else teach singers how to read music. [. . .] And now it would be the duty of Liceos and

Conservatories not to admit any voice students without having them study literature seriously.

As for the Società del Quartetto I beg you to leave me out of it. You know I am a jackass in music and do not at all understand what the learned baptize as classic. [. . .]
AB II, 744

On 11 November 1863, *I profughi fiamminghi* by Franco Faccio had its premiere at La Scala. Tepid success.

Franco Faccio to Verdi ; 16 November 1863

Countess Maffei has emboldened me to give you myself the news of the good outcome of my first opera. You can imagine that in writing these few lines I feel myself filled with that awed shyness that the very small feels beside the very great; but also, I dare say to you, close to You, who with bold words of faith and hope urged me on, my shyness becomes self-confident and trusting. And I remember always with an artist's emotion your final advice, your final wish, and I know that, moving away from you, I felt myself filled with youthful boldness, and I dared, and I wrote. [. . .]

I beg you to accept also the respectful greetings of my Boito who, like me, hopes and works. [. . .]
AB II, 761

A few days after this letter was written, some friends of Faccio's gave him a festive dinner. On the occasion, Boito read some verses, which were then published.

Museo di famiglia, Milan, 22 November 1863

Alla salute dell'Arte italiana!
Perché la scappi fuora un momentino
Dalla cerchia del vecchio e del cretino,
      Giovane e sana. [. . .]

Forse già nacque chi sovra l'altare
Rizzerà l'arte, verecondo e puro,
Su quell'altar bruttato come un muro
      Di lupanare. [. . .]

To the health of Italian Art!
May it escape for a moment
From the grip of the old and the idiotic,
      Young and healthy. [. . .]

Perhaps he is already born, who, upon the altar
Will set art erect, he, truthful and pure,
On that altar, befouled like the wall
      Of a brothel. [. . .]

NARDI, 128

Verdi to Clarina Maffei ; 13 December 1863

For about a fortnight I have been travelling here and there like a madman, doing nothing, as usual, just for the pleasure of being bored, and of boring some friends I met, and for this reason I have not previously answered your letter or Faccio's. I will tell you, for that matter, with my usual frankness, that the latter embarrasses me. What to answer him? A word of encouragement, you say: but what is the need of this word to someone who has presented himself, and has made the public his judge? Now it is a matter

between them, and every word becomes futile. I know there has been much talk about this opera, too much, if you ask me, and I have read some articles in the papers, where I found big words about *Art, Aesthetics, Revelations, Past, Future,* etc. etc. and I confess that I (great ignoramus that I am!) understood nothing. For that matter I do not know Faccio's talent, or his opera; and I would not like to know it, so as not to discuss it, express an opinion on it, things I detest because they are the most futile in the world. *Discussions* never convince anyone; *opinions* are most often erroneous. Finally, if, as his friends say, Faccio has found new paths, if Faccio is destined to set art erect on the altar now *ugly as the stink of a brothel,* so much the better for him, and for the public. [. . .]

Ah. you have read Escudier's nonsense about me [*Mes souvenirs*]! There is much truth, but he exaggerates everything to be more readable. It's a commercial matter and nothing more.
COP, 506

Verdi finally wrote a chilly, formal reply to Faccio. And for some years he had no more to do with the future conductor of his *Otello* or with Boito, its future librettist. Verdi was more concerned, during 1864, with trying to find a new solution for the *Forza* libretto and with a forthcoming French premiere of *Macbeth*, for which he was supposed to write ballet music.

Verdi to Escudier ; Sant'Agata, 22 October 1864

I have looked over *Macbet* to write the ballet, but alas! In reading this music I was struck by a number of things I would not have wanted to find there. To say everything in a word, there are various numbers that are either weak or lacking in character, which is even worse. There would be needed:

1. An aria for Lady Macbet in Act II.
2. Various passages to be revised in the vision [show of kings] Act II.
3. Completely redo Macbet's aria Act III.
4. Retouch the first scenes of Act IV.
5. Rewrite the last finale, removing the death of Macbet.

To do this work, besides the Ballet, will take time and it would be best for Carvalho to abandon the thought of giving *Macbet* this winter. [. . .]
AB II, 801

Verdi to Tito Ricordi ; 15 December 1864

Let me finish this *Macbet*, and then I'll do something or other for *La forza del destino*. Tell me: have you no poet, no literary friend who is capable of finding me a denouement for that opera? [. . .]
AB II, 803

Verdi to Tito Ricordi ; 1 January 1865

It's a poor idea . . . to write to Gutiérrez when in Madrid there is the Duque de Rivas, to whom I can write when I wish? But neither Gutiérrez nor the Duke would think of anything. For a thousand reasons it would be wrong to turn to Ghislanzoni or Marcello, and Boito would not do. In the end I will find something, you'll see, meanwhile, if you like, rent the opera as it is.
AB II, 804

Verdi to Piave; Sant' Agata, 28 January 1865

I am about to set the last Chorus [for *Macbet*], but it is one of the thousand and one things that are everywhere and have no effect. I have conceived one where there could be something exciting and I submit it to your approval.

After the battle I have enter some *Bards* who sing the Hymn of victory. The Bards (you know) followed the armies in those times. [. . .] Turn the page and you will find everything written out. [. . .]

AB II, 812

Verdi's sketch of the final scene was much as it has now remained.

Verdi to Escudier; Sant' Agata, 23 January 1865

You received some time ago the first two acts of *Macbet*. The other day I sent the third to Ricordi, so you will perhaps receive it at the same time as this letter. Except for a part of the 1st chorus and a part of the dance of the Sylphs when Macbet has fainted, all the rest of this third act is new.

The act ends with a *Duo* between Lady and Macbet. It doesn't seem to me illogical that Lady, always intent on keeping an eye on her husband, should have discovered where he is. The act ends better. The prima donna is made to appear and Macbet is thus relieved of some of the great work.

You will see that in the Ballet (*Divertissement*) there is a little action, which connects very well with the Drama. All is marked in the score and you will also find the programme of the *Divertissement*.

The apparition of Hecate, Goddess of the night, works well, because it interrupts all those diabolical dances and makes room for a calm and severe Adagio. I needn't tell you that Hecate should never dance, but only strike poses. I also needn't warn you that this Adagio must be played by the Clarone or bass-clarinet (as indicated) so that in unison with the 'cello and the bassoon a grim, severe sound is made as the situation demands. Please ask the conductor to supervise at every stage the studying of the dances, so that he can indicate the tempos I have marked. Dancers always change all movements and, so doing, this ballet would lose all character and would not produce that effect that I feel it has.

Another thing I urge on you, namely to use the specific instruments indicated for the little orchestra beneath the stage at the apparition of the eight Kings. That little orchestra of two oboes, six A clarinets, two bassoons, and a double-bassoon forms a strange, mysterious and at the same time calm and quiet sonority, which other instruments could not produce. They must be placed below the stage, near a *trappe*, open and fairly broad, so that the sound can emerge and spread through the theatre, but in a mysterious way, as if in the distance.

Another observation for the scene of the Banquet in the second act. I have seen this play performed several times in France, England, Italy. Everywhere Banco is made to appear from a *coulisse*; he turns, waves his arms about, inveighs against Macbet, then calmly goes off into another *coulisse*. This, in my view, has no illusion, makes no sensation at all, and you can't tell clearly whether he's a ghost or a man.

When I staged *Macbet* in Florence I had Banco (with a broad wound on his forehead) appear from an under-

ground *trappe* precisely in Macbet's place. He did not move, only at the right moment he raised his head. He inspired terror. [. . .]

If you think of something better, do it, but make sure the public understands clearly the ghost of Banco. Final observation. In the duet of the 1st act between Macbet and Lady there is the first section that always has great effect and there is a phrase where the words say:

> 'Follie follie che sperdono
> I primi rai del dì.'
> [Follies, follies that the first
> rays of the day dispel.]

The French translator must retain the words *Follie follie* because perhaps in these words and in Lady's infernal derision lies the secret of the effect of this piece. [. . .]

AB II, 816

Verdi to Escudier; Sant' Agata, 3 February 1865

[. . .] You will laugh when you hear that for the battle I have made a *Fugue*! ! ! A *Fugue*? . . . I who loathe anything that smells of the scholastic and hadn't written any for almost thirty years! ! ! But I will tell you that in this case that musical form works very well. The rushing after one another of subjects and counter-subjects, the clash of the dissonances, the racket, etc. etc. can fairly well express a battle. Ah if there were our trumpets, so resounding, ringing! ! Those *trompettes à pistons* of yours are neither flesh nor fowl. For the rest the orchestra will enjoy itself. [. . .]

I see the papers are already beginning to speak of this *Macbet*. For the love of God, *ne blaguez pas trop*. It's perfectly futile.

AB II, 819

Verdi to Escudier; 28 March 1865

M. Carvalho's notion of having the Brindisi sung by the Tenor is surely ingenious, but for myself I am still of the opinion that this harms the general effect of the Finale. It seems to me far more beautiful and theatrical that Lady, accepting the invitation of Macbet himself 'il brindisi lieto di nuovo s'intuoni' [let the joyful toast resound again], should resume the Brindisi and finish it. Then if Macduff says words of suspicion, these words will not go well with the brilliant notes of the Brindisi. And what will Lady do meanwhile? Turn into a super? That cannot be: Lady in this scene is, and must be, the dominant character both dramatically and musically. [. . .]

AB II, 822

On 21 April 1865, premiere of *Macbeth*, revised version (French translation by C. L. E. Nuitter and A. Beaumont), at the Théâtre Lyrique, Paris.

Telegram from impresario Léon Carvalho to Verdi; Paris, April 1865

Maestro, I write you under the effect of one of my greatest musical emotions. *Macbeth* has just obtained at the Théâtre Lyrique an immense success. Thank you, dear Maestro, for the faith you had in me. [. . .]

ALB, 51

Telegram from Escudier to Verdi; Paris, April 1865

Macbeth immense success. Finale first act, Brindisi encored.

Admirable performance. Marvellous production. General enthusiasm. Writing to Busseto.
ALB, 51

Verdi to Escudier, 28 April 1865

[. . .] I have noticed in some French papers some sentences that would allow doubts. Some remark on one thing, some on another. Some find the subject sublime, and some not suited to music. Some find that I did not know Shachspeare when I wrote *Macbet*.

Oh, in this they are greatly wrong. I may not have rendered *Macbet* well, but that I do not know, that I do not understand and do not feel Shachspeare, no, by God, no. He is one of my favourite poets, whom I have had in my hands since my first youth and whom I read and reread constantly.

I would like to know what happened later, and I would be obliged to you if you will tell me sincerely and frankly, and you will do me the favour of sending me also (let them say what they will) the *Débats*, the *Siècle* and all the big newspapers.
AB III, 8

The summer of 1865 for Verdi was marked by a local nuisance. The citizens of Busseto had erected a theatre in a wing of the old fortress, the Rocca di Busseto. They wanted to give it Verdi's name, but at the same time they wanted him to persuade famous artists to come there, at less than their usual fees. When Verdi refused to act as intermediary, there were accusations of ingratitude, and he was reminded of his stipend of 25 francs from the Monte di pietà. Verdi dictated his annoyance to Giuseppina.

From Giuseppina's notebook; Sant'Agata, July 1865

To say at every moment this phrase, which, if ridiculous, is still offensive: '*We made him.*' It's the business of the 27 [*sic*] francs again. And why didn't they 'make' the others, since the means were the same?

If I in this connection, without departing from the truth, were to write a short letter for publication, I could make them look ridiculous before all Europe.

It's better to have done with it – both with the 27 francs 50 centimes and with the kind of inquisition that has been practised for sixteen years.

I have, so to speak, withdrawn from Busseto. If my annoyance increases I shall withdraw from Sant'Agata, and I shan't be the one that will cut the worst figure. [. . .]

Our opinions are at the antipodes. I am Liberal to the utmost degree, without being a Red. I respect the liberty of others and I demand respect for my own. The town is anything but Liberal. It makes a show of being so, perhaps out of fear, but is of clerical tendencies.
WAL, 256

At the end of August 1865 Verdi signed a contract with Paris, to produce *La forza del destino* there, and to write a new work for the Opéra.

Verdi to Arrivabene; Paris, 31 December 1865

Dog, dog, dog! I have been here a month and I have no sign of life from you! And you cannot complain about me this time, since I wrote you a day or two before leaving

Sant'Agata. I am pleased to find you at fault; as punishment you will write me a letter of at least four pages, speaking to me at length first of yourself, then of our country's affairs.

I roam through the length and breadth of Paris and I examine carefully the new part which is truly beautiful. How many *boulevards*, how many *Avenues*, how many gardens, etc. etc. Too bad the sun doesn't shine more frequently! I have been four times to the *Opéra*!!! Once or twice to all the musical theatres, and I was bored everywhere. *L'Africaine* is certainly not Meyerbeer's best opera. I have heard also the overture to *Tannhaüser* by Wagner. He's mad!!! You know that I came here to stage at once *La forza del destino* and to write a new opera for the end of '66. There was too much to be done for *Forza* and it was impossible for me to do so much work in the space of a year. We have agreed to give first the new opera, which will be *Don Carlos* taken from Schiller. The poet will be Méry. Once things are properly settled with the poet I will go back to Sant'Agata to work in peace and will be back here again towards the end of August or in early July. [. . .]
ALB, 61

Verdi to Piroli; Paris, 31 December 1865

[. . .] Paris becomes more beautiful every day. There is a new Paris constructed in the past two years around the *arc de l'Etoile* which is truly marvellous. The inhabitants are no crazier (which is to say all) than usual.

I will write as first opera *Don Carlos* for the *Opéra*. It is taken from Schiller: the poet will be Méry.
CV III, 34–5

Verdi to Escudier; Sant'Agata, 6 May 1866

I expect any moment to hear cannon, and I am so close here to the army's camps, that it wouldn't surprise me one fine morning to see a cannonball roll into my room. War is inevitable. Things have been driven to such a point, that even if the whole world were against it, we would want it. The masses can no longer contain themselves; it is no longer even within the power of the King, and what will be will be, but the war must be waged. [. . .]

When the war breaks out, I will have to abandon this locality, which is too exposed, but I lack the heart to abandon Italy! What will I do? . . . Who knows! . . . A pity! The opera had been going so well for about a fortnight! I have finished the Third act and begun the Fourth. When this is finished, I consider the opera finished, because the Fifth act can and must be done in a moment. I realize this *moment* doesn't arrive every day, but in a week or two this moment should be found. [. . .]
AB III, 79

Verdi to Piroli; Sant'Agata, 9 June 1866

[. . .] I am still here, but at the first cannon shot I shall leave, because the very idea that the Austrians might put in an appearance even here, would make me run a thousand miles without stopping for breath, only to avoid seeing those ugly faces. For the moment I shall go to Genoa, and will stay there till the last, very last moment when I must or should leave for Paris.

I say *should* because leaving Italy at this moment weighs on me like remorse. It is quite true that I have neither age nor strength to go to war; I have no head for offering counsel, finally I am good for nothing, but still I would have stayed here, I would have bestirred myself, I would

have done what little good I might have been able to, and like so many others I would have rejoiced and suffered with my people. If the Paris *Opéra* belonged as in the past to the *Maison de l'Empereur* I would write to the Minister, begging him to leave me in Italy for the present. The Minister would perhaps have granted it me. But now that the *Opéra* is in the hands of an *Entrepreneur* a lawsuit would be very probable if I remained here. What do you say? What would you do in my place? And you, my dear Piroli, have with the palpitation and anxiety of every Italian the affliction of having seen your son go off. Glorious affliction which I hope will be converted to joy, when you embrace this son again among the redeemers of poor Venice.
CV III, 39

Verdi to Piroli; Genoa, 5 July 1866

I have just this moment arrived in Genoa and I read a bulletin that says: '*Austria has decided to cede Venice to the Emperor of the French*', etc. etc. Why to the Emperor of the French? Austria, beaten in Prussia, wants to gain time. I still understand nothing. [. . .]
CV III, 41

During his stay in Genoa, Verdi – with Giuseppina – set about looking for a permanent winter residence there. For some years he had been spending long periods in the city.

From Ferdinando Resasco's study of Verdi in Genoa

Verdi decided after 1859 to establish more permanent residence in Genoa, reserving his hermitage in Busseto for the summer season of the fields. His wife finding Genoa's climate also very beneficial to her health, they chose in 1866 one of the most pleasing and healthful localities, namely the Carigano hill. [. . .]

176   Angelo Mariani lived on one floor of the Palazzo Sauli; hence a greater attraction for Verdi in selecting his residence in another of the apartments of that sumptuous palace. Since that apartment was supplied also with a grand and resonant salon, it was believed, at first, that the great maestro would not be averse to opening his home now and then for receptions, comforted by that divine art which had in him its resplendent apostle. But the fact was, on the contrary, that on the Carignano hill the industrious artist wanted calm and meditation, far from the centre of the city's life and business.
RES, 16–17

Verdi to Piroli; Genoa, 14 July 1866

Poor us! The situation is so depressing that I haven't even the strength to curse that bunch of inept, stupid, word-spinning rogues who have brought us to ruin. Can we hope for a victory from Cialdini? But is it possible if now the Austrians abandon everything? . . . And the future? When the reds ask: You Moderate gentlemen, what were you able to do in the 6 years of your Government? An army without organization and without leaders, a navy that doesn't exist, and Finance in ruins!
    I wrote yesterday to Paris asking for the dissolution of my contract. [. . .]
CV III, 41

Verdi to Arrivabene; Genoa, 22 July 1866

I leave tonight for Paris. I did everything possible to break my contract with the *Opéra*, but in vain.
    Imagine what pleasure for an Italian who loves his country to be in Paris now!
    I will not speak to you of our situation! For me it is too sad, because, even assuming that now things will be settled more or less well, the future will be very nasty.
ALB, 71

Verdi to his estate-agent Paolo Marenghi; Paris, 28 September 1866

Have them cut the poplars you believe necessary to make timber for construction. Only you must give an account, both of the quantity and the quality, to Dr Carrara.
    [. . .] From your letters I realize you are not working *Milord* very much and you are not having the filly broken. I do not like this because the horses will not remain healthy or at least they will become fat and heavy like Rosso's. I also want my horses to eat the Sant'Agata hay. I hope you will take care of the manure pile, on which I am counting greatly. . . .
AB III, 107

Verdi to Ricordi; Paris, 25 September 1866

We must not speak for the present of *D. Carlos*: it will not go on in October, or in November, or in December, and perhaps not even in January. [. . .]
AB III, 109

Giuseppina to Corticelli; Paris, 7 December 1866

Verdi, with his opera, cannot give a thought to anything that might distract him. You know that we have settled on an apartment at Genoa, and that this apartment has to be furnished and decorated . . . and all that with the least possible expense, because money doesn't rain on us from the sky as it does on you people. So I have had, and still have, to run to right and left, and, God willing, in eight or ten days everything will be packed up and I shall be able to breathe a little. Add that, through I don't know what aberration, we have begun to give a little dinner-party every week! . . . *Don Carlos*, God and the Tortoises of the Opéra willing, will perhaps be put on at the end of January. What a punishment for a composer's sins is the staging of an opera in that theatre, with its machinery of marble and lead! Just think! I am burning with impatience to go to Genoa and put in order and enjoy the apartment, and at the Opéra they argue for twenty-four hours before deciding whether Faure or la Sasse is to raise a finger or the whole hand.   178–79
AB III, 113

Giuseppina to De Sanctis; Paris, 19 January 1867

Though you haven't answered my last letter, I have too much faith in your old friendship not to believe that you share in our misfortunes. Verdi's father, already ill for many years, and when a tendency towards improvement seemed to be evident, suddenly took a turn for the worse and died in less than three days. You who know us can imagine how this loss grieves our hearts! Take as a friend your part of sorrow and pray with all your family for the peace of the poor old father we shall never see again, never . . . What a fearsome word! . . .

Verdi and I, weeping, embrace you.

CV I, 99–100

Verdi to Clarina Maffei; Paris, 6 February 1867

[. . .] I can't wait to leave and to arrive home, where my poor father has left a sister aged 83, and a [great-]niece aged 7. And these two poor creatures are in the hands of two domestics!! Imagine: I who have so little faith, if I can have faith in the virtue of two domestics who are, you might say, masters in my house. . . .

AB III, 116

232 The seven-year-old was Filomena Maria 'Fifao' Verdi, whom Verdi and Giuseppina took in, and who eventually became his heiress.

On 24 February 1867 a closed dress-rehearsal of *Don Carlos* took place at the Opéra. There were problems of length.

Gazzetta musicale di Milano, 3 March 1867

Having begun at 7 in the evening the performance ended around midnight. It is true that the intervals or *entr'actes* lasted longer than normal; but even abbreviating them as much as possible, the opera would still be a quarter-hour longer than it should be. In Paris the duration of an opera is established, and the rule cannot be broken. The performance cannot run beyond midnight, because the last departure of the suburban trains and that for the surrounding regions is at thirty-five minutes past midnight. For the convenience of those who live in the suburbs or environs of Paris, the performance must therefore be shortened, so that it does not run past midnight. Nor can the time of the curtain-rise be moved forward, because they do not wish to hasten the dinner of the people who go to the Opéra! All these considerations, or rather all these servitudes, if not *slaveries*, have prompted the composer, or rather have obliged him, to shorten the length of the music by a quarter-hour.

177–9 The most troublesome thing was to find a way to shorten it. Everything is calculated for the arrangement of the effects and the requirements of the musical drama. Already a duet between Mme Sasse and Mme Gueymard, that is to say between the Queen of Spain and the Princess of Eboli, had been sacrificed. What else could be cut out, except to remove a bar here, some more there? And this is precisely the thankless task with which Verdi is occupied as I write. Sad necessity that sacrifices the wholeness of a work to such puerile considerations! How can a quarter-hour of music be cut, especially from an opera among whose thousand merits is the rapidity of the action? Verdi has not indulged himself by repeating the same phrases, according to the usage of the old composers . . . and many of the moderns. Having above all the dramatic action in view, he is particularly attentive to this and not to have it languish with the customary *tricks*, which so many composers use, sacrificing dramatic truth to ephemeral and facile but illogical musical effects.

ATTI II, 102

Verdi made the necessary excisions. The material he cut has been rediscovered only recently and, to varying

Verdi, *Don Carlos*, 1867. Title page of piano score published by Escudier, Paris. Bibliothèque de l'Opéra, Paris.

degrees, restored in productions of the opera in Britain, Germany, Italy and the United States.

On 11 March 1867, premiere of *Don Carlos* at the Opéra, Paris.

180

Verdi to Arrivabene; Paris, 12 March 1867

Last night *Don Carlos*. It was not a success!! I don't know what will happen later, and I wouldn't be surprised if things changed. Tonight I leave for Genoa. [. . .]

ALB, 75

Ernest Reyer, Journal des débats, Paris, March 1867

When an individuality is so deservedly and universally recognized as that of Verdi, it is preserved like a precious possession, whose advantages are such as to compensate for the harshest and sometimes most unjust criticisms. So, at the same time as I render homage to the bold attempts of the author of *La forza del destino*, *Il trovatore*, and *Rigoletto*, it is my duty to observe that in *Don Carlos* he has not lost his most salient and personal qualities: the public showed itself highly satisfied, and those pieces that most especially bear the composer's habitual imprint were not less applauded. I will cite in the 1st act the romanza of *Don Carlos* preceded by a very interesting recitative; the ensuing duet between the Infante and Elisabeth [. . .].

The Introduction of the 2nd act, for four horns, is of a magnificent character, and in the chorus of friars in San Yuste the grim accents of the 'Miserere' [in *Trovatore*] are found again. [. . .] There is warmth and passion in the duet between Rodrigo and Carlos. The veil song was repeated. [. . .] The trio of Elisabeth, Rodrigo and Eboli is conceived with the same feeling as the quartet of *Rigoletto* and is no less successful. The duet between the Marquis of Posa and Philip, with the imitative effects that accompany the singing of Rodrigo, is one of the most beautiful pages of the score. But I wish especially to draw attention to the coronation scene [actually the *Auto da fé*] handled with such vastness, so full of happy contrasts, and in which the instruments and voices have a power of sonority truly fascinating. The entire hall was electrified by the effect of this piece. [. . .] The orchestration in this final number [last act duet between Elisabeth and Carlos], as in many other pages of the score, is handled with a delicacy and a care to which even Verdi had not accustomed us till now.

ALB, 75n

Théophile Gautier, Le Moniteur, Paris, March 1867

[. . .] At the second performance the main pieces were marked, and the public, knowing at which points to focus its attention, could more fully enjoy, and receive with enthusiasm, this considerable work.

Now that the old school still counts a majority of partisans, this near-conversion of Verdi will gain him a good number of reproaches: but the Maestro knows that not long ago the music of [Rossini's] *Otello* and *La gazza ladra* was called noise and confusion, and so he has understood that an opera destined to live in the future must take inspiration from the newest forms of art and that thus it will keep old age ever farther away. [. . .]

ALB, 77n

Verdi to Escudier; Genoa, 1 April 1867

[. . .] I have read in Ricordi's *Gazzetta* the resumé on *D. Carlos* of the chief newspapers of France. So I am an almost perfect Wagnerian. But if the critics had paid a bit more attention they would have seen that there were the same intentions in the trio of *Ernani*, in the sleep-walking scene of *Macbet* and in many other pieces etc. etc. . . . But the question is not whether *D. Carlos* belongs to a system, but whether the music is good or bad. The question is a clear and simple, and, above all, a fair one.

AB III, 131

In May 1868 Giuseppina went to Milan to buy furniture for the Genoa apartment. For many years Verdi had stayed away from Milan, and although he had maintained his correspondence with Clarina Maffei, she and Giuseppina had never met. During her visit to the city, Giuseppina called on Clarina, and the two women became immediate friends.

Giuseppina to Clarina Maffei; Sant'Agata, 21 May 1867

The fatigue and the emotions of the last few days heated my blood to 80 degrees, and I arrived home with a magnificent headache which, if it prevented me from writing to you yesterday, allowed me still to pour out to Verdi all the events of Milan. He was waiting for me at the Alseno station with little Filomena, and as soon as we were in the carriage he asked me about my family and what I had done in Milan for the furniture. I said I had searched all about, not finding anything of what I wanted: that I had seen the

Ricordis, Piave, and his delights, and that, though pressed for time, if he had given me a letter for you I would have introduced myself, despite a certain repugnance for the *embonpoint* which for three years has not allowed me to sit in the circle of sentimental women.

While he, laughing, gave me the flattering epithet of *capricious* (it is given only to young women, and I haven't been that for some time), I slowly took from my purse your note, threw it in his lap, and as soon as he had glanced at it, it gave me the sight of a great row of teeth, including the wisdoms! I told him quickly, at the pace of a charge, how you had received me; how you (something extraordinary for you) had gone out with me; how I had been silly to wait so many years before knowing you, and he kept repeating: 'I'm not surprised, not surprised; I know Clarina.' Wanting to drive the machine at full steam, I said with affected indifference: 'If you go to Milan, you must introduce yourself to Manzoni. He is expecting you; I was there with her the other day.'

Bang! here the bombshell was so great and unexpected, that I didn't know whether to open the doors of the carriage to give him air, or whether to close them, fearing that in the paroxysm of surprise and joy he might jump out! He turned red, pale, sweating; he took off his hat, he rubbed it in such a way that he almost reduced it to a pancake. Moreover (and this must remain between us) the stern and ferocious Bear of Busseto had his eyes filled with tears, and both moved, overcome, we remained ten minutes in complete silence.

[. . .] Now Verdi is concerned about writing to Manzoni, and I laugh, because while I remained confused, awkward, and foolish when you obtained for me that great honour of finding myself in *his* presence, I am pleased that also those who are much more than I experience a bit of embarrassment, smooth their moustaches, and scratch their ears, to find words worthy of being said to colossi.

AB III, 140

Verdi to Clarina Maffei, 24 May 1867

I am still gaping at Peppina's tale of what happened between you two and with you two. And I am all the more surprised, because before my better half left Sant'Agata, I asked her if she wanted a note to you: 'No,' she answered, 'do you imagine that with these dimensions and with this housewifely air I want to present myself to a very elegant lady, a wisp of air, to one who lives on enthusiasms, etc. etc., etc., *n'en parlons plus*.' And I, who believe so little (without making exceptions, excuse me, for the fair sex), this time believed [. . .]. You are great devils, you women! But I rather love this kind of boldness, which embarrasses no one . . . If I was amazed at the first part of the story, you cannot imagine the sensation produced in me by the second.

How I envy my wife having seen that Great Man! But I don't know if, even coming to Milan, I will have the courage to present myself to Him. You well know how great and how deep is my veneration for that Man who, in my opinion, has written not only the greatest book of our time but one of the greatest books that have ever emerged from the human brain. And it is not only a book but a consolation for mankind. I was sixteen when I read it for the first time. Since then I have read many others, on which, when reread, the advance of age has modified or erased [. . .] the opinions of my young years: but for that book my enthusiasm remains still the same; indeed, as I know men better, it is grown greater. The fact is that is a *true* book, as true as *truth*.

Oh if artists could once understand this *true*, there would no longer be musicians of the future and of the past; nor purist, realist, idealist painters; nor classic and romantic poets; but true poets, true painters, true musicians. [. . .]
AB III, 141

Giuseppina to De Sanctis; Sant'Agata, 25 May 1867

[. . .] . . . Though we have fixed our winter residence in Genoa, the way to Naples is always open by sea or by land. You must understand, dear Cesarino, you who are a man of business, why Genoa is for us much more convenient than Naples, since Verdi can keep an eye on the little property he has acquired; if he likes, he can leave Genoa in the morning, attend to his affairs at Sant'Agata, and be back comfortably for dinner the next day.

The estate agents, knowing he is so close to their backs, will take a bit less advantage. At least we have this illusion. I will tell you that we are tempted to adopt a dear little girl aged seven: she is a distant relative of Verdi's, and her name is also Verdi. We will decide yes or no when we come back from Paris and from Cauterets in the Pyrenees, where Verdi plans to return to take the waters. It would be curious if we were to adopt her and if one of your sons [. . .] were to turn out as good as Papà Cesare, and she were to become a De Sanctis. [. . .]
CV I, 100

Giuseppina to Clarina Maffei; early July 1867

Poor Signor Antonio [Barezzi] is still in a pitiful state, and for a few hours of relief he has many in which his life is in the gravest danger! The other evening they called us at midnight; we left in all haste for Busseto and we found him so worsened, that some *zealous* souls had thought to have ready a *priest*! . . . Towards two in the morning the fever calmed down, and the dear old man regained a bit of life.

This morning Verdi and I went there to act as up-holsterers, adjusting a certain green curtain, so that the air can circulate in the room, without the light hurting him. If you could see how his eyes filled with affection look at us! . . . how he presses our hands, when we are about to leave, as if he wanted to keep us by force at his side! [. . .]
AB III, 145

Verdi's humour during this period was understandably grim, and Giuseppina – and the Sant'Agata domestic staff – sometimes paid the consequences.

From Giuseppina's notebook, early July 1867

[. . .] I try to raise Verdi's morale over the indisposition that perhaps his nerves and his imagination make seem worse than it is. He says I don't believe it, that I laugh, etc. etc., and holds it against me. He is subject to affliction of the intestines, and the emotions, the journeys, the effort of these days because of the hydraulic pump, and his natural restlessness cause him some upsets of the bowels. . . . He comes often into my room without standing still ten minutes. [. . .]

Finally he is enraged against the servants and against me, and I don't know what words and what tone of voice to speak to him so as not to offend him! Alas, how things will end I don't know, because his mood becomes more and more restless and wrathful. . . .
AB III, 146

On 21 July 1867, Antonio Barezzi died in Busseto. He was in his eightieth year.

Verdi to Arrivabene; Busseto, 25 July 1867

Sorrows follow sorrows with a frightful rapidity! Poor Signor Antonio, my second father, my benefactor, my friend, he who so loved me, is no more! His great age does not help to mitigate the grief that is very great for me! Poor Signor Antonio! If there is a second life he will see how I loved him and how grateful I am to him for what he did for me. He died in my arms and I have the consolation of never having caused him any sorrow.
ALB, 79

Meanwhile preparations were in progress for the Italian premiere of *Don Carlos*. It was to be conducted by Angelo Mariani.
186

Mariani to Ricordi, late April 1867

[. . .] Now to come to *Don Carlos*, I will say frankly that for the part of Elisabetta we must stick to la Fricci. For that of Eboli, if we find no better, la Ferni can do, since she is a good artist, excellent musician, and moreover endowed with great intelligence . . .

La Stolz is a fair artist, she has the vocal means to draw advantage from the part, but la Fricci is still preferable, indeed one leg of la Fricci is preferable to an entire Stolz. [. . .]
185
AB III, 134

Obviously, Stolz and Mariani were not yet lovers. Shortly after Barezzi's death, Mariani went with the Verdis to Paris, to hear *Don Carlos* there.
On 27 October 1867, *Don Carlos* was given in Bologna, with Stolz as Elisabetta.

Verdi to Escudier; Genoa, 30 October 1867

[. . .] Let us talk of *D. Carlos*, which, it seems, had a very great success in Bologna. All say the performance is marvellous and there are some very powerful effects. I cannot help but make some considerations: here they rehearsed not even a month and they achieve great effects; at the Opéra they rehearse eight months and end by achieving a bloodless, frozen performance.

You see how right I am to say that one, single, secure, powerful hand can work miracles! You saw it with Costa in London [where *Don Carlos* had been given in June], you see it even more with Mariani in Bologna. Will the Opéra never be convinced that its performances, on the musical side, are less than mediocre? And will they never believe that there is need of a reform, and of a musical direction, powerful and *single*?
AB III, 155

From Giuseppina's Diary, January 1868

1 January. Apart from the fairly serious quarrel yesterday about the house in Genoa [. . .] the day passed fairly well and he absolutely insisted on giving me a New Year's present . . . for he is a *grand seigneur* and generous. I was touched, as by all the good he has done me and that he has always done without ostentation and without reproaches . . . exemplified three times in these past few days!

2 January. Peaceful day! The dinner met with approval. I am happy. He is calm.

3 January. We played billiards, as almost always lately. [. . .] He busied himself acting as carpenter, locksmith, and playing the piano. He found nothing to criticize or to scold! . . . It would be so easy to be happy, when one has one's health and a little property. Why isn't he always like that, instead of finding fault with all that I do, that I do with the single intention of making his life comfortable, agreeable and peaceful?!

4 January. Alas! the clouds are back! . . . Verdi becomes irritated at tones of voice that are too soft or too lively, so that I wonder what might be the happy medium that would suit him! [. . .]

I wanted to become a *new woman* to respond worthily to the honour I received in becoming his wife and the good that I receive constantly from that man, who, to be perfect, is lacking only a bit of sweetness and of charm [. . .] 2.30 p.m. Now he is playing the piano and singing with Mariani.

AB III, 157

That summer was marked by a surprise visit (a surprise arranged, of course, by Giuseppina).

67   *Clarina Maffei to Carlo Tenca; Sant'Agata, 19 May 1868*

From this place where the soul is truly refreshed and the heart's faith in Good and Good people is strengthened, I want to write to you, excellent friend, who are one of the people whom I most love and respect. I am truly happy to have carried out the idea of coming to visit Verdi. He welcomed me like a sister; he recognized me at once, but he couldn't believe his eyes. He looked at me, dazed: then let out some exclamations; he embraced me; there was such a moved rejoicing that it proved to me that his deep and great affection for me is out of sheer fondness. He promised me immediately to come to Milan and will come soon. [. . .] The house is elegant and very comfortable; the garden vast and beautiful; we will bring to Milan forests of flowers. This morning Verdi spoke to me of the rose-bushes, of which I send you a leaf as souvenir. Today we will go to Busseto; then to visit the house where he was born. All is dear and sacred with us.

BARB, 360

Verdi to Clarina Maffei; after his visit to Milan in June 1868

What could I say to you of Manzoni? How to explain the very sweet, indefinable, new sensation produced in me, in the presence of that Saint, as you call him? I would have knelt before him, if men could be worshipped. They say it must not be done, and so be it: although we venerate on altars many who did not have the talent or the virtues of Manzoni, and who indeed were downright rascals. When you see him kiss his hand and for me tell him all my veneration.

AB III, 215

Verdi to Escudier; Sant'Agata, 9 July 1868

Last week I was in Milan. It had been twenty years since I last saw the city, and it is completely changed. The new Galleria is truly a beautiful thing. A true artistic, monumental thing. In our country still there is the sentiment of the *Great* united to the *Beautiful*.

I visited there our great *Poet*, who is also a great citizen, and a saintly man! Absolutely in our Great there is a somehow natural quality, that is not found in those of other countries. Now I am here and I don't know what I'll do till winter. And are you still in the country? Give me your news; do not speak to me of music, and imagine that I am not a composer, nor you a publisher. Speak to me as friend to friend.

AB III, 215

A sad event of that summer was the terrible illness of Piave, who for some years had been living in Milan and working as stage director at La Scala. In 1868 he was stricken by a paralysis that left him mute and helpless (he survived another eight years). Verdi contributed to the support of his wife and daughter and persuaded other Italian composers to contribute, with him, to an album of songs, the proceeds of whose sales went to the Piave family. With Piave incapacitated, and with a production of *La forza del destino* scheduled for La Scala the following winter, Verdi had to call on another writer for adaptations. This was Antonio Ghislanzoni (see above, p. 152).   193

From Antonio Ghislanzoni's account of Verdi at home

It had been almost twenty years since I had last seen Maestro Verdi. In 1846 or 1847, I had found myself with him, in Milan, at a supper among friends, and the features of that stern and pensive face had been impressed in indelible characters on my youthful imagination. At that table, among many journalists, writers, artists and good-timers of every sort, there sat also Cavaliere Andrea Maffei, the   70 elegant translator of Schiller, Moore, and Goethe, the Virgilian poet whose verses are a music. In the midst of the noisy gaiety of us all, the poet and the Maestro maintained a depressing taciturnity. Both seemed absorbed in grave thoughts; I believe at that period the score of *I masnadieri* was in gestation, which then was performed [. . .] in London.

After that day, as I said, I did not have the good fortune to see the Maestro again, and he too, after a few months' stay in Milan, abandoned the city of his first triumphs, to return there only about twenty years afterwards, in early July 1868. [. . .]

But let us come to the villa of Sant'Agata. [. . .] Beyond   226–30 the garden, crossed by a long avenue in which the eye is lost, there extend the vast land-holdings of the Maestro, scattered with peasant huts, and with very well-built farmhouses. The cultivation reveals that perfect art that is learned on foreign fields, less favoured by nature. Verdi's observant spirit has gathered, to pour them on this field, all the progresses of agricultural science in England and France. Whereas the garden with its willows, the thick trees and the opaque kiosks, and the tortuous and melancholy lake, portray the impassioned nature of the artist, the cultivation of these broad lands seems to reflect on the other hand the orderly mind of the man, that practical and positive judgment which in Verdi, a case unique rather than rare, is paired with an exuberant imagination, a lively and sensitive temperament.

This practical and positive judgment is shown all the more in the architecture of the house, in the choice of furniture, in everything that constitutes the comfortable and internal order of the family. There is only one word, a musical word, which can express this marvellous order, this most happy marriage of art with the material necessities of life – the word *harmony* [. . .].

The Maestro ordinarily composes in his bedroom – a room on the ground floor, spacious, full of air and of light, furnished with artistic profusion. The windows and glass doors give on to the garden. Yonder, a magnificent piano, a bookcase, and a massive desk of eccentric shape which, dividing the room into two compartments, displays to the gaze a delightful variety of sketches, statuettes, artistic trinkets. Above the piano there hangs the oil portrait of old Barezzi, Verdi's true friend and patron, for whose name, for whose revered image, the Maestro professes a kind of cult. [. . .]

Malevolent biographers, and above all that most ignorant savant that was Fétis, not satisfied with having tried through the most unhappy sophisms of criticism to demolish the talent and the glory of the illustrious Italian Maestro, also enjoyed depicting him physically and morally as a savage, I would almost say a bear. Nothing is more foolish than caricature which falsifies a portrait.

Maestro Verdi at that time was fifty-six. Tall of person, slim, vigorous, endowed with an iron constitution and iron energy of character, he promised an eternal virility. Twenty years before, when I had found myself with him in Milan, the general impression of his person showed some alarming symptoms. If in those days the frail structure of his limbs, the pale face, the hollow cheeks and sunken eyes could prompt sinister presages, today in his aspect you find only the glow and the sturdiness of those predestined to a long career.

And like his person, so also the spirit and character of Verdi have undergone a favourable transformation. No one could be more elastic towards impressions, more cordial, more expansive. What a difference between my taciturn dinner-companion of the year 1846 and my lively and sometimes most jovial host of the year 1868! I have known artists who, after having been heedlessly prodigal of gaiety and affability in their youth, later, under the veneer of glory and honours, became opaque and almost intractable. One would say that Verdi, moving through a career of triumphs, had shed at every stage a part of that rough bark that was his in the years of his youth. [. . .]

At five in the morning he moves through the avenues of the park, visits the fields and the farms, amuses himself by navigating the lake in a little boat which he conducts and directs as an able pilot. Not a moment's pause. To rest from music, Verdi turns to poetry; to temper the strong emotions of both, he takes refuge in history and philosophy. There is no area of human learning into which his restless mind, greedy for culture, does not fling itself enthusiastically.

A wife endowed with the most exquisite gifts of heart and mind, as cultivated as she is lovable, Signora Giuseppina Strepponi shares with this man of the old school, with this privileged artist, the serene tasks of the villa. Harmony reigns in the two hearts, and this harmony produces order and well-being in the house.

Meanwhile from every part of the civilized world letters and telegrams arrive at the villa, asking for scores, offering incredible fees, promising honours and triumphs. Will Maestro Verdi be able to resist for long so many seductions of money and glory? – What I believe impossible is that the author of *Don Carlo* can restrain the outbursts of his own genius, that overwhelming need of expansion that still stirs and drives him. The volcano has its pauses, its truces, but the latent fire sooner or later must erupt. [. . .]
GHIS LS, 152FF

On 13 November 1868, Rossini died in Paris. 182

Verdi to Clarina Maffei, 20 November 1868

[. . .] A great name has disappeared from the world! His was the most extensive, the most popular reputation of our time, and it was an Italian glory! When the other who still lives [Manzoni] is no more, what will we have left? Our ministers, and the exploits of Lissa and Custoza!
AB III, 224

The second Battle of Custoza (the first having been in 175 1848), and the naval débâcle of Lissa, had been Italian defeats in the war of 1866 against Austria.
Four days after Rossini's death Verdi wrote to Ricordi, who published the letter in the *Gazzetta musicale*.

Verdi to Tito Ricordi; Sant' Agata, 17 November 1868

To honour the memory of Rossini I would wish the most distinguished Italian composers (Mercadante at the head, if only for a few bars) to compose a *Requiem Mass* to be performed on the anniversary of his death.

I would like not only the composers, but all the performing artists, in addition to lending their services, to offer also a contribution to pay the expenses.

I would like no foreign hand, no hand alien to art, no matter how powerful, to lend us assistance. In this case I would withdraw at once from the association.

The *Mass* should be performed in San Petronio, in the city of Bologna, which was Rossini's true musical home.

This *Mass* would not be an object of curiosity or of speculation; but as soon as it has been performed, it should be sealed and placed in the archives of the Liceo Musicale of that city, from which it should never be taken. Exception could perhaps be made for His anniversaries, if posterity should decide to celebrate them.

If I were in the good graces of the Holy Father, I would beg him to allow, at least this once, women to take part in the performance of this music, but since I am not, it would be best to find a person more suitable than I to achieve this end.

It would be best to set up a Committee of intelligent men to take charge of the arrangements for this performance, and especially to choose the composers, assign the pieces, and watch over the general form of the work.

This composition (however good the individual numbers may be) will necessarily lack musical unity; but if it is wanting in this respect, it will serve nonetheless to show how great in all of us is the veneration for that man whose loss the whole world mourns.
ASR, MILAN

Verdi's project was undoubtedly noble, but it was to cause him endless problems and contribute largely to his rupture with Mariani. The story is complex, and has been ably unravelled by Frank Walker in his *The Man Verdi*.
In December 1868 Verdi finally began revising *La forza del destino*, which was to mark his return to La Scala: the first time he had worked for Milan since *Giovanna d'Arco* (1845).

Verdi to Tito Ricordi; Genoa, 15 December 1868

I will come myself to Milan to take the rehearsals I shall

believe necessary for *La forza del destino*, changing the last finale and various other passages here and there in the course of the opera.

I want nothing to do with the Management of La Scala; I don't want to appear on the posters; and I will not stay for the premiere, which cannot be given without my permission. [. . .]
AB III, 235

Giuseppina to Verdi; Genoa, 3 February 1869

[. . .] I have pondered your profound silence before leaving Genoa, your words in Turin, your letter of Tuesday, and my feelings counsel me to decline your offer to me to come and hear some rehearsals of *La forza del destino*. I sense all that is forced in this invitation and I believe the wise decision is to leave you in peace and stay where I am. If I do not amuse myself, at least I am not exposing myself to further and useless bitternesses, and you moreover will be completely *à ton aise*.

Last spring when my heart gave me the boldness to present myself to la Maffei and to Manzoni to return to you with hands full of welcome things – when we made the trip to Milan together, the visit to Manzoni, the excursion to the Lake, and the consequence of all this was your rapprochement with the city of your first successes . . . certainly I did not think of the strange and harsh result of being rejected. [. . .]

Permit at least that my sore heart find at least the dignity of refusal and may God forgive you the sharp and humiliating wound you have caused me.
AB III, 248

In the end, Giuseppina did go to Milan. The revised *Forza* opened on 27 February 1869 at La Scala, conducted by Verdi, with Stolz as Leonora and Mario Tiberini as Alvaro.

174

Verdi to Arrivabene; Genoa, 1 March 1869

I returned here last night from Milan at midnight, dead tired from work.

I need a fortnight's sleep to recover. By now you will know about *La forza del destino*: there was a good performance and a success. La Stolz and Tiberini superb. The others well. Chorus and orchestra performed with indescribable precision and fire. They had a devil in them. Good, very good. [. . .] The new pieces are an Overture, marvellously performed by the orchestra, a little chorus of a Patrol, and a Trio that closes the opera. [. . .]
ALB, 99

Verdi to Draneht Bey, Director of the Khedival Theatres in Cairo; Genoa, 9 August 1869

198

I am aware that the new theatre in Cairo is about to open, on the occasion of the celebration that will take place for the cutting through of the isthmus of Suez.

While I appreciate that you, M. le Bey, were so kind as to do me the honour of thinking of me to write the hymn that will mark the date of the opening, I regret that I must decline this honour both because of my numerous present occupations and because it is not my custom to compose occasional pieces. [. . .]
QISV IV, XV

222

While Verdi continued with his plans for the collective *Requiem* for Rossini, he heard that his friend Mariani had consented to organize and conduct an elaborate Rossini commemoration, that same summer, in the composer's birthplace, Pesaro. Verdi clearly regarded this as a rival initiative.

Verdi to Arrivabene; Genoa, 3 August 1869

[. . .] I know nothing about the Pesaro announcement because Mariani is in Vicenza. It's a badly organized festival. [. . .]

I am writing my piece for the *Messa da Requiem*.
ALB, 107

217

Mariani to Verdi; Pesaro, 17 August 1869

This morning I heard the choir that is to perform the Cherubini *Mass*. It's truly stupendous, being made up of the best singers from all the choirs of the neighbouring towns. [. . .] Shall we have such a choir in Bologna? What will the Milanese committee do to procure it? Do they think they can make use of the theatre chorus? I don't consider them competent for that sort of music!!! I will keep you informed of how everything goes, and if I can be of use to you, you have only to command me.
WAL, 353

Mariani to Verdi; Pesaro, 19 August 1869

I have received your two letters. You can imagine how happy I should be if you really decided to come to Pesaro. Come, come, and come! [. . .] I am at your disposal. Here you won't find hotels, but you will have the hospitality you deserve. You will be lodged in one of the principal private houses. [. . .]
AB III, 295

Verdi to Mariani; Genoa, 19 August 1869

Sleep in peace, for I have already answered that I cannot come to Pesaro. I return to your letter of yesterday because there are two sentences I don't clearly understand: 'What will the Milanese committee do?' and, below: 'If I can be of use to you, command me.' Does this mean we have to beg you in order to have the chorus you have in Pesaro? First of all you should already have realized that my *ego* has vanished, and that now I am only a pen writing as best it can a few notes and a hand to offer my contribution to the fulfilment of this *National Celebration*. Further I will say to you that nobody in this case should beg or be begged, because it is a duty that all artists must or should carry out. [. . .]
AB III, 296

The letter goes on at some length, excoriating poor Mariani.

Verdi to Tito Ricordi; Genoa, 20 August 1869

Tomorrow I will send you my piece for the Rossini *Mass*: 'Libera me, Domine'. In the inadmissible event that this solemnity should not take place, I urge you to take good care of the piece and have it returned to me.

Mariani writes that in Pesaro he will have a marvellous chorus. After having told me the wonders of their performances he says to me, with a certain air . . . 'What will the Milanese committee do to procure it?'

For anyone who knows Latin this sentence should be translated: 'You have to turn to me to do anything good.' He's the usual *dadà*. . . . [. . .] It is best for the Committee to know that he will not be very warm towards this *Mass* of ours, because he wasn't its promoter, and more because the Committee didn't assign him a piece to compose. [. . .]

AB III, 298

Mariani to Verdi; Pesaro, 24 August 1869

Your last letter of the 19th caused me much grief, and you cannot believe how sorry I am not to have been able to reply at once.

I didn't ask you – *what will the Milanese committee do* – in order to be begged for anything, not, *as you write*, to give you the chorus that is now in Pesaro: I was not the one who united it, it doesn't depend on me, and I would have no power over it. Since I know the chorus of the Teatro Comunale [of Bologna], I asked only if the Committee intended to use it [. . .]. If then I offer you my services, you must not believe, O my maestro, that I consider myself worthy of serving you: I believe no explanation is necessary to show what veneration I have for you!

AB III, 298

In the event, the impresario of the Comunale refused to allow his chorus to perform free, and for that and other reasons, Verdi's Rossini *Requiem* project fell through.

Verdi to Arrivabene; Genoa, 30 December 1869

[. . .] The *Messa a Rossini* was not performed, and I am sorry because of my colleagues who lent themselves with such solicitude, through the fault of the authorities of Bologna, the theatre's management, and a bit also of our illustrious friend Signor Angelo. He did not do what he should have both as artist and as my friend; perhaps a bit hurt because he wasn't in the roster of composers, *vanitas vanitatis*, etc. Ah! men of talent are almost always big children. [. . .]

ALB, 114

190 In December Camille Du Locle, soon to become director of the Opéra Comique, was in Genoa. He mentioned to Verdi that the Khedive (or Viceroy) of Egypt was planning to commission an opera for his new theatre in Cairo. This was the first germ of the future *Aida*. But, in writing to Du Locle afterwards, Verdi did not mention it.

Verdi to Du Locle; Genoa, 23 January 1870

Most wicked Du Locle! You have forgotten to send me the literary writings of Wagner. You know I wish to know him also from this aspect, and so I beg you to do that which you have not done. Please add also *Acte et Néron* [by Dumas père].

I still believe that *Nerone* can be the subject of a grand opera, done my way, mind you. Thus it would become impossible for the Opéra, but quite possible here. [. . .]

AB III, 328

Du Locle to Verdi; Paris, January 1870

Do not accuse me of negligence. The works by Wagner that you wish have never been translated into French: what I have read of them has been partially in papers now old, whose dates it has been impossible for me to find [. . .] The only thing of Wagner's that can be procured is his famous preface to his librettos (I believe I saw that volume in your house): as to the others, *Art and Music, Politics and Music, The Jews and Music*, they have not been translated. To make sure, I finally had someone write to M. Wagner himself, without telling him, of course, who wanted those translations. [. . .]

AB III, 329

Du Locle was, with Ricordi, one of the most insistent of those prodding Verdi to return to composition. The Frenchman sent Verdi various subjects, but Verdi objected to them all. The talks continued during a spring visit of the Verdis to Paris, as the composer informed Giulio Ricordi, now very active in the family firm. 240

Verdi to Giulio Ricordi; Paris, 13 April 1870

The day before yesterday I saw Sardou [. . .].

I will not repeat to you everything that was said during this conversation, at which [the director of the Opéra, Emile] Perrin was also present: myself saying that the *Opéra est une affreuse boutique*, they insisting that it is the only possible imaginable theatre of times past present and future . . . The pretensions of the French have no limits! [. . .]

I am dead tired. I wanted to see everything, and go the rounds of all the theatres in the evening. La Patti marvellous 181 in *Rigoletto* and in *La traviata*: the rest dreadful. In the other theatres all below the level of mediocre, except for the Opéra Comique, where there is a good chorus and especially a delightful orchestra. [. . .]

AB III, 335

Among the projects discussed in Paris, evidently, was *Aida*.

Verdi to Du Locle; Sant'Agata, 26 May 1870

[. . .] I have read the Egyptian scenario. It is well made; the *mise en scène* is splendid, and there are two or three situations which, if not very new, are surely very beautiful. But who did it? It shows a very expert hand, accustomed to this craft, and one who knows the theatre very well.

Now let us hear the pecuniary conditions of Egypt, and then we will decide. The Italian libretto would have to be made, and naturally I would have to have it done myself.

AB III, 371

Du Locle to Verdi; Paris, May–June 1870

[. . .] The Egyptian libretto is the work of the Viceroy 197 and of Mariette Bey, the famous archaeologist, nobody else 191 has touched it. [. . .]

AB III, 371

Verdi to Du Locle; Sant'Agata, 2 June 1870

Here I am at the Egypt business; and first of all I must be allowed time to compose the opera, because it is a work of very vast dimensions (as if it were for the *Grande Boutique*) and because the Italian poet must find first the thoughts to put into the mouths of the characters, and then write the poem. Assuming then that I can arrive in time, here are the conditions:

1. I will do the libretto at my expense.

2. I will also send at my expense a person to Cairo to rehearse and conduct the opera.

3. I will send a copy of the score and will concede absolute property of libretto and music only for the kingdom of Egypt, retaining for myself the property of libretto and music for all the other parts of the world.

In compensation, I will be paid the sum of one hundred and fifty thousand francs, payable in Paris by the Banque Rotschild, when the score is delivered. [. . .]
AB III, 372

The terms were accepted. In the latter part of June Du Locle came to Sant'Agata and, with Verdi, completed a prose libretto of *Aida* in French, which Ghislanzoni was to versify in Italian.

Giulio Ricordi to Verdi; Milan, 8 July 1870

[. . .] Ghislanzoni, overjoyed at the assignment, will devote himself to it with all his zeal and all his soul . . . I asked him about payment, and as I foresaw, he wouldn't say anything to me, declaring himself completely content with whatever you decide to do.

Meanwhile I will find out what you wish concerning the various historical facts and will write to you about them.
AB III, 374

Verdi to Ricordi; Sant'Agata, 1–10 July 1870

[. . .] I keep rereading the scenario of *Aida*. I see some notes by Ghislanzoni that (be it said between us) frighten me a little, and I would not wish him, to avoid imaginary dangers, to end by saying what is not in the situation and in the scene, and I would not like him to forget *parole sceniche*.

By *parole sceniche* I mean those words that sculpt a situation or a character, which are always also most powerful in their effect on the public. I know that at times it is difficult to give them lofty and poetic form. But . . . (forgive the blasphemy) both poet and composer must have, when required, the talent and the courage to write neither poetry nor music . . . Horror! horror! [. . .]
AB III, 348

Ghislanzoni sent Verdi the text for Act I on 15 July 1870. At the end of the summer the poet paid another visit to Sant'Agata, for further discussions, and by the end of September Verdi had composed the first two acts.

Verdi to Du Locle; Sant'Agata, 15 July 1870

I haven't written before because Giulio Ricordi was here with the poet who will versify *Aida*. We have agreed on everything and I hope to receive as soon as possible the verses of the first act, so I will be able to start work myself. We have made some changes in the Duet of the third act between Aida and Radamès. The treason no longer seems so odious, but nothing of the stage effect has been removed.

I thank you for the information you give me about Egyptian musical instruments, which can serve in several places. I would also like to use them for the fanfare in the

third act, in the finale, but the effect, I fear, will fail. I assure you that to put in, for example, the instruments of Saxe, revolts me horribly. It is bearable in a more modern subject . . . but among the Pharaohs!!. . .

Tell me also: were there Priestesses of Isis and other divinities? In the books I have leafed through I find instead that this service was restricted to men. [. . .]
AB III, 376

War broke out between France and Prussia on 19 July 1870. The month of September was crucial. On the 2nd came the crushing defeat of the French at Sedan; then, on the 22nd, the Papal defences of Rome (now without its French garrison) were breached at Porta Pia, and the city was occupied by the forces of the King of Italy.

Verdi to Clarina Maffei; Sant'Agata, 30 September 1870

This disaster to France fills my heart, as it does yours, with desolation. It is true that the *blague*, the impertinence, the presumption of the French were and are, despite all their misfortunes, unbearable: but after all France gave liberty and civilization to the modern world. And if she falls, let us not deceive ourselves, all our liberties and civilizations will fall. Let our literary men and our politicians sing as they will the praises of the knowledge, the sciences and even (God forgive them) the arts of these victors; but if they looked a bit more closely, they would see that in their veins the old Gothic blood still flows; that they are of boundless pride, hard, intolerant, contemptuous of all that is not Germanic, and of a rapacity without limit. Men of head, but without heart; a strong race, but not civilized.

And that King, who is always talking of God and Providence, and who with the latter's help destroys the best part of Europe! He believes himself predestined to reform the habits and punish the vices of the modern world! What a brand of missionary! The ancient Attila (another missionary *idem*) halted before the majesty of the capital of the ancient world; but this one is about to bombard the capital of the modern world, and now that Bismarck is letting on that Paris will be spared, I fear more than ever it will be, at least in part, ruined. Why? I couldn't say; perhaps so that there will no longer exist a capital so beautiful that they will never succeed in making one its equal. Poor Paris! which I saw so gay, so beautiful, so splendid last April.

And us? I would have liked a more generous policy, and one that *paid a debt of gratitude*. A hundred thousand of our men could have perhaps saved France and us. In any case I would have preferred suing for peace, after being vanquished alongside the French, to this inertia that will one day make us despised. We will not avoid a European war, and we will be *devoured*. It will not come tomorrow, but it will come. A pretext is easily found: perhaps Rome . . . the Mediterranean. . . . And besides, isn't there the Adriatic, which they have already proclaimed a Germanic sea?

The Rome business is a great deed, but it leaves me cold, perhaps because I feel it could be the cause of trouble, both abroad and at home: because I cannot reconcile Parliament and College of Cardinals, freedom of the press and Inquisition, Civil Code and Syllabus: and because it frightens me to see that our Government has no policy and is relying on . . . time. Let a dextrous, astute Pope, a real sly man, such as Rome has had, arrive tomorrow, and he will

ruin us. I can't see the Pope and the King of Italy coming together, not even in this letter. [. . .]
AB III, 360

At the end of October, Act III of *Aida* was finished. In November another visit from Ghislanzoni, and by mid-November, before the composer left to winter in Genoa, the opera was complete except for some of the scoring. Meanwhile the Franco–Prussian war was raging. Paris, besieged, was cut off from the rest of the world. And in Paris, besides Du Locle, there were the sets and costumes being prepared for Cairo. Verdi was understandably concerned and wrote to Mariette about the situation.

Draneht Bey to Verdi; Cairo, 16 December 1870

In the absence of Mariette Bey, I have had to take cognizance of the letter that you addressed to him dated 12 November last. I presumed correctly that it had to deal with your agreement with him for the music of *Aida* and that makes my indiscretion legitimate.

I knew of the existence of your contract, and no more. I knew the terms only vaguely; but I learn from your letter that Mariette Bey was responsible for carrying it into effect, and that this was to be done in Paris, the funds having in fact been deposited with a banker in that city to be delivered there to you. Now Mariette Bey is shut up in Paris, all communication with him is for the present impossible; we must perforce await the raising of the siege or its final outcome to fulfil the final clauses of the contract.

At the time of the conclusion of that agreement we enjoyed a peace that seemed indefinite, and nothing, surely, could have foretold the present events. Here, in consequence, is a case of *force majeure* to which we are obliged to bow. [. . .] As soon as I had examined your letter, I informed His Highness the Khedive, and his view was identical with mine as to the execution of the agreement. It is this view that I have the honour to transmit to you here, begging you to be quite persuaded that, on our part, we will do everything in our power to hasten the execution of a contract that His Highness is happy and proud of having had concluded in his name with the most celebrated musical genius of our epoch. [. . .]
QISV IV, 28–9

Draneht Bey to Verdi; Cairo, 22 December 1870

I have just received a letter dated the 5th of this month from M. Muzio, who tells me that you have chosen him as your delegate to us for the staging of *Aida*. In this letter M. Muzio, to my great astonishment, informs me of your intention of presenting the new opera at the Teatro alla Scala, in Milan, with la Fricci and Tiberini; and this in the near future, supposing no doubt that the first performance in Cairo will take place next January.

I have told His Highness the Khedive of this letter, and He asks me to say to you that if this is the case, he would be extremely distressed by this decision on your part. We have done everything in our power to stage your Opera next January, but, as I had the honour of telling you in my last letter dated 16th of this month, after the declaration of war, unforeseeable at the time when your agreement was signed, events have taken a turn such as the attack on Paris, and our suppliers are unable to fulfil their contract with us, sending us at the fixed dates the costumes and sets ordered from them for *Aida*. [. . .]

In selecting you, dear Maestro, to write the score of a new work whose action takes place in His States, His Highness had conceived the thought of creating a national work which could later be one of the most precious memories of his reign. Must he be the victim of a question of dates caused by events completely alien to him?

I do not wish to invoke here our right of priority or the case of *force majeure* of which I spoke above. It is to your loyalty, dear Maestro, that I wish to appeal. [. . .]
QISV IV, 30

Muzio to Draneht Bey; Brussels, 4 January 1871

I received your kind and courteous letter. At the same time I had one also from my Maestro and friend Verdi who tells me he had an answer from you. Let us wait then until the gates of Paris open. We will not have long to wait!

It would be a great loss for art if this opera were condemned to silence.

Let us hope that the theatre which Your Excellency directs and manages with such intelligence will have the fortune of hearing this beautiful music in this season. [. . .]
QISV IV, 32

Meanwhile, after the death of Mercadante, Verdi was offered the directorship of the Naples Conservatory, in private letters and in an 'address' signed by the professors of the institution. He refused the post, in a letter to Francesco Florimo, archivist of the Conservatory.

Verdi to Florimo; Genoa, 4 January 1871

[. . .] It is quite painful for me to be unable to respond, as I would like, to this trust; but with my occupations, my habits, with my love of an independent life, it would be impossible for me to take on such a heavy task. You will say to me: 'What of art?' Well and good, but I have done what I could, and if from time to time I can do something, I must be free of any other occupation.

If that were not so, imagine whether or not I would be proud to occupy that post once occupied by those founders of a school, A. Scarlatti and then Durante and Leo. I would have gloried in training pupils in those grave and severe studies, at once so clear, of those early fathers. I would have like to place, so to speak, one foot in the past and the other in the present and future (for the *music of the future* does not frighten me); I would have said to the young pupils: 'Practise the *Fugue* constantly, tenaciously, until you have had your fill, and until your hand becomes easy and strong in bending the notes to your will. Thus you will learn to compose with confidence, to arrange the parts well and to modulate without affectation. Study Palestrina and a few others, his contemporaries. Then skip to Marcello and pay special attention to recitatives. Attend *few performances* of modern works, not letting yourselves be fascinated by the many harmonic and instrumental beauties or by the *diminished seventh* chord, rock and refuge of all of us who cannot compose four bars without half a dozen of these *sevenths*.'

Having completed these studies, accompanied by a broad literary culture, I would say finally to the young: 'Now put your hand on your heart; write, and (assuming the artistic organization) you will be composers. In any case do not swell the horde of imitators and of the *sick* of our time, who seek, and seek, and (sometimes doing well) never find.' In the teaching of voice I would also have liked the old studies, accompanied by modern declamation.

225

To carry out these few maxims, apparently easy, the teaching would have to be supervised with such assiduousness, that the twelve months of the year would, so to speak, be few. I, who have home, interests, fortune . . . everything, everything here, ask you: How could I do it?

So, my dear Florimo, please be interpreter of my very great sorrow to your colleagues and to the many musicians of your beautiful Naples, if I cannot accept this invitation which does me such honour. I hope you find a man who is learned above all and severe in studies. Licence and errors of counterpoint can be allowed and are sometimes beautiful in the theatre; in the Conservatory, no. Let us return to the ancient: it will be a step forward.

AB III, 355–6

Even before *Aida* was performed, Ricordi wanted to make sure Verdi had some project for the future. Verdi's interest in the subject of *Nerone* was known, but there was a possible obstacle: Boito's announced intention of writing an opera on the subject, to a libretto he was drafting. Ricordi sought to remove the obstacle and interest Verdi in Boito by sending a copy of *Amleto*, a libretto the younger man had written for his friend Faccio.

Giulio Ricordi to Verdi; Milan, 26 January 1871

I have sent you a libretto of *Amleto* and on this subject I will come straight to a *Great project*!! which you know I ruminate worse than an ox!! . . .

Now then, two or three times you mentioned to me *Nerone* . . . and I saw that you were not averse to this subject. Yesterday Boito was at my house and *wham* I fired the broadside: Boito asked me for a night to think it over, and this morning he was here, and he discussed the matter at length with me. The conclusion is that Boito would consider himself the *happiest, most fortunate* of men if he could write the libretto of *Nerone* for you; and he would gladly and immediately give up the idea of composing it. Boito told me frankly that he would feel ready to satisfy all your demands, that he would never have worked with such a will, with such enthusiasm as for this work, with the *very rare* combination of poet and composer both convinced of the beauty of the subject, and he believes that never was there a subject so vast, so beautiful, so adapted to the genius of Verdi, as this one of *Nerone*. . . .

AB III, 357–8

Verdi to Giulio Ricordi; Genoa, 30 January 1871

I am writing to you about *Nerone*. I needn't repeat to you how much I love this subject. It is also useless for me to add how happy I would be to collaborate with a young poet, whose abundant talent I have also had lately, with this *Amleto*, occasion to admire.

But you know my affairs and my commitments well enough to understand what a grave thought it would be for me to take on this new task. I am in quite a singular position. I have not the courage to say: *let us do it*, nor do I dare renounce such a beautiful project. But tell me, dear Giulio, could we not leave this matter in suspense for a while, and take it up later? [. . .]

AB III, 359

Alberto Mazzucato, of the Milan Conservatory, saw the 'Libera me' of the ill-starred Rossini *Requiem* in Ricordi's office, and wrote Verdi a letter of praise.

Verdi to Alberto Mazzucato; Genoa, 4 February 1871

If at my age one could still decently blush, I would blush at your praise of that piece of mine; praise which, I will not deny, coming from a Maestro and a critic of your value, has a very great importance and greatly flatters my amour propre. And – you see what a composer's ambition is! – those words of yours would almost have caused to be born in me the desire to write, later, the whole *Mass*; especially since, with some greater development, I would find myself already having written the 'Requiem' and the 'Dies irae', whose recapitulation is in the 'Libera', already composed.

Think then, and feel remorse, what deplorable consequences that praise of yours could have! – but don't worry: it's a temptation that will pass like so many others. I do not like superfluous things. There are so many, many, many *Masses* for the dead!!! It is superfluous to add another. . . .

AB III, 433

The spring and summer of 1871 were spent largely in a search for singers for *Aida* for the Scala premiere, which was to follow that of Cairo. Stolz, after some questions of money, was engaged for Aida (she had been briefly considered as a possible Amneris). Verdi refused to sign a contract until the casting was complete.

Verdi to Tito Ricordi; Sant'Agata, 10 July 1871

[. . .] You must know the libretto of *Aida* and you know that for Amneris we need an artist of highly dramatic feeling, and mistress of the stage. [. . .] The voice alone, however beautiful, is not enough for that part. I care little for so-called refined singing: I like to have parts sung the way I want: however, I cannot give anyone voice or soul, or that certain something that is commonly called having a devil in one. [. . .]

This arrangement of the orchestra is far more important that is commonly believed, because of the mingling of the instruments, the sonorities, and the effect. These little improvements will open the way then to other innovations that will surely come one day, and among these that of removing spectators' boxes from the stage, bringing the curtain to the footlights: the other, making the orchestra invisible.

This idea is not mine; it is Wagner's. It is very good. It seems impossible that nowadays we can bear seeing our wretched tailcoats and white ties, mixed, for example, with a Egyptian, Assyrian, Druid costume, etc. etc., and to see, moreover, the mass of the orchestra 'which is part of the fictitious world' almost in the midst of the stalls amid the world of the booers or applauders. [. . .]

AB III, 461

On 1 November 1871, premiere of *Lohengrin* at the Teatro Comunale, Bologna, the first performance of a Wagner opera in Italy. 187–88

From Enrico Panzacchi's 'Riccardo Wagner'

Who does not remember it, who saw it? The Teatro Comunale towards eight in the evening was filling with eager people, serious and almost grave. Many had the thick volume [of the score] under their arm. Even the ladies gradually entered their boxes and sat in the front, silent, with a certain air of composed, solemn expectation. Stalls, benches, standing room, boxes, galleries, all crowded. Everyone was in his place; the men almost all in full dress and white tie, the ladies, décolletées and very elegant.

In those ten minutes of waiting Bibiena's auditorium resounded with a contained, deep hum, like a gigantic hive; up in the top gallery every now and then a rougher grumbling burst out, a laugh, a cry: Viva Verdi! Viva Rossini! But it was a matter of a moment. – The theatre clock marks eight sharp: in the hall a sepulchral silence has promptly fallen. There, Angelo Mariani has climbed on to his podium; he turns slowly to right and left his handsome head with its flowing hair; he smiles calmly at Camillo Casarini, who from his mayoral box, responds with a nervous smile; and in the orchestra the Prelude begins.
PAN, 65 FF.

Mariani to Richard Wagner; Bologna, 2 November 1871

With an overjoyed spirit I am glad to communicate to you myself the very happy outcome obtained here by your exquisite *Lohengrin*.

I say with an overjoyed spirit, because my faith was completely justified; and as I take endless pleasure in the glory that comes from it to you, so I am pleased, and I will say so, to have to some small degree contributed to the complete fulfilment of our common wish.

As to the details, I would like you to receive full and free news, as you will, from a hundred other people and from impartial judgments.

I will sum up briefly, and I will say: the singers were good, and especially the protagonist. The orchestra confirmed its reputation, a merited one, of first rate excellence. The chorus reached the apex of excellence [. . .]

Applause, ovations, encores, everything in short combined to make one of the most beautiful days of my life!

From many Italian provinces came the flower of musical knowledge. I can thus only add my sincere congratulations to the praise of the many, who are worth far more and understand far more than I, and proudly shake your hand. [. . .]
PANIZ II, 31

On 19 November Verdi went to Bologna to hear *Lohengrin* for himself. He tried to maintain his incognito, but failed.

Mariani to his friend Carlino Del Signore; Bologna, 20 November 1871

To avoid new rancours or misunderstandings, and apart from any other interpretation which might perhaps fall, like so many others, on my shoulders, I must tell you something, because if the Maestro should ever talk to you about it, it is well that you know the pure truth of it.

Yesterday at three p.m. I was at the station, called there by a friend of mine who was in the suite of the Grand Duke Michael of Russia. I saw there Signor Luigi Monti, the Ricordi agent [in Bologna]. I asked him what he was doing, he replied that he was waiting for someone, but he hadn't arrived. No sooner had he said these words, when I see, a few paces off, the Maestro. I go to him, greet him, and try to relieve him of the burden of his case: he doesn't allow me. I realized that he was not pleased that I had seen him arrive. I gave him my word of honour that not a living soul would learn from me. He went off, I remained at the station. Half an hour later I went home by carriage, lay down as usual on my bed, got up at dinner time, did not speak with a living soul, and, at the usual hour, went to the theatre.

I realized from certain imperfections in the performance of the chorus and the singers that there was some emotion on stage. After the first act, complaining of this, I was told that Maestro Verdi was in the theatre, and, to be precise, in box 23 of the second tier. I answer that it is not true, I am told to go and see from the little pass-door, but I don't go. I encounter la Sacconi and she also told me she had seen him, and in reply I call her imbecile. After the second act I hear from the management's box Luigi Monti shout: Viva il Maestro Verdi, to which a general applause from the public replies, prolonged for about a quarter-hour. You can imagine the impression I received! *Now I am in a fine fix* (I said to myself). *The Maestro will believe I told and will think me one who doesn't keep his word.*

The Maestro, naturally, did not show himself, and I believe he was absolutely right. I know that even the Mayor asked him, but all to no avail. I asked how it was known; I was answered, *from some Milanese who arrived on the same train and who had seen him enter, and then in the box.* [. . .] The Maestro then left the theatre at the end of the opera; I was told he left last night [. . .]

The Maestro's presence had alarmed singers, chorus, and orchestra, because there were here and there imperfections in the performance that had not happened the previous evenings [. . .].
AB III, 506

Verdi's annotations in his score of Lohengrin

> *too loud* [opening of the Prelude]
> *can't understand* [end of first page] [. . .]
> *beautiful but proves heavy with violins' constant high notes* [end of Prelude]
> *as a scene, the sight is beautiful at the beginning, but all the stage movement slow*
> [. . .]
> *ends well, one curtain call* [end of Act II]
> *well played the second time* [end of Act III Prelude]
> [. . .]
> *beautiful, badly sung, quarter-tone flat* [end of Act III]
> TOTAL

Mediocre impression. Beautiful music, when it is clear and there is thought. The action flows slowly like the text. Hence boredom. Beautiful instrumental effects. Abuse of suspensions and result heavy. Mediocre performance. Much *verve* but without poetry and refinement. In the difficult passages always bad.
AB II, 508–11

Verdi to Giulio Ricordi; Genoa, 8 December 1871

In receiving your letter this morning, you cannot imagine my amazement in receiving another from Filippi, in which he tells me he is going to Cairo, invited by the Viceroy. Ahhhh! . . . [. . .]

Listen, my dear Giulio! At this moment I feel so disgusted, so revolted, so irritated that I would a thousand times set fire to the score of *Aida* without a sigh! Shall I? . . . We are still in time! . . . the contract is not yet signed, and if you want to destroy everything . . .

But if this poor opera must still exist, for the love of heaven no *réclames*, no machinations which for me are the most humiliating humiliation. Oh everything I saw in Bologna and hear now in Florence revolts me! No no . . . I don't want *Lohengrinades* . . . Rather the fire!!
AB III, 517

In September–October 1871 Teresa Stolz had paid her first visit to Sant'Agata. In November–December she was in Genoa, with other singers, to study her role of *Aida* with Verdi for La Scala. Her engagement to Mariani was by now broken, and their relationship at an end. She was by now in fairly regular correspondence with Giuseppina and with Verdi.

Teresa Stolz to Giuseppina; Milan, 12 December 1871

Dear Signora Peppina, I cannot help but thank you for the kindness you showed me during the time I remained in Genoa, and if occasionally I took advantage of this kindness, annoying you too much, attribute it only to the sincere affection I bear you. . . . From the letter I wrote the Maestro you will know that I have been obliged to take a flat in Via Agnello, no. 8.

[. . .] The few people I see always speak to me of Mariani, all say that he is very ill and that he must seriously take care for his health . . . It seems that Mariani really was ill in Florence. [. . .]

I don't know what course to take, if I am to believe these things or not. I unfortunately know his way of always exaggerating his ailments, so I wouldn't be the least surprised to hear that Mariani has arrived in Genoa all fresh as he was a few months ago!! . . .

I wish we were already in the month of January, to have the pleasure of seeing you and embracing you here in Milan. . . .

AB III, 251

195–6 On 24 December 1871, premiere of *Aida* at the Khedival Opera, Cairo. The Milan critic Filippo Filippi went to Cairo, despite Verdi's disapproval (see p. 227), and sent a series of long articles about Egypt, the opera house and the opera.

Verdi, *Aida*, 1871. Title page of Arabic libretto. Formerly in Opera House, Cairo.

194 *Filippo Filippi, La Perseveranza, Milan, 27 December 1871*

Archaeology in *Aida* is all for the eyes, and here in Cairo, for richness and scrupulosity well combined with elegance, the production has succeeded with a perfection which no other theatre will be able to achieve, unless it reproduces

199 exactly the sets, costumes, jewels, all the accessories of Cairo, and it is not easy, for Mariette Bey, happy with the

201–6 triumph, keeps the designs well preserved, to have them
191 photographed eventually, and to make with them a handsome bibliographical souvenir.

I attended many stage rehearsals and production rehearsals, in which all took part with exemplary assiduousness and care, even the masses [orchestra and chorus], accustomed in these theatres to hasty rehearsals of

189 repertory operas. Bottesini for the orchestra, Devasini for the chorus, D'Ormeville for the staging, have not had a moment's rest for a fortnight. The musical rehearsals always proceeded regularly; those of the staging, on the contrary, were slow, incomplete, so that at the pre-dress rehearsal not one set, one wing, one platform was in place, and the big moving platform for the final scene was still to be finished, the one where above there is the temple of Vulcan, below the cave where Aida and Radamès die.

When, at the pre-dress rehearsal, I saw the production so unready, I could not believe that a good dress rehearsal could be held on Saturday and that, on Sunday they could risk the premiere. But a higher will ordained the miracle, and the miracle took place. The Viceroy had said he was leaving on Tuesday for a long excursion to Upper Egypt, and that on Sunday he wanted to attend the premiere of *Aida*. No sooner said than done. Saturday's dress rehearsal was an heroic effort for all; suffice it to say that it lasted from seven in the evening to three-thirty in the morning, with the presence of subscribers, almost all of whom stayed in their places till the end, including the ladies in the boxes, and the Viceroy himself with his suite.

This dress rehearsal decided the success, because, with the subscribers there, the theatre illuminated, the artists dressed in their costumes, it differed from the first performance only in the far longer intervals between the acts, caused by the still incomplete and untried stage machinery. As at the performance, there was applause, ovations, cries of enthusiasm, and then, in the animated conversations during the intervals, exchanges of admiration for the great work and a private satisfaction at this signal honour bestowed on the Cairo theatre, that of giving life to such a grand and beautiful musical composition. All the numbers, from the prelude to the final duet, were applauded and even interrupted by the excessive fervour of the impatient. In the hymn that closes the first part of Act One there is a loud suspended chord, which was followed by a burst of applause; Bottesini, irked by the untimely interruption, turned to the audience, shouting in distinct Milanese accent: 'L'è minga finì!' [It's not over!].

At three-thirty, when we left the theatre, after the end of the dress rehearsal, we were all overjoyed and happy at having heard the great Maestro's new music, which, even

228

to those who already knew it by heart, having heard it at the rehearsals, with the prestige of the beautiful sets, the sumptuous decorations, the glow of arms and jewels, and specially the action, seemed to increase and redouble a thousand times in beauty and dramatic efficacy; for theatrical effect is a distinct, salient character of the operas of Verdi, and it is singular how they gain in performance, whereas many very beautiful compositions, admirable when read at the piano and in score, on the stage become faded, monotonous, boring; in this respect the genius of Verdi has a great affinity with that of Wagner, *mutatis mutandis*, naturally. [. . .]

The curiosity, the eagerness of the Egyptian public to attend the premiere of *Aida* were such that, for about two weeks, all the seats had been snatched up, and, at the last minute, speculators made people pay pure gold for the boxes and stalls. When I say Egyptian public, I refer especially to the European colony; for the Arabs, even the wealthy, do not like our theatre; they prefer the miauing of their chants, the monotonous banging of their drums to all the melodies of past, present and future. It is a true miracle to see a fez in the theatres of Cairo [. . .]

197 For this splendid Italian creation [*Aida*] the Viceroy had the satisfaction not only of the excellent result but also of seeing how all the public which crowded into the theatre, on Sunday evening, recognized at once what a debt of gratitude art and civilization owe to this rare prince, unique in his intelligent munificence. The applause for him, universal, long, frenzied, was not long in exploding; the softly high, last notes of the violins had hardly died away when a cry of 'Long live the Khedive!' was heard reechoing throughout the theatre; in the midst of that polyglot mob the Italian accent dominated; all the ladies stood up; handkerchiefs waved, a thousand voices acclaimed, and the Khedive, rising, greeted with a smile, at once of thanks and of personal satisfaction. [. . .]
MM, 353 FF.

Ernest Reyer, Journal des débats, Paris, 31 December 1871

[. . .] When I accepted the invitation to come to Egypt, to attend the premiere of *Aida*, it was clearly agreed that I would not submit to any influence and that I would express my opinion with the greatest frankness. Had M. Verdi's opera been mediocre, I would have said so directly; it has succeeded; it deserved to succeed; I am happy to spread the good news and to congratulate the composer, towards whom, as is well known, I have never shown either great admiration or much fondness.

This then is a very interesting, very remarkable work, which will surely be appreciated in France as in Italy, and which was written at the instigation of an Egyptian prince. No matter how magnificent and absolute the sovereign of this country may be, he did not have the power to decree a masterpiece, and he knew this well when, to give a novelty to the Cairo theatre, he asked for a new score from the most popular of Italian composers. With the best intentions in the world, M. Verdi could easily have responded to the Khedive's wish as he responded, some years ago, to the invitation of the Czar, with *La forza del destino*. Happily the subject of *Aida* is worth far more than that one and has far better served the composer's inspiration. He has even found in it the opportunity to create some local colour, which does not happen to him often, and which he did not seem to seek in his previous works. [. . .]

To those who deny movement in music, M. Verdi has just replied like the ancient philosopher: it has walked. To

be sure, the old Verdi still survives; one finds him in *Aida* with his exaggerations, his brusque oppositions, his carelessnesses of style and his transports. But another Verdi tinged with Germanism is also shown, very skilfully using, with a learning and a tact that one did not suspect in him, the artifices of fugue and counterpoint, combining timbres with a rare ingeniousness, breaking the old melodic moulds, even those which were peculiar to him, caressing in turn the grand recitatives and the long melodic lines, seeking the newest harmonies, at times the strangest, the most unexpected modulations, giving the accompaniment more interest, often more value, than the melody itself. [. . .]

No one can tell me any more that M. Verdi lives in the most complete isolation and remains absolutely indifferent to all new works, to any new system. A few years ago I was assured that he had never read *Don Giovanni*. That is quite possible, but he has read it since, and has even ventured much farther. I am quite certain that the works of Richard Wagner are familiar to him, and those of Berlioz as well. He must also have studied the scores of Meyerbeer a bit and have considered the procedures of M. Gounod, which are not those of just anyone. His studies in these different genres were perhaps only sketched when he wrote *Don Carlos*; they are much advanced, if not absolutely complete today. And if he persists in his new manner, Maestro Verdi, while some enthusiasms will cool around him, will make many conversions and will win many adepts, even in the circles where until now he was not admitted. [. . .]
REY, 185FF.

A dancer describes Verdi rehearsing *Aida* at La Scala, where it was first performed on 8 February 1872.   207 209

'An unknown artist' to Gaetano Cesari, critic of Corriere della Sera; Milan, 23 November 1923

In your valuable article of yesterday on the premiere of *Aida* at La Scala, I read, concerning the choreographic part of the 2nd scene of Act II, the observation that 'here the scenic action at a certain moment towards the end of the act seems even to attract towards itself the centre of gravity which is in the music'. Your observation is correct, and it seems useful to me to recall an event, which I believe unknown, which I had occasion to know because I too was an artist then (how many years ago, alas!) and I was a witness, and it might also interest the readers of the *Corriere*.

When *Aida* was given the first time at La Scala, the dances were devised and the triumphal march staged by Maestro Giovanni Casati, then illustrious director of the ballet school of La Scala. He, a true artistic temperament [. . .], made of the grand triumphal march a true cinematograph of movement, grandeur, with various and picturesque groupings of ballerinas, entwinings and weavings of masses of swordsmen, of dancers following one another so as to form a marvellous and spectacular apotheosis of glory.

At the pre-dress rehearsal Verdi was sitting in the centre of the stalls, surrounded by members of the Artistic Committee, to observe the stage effect, which he was seeing in complete action for the first time, and obviously that great movement seemed excessive to him and perhaps harmful to the musical demands, so with a sudden start he sprang to his feet and shouted, interrupting the rehearsal: 'Away with those ballerinas! Away with these people. . . . There's too much movement!' and he quickly climbed on to the stage to prompt the desired changes. But Casati, a very proud little man and convinced of his conscientious and effective work, considered himself offended by the maestro's outburst, though he was a great friend and admirer. He rushed from the theatre, leaving the rehearsal half-done, and went home. As soon as Verdi learned that Casati was no longer in the theatre, he was very sorry and sent Giulio Ricordi to his house [. . .]. Ricordi exerted himself and persuaded Casati to come back. So he and Giulio Ricordi between them worked out the changes and simplifications of effect that the Maestro wished and which have always been retained, more or less, in the later productions of *Aida*.

For the record I might add that Casati always bore Verdi a bit of a grudge over this, a grudge which, however, completely vanished at the first night of *Otello* at La Scala, when Casati, in an interval, in the electrifying enthusiasm of that unforgettable evening, encountering Verdi on the stage, threw his arms around this illustrious friend and contemporary, who, moved, cordially returned the embrace with a feeling of affection as of respect.

MS, EREDI CESARI, PARMA

After Milan, *Aida* was given in Parma, again with Stolz in the title role. And during these months there were long negotiations between Verdi, the singers, and the management of the Teatro San Carlo in Naples. The contract was finally concluded (engaging Stolz had been one of Verdi's conditions), and in early November 1872 Verdi and Giuseppina went to Naples, where a new production of *Don Carlos* was to precede the *Aida* premiere.

Verdi to Tito Ricordi; Naples, 2 January 1873

Stupid criticisms, and even more stupid praise: not one elevated, artistic idea; not one who chose to point out my intentions; blunders and nonsense always, and basically a certain vexation as if I had committed a crime in writing *Aida* and having it well performed.

Nobody, finally, who chose to underline at least the material fact of an exceptional performance and *mise en scène*! Not one who said to me: *thanks, dog*!

COP, 280

213–15   Because of an indisposition of Stolz's, the opera was delayed, and the Verdis' stay in Naples prolonged until early April.

Verdi to Arrivabene; Sant'Agata, 16 April 1873

[. . .] In my moments of idleness in Naples I actually wrote a quartet. I had it performed one evening in my house without attaching the slightest importance to it, and without issuing invitations of any kind. Present were only seven or eight people accustomed to visiting me. Whether the quartet is beautiful or ugly I don't know . . . All I know is that it's a quartet!

ALB, 156

'Un dilettante', Gazzetta musicale di Milano, April 1873

[. . .] The other evening we go to Verdi's and . . . wonder: there lined up two classic music-stands, with the classic candles, the classic chairs. What is this? . . . and the Maestro, smiling, begging us to keep talking about our

230

Verdi, Quartet in E minor, 1873. First page of score published by Ricordi, Milan. William Weaver Collection, Monte San Savino (AR).

own affairs, to avoid the danger of falling asleep through having to digest the hearing of a quartet. Protests, declarations, counter-protests, negotiations, finally a settlement is reached, as we agree to sit down in soft armchairs where Morpheus could gently rock us *si casus erat*. It seems to me that this time it was not the case, because not only did we hear the quartet once, but insisted at all costs on hearing it over again completely.

[. . .] All four movements of his quartet are four creations of genius. The first and last movements are more severe, more learned, especially the Finale which is a splendid and very bold fugue. More genial, more moving are the [. . .] Scherzo and Andante. [. . .]

AB III, 624

On 22 May 1873, Alessandro Manzoni died in Milan.   216

Verdi to Giulio Ricordi, 23 May 1873

I am profoundly saddened by the death of our Great Man! But I shall not come to Milan, for I would not have the heart to attend his funeral. I will come soon to visit his grave, alone and unseen, and perhaps (after further reflection, after having weighed my strength) to propose something to honour his memory.

Keep this secret, and do not say a word about my coming, for it is so painful to hear the newspapers speak of me, and to make me say and do what I do not say and do not do. Greet Clarina! Addio.

AB III, 642

Verdi to Clarina Maffei, 29 May 1873

I was not present, but there will have been few on that morning more sad and moved than I was, though far away. Now all is ended! and with him ends the most pure, the most holy, the most lofty of our glories.

I have read many papers! None speaks of him as it should. Many words, but not deeply felt. And the bites are not lacking. Even for Him! Oh what an ugly race we are!

AB III, 643

Verdi to Giulio Ricordi; Milan, 3 June 1873

217–19 I would also like to demonstrate what affection and veneration I bore and bear that Great Man who is no more, and whom Milan has so worthily honoured. I would like to compose a *Mass for the dead* to be performed next year for the anniversary of his death. The *Mass* would have rather vast dimensions, and besides a big orchestra and a big Chorus, it would also require (I cannot be specific now) four or five principal singers.

Do you think the City would assume the expense of the performance? The copying of the music I would have done at my expense, and I myself would conduct the performance both at the rehearsals and in church. If you believe this possible speak of it to the Mayor; give me an answer as soon as you can, for you can consider this letter of mine binding.

AB III, 643

Verdi to Giulio Bellinzaghi, Mayor of Milan; Sant'Agata, 9 June 1873

No thanks are owed me by you or by the Council for the offer to write a funeral *Mass* for the anniversary of Manzoni. It is an impulse, or better, a need of the heart that impels me to honour, insofar as I can, this Great Man, whom I so admired as a Writer, and venerated as a Man, model of virtue and of patriotism!

When the musical work is well advanced I shall not fail to inform you as to what elements will be necessary to make the performance worthy both of the country and of the Man whose loss we all mourn. [. . .]

AB III, 644

Verdi to Giulio Ricordi; Sant'Agata, 6 June 1873

Now that the matter is public, what is being said of the *Mass* I shall write? Surely there is nothing wrong with this, but *I know my chickens*, as Giusti said, and I am sure there will be heaps of *ifs* and *buts*. Keep me informed. [. . .]

How many tiresome and irritating things in these days! Oh blessed a thousand times is the peasant, who is born, eats, and dies without anybody taking interest in his affairs! and we, stupid gypsies, cannot take a step without its being remarked on a thousand ways! But people are right to treat us like this . . . we who wear out our brains to be their buffoons, and to amuse them. . . .

AB III, 644

Verdi to Giulio Ricordi, 6 September 1873

[. . .] P.S. I receive a letter from the Management of Trieste inviting me to go there for the first performance of *Aida*!!! By the Holy God am I then considered a charlatan, a clown who likes to display himself like a *Tom Pouce*, a *Miss Baba*, an *ourangothan* or some other monster!! Poor me! Poor me! [. . .]

AB III, 648

Clarina Maffei to Verdi; Clusone, 13 September 1873

[. . .] Before leaving Milan, which was 20 July, I knelt before that Tomb, and what I felt, you can understand . . . I also went to visit poor Piave, what a touching sight, it was early in the morning, the bedroom still not done, and yet he was clean, white linen, his person very tidy, and this to the honour of that good Elisa [Piave's wife], who called out to that unfortunate, what we say when we go to bed and when we wake, *viva Verdi*, and when we go to table, *viva Verdi*, and He, with tears in his eyes, but, but, but. . . . [. . .]

AB III, 652

Verdi to Escudier, 19 October 1873

[. . .] Since I returned from Paris I have done nothing but move up and down through the fields, eat, and sleep. I have almost not read the papers, because I have been falling asleep as soon as I stick my nose into them. But now, if the weather, as it seems, turns bad, I will be forced to stay in the house, and I will return to my *Mass*, which I would like to finish before going to Genoa, at least I would like to finish the creative part.

AB III, 654

Verdi to Du Locle; Genoa, 28 February 1874

[. . .] I am working on my *Mass*, and it really is with great pleasure. I feel as if I had become a serious man, and am no longer the public's clown who with a great bass-drum . . . shouts: 'Come on in, step right up, etc.' You will understand that on hearing operas mentioned now, my conscience is scandalized, and I quickly make the Sign of the Cross!! What do you have to say to that? [. . .] Aren't you edified by me? [. . .]

AB III, 679

Giuseppina to Clarina Maffei; Genoa, 5 March 1874

[. . .] Verdi, I believe, will make another quick trip to Milan in a few days; but I shall stay in Genoa. He has many things to settle for his *Mass* and he will settle them better in person than by writing letters for two months on end.

It is true: when one reaches a certain age, one lives much on memories. All of us have happy, sad, and dear ones, but alas! not all are fortunate enough to maintain unchanged the affections and the friendship of the living, or at least the illusion of possessing these riches that make life dear. Lucky you, who believe, possess and deserve to possess the affection of your old and new friends!

As for me, I will tell you in profound disillusionment, I hardly believe in anything or anyone any longer. . . . I have undergone so many and such cruel disappointments that I am disgusted with life. . . .

AB III, 670

The singers for the *Requiem* included Stolz and Maria Waldmann, the Aida and Amneris of La Scala. 218 / 210–12

Teresa Stolz to Verdi; Milan, early 1874

[. . .] If you were coming soon to Milan (which I wish very much), then I would not need the part, and I would prefer to study it with the Maestro, I believe it would be better for me, and also for you [singular], because, *true pumpkin-head that I am*, I might make some big blunder if I go through it and study it on my own. . . .

La Waldmann would also like to know when rehearsals begin . . . I write to Sant'Agata assuming that you [plural] are there to enjoy the pure and cool air. . . . When you [singular] are in Milan I will ask you for some good advice about the contracts that are being offered me for next year.

AB III, 687

Verdi to Giulio Ricordi; Sant'Agata, 26 April 1874

What! You haven't yet begun rehearsing the chorus? Ah, you are a bit too confident! I realize it may be as easy as you like, but there are matters of expression, and above all of character, that are not so easy. You will understand better than I that this *Mass* must not be sung the way an opera is sung, and thus colours that can be good in the Theatre will not satisfy me at all. The same can be said of the accents, etc. etc.

[. . .] La Waldman[n], you will know by now, is at the Europa. I was planning to begin the rehearsal on 1 May with the singers but we will begin Saturday evening (2 May). I will be in Milan that same Saturday at 5.30; invite the four Singers to the Hall that the City selects for 8 o'clock sharp. If Capponi [the tenor] is not in Milan by Saturday we will begin all the same. . . .

I do not want the parts to be distributed beforehand. Saturday evening will be spent having them hear their parts without their singing . . . in fact perhaps for this reason it would be better to invite first the men at 8, and the ladies afterwards at 9 . . . I said not to distribute the parts, but if [the bass] Maini (whom I believe very slow) asks for his, you can give it him. But do not give it to la Stolz or to la Waldman[n]. I am afraid of mistakes in the words. [. . .]

AB III, 688

219   On 22 May 1874, first performance of the *Messa da Requiem*, in the Chiesa di San Marco, Milan.
The conductor Hans von Bülow, in Milan that May, attached more importance to the first production outside Russia of Mikhail Glinka's opera *A Life for the Czar (Ivan Susanin)* – a fiasco – than to the Verdi *Requiem*, from which he absented himself.

Hans von Bülow, Allgemeine Zeitung, No. 148, 1874

[. . .] The second [event], in the Church of San Marco, which has been decorated to look like a theatre, is the monster performance, exceptionally under the direction of the composer, Senator Giuseppe Verdi, of his *Requiem* commissioned by the city authorities to commemorate the first anniversary of the death of Alessandro Manzoni (22 May 1873). With this work the all-powerful despoiler of
221   Italian artistic taste – and ruler of the taste he has despoiled – presumably hopes to eliminate the last remains, irksome to his own ambition, of Rossini's immortality. As is well known, this last remnant resides, as far as Italy is concerned, solely in his ecclesiastical music – the *Stabat Mater* and the *Petite Messe solennelle* – seldom though his compatriots ever have a chance to hear these works. For more than a quarter-century the Attila of the larynx has been exerting himself – with total success – to ensure that Rossini operas such as *Tell, Barbiere, Semiramide* and *Mosé* are simply no longer playable in Italy. His latest opera in ecclesiastical

dress will, after the first token obeisance to the memory of the poet, be straightway exposed to secular enthusiasm at La Scala for three evenings, after which it will set off for Paris, with the soloists he has trained up himself, for its coronation in the aesthetic Rome of the Italians. Surreptitious glances at this newest manifestation of the composer of *Trovatore* and *Traviata* have not exactly whetted our appetite for this so-called 'Festival', although to give the Maestro his due he hasn't exactly given himself an easy time of it. Among other things, the concluding fugue, in spite of many student faults, lapses of taste and ugly blemishes, is an elaborately worked-out piece that will come as a surprise to many a German musician. In general, however, the style is that of his latest period, as Berlin and Vienna have heard it in *Aida*: that style of which a singing-teacher on the Danube wittily observed that it had 'improved, much to its detriment'. But in the end the sorry spectacle of yesterday's defeat of Slavonic culture (which from the musical point of view is as much as to say German culture) has made us incapable of maintaining our *sang-froid* through a triumph – artificially contrived – of Latin barbarism. It is to be hoped that Verdi's *Requiem* in Paris will not receive the attentions of German theatrical impresarios, who even from the purely commercial point of view would do well to look eastward for a change instead of westward. [. . .]

BÜLOW V, 341

Verdi to Giulio Ricordi, May 1874

[. . .] It would be better for all, and more dignified, to speak no more of the Bulow affair; and, to tell the truth, if these Germans are so insolent the fault is chiefly ours. When they come to Italy we so swell their natural vainglory with our ravings, our enthusiasms, with our mindless epithets, that they naturally must well believe we cannot breathe or see the light without their bringing us their sun.

And let us speak the whole truth: isn't the enthusiasm, especially in Milan, for Bulow and Rubestein [Rubinstein] 99 degrees above their merit? What are they after all?

Pianists at an immense distance from Liszt and Chopin, and third-rate musicians. . . .

AB III, 690

Almost immediately after the Milan performances, the *Requiem* was given in Paris at the Opéra Comique, with Verdi conducting. Arrangements were going forward for further performances there, and in other European cities, the following year. Verdi spent the summer at Sant'Agata, and in the autumn moved into his new Genoa residence, the Palazzo Doria.

From Resasco's study of Verdi in Genoa

Of the Verdi residence in Palazzo Doria, besides the   233–34
monumental terrace with its marble balustrade, from which the maestro cast so often his eagle's gaze on the immensity of the horizon, three rooms were particularly memorable: the great reception salon, the bedroom containing the piano, and the Turkish chamber. There, in the dazzling reception salon [. . .], Giuseppe Verdi, as sovereign of art, received not only his admirers, sons of the same fatherland, but the foreigners who came to urge him warmly to grant the treasure of his genius also to their theatres. [. . .]

RES, 16–17

Verdi to Piroli; Genoa, 21 November 1874

I receive your letter that announces my being named Senator. Yesterday I received the despatch of the Prefect of Parma by order of the Minister. I am very sensitive to this high honour they have chosen to give me; but what have I ever done to deserve it? And besides . . . what a poor Senator! In any event tomorrow I will write to the Minister and thank him: meanwhile I thank you because you are surely the one behind the whole business.

The despatch tells me to come and take the oath at the Royal session, and I would come at once, but you know that at the Apollo the first opera is *Aida*, and perhaps by now they are rehearsing. If I came to Rome, it would be quite difficult for me to evade these musical nuisances, and I don't want to be bothered now with the performance of *Aida*. [. . .]

AB III, 721

Verdi to Giulio Ricordi; Genoa, 6 February 1875

I send you the new 'Liber scriptus' for mezzosoprano. [. . .] As you see, the piece follows without a break immediately after the bass solo 'Mors stupebit', etc. etc., and is followed by the big forte bar 1, page fifty of the printed score. *Amen.* [. . .]

AB III, 736

Verdi to Maria Waldmann; Genoa, 5 March 1875

[. . .] Another thing: you know that I have written a solo for you, but I would advise against performing it in Paris. You know that for an audience the first impressions are always terrible, and even if that piece were effective, all would say: '*It was better as it was before.*' This would be the return you and I would surely have. [. . .]

AB III, 740

Verdi to Giulio Ricordi; Sant'Agata, 4 April 1875

You speak to me of results obtained!!!!!!!!! What?... I'll tell you. After 25 years that I had been absent from La Scala I obtained booing after the first act of *La forza del destino*. After *Aida* infinite gossip: that I was no longer the Verdi of *Ballo* (of that *Ballo* that was booed the first time at La Scala); that it would have been terrible if it hadn't been for the fourth act (according to d'Arcais); that I *didn't know how to write* for singers; that there was only something tolerable in the 2nd and fourth acts (the third nothing) and that finally I was an imitator of Wagner!!! Fine result after 35 years of career to end an *Imitator*!!! [. . .]

AB III, 745

Verdi to Piroli; Paris, 6 May 1875

[. . .] the *Mass* is going really well in every respect. The quartet of singers has gained much because this year we have a tenor who has a delightful and true voice. Oh if only he were an artist! Tomorrow evening, Friday, we will have the last *audition* and Saturday we leave for London.

The premiere in London will be on the fifteenth and after four or six performances, I'm not sure which, we will go to Vienna. [. . .]

AB III, 750

211   Blanche Roosevelt met Verdi in Paris on 5 June 1875.

From Blanche Roosevelt's life of Verdi

The mouth is large and pleasant, but it is almost totally concealed by a dark moustache, which gives the face a very young look. The forehead is very broad and high, denoting great character and quickness of perception; the eyebrows are heavy, also gray and black. The hair is very long, lying lightly on the forehead; it, also, is slightly mixed with gray. There are a wonderful firmness and hidden strength in Verdi's countenance, which made me think of a picture I had once seen of Samson.

In one way I was disappointed in his looks. He has the air and figure of anything but an ideal composer. I do not know what I expected to find, but certainly he has the frank, social manners of an ordinary individual rather than the exclusive and sometimes painful diffidence characteristic of men of great talent. I cannot say he lacks dignity, but there was so utter an absence of self-consciousness in his bearing, and such a happy, gracious smile on his face, that I was charmed with his whole manner.

ROOS, 78

Eduard Hanslick on Verdi's Requiem

In June of 1875, Verdi conducted four performances of his *Requiem* in Vienna, scoring a series of triumphs over a combination of summer heat and high admission prices. The public received the work with unwonted enthusiasm; our best connoisseurs and laymen, among them many a sworn anti-Verdian, participated unreservedly in the applause. Verdi, already so ill-considered as an opera composer in German countries, must have been prepared for the most bitter opposition as a church composer, the more so since it is one of the delights of the German critic to dampen the public's pleasure by merciless fault-finding in trivial and superficial matters. But in these days of *succès d'estime*, a real, genuine success is so rare that the critic, too, is disposed to share in the general enthusiasm, even if the festivity is not without certain improprieties and some of the enthusiasm unnecessarily boisterous.

Verdi's *Requiem* is a sound and beautiful work, above all a milestone in the history of his development as a composer. One may rate it higher or lower as one pleases; the cry, 'We never expected this from Verdi', will never end. In this sense it is a companion piece to *Aida*, which still seems more significant both in invention and execution. How far it is from *Ernani* or *Il trovatore*! And yet it is unmistakably Verdi, wholly and completely. The study of old Roman church music shines through it, but only as a glimmer, not as a model.

To be sure – and this must be stated at the outset – the theatre has greater need of Verdi than has the church. If he has shown in the *Requiem* what he can do on foreign soil, he remains, nevertheless, far stronger on his home ground. Not even in the *Requiem* can he deny the dramatic composer. Mourning and supplication, awe and faith – they speak here in language more passionate and individual than we are accustomed to hear in the church.

The 'unchurchliness' of the Verdi *Requiem* is the first of its qualities to invite criticism. And yet there are few subjects about which it is so risky to pass judgment. The subjective religiousness of the artist must be left out of the question; criticism is not inquisition. [. . .] The essential factor remains: the composer, with due regard for his mission, must remain true to himself.

One must grant Verdi this testament of sincerity: no movement of his *Requiem* is trivial, false, or frivolous. He proceeds incomparably more earnestly, more sternly, than

Rossini in his *Stabat Mater*, although the kinship of the two works is not to be denied. Both composers have hitherto worked exclusively in the opera idiom. That Rossini's special field was comic opera, while Verdi's has been the serious and the tragic, is to the latter's advantage in his *Requiem*. In sweet melodic charm the *Stabat Mater* is superior to Verdi's *Requiem*, if one may say 'superior' where 'inferior' would be more pertinent. Verdi, following the better Neapolitan church music, has denied neither the rich artistic means of his time nor the lively fervour of his nature. He has, like many a pious painter, placed his own portrait on his sacred canvas. Religious devotion, too, varies in its expression; it has its countries and its times. What may appear so passionate, so sensuous in Verdi's *Requiem* is derived from the emotional habits of his people, and the Italian has a perfect right to inquire whether he may not talk to the dear Lord in the Italian language!

PL, 178 FF.

In the summer of 1875 a storm that had been brewing finally exploded. During the *Requiem* tour, Verdi had a disagreement with his publishers about the tour's financing. He began to suspect also that there were 'irregularities' in Ricordi's royalties. So he demanded to see the records. Tito Ricordi fled to the spa of San Pellegrino, leaving matters in the hands of his son. Verdi made Giuseppina act as secretary and go-between.

Giuseppina to Giulio Ricordi; Sant'Agata, 11 July 1875

I answer briefly your letter of yesterday and the two received today from you and your father. Signor Tito did very well to go to San Pellegrino and take advantage of the favourable season to take the cure there. . . . Verdi asks me to say to you that he is surprised that he is consulted about settling the Trieste business. Casa Ricordi must make – and it has every right – all contracts it believes opportune, only they must be made in a *regular way*.

Verdi wants to see all the Contracts of his Operas, from *Rigoletto* to today. Corticelli, who will deliver this to you, leaves for Milan for this reason. They can give him said contracts, for which he will sign a receipt. . . .

Believe in my loyal promise (as I said to you yesterday) I will, in just and honest fashion, do everything possible to restore calm to this still very agitated sea.

AB III, 766

Verdi to Piroli; Sant'Agata, 29 December 1875

First of all happy new year and all good wishes. We spent a very sad Christmas. Peppina was and still is in bed with a light bronchitis; but today she will get up and I want to hope it is over.

[. . .] I have settled things with Casa Ricordi. The firm will pay me 50,000 lire. It is not what would be owed me, but that does not matter. The bad thing is that there will no longer be between us the relationship there was. [. . .]

CV III, 115

224
220   The situation between Verdi and Giuseppina was also troubled still. In one of his absences, at about this time, she drafted a letter to him.

234

From Giuseppina Verdi's notebook, January 1876

You will perhaps recall how lately I have several times mentioned to you the necessity of a conversation between us on certain matters which concern us both, and which it would be well to resolve without hesitations, since time is pressing for us. The opportunity presents itself and I seize it, able to deal with it in a letter because a perfect calm allows me to.

It is certain that for you the climate of Genoa is not favourable. The coal smoke which, with the new commercial installations, now reaches us, has worsened so to speak the atmospheric conditions of this locality, and made very probable, almost inevitable, the necessity of moving house sooner or later. It is true that you have made no efforts to meet Genoese society, but instinctively it is disagreeable to you. We will then have the inconvenience of moving, we will have to go away from the sea, the light, the free air, without society's compensating us for these sacrifices.

Listen well, my Verdi, hear me with a bit of patience, and believe that what I am about to say to you is the result of long reflection, which I expound to you with all sincerity of soul [*erased:* and I have the right to be believed by you]. You love Milan, and its climate is not harmful to you. You like its society, you have in that city your old friends, the memories of your first glories – and to use a modern word – there is in Milan the ambiance suited to an artist.

I propose to you that we go to Milan. The climate cannot harm me, being almost my native climate; you will be able to have, at least in the evening, a bit of company, and when there isn't any, you can go to pay some visits or to a café to spend an hour pleasantly. I, you know, have no need of society, and some good person with whom to exchange words now and then suffices. I love to stay at home; I ask of you only an apartment with light and air and that you do not abandon me completely in these last years of life; by that I mean not to desert the house completely. In that flat city I can take some walks, make some visits, and I will have the opportunity of spending a little money also for myself, for in Genoa I have neither opportunity nor desire. [. . .]

AB III, 783

Verdi to Arrivabene (who had written to him about younger composers); Genoa, 5 February 1876

[. . .] Of those I know the one who can do best is Ponchielli, but alas, he is no longer young, I believe he is about forty and has seen and *heard* too much. You know my opinions on *hearing too much*. . . . I told you in Florence. When the young realize that the light must not be sought in Mendelssohn, or in Chopin, or in Gounod, then perhaps they will *find*. It is a curious thing, however, that they take as model for Drama authors who are not dramatic.

You will be surprised that I speak in such a way of the author of *Faust*! What can I say? Gounod is a very great musician, the first composer of France, but he does not have dramatic fibre. Stupendous music, likeable, magnificent details, the word almost always well expressed . . . mind you, the word, not the situation, the characters not well drawn, and no imprint of particular colour in the drama, or the dramas [. . .].

ALB, 185–6

On 22 April 1876, Verdi conducted *Aida* at the Théâtre   222
Italien, Paris.

Verdi to Tito and Giulio Ricordi; Paris, 28 April 1876

AIDA

1st perf.	Takings Fr. 18,000 plus
2nd perf.	Fr. 17,700 plus
3rd perf.	Fr. 17,796

The takings would have risen to 20,000 and perhaps more, if Escudier had had the courage to eliminate completely the so-called *service de presse*. From the takings then it seems a success. The press treated the women a bit badly, especially la Stolz, but for the rest very favourable. Naturally here, as in Germany, I learned to write well only three or four years ago, but at least they haven't accused me of Wagnerism, as I was so kindly accused then by the Italian press, the Milanese in particular. [. . .]
AB III, 798

At about this time, Giuseppina again drafted a letter to Verdi, summing up the situation between herself and Verdi on the subject of his relationship with la Stolz. The translation is by Frank Walker.

From Giuseppina's notebook; Paris, April 1876

'It didn't seem to me a fitting day for you to pay a call on a lady who is neither your daughter, nor your sister, nor your wife!' The observation escaped me, and I perceived at once that you were annoyed. It's quite natural, this ill-humour of yours hurt me, for, as she's not ill and there's no performance, it seemed to me you could spend twenty-four hours without seeing the said lady, all the more since I had taken the trouble, so as not to fail in my attention towards her, of asking her personally how she was; I told you as soon as I reached home again.

I don't know if there's anything in it, or not. . . . I do know that since 1872 there have been [*added and erased*: febrile] periods of assiduity and attentions on your part that no woman could interpret in a more favourable sense. [*Erased*: I know that I have never failed to show cordiality and courtesy to this person.] I know that I have always been disposed to love her frankly and sincerely.

You know how you have repaid me! [*Erased*: There is no biting word . . .] With harsh, violent, biting words! You can't control yourself. [*Partly erased*: But then I open my heart to the hope that you will see this person and things as they are.]

If there's anything in it . . . Let's get this over. [*Erased*: If you find this person so seductive] Be frank and say so, without making me suffer the humiliation of this excessive deference of yours.

If there's nothing in it . . . Be more calm in your attentions, [*added and erased*: don't display such agitation], be natural and less exclusive. Think sometimes that I, your wife, despising past rumours, am living at this very moment *à trois*, and that I have the right to ask, if not for your caresses, at least for your consideration. Is that too much?

How calm and gay I was the first twenty days! And that was because you were cordial. . . .
WAL, 431

Gossip about Stolz and Verdi had already reached print, in a pair of scurrilous articles published in a Florence paper that past winter. Giuseppina had put on a brave front, continuing to write to Teresa. Whatever Verdi may have answered to Giuseppina, we cannot know. Nor can we know the exact nature of his relationship with Teresa Stolz. Certainly, some months later Giuseppina's attitude began to change to one of resignation: a resignation that was later to mellow into warm friendship. The *menage à trois* continued, but it was a threesome of friends growing old together. Stolz retired from the stage in 1877, settled in Milan, and became a regular visitor to Sant'Agata, as she continued to be after Giuseppina's death in 1897. Stolz was at Verdi's deathbed. Meanwhile the correspondence went on.

Teresa Stolz to Giuseppina; Paris, 21 June 1876

[. . .] It is a very sad thing to see dear ones leave! ! I would have liked to say so many things to you [singular] in those last moments, instead I stood there like a plaster statue, and I didn't say even a word to express my gratitude for all the kindnesses you did me in allowing me to live in your dear company. These three months were for me delightful, there were some ailments, some artistic emotions, but in the end I felt so happy with you [. . .].

Dear Peppina, I tried to perform your errands; but unfortunately I couldn't find the same coffee colour that you gave me as a sample; everyone told me the colour is no longer in fashion . . . Today I am packing my trunks [. . .].
AB IV, 8

In August, Teresa Stolz was at Tabiano, a spa not far from Sant'Agata. According to a previous plan, Giuseppina was to have joined her there, with Filomena Maria Verdi and with Barberina Strepponi (Giuseppina's perennially ailing sister, who was to survive another forty years).

Giuseppina to Teresa Stolz; Sant'Agata, 8 August 1876

I'm sorry, but it's impossible for me to come to Tabiano this year. Without seeking other reasons, there are the following two, which you will easily understand: It's too early – It's too late. Too early, because since the baths are still crowded, besides being badly lodged, one would have to bother about one's *toilette*, and I don't really feel disposed to put up with that frivolous tyranny. Too late because Maria, who is not at Sant'Agata, has to take her final examinations about 20 or 25 August and I shall have to spend some days in Turin, both to attend some of the examinations and to complete the formalities required by such an occasion. Besides, even if I did burden myself with the disagreeable task of packing and making my *toilette*, there would be left only a few days to take the cure, so I definitely give up the idea of Tabiano. Bathe and enjoy yourself, for one only lives once. [. . .] You will not need news of Verdi, because he gives it to you himself. I still have pains in my knees and my liverish spots, which will pass away, if they do pass away, even without bathing. For the rest, good or bad health matters little to me.
WAL, 434

In the end Giuseppina and Maria did go to Tabiano briefly, and Teresa came back with them to Sant'Agata for a visit. Then she went off for a season in Russia, and for a while she was safely out of the way. After her return, the decline of Verdi's passion – if passion it had been – into friendship began.

The year 1877, for Verdi, was fairly uneventful. In January he received an invitation to conduct his *Requiem* at the Cologne festival, and in May he did so.

Verdi to Arrivabene; Cologne, 22 May 1877

I had said I would write you before leaving Italy, and I am writing only now after I have been here a week. But now I can tell you so many things . . . I can tell you first of all that I am half dead with fatigue, not so much from the rehearsals as from a constant coming and going, excursions, invitations, visits, dinners, suppers, etc. etc. that I have refused as many as I could. I couldn't refuse, however, to go to a concert of the Choral Society, which sang various compositions of their greatest masters. Marvellous performance. The Quartet Society wanted to have me hear *mine*, also marvellously performed. [. . .] Finally last night the *Mass* with a chorus of 300 and orchestra of 200. . . . Most excellent performance on the part of the masses, but not on the part of the four soloists. Very good success. The Ladies of the Chorus (amateurs from Cologne and the nearby cities, *gratis*) have given me a silver-decorated ivory baton. The Ladies of the City a magnificent wreath of silver and gold; on each leaf is written the name of the Lady . . . [. . .]
ALB, 203

The impact of Verdi on one famous German is recorded in a letter from the art historian Jakob Burckhardt.

Jakob Burckhardt to Max Alioth; Munich, 15 August 1877

[. . .] Yesterday again *Aida*! Everyone divinely in voice! Nachbauer as Radamès sent forth the most marvellous rockets. This time the finale of the second act swept me along to the heights, then again the wonderful third act with Reichmann as Amonasro – one of the most gentle and yet powerful baritones God's grace created. Not to mention the towering moments in the fourth act! One can go mad over this. – Afterwards I went to the Ratskeller and drank two pints of Affenthaler in solitary enthusiasm.
BUR, 401

Verdi to Arrivabene; Sant'Agata, 22 October 1877

[. . .] As for me I lead my usual peasant's life, or rather now I act as bricklayer, because I build, knock down, remodel houses etc. etc. just to be doing something. After Cologne, I nailed up, so to speak, the piano, and music seems to me something of another world. I am not even interested in politics. I read or rather skip through some newspapers. [. . .]
ALB, 204

In 1878 Paris, recovered from the war, was holding another great international Exposition, and to represent Italy the orchestra of La Scala was to perform, under Franco Faccio, now Italy's leading conductor and a much-praised interpreter of the *Messa da Requiem*.

Faccio to Verdi; Ravenna, 22 May 1878

For some time I have wanted to write to you, but so far I have always restrained myself because the profound emotion that grips me every time I address you is equalled by my fear of disturbing you. But now I would really need

236

your paternal, authoritative opinion. [. . .] The Orchestra of La Scala (which has found a group of capitalists with the necessary funds for the heavy expense) has agreed to give some concerts in Paris. [. . .]

What pleasure, and at the same time, what anxiety! Allow me to transcribe part of article 32 of the General Regulations of the Exposition. 'Representatives from abroad are requested to base themselves, in the composition of their programmes, on the following principle: that they are to present in particular the music of their compatriots. The programmes of the performances of foreign music will be made up of national works by living composers, and of works by dead composers without distinction of origin.' Following this article I would have in mind to prepare three programmes of twelve pieces each (would ten suffice?), in which we would perform Sinfonie by our great Italian masters: Cimarosa, Boccherini, Rossini, Verdi, Donizetti, Mercadante, not excluding the works of Foroni, Bazzini, and the young composers [. . .] then in each programme I would put two pieces, Overtures and fragments of symphonies of the unique Beethoven. [. . .]
DE R, 157

Verdi to Faccio; Sant'Agata, 26 May 1878

I would not know what to answer and there seems to me no answering your esteemed letter of 22 May. Since you have agreed to go to Paris to give concerts with the orchestra of La Scala, since the Commission there imposes a programme, you can only conform, and any opinion would be an obstacle. I can only send my warmest best wishes for a splendid success to the honour of our country. . . .
AB IV, 59

Verdi to Clarina Maffei; Sant'Agata, 19 June 1878

[. . .] Faccio wrote me asking my *paternal advice* (as he says!) on the repertory. Two days later I saw announced in the *Gazzetta musicale* the programme of the 1st Concert. *A quoi bon* my paternal advice? It was a joke that would have offended me if it had not come from Faccio. Finally let us hope that the fire, the impetus that Faccio will be able to communicate to the orchestra (provided it goes no farther) will save everything. There is nothing else to be hoped. There is no counting on the *recettes*, and there will be slim pickings. [. . .]
AB IV, 60

Faccio to Verdi, after the first concert; Paris, summer 1878

The triumph of the orchestra of La Scala was complete, and in giving you the festive news I feel as if relieved of a huge weight. Three pieces were repeated, among them the Overture of *Vespri* which had the broad hall of the Trocadéro cheering [. . .]
AB IV, 61

Verdi to Arrivabene; Sant'Agata, 14 October 1878

[. . .] Do you remember that girl, or rather that child you saw here 10 or 12 years ago? On the 17th of this month she will be the bride of an excellent young man of the Carrara family of Busseto. I am very pleased. I believe she will be happy in this family, well-off and a bit patriarchal [. . .]
ALB, 222

243

232

Teresa Stolz to Giuseppina; Milan, 24 December 1878

[. . .] My dear Peppina, I wish you all happiness, health, every satisfaction your heart desires, these are the wishes of my sincere heart.

[. . .] Chance willed that at the Teatro Comunale [Bologna] (where I had gone to hear the new opera *Creola* by Coronaro) I ran into the Contessa Massari [Maria Waldmann] with her husband. Imagine the surprise of both of us! ! It was then immediately agreed between us to pay a visit to little Cecchino [Waldmann's infant son], and in fact after a two-day stay in Bologna I left for Ferrara. Maria and her Count preceded me by 24 hours, and Maria came to fetch me at the Station with her beautiful equipage.

What can I tell you, dear Peppina, of the grandeur, the riches, the sumptuousness of Count Massari! ! ! [. . .] As soon as I got out of the coach I saw lined up a number of servants all in livery. . . . Immediately I was presented to the *Contessa madre*. . . . Maria was at the peak of happiness in showing me all the grand Palazzo. [. . .]

The Count showed me his stables . . . there I saw at least thirty beautiful horses, afterwards he led me to the coach house, where there were at least twenty carriages of every kind and size. . . . In the garden too there are beautiful hothouses with rare plants. . . .

AB IV, 68

Giuseppina to Teresa Stolz; Genoa, 26 December 1878

Thank you for your unfailing thoughtfulness and the wishes you make me for the future. Though I have *little faith*, as you know, and have completely lost trust in the world, still I should and do believe in your protestations, which [*erased*: if I have never done you harm] you would have no reason not to offer sincerely and cordially. [. . .]

AB IV, 69

In the early summer of 1879 there were terrible floods in Italy, causing many victims. For the benefit of those victims, Verdi agreed to conduct, at La Scala, a special performance of the *Requiem*. For the occasion, Teresa Stolz and Maria Waldmann emerged from retirement.

Filippo Filippi in La Perseveranza, Milan, 1 July 1879

[. . .] At the end of the *Mass* there was a colossal demonstration; from the boxes began a rain of flowers flooding the stage, and covering the maestro, the artists, everyone. When the ladies of the chorus had their hands full, the bouquets passed from the stage to the stalls, collected by the ladies there. [. . .]

If art triumphed, charity enjoys the fruits of the triumph, with the more than 30,000 lire taken in for the benefit of the flood victims.

Immediately after the *Mass* a great crowd formed in front of the Hôtel Milan, and Maestro Verdi, when he arrived there from the theatre, was received by lively applause and enthusiastic cheers. He had to appear on the balcony to respond to the insistent acclamations of the public.

The Hôtel Milan was festively decorated. Over the door of the lobby, where the maestro entered there was a trophy, with, inside a wreath, some flowers forming *Viva Verdi*.

A little later some space was cleared in front of the Hotel to place the Scala orchestra there for the serenade. It was not an easy undertaking, since Via Manzoni was crowded.

The orchestra was conducted by Maestro Faccio. [. . .]

ALB, 238 FF.

Verdi stayed on in Milan for a few days. On one of those evenings, Giulio Ricordi came to dinner, with Faccio.

Giulio Ricordi's account to his biographer Giuseppe Adami

The idea of the opera came up during a friendly dinner, in which, by chance, I had the conversation turn to Shakespeare and to Boito. At the mention of *Othello* I saw Verdi stare at me with mistrust, but with interest. He had certainly understood, had certainly responded. I believed the time was ripe. My able accomplice was Franco Faccio. I was over-confident. The next day when, on my advice, Faccio took Boito to Verdi with the plan for the libretto already outlined, the Maestro, after examining it and finding it excellent, would not commit himself. He said: 'Now write the poem. It will always be good, for me . . . for you . . . for someone else.'

AD, 93

Verdi to Giulio Ricordi; Sant'Agata, 4 September 1879

[. . .] A visit of yours will always be welcome, accompanied by a friend, who now, obviously, would be Boito. Allow me, however, on this subject to speak to you very clearly and without ceremony. A visit of his would commit me too much and I absolutely do not wish to commit myself.

How this plan for the Chocolate [this was Verdi's and Ricordi's code-name for *Otello*] was born, you know. You were dining with me, with some friends. We spoke of *Othello*, of Shakespeare, of Boito. The next day Faccio brought Boito to the Hotel. Three days later Boito brought me the sketch of *Otello* which I read and found good. Write the poem, I said to him; it will always be good for you, for me, or for someone else, etc. etc.

Now, if you came here with Boito, I would find myself obliged to read the finished libretto he will bring. If I find the libretto completely good I find myself somehow committed. If, finding it good, I suggest changes that Boito accepts, I am even more committed. But if it is very beautiful, and I still don't like it, it would be too difficult to tell him to his face.

No, no . . . you have already gone too far and this must stop before gossip and aversion are born. In my opinion, the best course (if you believe it and this suits Boito) is to send me the finished poem, so that I can read it and express my opinion calmly without its committing either of the two parties. Once these touchy difficulties have been smoothed out, I will be happy to see you here with Boito. [. . .]

AB IV, 86

The correspondence about *Otello*, which continues for another seven years or so, is voluminous (in fact, it will appear in a separate volume, being prepared by the Instituto di studi verdiani, Parma). Not only did Verdi and Boito exchange countless letters, but there are also letters exchanged between Boito and Ricordi, between Ricordi and Verdi, and between Giuseppina – another catalyst in the opera's creation – and Ricordi. Here it is impossible to give more than a brief sampling.

Giuseppina to Giulio Ricordi, 7 November 1879

[. . .] Now let us come to the serious part of your letter. I know Boito very slightly, but I believe I have figured him out. A nervous, highly excitable nature! When invaded by admiration, capable of boundless enthusiasm and perhaps also sometimes, *through effect of contrast,* capable of excessive antipathies. All this, however, in brief paroxysms and only when there is a struggle between mind and heart, or rather between contrasting passions, or powers. The honesty and fairness of his character must quickly gain dominion and balance all his faculties. A firm friend and, at the same time, mild and impressionable as a boy, when his fibre is not, so to speak, *piqued.* I say all this to make you *understand,* that I seem to have *understood* the man; so I am not surprised at his febrile state in the present moment.

In the hope of bringing a bit of calm, I will whisper into Giulio's ear a little confidence, on condition that it doesn't become the secret of Pulcinella. Towards the 20th of this month of November, we will come to Milan to spend a few days, and I would be of the opinion to wait till that moment, which seems to me most opportune, because, without attracting attention, or arousing the interest of the curious, Boito could speak at length and calmly with Verdi.

Inter nos, what has been written so far of the *African* [another code-name for *Otello*] is apparently to his [Verdi's] taste and very well done; surely the rest will be just as well done. Let him then finish the poem calmly, abandoning himself to his fantasy (without torturing it); as soon as it's finished, let him send it without delay or hesitation to Verdi, before he comes to Milan, so he can read it in peace and if necessary make his observations in advance. I repeat: the impression is good; the changes and polishing will come later.

I wish and believe we can say: All's well that ends well, and so it will end. [. . .] Do not tell Verdi I have written you on this subject. I believe the best way is not to arouse in Verdi's spirit the idea of even the most remote pressure. [. . .]

AB IV, 113

From Milan Verdi went to Genoa and from there, 12 February 1880, to Paris, where he conducted the first performance of *Aida* at the Opéra, sung in French, on 22 March. Giuseppina and Teresa were with him.

Giuseppina to her sister Barberina Strepponi; Turin, 11 April 1880

[. . .] Tomorrow we leave for Milan, where, as you will see from the papers, the most outstanding citizens have decided to erect to Verdi, still living, thank God, a solemn testimony of admiration, of affection for his genius, for his character, and for having gloriously borne the name of Italy to the most distant regions of the civilized world. This solemn tribute of honour is deserved; and I, though I find it difficult to display my feelings, am moved at the sole thought of it, impossible as it would be for me to put it in words! It will not be one of the usual noisy festivities, too dear to the Italians, but a serious, dignified, extraordinary event, for HIM, who, though great, has not passed to immortality, leaving his mortal remains to the world.

A statue will be erected to the greatest living composer of his time, in the foyer of La Scala, and Verdi will be able to witness, as it were, with his own eyes, his own apotheosis! May God bless him a thousand times, as my heart desires.

AB IV, 118

For the solemn occasion there was the first performance of two new pieces by Verdi, the *Pater noster* and the *Ave Maria.* Needless to say, they were a great success, and both had to be sung twice. Among those present on the occasion were Muzio, the old painter Hayez, and Faccio, who conducted. Verdi made a well-received speech. He then returned to Sant'Agata, while Giuseppina went to Genoa.

Giuseppina to Verdi; Genoa, 21 April 1880

[. . .] I got up more tired than yesterday and absolutely without the wish to say a word. I am happy, however, that, except for the donkeys braying at this moment, nobody for today at least will come to disturb the profound peace of this Wednesday 21 April. If the weather is good, starting tomorrow I will busy myself with the furs and winter things to put away in pepper and camphor. [. . .]

Don't tire yourself, my dear Pasticcio, and [. . .] try to arrange to live to the age of Methuselah (966 years) if for no other reason than to please those who love you. [. . .]

Now I leave you, I kiss and embrace you. I wish you good appetite and for myself I wish to see you turn up soon, very soon, because I still love you madly and sometimes when I'm in a bad humour, it is a kind of *amative* fever, not known to any physician. [. . .]

AB IV, 123

Verdi to Boito; Sant'Agata, 15 August 1880

Giulio has surely told you that I received your verses a few days ago and wanted to read and study them with care before replying.

They are certainly better than the first, but to my way of thinking it's still not a dramatically effective piece, because the possibility of that does not exist. After Otello has insulted Desdemona, there's nothing more to be said, at most a phrase, a reproach, a curse against the *barbarian* who has insulted a woman! And here, either bring down the curtain, or come up with an *invention* not in Shakespeare! For example, after the words: 'Silence, Devil!' Lodovico, with all the pride of a patrician and dignity of an ambassador, could remonstrate with Otello: 'Unworthy Moor, you dare insult a Venetian patrician, my relative, and do not fear the wrath of the senate.' (a stanza of 4 or 6 lines)

Iago gloats over his handiwork (a similar stanza)
Desdemona laments (a similar stanza)
Rodrigo (a stanza)
Emilia and chorus (a stanza)
Otello silent, motionless, awesome, says nothing . . .

Suddenly in the distance drums are heard, trumpets, cannon fire, etc. etc. – The Turks! The Turks! – Soldiers and populace invade the stage; surprise and fear on all sides. Otello stirs himself and draws himself erect, lion-like; brandishes his sword . . . : Let us go! I will lead you again to victory! All leave the stage except Desdemona. Meanwhile the women, rushing in from all sides, fall on their knees while offstage are heard the warriors' cries, cannon fire, drums, trumpets, and all the fury of battle. Desdemona in the centre of the stage, isolated, motionless, her eyes fixed on Heaven, prays for Otello, Curtain. The musical number would be there, and a composer might be satisfied. The critic would have many remarks to make. For example: If the Turks have been defeated (as is said at the beginning) how could they now fight? This, however, is not a serious criticism because one could suppose, and say so in a few words, that the Turks suffered damage and were scattered by the storm, but not destroyed. There would be a more serious objection: Can Otello, overcome with sorrow, gnawed by jealousy, disheartened, physically and morally ill – can he suddenly pull himself together and become again the hero that he was? And if he can, if glory can still fascinate him, and he can forget love, sorrow, and jealousy, why should he kill Desdemona and then himself?

Are these scruples, or serious objections? [. . .]

WAL, 477

Boito to Verdi; Milan, 18 October 1880

[. . .] When you ask me, or rather yourself: Are these scruples, or serious objections? I reply. They are serious objections. Otello is like a man moving in circles, under an incubus, and under the fatal and growing domination of that incubus, he thinks, he acts, he suffers, and commits his tremendous crime. Now if we invent something that must necessarily excite and distract Otello from this tenacious incubus, we destroy all the sinister spell created by Shakespeare and we cannot logically reach the climax of the action. That attack by the Turks is like a fist breaking the window of a room where two persons were on the point of dying of asphyxiation. That intimate atmosphere of death, so carefully built up by Shakespeare, is suddenly dispelled. Vital air circulates again in our tragedy and Otello and Desdemona are saved. In order to set them again on the way to death we must enclose them again in the lethal chamber, reconstruct the incubus, patiently reconduct Iago to his prey, and there is only one act left for us to begin the tragedy over again. In other words: *We have found the end of an act, but at the cost of the effect of the final catastrophe* [. . .].

AB IV, 173

Towards the end of 1880 the *Otello* project was temporary shelved, while Verdi engaged Boito's assistance in another, less demanding assignment: a revision of *Simon Boccanegra*, which was to be given at La Scala that season. Boito quickly dedicated himself to the revisions which involved, among other, smaller things, an entire new scene. He made several suggestions.

Verdi to Boito; Genoa, 11 December 1880

Either the Council chamber . . . or the Church of San Siro . . . or do nothing. To do nothing would be the best thing; but reasons that are not commercial, but, I will say, professional, prevent me from giving up the idea of revising this *Boccanegra* – at least without having first tried to do something with it. Parenthetically, it is in everyone's interest that La Scala live! The programme for this year is deplorable! Very good the opera of Ponchielli [*Il figliuol prodigo*], but the rest . . . Eternal Gods!! There would be the opera to awaken great interest in the public, and I don't understand why author and publisher stubbornly refuse it. I am speaking of [Boito's] *Mefistofele*. The moment would be propitious and you would be doing a service to art and *to all*.

The act you have invented in the church of San Siro is stupendous in every respect. Beautiful in its novelty; beautiful in historical colour; beautiful from the dramatic-musical point of view; but it would demand too much of me and I could not undertake so much work. Unfortunately renouncing this act, we must stick to the scene of the Council chamber, which, written by you, I am sure cannot prove cold.

Your criticisms are just, but you, involved in more elevated works and having *Otello* in mind, aim at a perfection that here it would be impossible to achieve. I set my sights lower, and, being more of an optimist than you, do not despair. I agree that the table is rickety, but adjusting a leg or two, I think it can stand. I agree further that there are none of those characters (always very rare) that make you cry: 'he is sculpted in the round'; nevertheless it seems to me that in the characters of Fiesco and of Simone there is something that can be well exploited. [. . .]

MS, ISV, PARMA

Boito to Giulio Ricordi; 21 January 1881

When the Management of La Scala decides to publish the appendix to the season's programme with the announcement of *Boccanegra*, care must be taken and neither by error nor by indiscretion must my name or my anagram [Tobia Gorria] be printed.

You know that I have agreed to work on the libretto of *Boccanegra* because I am devoted to Verdi's wishes, you know that I have been consistently opposed to the idea of staging this opera at La Scala now, you know that I attribute no artistic or literary merit to those revisions I have made to the work of poor Piave.

So I beg you to watch out for this: the new *Boccanegra* must appear with the name of F. M. Piave, pure and simple, and my name must not be added in any way.

AB IV, 175

On 24 March 1881, premiere of *Simon Boccanegra* (revised version) at La Scala, Milan. The cast included the tenor Francesco Tamagno, the future Otello, and the baritone Victor Maurel, the future Iago. Verdi, however, was in no hurry to begin work on his new opera. That summer Ricordi and Boito came to Sant'Agata for a visit, and the third act of the libretto was discussed. For some time, too, the composer had been urging his friend, the Neapolitan painter Domenico Morelli, to paint him an *Iago*.

241
258

Domenico Morelli to Verdi; Naples, 1 September 1881

215

[. . .] Iago – easier said than done – how to paint him? Now it seems to me that I have found him in a kind of figure, in a certain face, in a proportion I would say of underdeveloped limbs; now it seems to me he is not [the Iago] of the author; and I must forget all I have toyed with for so long, and find another. If Shakespeare had not made him a soldier, or at least if he had not made him say he had been to war, I would be freer to imprint his Jesuitism on his figure and face: and then? There is more, the dramatic, *true* action, of one who contemplates with (*apparent*) concern a man who suffers. The more hypocritical, the more hidden, the less visible his wickedness – and in painting where all is apparent you know how difficult this is. I realize that when the conception is right, one can paint anything, but in the case of a subject found, conceived by another, one's own conception can be correct only up to a certain point, and especially when dealing with that friend of ours [Shakespeare], who cannot be surpassed or matched.

AB IV, 182

Verdi to Morelli; Sant'Agata, 24 September 1881

For the type of figure of Iago, . . . you would like a small figure, of (you say) underdeveloped limbs, and, if I have understood correctly, one of those sly, malignant figures, I would say *pointed*. Very well: if you feel him like that, do him like that. But, if I were an actor and had to play Iago, I would rather have a long and thin figure, thin lips, small eyes set close to the nose like a monkey's, broad, receding brow, and the head developed behind; an absent, *nonchalant* manner, indifferent to everything, witty, speaking good and evil almost lightheartedly, and having the air of not even thinking of what he says; so that, if someone were to reproach him: 'What you say is vile!' he could answer: 'Really? I didn't think so . . . we'll say no more about it! . . .'

A figure like this can deceive everyone, and even up to a point his wife. A small, malicious figure arouses everyone's suspicion and deceives nobody! *Amen.* [. . .]
AB IV, 183

Muzio to Giulio Ricordi; Paris, 2 May 1882

Verdi and the Signora have arrived, they are resting today, and tomorrow they will be visible. [. . .]
AB IV, 200

Verdi was in Paris to look after his copyrights, after the death of Escudier. He also was thinking of a revised *Don Carlos*, in four acts; the revisions were to be done by Charles Nuitter, archivist of the Opéra, in collaboration with Du Locle, with whom Verdi was not on speaking – or even writing – terms by then, since the financial failure of Du Locle's management of the Opéra Comique (1870–74) had lost Verdi a great deal of money in royalties. This work occupied Verdi through the late summer, autumn, and winter, with the prospect of a performance in Vienna (which did not, in the event, come off). One interesting problem concerns the still-debated end of the opera.

Verdi to Charles Nuitter; Sant'Agata, 14 June 1882

Charles V's being alive has always jarred upon me. If he is alive, how is it that Don Carlos does not know it? Moreover (always supposing him to be alive) how can Philip II be an old man, as he describes himself. [. . .] We must decide whether it suitable or not to omit this *Monk* who is half ghost and half man; or whether instead it might not be better to transform this *Monk* into an old colleague of Charles V, long since dead: a monk who could come to pray at Charles V's tomb.
PORT, 11

Du Locle replied in a third-person memorandum.

From Du Locle's 'Notes on projected modifications to the libretto of Don Carlos'; Paris, 1882

[. . .] The death of Charles V, which was for a long time kept hidden, is not a date in history, since for many years he had disappeared from the world's stage on which he had played so large a part. He himself, retiring to the monastery of Yuste, liked to wrap himself in a kind of funereal mystery. He had his obsequies celebrated with great pomp, attending them dressed in a monk's robe, hidden amid the friars of the monastery. This is more than enough to justify the operatic role which the authors of the *Don Carlos* libretto have assigned to the great Emperor. [. . .] For the

rest nothing could be less historical than the whole tale of *Don Carlos*, and the way it is handled by Schiller, whose play is the starting-point of the opera.

[. . .] To suppress the character of Charles V would be to diminish the grandeur and effectiveness of the introduction to the new first act, so striking from a musical point of view, and would be a more than regrettable sacrifice. If *the monk* were to become an ordinary monk, how could one justify the journey, made twice during the course of the drama, by all the Spanish court from Madrid and from Valladolid to Yuste, deep in the mountains of Estremadura. [. . .]

[. . .] The author of this note thinks it desirable that the role of Charles V should be retained. Perhaps the secret of his life continuing among the monks, while he prays beside his empty tomb, should and could be better explained [. . .] then at the end, after Carlos is sentenced, Charles V could appear perhaps having reassumed the Imperial attributes; he could intervene like a God at the denouement of a classical tragedy, to conclude the action either by saving or condemning Carlos. That is where a happy invention would be needed. One could hope for it from no one better than the master who devised the admirable scene of the last act of *Aida*.
PORT, 11 FF.

Verdi to Giulio Ricordi; Genoa, 15 February 1883

Sad! Sad! Sad! Wagner is dead!!! Reading the despatch about it yesterday, I was, I might almost say, terrified! No question. It is a great individual who has gone! A name that leaves a very powerful imprint on the history of art!!
AB IV, 208

Returning to Busseto that summer after taking the waters at Montecatini Terme, the three travellers stopped off in Florence. A young librarian, Italo Pizzi (later to become a distinguished Orientalist), showed them round.

From Italo Pizzi's 'Ricordi verdiani'

On Saturday 14 July 1883, a day memorable for the great heat, I was in the Laurentian Library in Florence, spending, somnolent and lazy, the afternoon hours. A public guide, one Battaglia, entered, accompanying a handsome gentleman, already well-along in years, followed by two ladies. It was the Maestro, coming back from Montecatini, and he had with him Signora Strepponi, his wife, and Signora Teresina Stolz, formerly a famous singer.

Verdi observed with great attention the precious things housed in that distinguished library, the illuminated pages displayed, the autographs of Petrarch, Cellini, Alfieri, the second-century Virgil, the Tacitus found in Westphalia, the Paulus Orosius. He asked about many things and, among others, also about the celebrated Foligno edition of the *Divine Comedy. . . .* I showed the Maestro the most dear and prized possessions of the library, those that are kept jealously locked away and which are not shown to all [. . .].

But he did not reveal himself simply as an admirer, he was also erudite. . . . I was amazed at him when, showing him a very rare edition of the works of Aristotle in Greek, made in Venice and adorned with beautiful miniatures of animals, he said: 'I know no Greek, but this must be the History of animals of Aristotle.' And he was right.
PIZZI, 9–12

Later that year Carlo Tenca died, Verdi's friend and for many years the lover of Clarina.

Verdi to Clarina Maffei; Sant' Agata, 11 October 1883

I have been told everything. I admired your courage, and I can well understand now, after the first nervous excitement, all the dejection of your spirit. There are no words that can bring comfort to this sort of misfortune. And I will not say to you the usual stupid word 'courage': a word that has always aroused my wrath when addressed to me. It takes something quite different! You will find comfort only in the strength of your spirit and the steadfastness of your mind. [. . .]

The years are really beginning to be too many and I think . . . I think that life is the most stupid thing, and worse still, useless. What do we do? What have we done? What will we do? Summing up everything, the answer is humiliating and very sad:

NOTHING!

AB IV, 226

On 10 January 1884, premiere of *Don Carlos*, revised version in four acts, at La Scala, Milan.

Verdi to Clarina Maffei; Genoa, 29 January 1884

[. . .] I'm sorry that on this last occasion I wasn't able to spend more time with you. But you know how it is. When one has to deal with that galley that others call the theatre, one is never master of one's own time. Poor artists, whom many have the . . . I will say, the kindness to envy; slaves of a public most often ignorant (thank goodness), capricious, and unfair.

I laugh when I think that I too have had some moments of weakness. . . . I was 25 years old . . . but they were of brief duration. A year later the blindfold fell away; and when, later, I had to deal with the public, I armed myself with cuirass, and prepared for the rifle-shots, I said: *A noi!* Have at you! In fact, there were always battles. Battles that never gave satisfaction, even when one conquered!! Sad! Sad! . . .

I have twice seen Boito, who is having a peaceful time at Nervi. [. . .]

AB IV, 231

Boito to Giulio Ricordi, 20 March 1884

[. . .] I have good news for you, but for heaven's sake don't tell anyone, don't even tell your family, don't even tell yourself; I fear I have already committed an indiscretion. The Maestro is writing, indeed he has already written a good part of the opening of the first act and seems to be working with fervour. [. . .]

WAL, 488

But Boito's jubilation was to be short-lived. That same month of March his *Mefistofele* was triumphantly given in Naples. There, at a banquet given by the professors of the Conservatory, a journalist asked him why he had given his libretto of *Otello* (then called *Iago*) to Verdi instead of composing it himself. Boito's answer, which was meant to be evasive, was reported in the press.

Verdi to Faccio; Genoa, 27 March 1884

[. . .] *Il Pungolo* quotes from *Il Piccolo* of Naples these sentences: 'On the subject of *Iago*, Boito said that he had dealt with the subject almost reluctantly; but that, once finished, he regretted not being able to compose it himself.'

This words, spoken at a banquet, admittedly may not have great value; but unfortunately they lend themselves to talk. It could, for example, be said that I forced him into dealing with this subject. That would be no great harm; and you know, for that matter, how things went.

The worse thing is that Boito, *regretting* not to be able to compose it himself, leads the reader naturally to suppose that he does not hope to see it composed by me as he would like. I accept this perfectly, I accept it completely, and that is why I am addressing you, Boito's oldest, firmest friend, so that when he returns to Milan you can say to him, not in writing, that I, without a shadow of resentment, without any sort of bitterness, return his manuscript to him intact. Moreover, since the libretto is my property, I offer it to him as a gift if he intends to set it. If he accepts, I will be happy in the hope of thereby making a contribution to and furthering the art that we all love. [. . .]

AB IV, 236

Faccio met Boito in Turin and gave him the message.

Boito to Verdi; Milan, 19 April 1884

[. . .] If I had not gone to Turin who knows how many months I would have delayed learning what you wanted me to know from my friend's lips. Thank you with all my heart, my Maestro, thank you, but it seems to me already too much to be obliged to answer you in earnest that I do not accept, I do not accept your great and noble offer.

[. . .] Only you can compose *Otello*, all the Theatre that you have given us affirms this truth; if I have been able to sense the powerful operatic potential of Shakespeare's tragedy, which I did not feel before, and if I have been able to prove it in my libretto, this is because I have seen it from the Verdian point of view of art; because, in writing those verses, I felt what you would have felt, illustrating them with that other language, a thousand times more intimate and more powerful: music. And if I have done this, it is because I wanted to seize an opportunity, in the maturity of my life, in that age that no longer changes faith, an opportunity to show, better than with praises hurled in the face, how much I loved and felt the art you have given us. [. . .]

But for heaven's sake do not abandon *Otello*, do not abandon it. It is predestined to you, do it, you had already begun working on it and I was already all comforted and hoped already to see it, in a not too distant day, finished. You are more healthy than I, stronger than I, we have tested our strength, and my arm bent beneath yours, your life is calm and serene, pick up your pen again and write me soon: *Dear Boito, please change these verses,* etc. etc., and I will change them at once with joy, and I will know how to work for you, I who do not know how to work for myself, because you live in the true and real life of Art, I in the world of hallucinations.

AB IV, 239

Boito was forgiven, but Verdi did not resume work immediately. The librettist gently prodded him.

Boito to Verdi, 26 April 1884

Your letter, though wise and kind, yet left me, I don't know why, somewhat upset, and I had no peace until I set to work for you again. I remembered that you were not satisfied with a scene of Iago's in the second act, in double five-syllabled lines, and that you wanted a more broken, less lyrical form: I suggested to you to have a kind of *Evil Credo*, and I have tried to write it in an uneven, unsymmetrical metre.

[. . .] So I will transcribe for you the *Credo* of Iago. See how many knavish things I've made him say. [. . .]

CV II, 110

Verdi to Boito; Genoa, 3 May 1884

[. . .] Most beautiful this Credo; most powerful and wholly Shakespearian. You'll have to link it, of course, with a line or two to the preceding scene between Cassio and Iago; but you can think about that later. Meanwhile it would be well to leave this *Otello* in peace for a bit, since he too is on edge, as we are – you perhaps more than I. [. . .]

MS, ISV, PARMA

On 31 May 1884, premiere of *Le villi* in Milan. The first opera by the young Giacomo Puccini attracted immediate attention, and Giulio Ricordi promptly bought the rights to the opera and gave its composer a contract.

Verdi to Arrivabene; Milan, 10 June 1884

[. . .] I have heard the composer Puccini very well spoken of. I have seen a letter that says nothing but good of him. He follows the modern tendencies, and this is natural, but he remains attached to melody, which is neither modern nor ancient. It seems, however, that in him the symphonic element predominates; nothing wrong with that. Only one must proceed cautiously in this matter. Opera is opera; symphony is symphony, and I do not believe that in an opera it is well to have a symphonic passage, for the mere pleasure of making the orchestra dance. [. . .]

ALB, 311–13

For the rest of the year Verdi was mostly idle. Then:

Verdi to Boito; Genoa, 9 December 1884

It seems impossible, but it's true!! I am busy, I am writing!!

MS, ISV, PARMA

This burst of activity lasted until the following April. Then idleness set in again.

Boito to Verdi; Milan, 9 September 1885

My desire to see you again is great, but my fear of disturbing you is equally great.

If you assure me I shan't be a nuisance I'll make up my mind to descend on Sant'Agata next Sunday. [. . .]

WAL, 492

Verdi to Boito; Sant'Agata, 10 September 1885

You can never disturb! Come, and you will give such great pleasure to both me and Peppina. And have no fear of interrupting the course of my work, as you say! Alas! Since I've been here (I blush to say) I've done nothing! The land, to some extent, the baths, the excessive heat, and let us add, my unimaginable laziness have prevented it. [. . .]

MS, ISV, PARMA

But, as Frank Walker says, 'Boito's conversation seems to have had an immensely stimulating effect, for on 5 October, only three weeks after his visit, Verdi announced: "I have finished the fourth act, and I breathe again."' Essentially, *Otello* was completed.

Boito to Verdi; Villa d'Este, 9 October 1885

First of all an *Evviva* from the bottom of my heart. Then I must confess to you that I have an irresistible desire to hear what you have written on that page so full of fears, on that which is the most anguished page ever conceived by the human mind. [. . .]

AB IV, 266

Though revisions and modifications of *Otello* were to continue throughout 1886, much of Verdi's and Boito's time was spent in thinking about the premiere, planned for La Scala. Boito discussed the costumes with the designer Edel. Verdi had to fend off letters from singers.

Verdi to Victor Maurel, late 1885

Otello is not, as has been said, completely finished, but it is well advanced towards the end. I am in no hurry to finish the work, because I have not so far thought, nor am I thinking now, of having it performed. The conditions of our theatres are such that, even when one achieves a success, the expenses for the artists and *mise en scène* are so exorbitant that the impresario must almost always undergo a loss. I do not want therefore to have the remorse of being, with my opera, a cause of ruin for anyone. So things remain suspended between heaven and earth like the tomb of Mohammed, and I make no practical decisions.

Before ending this letter I wish to clear up and explain a misunderstanding. I do not believe I ever promised to write for you the part of Iago. It is not my habit to promise something which I am not sure of being able to maintain. But I may well have said to you that the part of Iago would be one of those that perhaps no one would interpret better than you. If I said this, I confirm that remark. That, however, does not comprise a promise: it would be only a wish, quite capable of being fulfilled, if unforeseen circumstances do not prevent it [. . .]

AB IV, 267

Boito to Verdi; Quinto, 16 May 1886

Bravo!!! I fully approve that cut of four lines that allows Otello's entrance to be shifted [. . .]. Now the entrance, which did not satisfy us and which we sought, is found, and is splendid. A powerful cry of victory which ends in the breaking of a storm and a shout from the people. Bravo! bravo! [. . .]

Edel has already decided, on his own, to start his research for the costumes of *Otello* [. . .]. He has asked me for instructions about the period and I thought it opportune to give him these instructions because Edel is as lazy as he is gifted and he needs much time to do a job. Meanwhile he will prepare himself, doing research and making sketches and buying photographs. [. . .]

So our period is set thus by [Shakespeare's source] Giraldi: *a short time before 1527*. I believe I was not mistaken in setting Edel the outside limit of 1525. A couple of years' margin between the event and the story of the event does not seem too many to me. Edel then, in my opinion, in his studies should not go beyond 1525, but before that outside date he must have a broad space of years to consult. Clothes then changed much less rapidly than they change now. Even today, where there are many people, we see perhaps thirty years of fashion represented; the Italian-style cape that you wear still is one proof and the high collars of your shirts are another proof; thirty years separate one from the other.

I have advised our Edel to study the Venetian painters of the last years of the fifteenth century and the first quarter of the sixteenth. Luckily for us, the two great documents in that space of years are Carpaccio and Gentile Bellini! From their paintings will come the costumes of our characters. [. . .]
AB IV, 284

On 13 July 1886, Clarina Maffei died in Milan.

Verdi to Piroli; Sant'Agata, 7 August 1886

[. . .] I wanted to write to you before leaving Montecatini, and I couldn't! I left in haste; I have been here and there; and I have had a great sorrow at the death of Clarina Maffei. She was my friend for 44 years ! ! . . . Sincere and sure friend! She didn't know how to write verses like her husband . . . but instead what a heart! And what nobility of character! and what loftiness of feelings! Poor Clarina! [. . .]
CV III, 178

Verdi to Piroli; Milan, January 1887

Poor Arrivabene! He too has gone! ! I learned of his death immediately though a telegram sent me by the family or rather by Giovanni. . . .

I have been here for two days. Rehearsals have begun and I hope we will open at the end of the month or the very beginning of February. [. . .]
CV III, 180

On 2 February 1887, premiere of *Otello* at La Scala, Milan.

From Blanche Roosevelt's life of Verdi

Otellopolis [Milan], February 5th, 1887. You may imagine the excitement was not lost on me. I hastily dressed, and before noon was in the streets. Streets? There were no streets – at least, no crossings – visible, and had the blocks of houses not divided the town architecturally, everything would have been run together, like honey, with human beings, human beings, human beings.

The Piazza della Scala was a sight to see, and the cries of 'Viva Verdi! viva Verdi!' were so deafening that I longed for cotton in my ears. Poor Verdi! had he been there, he would certainly have been torn to pieces, as a crowd in its enthusiasm rarely distinguishes between glory and assassination. [. . .]

Well, at last – after dinner – I didn't dine, I swallowed food – we started to the theatre. The carriage had to be sent off long before we reached the door, the horses could not make their way through the crowd. At best, human beings one by one between a line of police could struggle towards the entrance. I expected my dress would be in rags;

Verdi, *Otello*, 1887. Verdi and Faccio with the leading singers. Souvenir print. Museo teatrale alla Scala, Milan.

however, I managed to get in whole, and once there the sight was indescribable. La Scala has never before held such an audience, and although it was fully an hour before the time to commence, every seat was occupied. [. . .]

From pit to dome, the immense auditorium was one mass of eager faces, sparkling eyes, brilliant toilettes, and splendid jewels. The Italian Court was a rainbow of colours, and Queen Margherita's ladies of honour like a hothouse bouquet of rarest exotics. The first and second tiers of boxes were so packed with the Milanese high-bred women, so covered with dazzling jewels and filmy laces, that the house seemed spanned with a river of light, up, up, up to where the last gallery was lost in a dainty cornice of gold. The gleam of diamond tiara and corsage bouquet shot oblong rays on the black-coated background; while the new electric lights, imprisoned in their dead-white globes, shed so unearthly a radiance over the auditorium that we all looked like spectres uprising from some fantastic dead-and-gone rout. As to the platea or 'stalls', it was simply marvellous. I know of no city in the world which could present a spectacle of similar brilliancy. In the first place, it was packed with officers – certainly the handsomest men in the world – gorgeous in the varied and brilliant Italian uniform: staff-officers in full dress, and scarred veterans with their whole record in speaking breast-decorations; and the women – such pretty women as one could see only in Italy; for the Italians are a decorative race when seen in Italy, and picturesque, my dear friend, is the only word possible to describe them. The men look well anywhere; the women may not shine on the Corso, but at the play they will put women of every other nation in the shade. [. . .]

The present incumbent of the leader's place at La Scala is Franco Faccio, an admirable musician and composer, one who knows his band as a flautist knows his stops, and who for years has directed Verdi's operas under the maestro's own eye and dictation. Faccio's appearance in the conductor's chair, which he has filled so long and so well, was a signal for thunders of applause. The orchestra at once struck up a few glorious chords representing a tempest, which were followed by an instantaneous rise of the curtain.

The scenery, costumes, choruses, and orchestra were nearly perfect; the cast was certainly weak. Victor Maurel is the only real artist in the opera, and he is a Frenchman. In voice, acting, appearance, and dress he is the ideal of what an operatic artist should be, and the ideal of what any operatic Iago could be. He sang as even his best friends never dreamed he could sing, and his acting was the consummate work which we always have at his artistic hands. He entered at once into the fullest sympathies of the audience, and I could not help then and there contrasting the Iagos we have seen in other countries with the Iagos we always see in Italy. Iago even seems a *persona grata* to the public; the qualities which raise a thrill of horror in the righteous Anglo-Saxon are received by this susceptible nation with placid contentment and relief. [. . .]

Tamagno, the tenor, looked and acted Othello, but he did not sing – he bleated. Desdemona has never been a favourite of mine in history, and the present exponent of the rôle suggested to me all my thousand unavenged wrongs laid at the door of Brabantio's daughter. Madame Pantaleone is an excellent person, but as Desdemona she ought to have been suppressed the night before at her dress rehearsal. Her voice is naturally fine and dramatic, but she has no more knowledge of the pure art of singing than I have of the real science of astronomy. She has a vile emission of tone in the medium open notes; the upper notes are clear, but rarely in tune. The lovely music assigned to Othello's wife must have splendid resisting powers not to have fallen flat in her hands or throat. In appearance Madame Pantaleone is likewise unfortunate: she is short, slightly cross-eyed, and of a physical plainness, which dwarfed the already insignificant Desdemona. She acted very well in the first and third acts, but not so well in the last. [. . .]

244
245 The ovations to Verdi and Boïto reached the climax of enthusiasm. Verdi was presented with a silver album filled with the autographs and cards of every citizen in Milan. He was called out twenty times, and at the last recalls hats and handkerchiefs were waved, and the house rose in a body. The emotion was something indescribable, and many wept. Verdi's carriage was dragged by citizens to the hotel. He was toasted and serenaded; and at five in the morning I had not closed my eyes in sleep for the crowds still singing and shrieking 'Viva Verdi! viva Verdi!' Who shall say that this cry will not reëcho all over the world?
ROOS, 183–99

The indefatigable Blanche Roosevelt also interviewed Boito, a few days after the performance.

From Blanche Roosevelt's life of Verdi

I said to him. 'How did you feel at such enthusiasm and repeated recalls? It must have been a strange sensation coming out before that sea of faces, accompanied by such roars and billows of applause. Were you pleased? Were you nervous?'

'When I heard my name I was strangely touched,' he replied. 'I had not thought about it. I was up in a box with Signora Verdi when the maestro sent for us. We went to the

stage, and when we were called he started, then turned in a half-dazed way for me. He took my hand. No, I shall never forget it.' In spite of himself, Boïto's voice trembled, and his hand went half towards his eyes, which were filling with tears. 'I can never describe to you how he took my hand: his touch – there was something so kind, so paternal, so protecting in it, and the clasp of his fingers so thrilled me that I felt the shock to my heart's core: it was an electric thrill, and yet so delicate I could scarcely realise that our hands had come in contact. Ah! Verdi said more to me in that single hand-clasp than he has said in all our previous intercourse: more than any one ever will say. I shall never forget it!'

Now will you believe it that we all felt like crying? There was something so pathetic in Boïto's voice that it was impossible not to be impressed, and I really believe, without knowing why, we would have all fell a-weeping.
ROOS, 231

259 Verdi, though not open-handed, could be charitable, even generous, both to individuals and to institutions. He helped Piave, his widow and daughter. And in 1888 a little hospital – at Villanova d'Arda, not far from Sant'Agata – was inaugurated, built at his expense to save the sick peasants of the area a long journey to the nearest hospital, in Piacenza (many died along the way). But his charities brought him problems.

Verdi to Signor Borrani, President of the Verdi Hospital at Villanova; Genoa, 16 January 1889

I think it best to advise you that I have received information about the Hospital of Villanova, and I wish to believe it is not correct. Here is what is said:

1. That the food is scanty.
2. Even scantier the wine (the cellar is provided with this).
3. That the milk is not paid its worth, and hence is poor quality.
4. That the oil is the most ordinary, and hence harmful for the foods, as for the illumination.
5. That there was thought of buying half-spoiled rice and black *pasta* of our district.
6. That even those who have no means at all are made to pay funeral expenses.
7. Many other things which, for the sake of brevity, I will not say.

I, far away, can say nothing, I can neither believe nor disbelieve; but in any case these reports grieve me very much. [. . .]

But I hope that all this is not true, and you will kindly reassure me as soon as possible with a few words.
COP, 350

In late February or early March of 1889, Verdi was in Milan, to examine a piece of land on what was then the edge of the city. At the same time, from an old number of the *Gazzetta musicale*, he worked out the harmony of an 'enigmatic scale': C, D flat, E, F sharp, G sharp, A sharp, B.

Verdi to Boito; Genoa, 6 March 1889

Leaving Milan, I threw into the fire some papers among them that graceless scale. I have still the first part of the scale, but of the second, done on the spot, I have forgotten the modulations and the arrangements of the parts [. . .]. If you haven't burned it, send me the A and G chords.

You will say it's not worth spending time on this trifle, and you're right. But what can I say? When you are old, you become a child, they say; and these trifles recall the age of eighteen, when my teacher enjoyed breaking my brain with such basses.

And more, I believe that from this scale a piece with words could be derived, for ex. an *Ave Maria*. [. . .]

Another *Ave Maria*? It would be the fourth! This way I might hope to be beatified after my death.

AB IV, 375

Boito to Verdi; Milan, 7 March 1889

I was wise to copy out those two pages of the scrambled scale, on which you climbed up and down with such ease. Every difficulty overcome without effort is a grace. In those counterpoints that sing there is a sad sweetness that suggests evening prayer. Let this fourth *Ave Maria* come. Many *Ave Marias* are needed so that you can make His Holiness pardon you for the *Credo* of Iago.

AB IV, 376

Thus the first of the *Four Sacred Pieces* was born. But soon a more important work would begin gestation. In the summer of 1889, Verdi was again at Montecatini. Boito joined him there, and – as a surprise – showed him a sketch for a libretto: *Falstaff*.

Verdi to Boito; Montecatini, 6 July 1889

Excellent! Excellent!

Before reading your sketch, I wanted to reread the *Merry Wives*, the two parts of *Henry IV* and *Henry V*, and I can only repeat: *Excellent*, for one could not do better than you have done.

A pity that the interest (it's not your fault) does not go on increasing to the end. The climax is the finale of the second act; and the appearance of Falstaff's face amid the laundry, etc., is a true comic invention.

I'm afraid, too, that the last act, in spite of its touch of fantasy, will be trivial, with all those little pieces, songs, ariettas, etc. etc. You bring back Bardolfo – and why not Pistola, too, both of them to get up to some prank or other?

You reduce the weddings to two! All the better, for they are only loosely connected with the main plot.

The two trials by water and fire suffice to punish Falstaff: nevertheless, I should like to see him thoroughly well beaten also.

I am talking for the sake of talking – take no notice. [. . .] I'll write to you tomorrow or the next day.

MS, ISV, PARMA

Verdi to Boito; Montecatini, 7 July 1889

I said yesterday I would write today, and I am keeping my word at the risk of annoying you. As long as one roams in the world of ideas all is smiling, but when one sets a foot on the ground, becoming practical, doubts and dejections are born.

In outlining *Falstaff*, did you never think of the enormous number of my years? I know well that you will answer, exaggerating the state of my health, good, excellent, robust. . . . And so be it: all the same you will agree with me

that I could be accused of great temerity in taking on such a task. And if the effort were too much for me? And if I did not succeed in completing the music? Then you would have wasted time and work in vain! I would not want that, for all the gold in the world. This idea is intolerable to me, and all the more intolerable if you, writing *Falstaff*, should, I won't say abandon, but even distract your mind from *Nerone* or delay the period of its production. I would be blamed for this delay, and the thunderbolts of the public's malice would fall on my shoulders.

Now, how to overcome these obstacles? Do you have a good reason to oppose to my reasons? I wish it, but don't believe it. Still let us think about it (and mind you do nothing that could harm your career) and if you found one reason on your side, and I found a way of taking about ten years off my back, then . . . What joy! to be able to say to the public:

A noi! ! Here we are again! !

MS, ISV, PARMA

Boito to Verdi; 7 July 1889

[. . .] This love-making between Nannetta and Fenton must appear suddenly, frequently; in all the scenes where they are present, they will steal kisses secretly in corners, slyly, boldly, without letting themselves be seen, with fresh little phrases and brief little dialogues, rapid and clever from the beginning to the end of the play; it will be a most lively, merry love, always disturbed and interrupted and always ready to begin again . . . I should like, as one sprinkles sugar on a cake, to sprinkle the whole comedy with that gay love, not collecting it all together at any one point. [. . .]

WAL, 497

Boito to Verdi, 7 July 1889

[. . .] The fact is that I never think of your age when I speak to you or when I write to you or when I work for you. It's your fault. [. . .] I don't think it would tire you to write a comic opera. Tragedy makes the person who writes it *really suffer.* [. . .] But the joking and laughter of comedy exhilarates mind and body. [. . .] You have a great desire to work. This is an unquestionable proof of health and strength. *Ave Marias* are not enough. [. . .] There is only one way to end better than with *Otello*, and it is to end victoriously with *Falstaff*. [. . .]

AB IV, 384

Verdi to Boito; Montecatini, 10 July 1889

Amen. So be it!

We'll write this *Falstaff* then! For the moment we won't think of obstacles, of age, of illness!

I too wish to maintain the most profound *secrecy* – a word I too underline three times [. . .]

MS, ISV, PARMA

Verdi set to work at once. In August he was already composing. But he also had other plans in his mind. He was purchasing a large property on the outskirts of Milan, where he was eventually to build his Casa di Riposo for old and needy musicians.

263–66

Verdi to the architect Camillo Boito, Arrigo's brother, October 1889

I am sending the lawyer Dina the contract form today, which will then be given back to you by the lawyer himself as soon as he has examined it. I don't think there is anything to comment on except one phrase 'in order to begin construction as soon as possible', etc. . . . which I have marked in pencil.

So as soon as the lawyer has returned the form to you, you can have the contract drawn up in my name. After the 20th of this month the sum will be on deposit, and you have only to give me 48 hours' notice, to *be in Milan on such and such a day* [. . .].
AB IV, 392

Both Boito and Verdi were concerned about Faccio, whose health was beginning to decline, and whose mind was becoming clouded.

Boito to Verdi; Milan, 20 March 1890

[. . .] First of all a first *Evviva* for the news you give me of having completed the 1st act of *Falstaff*. *Fàlstaff*, like all English bisyllabic names, is accented on the first. Ask Signora Giuseppina if I am right or wrong. I cannot remember any English surname of more than one syllable accented on the last. Only the French, who are incorrigible distorters of foreign surnames, pronounce it *Falstàff*. [. . .]

Yesterday I saw Faccio again. . . . His money is safe. . . . I repeat my impression: this is a mind that is tired but not a mind that is becoming extinguished. Rest will make him healthier than before.
AB V, 397

Verdi to Teresa Stolz; Sant' Agata, 12 August 1890

With this letter you will receive by Rail a case containing two shoulders of ham, San Secondo style, which we are sending, one for you and one for the Ricordi family. Pick the one you want. Mind you, to cook this kind of shoulder well, you must:

1. Put it in tepid water for about 12 hours to remove the salt.

2. Put it afterwards in cold water and boil over a slow fire, so it won't blow up, for about 3 hours and a half, perhaps 4 for the larger one. To see if it's done, prick the shoulder with a *curedents* and, if it enters easily, the shoulder is done.

3. Let it cool in its own broth and serve. Take special care in the cooking; if it's hard, it's not good, if it's over-cooked it becomes dry and chewy. [. . .]
AB IV, 402

For some years Emanuele Muzio had been living in Paris, first as conductor at the Théâtre Italien, then, after the destruction of the building by fire, as a highly-respected voice teacher. In autumn 1890, he fell mortally ill.

200 *Muzio to Verdi; Paris, 22 October 1890*

My dearest Maestro and friend Verdi.
There is a little nuisance in my will; I beg you to do as I ask. Soon I will go off to the next world, full of affection and friendship for you and for your good and dear wife. I have loved you both, and remember that, since 1844, my faithful friendship has never wavered.

Remember me now and then, and au revoir as late as possible in the next world. Kisses and kisses from your faithful and loving friend.

E. Muzio.

COP, 359

246

Verdi to Giulio Ricordi, Sant' Agata, 4 November 1890

At the moment I have no mind to do anything, and I can hardly get my bearings. This poor Muzio on 25 October wrote me these very words: '*I have put my things in order.*' I know him for an orderly man, and he will surely have provided for everything; still, if anything were needed, ask Signor Pisa to do for me in this fatal circumstance everything that must be done in the best way.

Peppina and I are absolutely desolate! If I weren't 77 . . . and in such a harsh season . . . but I am 77! ! !
COP, 358–9

Muzio died on 27 November 1890.

Muzio's will

[. . .] I declare that I leave an income of L. 600 annually to the Monte di pietà e d'abbondanza of Busseto to assist in completing his studies a young man of promise in music, fine arts, ecclesiastical career, or other Sciences, and that in gratitude for the help received in finishing my studies and following the good example given by Maestro Verdi, hoping that the good example will be followed by other students who will receive the same help and will succeed in their career, accumulating great riches, or very modest like mine, since not to all is it given to be born with the genius of Verdi, great-hearted, and whose friendship and that of his good and dear wife I bear with me. . . . [. . .]

As for the letters of Maestro Verdi which are all collected in bound packets, it is my *absolute will* that they all be burned, for I do not wish them to be made gifts of, nor in time that commerce in autographs be made with them for profit. [. . .]
AB IV, 409

Verdi to Maria Waldmann Massari; Genoa, 6 December 1890

Your letters, my dearest Maria, are always a consolation for me; but the last was a relief, a balm at a moment that is so sad for me. In the space of about a fortnight I have lost my two oldest friends! Senator Piroli, a learned, frank, sincere man, of unparalelled rectitude. Constant, unswerving friend for sixty years! *Dead!* Muzio, whom you knew as conductor, in Paris, for *Aida*. Sincere, devoted friend for about fifty years. *Dead!* And both were younger than I!!

All ends! ! A sad thing is life! I leave you to imagine the grief I felt and feel! And so I have little will to write an opera I have begun, but have not gone far with. Pay no attention to the gossip in the papers. Will I finish it? Won't I finish it? Who knows! I write without plans, aimlessly, just to pass some hours of the day. . . .
AB IV, 408

Verdi to Giulio Ricordi; Genoa, 1 January 1891

[. . .] Now let us come to *Falstaff*. It seems to me that all plans are madness, sheer madness! I'll explain. I started writing *Falstaff* simply to pass the time, without any preconceived ideas, without plans, I repeat, *to pass the time!* Nothing else! Now the talk about it, and the proposals that are being made, however vague, words that are wrested from you and finally become obligations and commitments that I absolutely do not want to assume.

I told you, and I repeat, 'I am writing to pass the time', I told you the music was half done . . . but let's get this clear: 'half sketched' and in this half the hardest work still remains, the arrangement of the parts, revising and adjusting, apart from the orchestration which will be very toilsome. Finally, to say everything in a word: the whole year of 1891 will not suffice to reach the end. Why then make plans, take on commitments, even with vague words?

More, if I were to feel in any way, in the slightest way, bound, I would no longer be *à mon aise* and could do nothing well. When I was young, although sickly, I could stay at my desk 10, even 12 hours!! always working, and more than once I started work at 4 in the morning until 4 in the afternoon with just a coffee inside me . . . and always working without taking breath. Now I can't. Then I could command my physique and my time. Now, alas! I can't. [. . .]
AB IV, 414

Verdi to Boito; Sant'Agata, 12 June 1891

254 The Big-belly is on the road that leads to madness. There are days when he doesn't move, sleeps, and is in a bad humour; other times he shouts, runs, leaps, kicks up a fuss. . . . I let him rage a bit; but if he continues I'll put a muzzle and a strait-jacket on him. [. . .]
MS, ISV, PARMA

Boito to Verdi; Milan, 14 June 1891

Evviva! Let him have his way, let him run, he will break all the windows and all the furniture of your room, no matter. You will buy others. He will smash up the piano: no matter: you will buy another. Let everything be turned upside down! but the big *scene* will be done! [. . .]
AB IV, 419

On 21 July 1891, Franco Faccio died in a clinic in Monza.

Verdi to Boito; Sant'Agata, 23 July 1891

He too is gone! Poor Faccio!
Yesterday, arriving at Sant'Agata, we were all grieved at the sad news we found in the *Corriere*!
Though he had lost his artistic intelligence, and with it the other qualities of that good soul, I can imagine the heartache you must have felt at this loss!
Poor Faccio was your schoolmate, companion and friend in the stormy and happy times of your youth . . . (And he loved you so much!) – In the great misfortune that struck him, you rushed to him, giving him solemn, wondrous proofs of your effective friendship. You must be satisfied with yourself, as you have deserved the praise of all honest people!
Poor unfortunate Faccio! So gifted! So good!
MS, ISV, PARMA

Giulio Ricordi sent Verdi a score of Mascagni's *L'Amico Fritz.*

Verdi to Giulio Ricordi, 6 November 1891

Thank you for the score of *Fritz* which you sent me. In my life I have read many, many, very many bad librettos, but I have never read a libretto as *idiotic* as this. [. . .]
It is not difficult to hit the target a bit high or a bit low, but it is difficult to hit in the middle (Manzoni used to say), and so the characters are not well-drawn. The music may be beautiful in any case! I consider things from my point of

view . . . but I am old and reactionary . . . that is, old, yes, but not so much a reactionary.
AB IV, 426

Bülow to Verdi; Hamburg, 7 April 1892

Illustrious Maestro: Deign to hear the confession of a contrite sinner!
Eighteen years ago the undersigned was guilty of a great – great journalistic *stupidity* – towards the last of the five Kings of modern Italian music! He has repented, he has felt bitter shame, oh how many times! When he committed the above-mentioned sin (perhaps your magnanimity will have quite forgotten it) he was truly in a state of idiocy – allow me to mention this, so to speak, attenuating circumstance. My mind was blinded by fanaticism, by ultra-Wagnerian 'Seide'. Seven years later, light has gradually dawned. The fanaticism has been purified, has become enthusiasm.
Fanaticism = kerosene; enthusiasm = electric light. In the intellectual and moral world light's name is: justice. Nothing is more destructive than injustice, nothing more intolerable than intolerance, as the most noble Giacomo Leopardi said.
Having reached this 'point of knowledge', how fortunate I was, how enriched my life has become, the field has increased of the most precious joys: the artistic joys! I began by studying your latest works: *Aida, Otello,* and the *Requiem,* of which, recently, a rather weak performance – moved me to tears; I have studied them not only according to the letter, which kills, but according to the spirit, which gives life! Well then, illustrious Maestro, now I admire you, I love you!
Will you forgive me, will you avail yourself of the sovereign privilege of clemency? However that may be, since it lies within my power, and even if only to set an example to the lesser brethren, I must confess my past guilt.
And, in accordance with our Prussian motto, *Suum cuique* [to each his due], I exclaim in all sincerity:
Evviva VERDI, the Wagner of our dear allies.
BÜLOW VIII, 78

Verdi to Giulio Ricordi; Genoa, 11 April 1892

[. . .] And now, be amazed! Hans de Bulow sends me the letter I enclose and which you will return as soon as you have read it . . . He is definitely mad! [. . .]
AB IV, 439

Verdi to Bülow; Genoa, 14 April 1892

There is no shadow of sin in you! – and it is not necessary to talk of repentance and absolution! If your opinions once were different from those of today, you were quite right to express them; nor would I have dared complain. For that matter, who knows . . . perhaps you were right then.
In any case, this unexpected letter of yours, written by a musician of your worth and your importance in the artistic world, has given me great pleasure! And this not because of my personal vanity, but because I see that truly superior artists judge without prejudice of schools, nationalities, period. [. . .]
AB IV, 439

Verdi spent most of the year 1892 in scoring *Falstaff* and 248 in correspondence with Ricordi about the selection of singers. Maurel, the obvious choice for the title role, 249 caused some trouble.

258 *Verdi to Teresa Stolz; Sant' Agata, 9 September 1892*

[. . .] I have spent an infernal week with Maurel. His demands were so outrageous, exorbitant, incredible, that the only course was to consign the whole thing to the devil. Four thousand lire a night! Paid rehearsals at ten thousand lire! Rights for him alone to do *Falstaff* in Milan, Florence, Rome, Madrid, America, etc. etc.!

Then I bared my talons and said: 'The opera is mine, and I do not allow rights to my property. I do not want to allow you to be paid for rehearsals, something that has never been done; I don't want a management, even Piontelli [impresario of La Scala whom Verdi disliked intensely], to be ruined by an opera of mine.' [. . .]

AB IV, 457

Verdi to Giulio Ricordi; Sant' Agata, 18 September 1892

[. . .] *Falstaff* could open in the first days of February if I have the Theatre at my complete disposal on 2 January 1893. As for the rehearsals, we will do as we have always done other times. Only the dress rehearsal must be completely different from the other times. I have never managed to have at La Scala a dress rehearsal such as should be had in that Theatre. I will not complain, but if something is wanting, I will leave the Theatre and you will then have to withdraw the score. [. . .]

AB IV, 459

Giuseppina to her sister Barberina Strepponi; Milan, early 1893

255 It is incredible the work that Verdi has done and is still doing and will do after the premiere of *Falstaff* which, if illness or other obstacles do not intervene, will open, God willing, next week! Add the infinite number of letters, demands of every kind, which in the midst of this complication of constant work, material and moral, come to besiege him, oppress him, and you will have an idea of Verdi's life in these days! [. . .]

I went to the rehearsal yesterday evening for the first time, and, if I can judge by my head and my impression, it seems to me the advent of a new genre, indeed the date which inaugurates a new art, music and poetry! We will see what is said by the Grand Gathering, the respected Public!

AB IV, 472

251 On 9 February 1893, premiere of *Falstaff* at La Scala, Milan. Among the critics present was the British composer Charles Villiers Stanford, who was filing for both the *Daily Graphic* and the *Fortnightly Review*.

C. V. Stanford, Daily Graphic, London, February 1893

[. . .] With what curiosity has the musical world awaited Verdi's first comic opera! For his first it certainly is: *Un giorno di regno*, an opera written to order in his earlier life under the stress of peculiar misery and sorrow, cannot be considered as one of his spontaneous creations, and it has long passed from the memory of the public. Many were the speculations as to its possible style; whether it was to be a descendant of Mozart or of Rossini, of his earlier or later self. A glance at the score is sufficient to show that it is in comedy the sister of *Otello* in tragedy, written on the same 'advanced' lines, but if possible more uncompromising in its details than the tragedy which preceded it. There is absolutely no concession to popular effect, scarcely a

248

fragment which could be detached from its surroundings; in this respect it goes even farther from the old grooves of conventional opera than the later works of Wagner. The parallels to *Otello* and *Falstaff* in Italy are *Tristan* and the *Meistersinger* in Germany. But after first principles the resemblance ceases. Verdi's workmanship is as totally different from Wagner's as the Italian nation is from the German. The whole work is as sunny as the composer's garden at Busseto. Clear as crystal in construction, tender and explosive by turns, humorous and witty without a touch of extravagance or a note of vulgarity. Each act goes as quickly as lightning, without halt, almost without slow *tempi*; and the general impression is that not of an opera written for musical effect or for the glorification of the singers, but of an admirable comedy which music has helped to illustrate, to accentuate, and to idealize. It is rightly termed on the title-page *Commedia lirica*. [. . .]

STAN, 174–5

Among the many other critics present was Camille Bellaigue of the Paris *Revue des deux mondes*, a future biographer of Verdi, He became friendly with both Verdi and Boito, and with the latter soon began a correspondence that continued until the librettist's death.

Camille Bellaigue to Verdi, 12 February 1893

I received your score yesterday, with gratitude and with emotion. I open it, and it is as if spring entered my home. What rays of light, flowers, what life and what joys! I have read only the first scene so far, which is dazzling, and I am looking through the rest.

What verve and what clarity! What a masterpiece of the *Latin*, classic genius, which neither politics nor the Alps prevent (or will ever prevent) our two countries from understanding, loving and sharing. [. . .]

AB IV, 477

The score of *Falstaff* had been printed before the first performance. Among those who studied it was Bernard Shaw.

Bernard Shaw, in The World, London, 12 April 1893

Easter has afforded me an opportunity for a look through the vocal score of Verdi's Falstaff, now to be had at Ricordi's for sixteen shillings, a price which must obviously be reduced before the opera can get into the hands of the amateur at large. I did not go to Milan to hear the first performance for several reasons, the chief being that I am not enough of a first-nighter to face the huge tedium and probable sickness of the journey from Holborn to Basle (the rest I do not mind) in order merely to knock at the tradesman's door of Italy, so to speak, and turn back after hearing an opera half murdered by La Scala prima donnas with shattering tremolos, and witnessing a Grand Old Man demonstration conducted for the most part by people who know about as much of music as the average worshipper of Mr Gladstone does of statesmanship. In short, being lazy and heavily preoccupied, I cried sour grapes and stayed at home, knowing that the mountain would come to Mahomet soon enough.

Let it be understood, then, that since I have not been present at a complete performance of Falstaff I do not know the work: I only know some things about it. And of these I need not repeat what has already been sufficiently told: as, for instance, that Falstaff is a music drama, not an opera, and that consequently it is by Shakespear, Boito, and Verdi, and not by Verdi alone. The fact that it is a music drama explains the whole mystery of its composition by a man eighty years old. If there were another *Il balen* or *La donna è mobile* in it, I should have been greatly astonished; but there is nothing of the sort: the fire and heroism of his earlier works blazes up now only on strong provocation.

Falstaff is lighted and warmed only by the afterglow of the fierce noonday sun of Ernani; but the gain in beauty conceals the loss in heat – if, indeed, it be a loss to replace intensity of passion and spontaneity of song by fullness of insight and perfect mastery of workmanship. Verdi has exchanged the excess of his qualities for the wisdom to supply his deficiencies; his weaknesses have disappeared with his superfluous force; and he is now, in his dignified competence, the greatest of living dramatic composers. It is not often that a man's strength is so immense that he can remain an athlete after bartering half of it to old age for experience; but the thing happens occasionally, and need not so greatly surprise us in Verdi's case, especially those of us who, long ago, when Von Bülow and others were contemptuously repudiating him, were able to discern in him a man possessing more power than he knew how to use, or indeed was permitted to use by the old operatic forms imposed on him by circumstances. [. . .]
SHAW, II, 280–2

Verdi continued making little changes in the score after the Scala production, and other productions quickly followed. The most immediately important was in Rome, with the King and Queen in the theatre. The opera was also performed abroad, in Berlin, and early in 1894 it was announced for the Opéra Comique in Paris.

Verdi to Giulio Ricordi; Genoa, 23 March 1894

To sum up: when you were here, we said:
1. That if you do not find good the singers who are to perform *Falstaff* in Paris, and above all suited to their parts, you and Boito have given me your word of honour that you will tell me 'Stay in Genoa'. I seriously trust your word of honour.
2. If I come to Paris I need: a living-room – a bedroom for Peppina – a bedroom for me – a room nearby for the maid. We will arrive (we will decide the day) at the Gare de Lyon at about six in the morning. Alas what an hour! For the journey you told me you would make arrangements yourself. I don't know what these *Vagons Lits* are. We want to be isolated in order to be able to sleep freely. [. . .]

I have *not* finished! You promised me you would free me from nuisances! Oh thanks a thousand times and I trust your promise! Can I trust you? Don't forget that I am almost 81 and I cannot stand much fatigue! I hold you to your word! [. . .]
AB IV, 538

On 18 April 1894, *Falstaff* at the Opéra Comique. Verdi was present, and satisfied with the performance and its reception. The summer of 1894 was darkened by the illness of Giuseppina, and was burdened by the necessity of composing ballet music to be inserted into *Otello* for a Paris production at the Opéra in the autumn. *Otello*, on 12 October 1894, was a triumphant success.

Telegram from Prime Minister Francesco Crispi to Verdi, 12 October 1894

Proud that the name of Italy has been highly honoured in this congenial and great city I consider augury of fraternal affection between two neighbouring peoples and bless the art that has offered this opportunity. Glory to Verdi who with his harmonies has crossed the Alps and opened the way to an accord of hearts.
AB IV, 556

Verdi to Giulio Ricordi; Genoa, 25 October 1894

[. . .] I left the Opéra Friday evening; and I said goodbye to every one of the artists, who gave me the most cordial, friendly, moving welcome. And I myself was not a little *bouleversé*. [. . .]
In short all goes well. Only I am sorry about Crispi's telegram . . . Besides those who have baptized it a *Crispinade*, this morning *Le Ménestrel* says: 'Crispigiroutte – Quelle lyrisme! . . .' [. . .]
AB IV, 557

Verdi to the conductor Edoardo Mascheroni; Genoa, 21 April 1895

[. . .] You say you surprised on my desk some pages of score! . . . Perhaps it's true! I wanted to write a 'Te Deum'!! A *thanksgiving* not for myself, but for the Public at having been liberated after so many years of hearing my operas!! [. . .]
AB IV, 572

Work on the 'Te Deum' – which was to be the most substantial of the *Quattro pezzi sacri* and Verdi's last major work – continued into 1896. Meanwhile there were smaller problems: the daughter of Commendatore Spatz, proprietor of the Grand Hôtel et de Milan, was about to marry the young composer Umberto Giordano. There was the question of a wedding present.

Verdi to Giulio Ricordi; Sant' Agata, 7 November 1896

It's true; we spoke months ago of a *souvenir* for the future bride Signorina Spatz; but my former enthusiasm has now diminished. After all what is Signorina Spatz to me? The daughter of the owner of the hotel that I have been staying in for perhaps thirty years, always paying punctually, never quibbling about a cent, staying *bon gré mal gré* in the most expensive apartment of the hotel even when there was no need. Therefore *Give* and *Take* equal.
I agree though that, especially lately, they have beeen extremely kind! This makes me hesitate, not so much for the expenditure of a few hundred francs, but because the thing in itself seems excessive!
AB IV, 597

Giulio suggested flowers or a fan. Verdi decided on the fan.
That winter was spent in Genoa. One of their visitors there was the writer Edmondo De Amicis, who has left a pen-portrait of Giuseppina in old age.

From Edmondo De Amicis's description of Giuseppina

On her face [. . .] the lines of her first beauty had remained

unchanged; and the still-persistent blond in her handsome greying hair and the rosy colour of her complexion gave her, at first sight, a youthful appearance; although her pale eyes had a naturally severe expression, which contrasted with the gaiety of her spirit. Nothing had remained in her, and perhaps there had never been anything, of that which some people think to recognize of the stage artist, even many years after they have left the stage; and she never recalled, unless obliged to, her artistic past, as if, compared to her new glory, her old one seemed too poor a boast. And yet, seeing her beside the Maestro, it was impossible not to think occasionally that fifty years earlier she had given her golden voice to his first triumph, not to consider that a long and happy existence was comprised in this sentence: – She sang *Nabucco* and she witnessed the triumph of *Falstaff*. – She spoke with great simplicity, but slowly, not out of difficulty, but caution, as if weighing phrases and words, which were few, and always appropriate; she expressed every opinion in the form of doubt [. . .]. Also on the subject of books, not only because of that reserve which in certain women, even very cultivated ones, is a form of intellectual modesty, but also, and perhaps even more, because of her nature, all delicately feminine, she used to express not so much her opinion as her feeling. Which, when it was of liking and admiration, she expressed with a girl's impassioned phrases. I remember hearing her say, about a book of exploration by Livingstone: 'When one has finished reading it, one would like to seek out that man to beg him to give us his blessing.'
DE A, 227–8

Verdi to Giulio Ricordi; Sant'Agata, 21 October 1897

. . . Today I send only two pieces: the Enigmatic Scale ['Ave Maria'] and Te Deum. In a few days I'll send the Prayer from *Il Paradiso* ['Laudi alla Vergine Maria'].
AB IV, 616

Verdi to Giulio Ricordi; Sant'Agata, 25 October 1897

I am sending you, alas, also these other two pieces, the Prayer from *Il Paradiso* and the Stabat . . . with immense sorrow!

As long as they existed on my desk, I looked at them now and then with satisfaction and they seemed my property! Now they are mine no longer! ! [. . .]
AB IV, 616

On 14 November 1897, Giuseppina Verdi died at Sant'Agata. One of the first to visit the house after her death was the executor of her will, the lawyer Amilcare Martinelli.

From Amilcare Martinelli's Verdi memoir

The brief journey from Cremona to the Villa of Sant'Agata seemed to me, this time, a long, eternal pilgrimage. The gloomy day, the fine rain, the leaden sky, the muddy road, the leafless trees, the countryside squalid and as if exhausted: all added sorrow to sorrow in my spirit. After Villanova, the Verdi Hospital, with the windows open, seemed to ask heaven for a ray of sunshine [. . .] And there, at the end, on the right, the park of Sant'Agata, with its tall, slim, densely planted, skeletal poplars – there the verdant oasis of peace, changed suddenly into an icy cemetery! I could not get out of my mind, as if I had her before my eyes, the figure of that lady, whose advanced age had taken away none of her grace and, I would say, her old fascination: – as I had the fortune

250

and the honour of knowing her, fifteen years ago, in the sumptuous rooms of Palazzo Doria in Genoa, as I had seen her again last May at Sant'Agata and barely a month before in Cremona. [. . .]

The last time, however, she was less happy, less merry than usual – she was impatiently awaiting Verdi – she repeated to me for the hundredth time that the hour had come to 'pack the trunks for the next world', that she felt tired, that her strength was failing . . . [. . .].

At Sant'Agata I found gathered, in the Villa Verdi, only the affectionate Carrara family of Busseto, the great Maestro's only relatives. They told me, in tears, the pathetic stories of these last three days. On Thursday poor Signora Giuseppina had carefully made a note of the objects that were to remain in the Villa and those that were to be gradually packed in cases, to be sent to Genoa. On Sunday, Verdi and the Signora were to leave for Milan, and from there for the Superba [Genoa]. And Sunday, instead, at 4.30 p.m. Giuseppina Verdi drew her last breath! . . . A violent pneumonia attacked her that same Thursday. At dinner she felt a sharp chest pain and a great chill. The doctor judged the case desperate, especially since for some time the poor Signora had taken scant nourishment.

There was a consultation; and unfortunately the consultation confirmed the terrible sentence! But the patient did not show great suffering [. . .]. A few hours before serenely closing her eyes, her Verdi brought her a violet, saying: 'Smell the perfume!' And she said: 'Thank you, but I don't smell anything, because I have a slight cold! !' Verdi kissed her in her death agony, and kissed the lifeless body again. . . . [. . .]

As I was about to take my leave, the kindly Signora Maria Carrara told me that Verdi didn't feel up to talking, but wished to see me.

I entered, sustained by I don't know what superhuman spirit. The Maestro was standing erect, at his armchair, between the bed against the wall, the broad desk all covered with papers, and the closed piano. His chin was against his chest; his cheeks flushed a bright scarlet; his hair and beard very white, more silver than snowy. I ran to him, bowing, and using gentle violence, made him sit. He didn't want to. He stammered these few words [. . .]: 'I don't feel up to speaking. [. . .] Tell Barberina it was better that she obeyed and left yesterday; it was better.' . . .

[. . .] Verdi has arranged everything for the funeral, which will be held at 7 a.m. on the 17th. And it will be very simple, respecting the expressed will of the deceased. After the religious ceremony in the S. Agata chapel, the bier will be carried to Fiorenzuola and from there – by rail – to Milan. [. . .]
MART, 35 FF.

Giuseppina Verdi's will

Sound in mind and body, I invoke Divine Assistance that my last will, the final act of my life, may be just and fair.

Having already provided, during my lifetime, to benefit other persons dear to me, of all my remaining private means, as of all my reason and action, I establish and name as my universal heir my beloved husband Giuseppe Verdi, praying the Most High to protect him in life and death and to join him to me for eternity in a better world.

[There follow some small bequests to relatives and servants and the local poor.]
And now farewell, my Verdi! ! As we were united in life, may God unite our spirits in Heaven! !
AN, PARMA

Verdi to Mascheroni; Milan, January 1898

268–9 [. . .] I will stay here I don't know how much longer! The weather is relatively good, and for the present there is no need to go to Genoa for the climate; staying there would be even sadder for me! My health *idem*. I am not sick, but I am too old!! To live without being able to do anything! It's very hard!
AB IV, 621

That January, Ricordi published the *Quattro pezzi sacri*. On 7 April 1898, first performance of the 'Te Deum', 'Laudi alla Vergine Maria' and 'Stabat Mater' (the 'Ave Maria' on the enigmatic scale omitted) at the Opéra, Paris. Verdi was forbidden by his doctors to go, so Boito went in his stead.

Verdi to Boito; Genoa, 8 April 1898

My dear Boito, let us speak frankly, without reticence, without veils, like true friends, as I am for you and you are for me. To show you my gratitude, I could offer you an object . . . but what would be the use? It would be embarrassing for me, pointless for you.

Allow me then, now that you have returned from Paris, to clasp your hand here, and for this handclasp you will not say a word, nor will you say thank you. Furthermore, absolute silence about the present letter.
MS, ISV, PARMA

Verdi to Giulio Ricordi; Sant' Agata, 9 August 1898

It is now five in the afternoon and I read in the *Corriere* 'The Milan Conservatory will be named after Gius. Verdi.'

My God, this was all that was lacking to annoy the soul of a poor devil like me, who wishes for nothing but to be serene and die serenely! No, sir! Even this is not granted me! What wrong have I done to be tormented like this!??
[. . .]
AB IV, 632

Verdi to Giulio Ricordi; Sant' Agata, 13 August 1898

[. . .] Conservatorio 'G. Verdi' is a discord! A Conservatory that (I do not exaggerate) tried to kill me, and whose memory I should try to escape. And what if that sainted man my father-in-law, on hearing the sentence of the Conservatory Prophets in June 1832, had said: 'I hear music isn't for you, no use wasting time and spending money. Go back to your native village, be an organist again, work the land, and die in peace.' It would have been natural. [. . .]
AB IV, 632

In the winter season of 1898–99 a revival of *Falstaff* was announced at La Scala, with Arturo Toscanini as conductor. Verdi, as usual, was sceptical.

Verdi to Giulio Ricordi; Genoa, 27 February 1899

[. . .] If Toscanini is not experienced, the others are even less so. Soon the revival of *Falstaff*. Everything is against it. The Falstaff may be good (maybe) but Alice no. . . . And mind you the protagonist of *Falstaff* is not Falstaff, but Alice. [. . .]
AB IV, 637

Verdi, *Quattro pezzi sacri*, 1898. Cover of piano score published by Ricordi, Milan.

On 11 March 1899, *Falstaff* was performed at La Scala under Toscanini, who allowed the baritone Antonio Scotti to repeat 'Quand' ero paggio' [When I was a page] twice.

Verdi to Giulio Ricordi; Genoa, 18 March 1899

I have read an article of yours (*Falstaff*), vibrant, very beautiful. If things are as you say it would be better to go back to the modest conductors of the old days (and yet there were Rolla, Festa, De Giovanni, etc.)   24

When I began to shock the musical world with my sins, there was the calamity of the prima donnas, Rondòs, now there is the tyranny of the conductors! Bad, bad! Still, less bad the former!
AB IV, 638

Verdi wrote to the Minister of Education, Baccelli, on hearing he was to be decorated with the Collare dell'Annunziata.

Verdi to Dr Guido Baccelli; 29 September 1899

Excellency! The newspapers are talking again about a high honour that would be conferred on me on my approaching birthday. I am not a man of politics, but a simple artist who has never had nor could have such high aspirations.

And yet if there is one thing I desire, it would be to be, after my death, buried with my poor wife in the chapel of the Home for Musicians which I am now building in Milan.   266

My wife has been lying provisionally for almost two years in a separate plot of the Milan Cemetery. Can I hope for this? I address Your Excellency and call upon your constant kindness to me to satisfy the only wish I can still make at my grave age. My gratitude will not be long, but it will be immense, beyond expression.

AB IV, 649

285   The request was granted. In Milan, 14 May 1900, Verdi made his will. It included a number of bequests to charitable institutions, including the Monte di pietà in Busseto, various farms left to descendants of his aunts and uncles, and for the rest, the Villa Sant'Agata to Filomena Maria Carrara Verdi and several bequests – including the rights to his operas – to the Casa di Riposo.

Conclusion of Verdi's will

I oblige my heir to maintain the garden and my house in Sant'Agata in its present state, asking her to maintain in their present state all the meadows that surround the garden. This obligation is made also for her heirs [. . .].

272   I order that my funeral be very modest and be held at daybreak or at the evening Ave Maria, without singing or music.

I want no announcements of my death with the usual formulas.

The day after my death one thousand lire will be distributed to the poor of the village of Sant'Agata.

AN, PARMA

From Italo Pizzi's 'Ricordi verdiani'

On 12 September 1900 I found him very dispirited! From my usual cab driver I had learned that, the day before, he had not received the visit of a foreign gentleman, excusing himself because he felt unwell. I feared than I could not be received; I tried all the same, and was admitted. At that moment (it was noon sharp) beyond Sant'Agata a terrible storm was raging. The wind whistled among the tall and numerous poplars that surround the Maestro's villa; the cold, almost icy rain was coming down in buckets. I believe this contributed to making him that day, at that moment, 270–1   more melancholy and sad. He welcomed me kindly, with a brief affable smile, then said:

'Forgive me, Pizzi, but I can't give you the welcome of other years, for today I don't feel well, not at all well!' And, after a pause: 'I no longer talk, no longer read, no longer write, and no longer play!' – I tried to cheer him up and blamed his illness on the bad season, and he said: 'Season! It's the seasons that weigh on me!'

[. . .] As I was taking my leave, he complained again about the state of his health. 'My legs won't carry me!' he said and, truly, as he accompanied me towards the door, he leaned heavily on my hand and made very short steps with difficulty. I said to him: 'Courage, Maestro! Your doctor, Battistini, told me a couple of hours ago in Busseto that your constitution is very healthy and strong.' – And he said, almost with faint irritation: 'I know, I know, otherwise I wouldn't have reached the age of eighty-seven. But it's those eighty-seven years that weigh heavily!' – And so I left him, and went away from the villa with the presentiment, which unfortunately proved true, that I would never see him again.

PIZZI, 18–19

On 21 January 1901, while dressing in his suite at the Grand Hôtel et de Milan, Verdi suffered a cerebral 273–81   haemorrhage and fell, half-paralysed, on to his bed. He died at 2.30 a.m. on 27 January.

252

Boito to Bellaigue; Milan, spring 1901

This is the first time I have dared speak of him in a letter. You see, you must forgive me [for a long silence]. I was the victim of a kind of paralysis of the will; my thought moved towards you almost every day in the form of a true remorse. [. . .]

Verdi is dead; he has taken with him an enormous measure of light and of vital warmth, we were all brightened by that Olympian old age. He died magnificently, like a formidable and mute fighter. The silence of death fell on him a week before he died.

Do you know the admirable bust of the Maestro made by   213 Gemito? M. Ca[h]en (the composer you know) has it in his house. That bust, sculpted 40 years ago, is the exact image of the Maestro as he was the fourth day before the end. The head bowed on the chest and his brows severe, he looked downwards and seemed to weigh with his gaze an unknown and formidable adversary and to calculate mentally the strength needed to oppose him.

He also put up an heroic resistance. The breathing of his broad chest sustained him victoriously for four days and three nights. The fourth night still his breathing filled the room, but the effort . . . Poor Maestro! How good and beautiful he was to the last moment! No matter, the old reaper had to carry off his scythe well-battered. [. . .]

MS, MTS, MILAN

In obedience to Verdi's wishes, expressed in his will, his funeral was very simple. At 4.30 a.m. on 30 January 1901, Verdi's body was carried first to the church of San Francesco di Paola, then to a temporary grave, beside   282 Giuseppina, in the Milan cemetery. On 27 February, when the remains of the composer and his wife were moved to the crypt of the Casa di Riposo, a second funeral was held, a state occasion, with official delegates   283–4 and a vast crowd.

Recollections of the altar-boy at San Francesco di Paola

I will tell you that I saw both funerals of Giuseppe Verdi, and I remember them very well because of the deep impression they made on me. The first burial took place on a foggy morning around half-past seven, with a third-class hearse drawn by a very modest little horse, in front of which was the priest Don Modesto Gallone, accompanied by a single altar-boy. The cortege could barely proceed through the thick crowd that flanked it, along Via Manzoni [. . .]. Not a song, not the slightest sound: an awesome silence reigned. All bared their heads at the passage of the very humble cortege, and the comments on the contrast between the glory of the existence and the humility of that funeral were made more with eyes than with words. I observed the second funeral from a window of the residence of the Oblate Fathers in Corso Magenta, and here there was the apotheosis of his merit. One detail struck me greatly: behind the gilded hearse in which were the biers of Giuseppe Verdi and la Strepponi, four pages bore a great wreath of flowers which, in various colours, made up these two most eloquent words: TRIESTE IRREDENTA.   287

RO, 66–7

From D'Annunzio's Ode

Pianse ed amò per tutti!
He wept and loved for all!

D'ANN, 204

Index

Figures in *italic* refer to the captions in the plate section, pp. 17–144.

PERSONS

Accarini, Antonio 148, 150
Adami, Giuseppe 237
Albert, Prince Consort *102*
Alberti, impresario 199
Alexander II, Czar 207, 229
Alfieri, Vittorio 147
Alioth, Max 236
Alizard, Adolphe Louis Joseph 173
Almasio, Maestro 11
Ape (Carlo Pellegrini) *221*
Appiani, Giuseppina 171–2, 173, 174, 192, 194
Arcari, Carlo 145
Ariosto, Ludovico 191
Arrivabene, Count Opprandino, letters to 152, 156, 206, 208, 209, 210, 212, 215, 216, 217, 219, 222, 223, 230, 234, 236, 242; death 243
Auber, Daniel 183, 198, 209, 210; *146*
Avoscani, architect *195–6*

Baccelli, Guido 251–2
Balestra, Luigi 160; *51, 66*
Balfe, Michael 173
Ballarini, Gian Bernardo 149
Barbaglia, Giuseppe *245, 259*
Barbieri-Nini, Marianna 161, 168, 169, 170; *93*
Barbot, Caroline 211
Bardare, Leone Emanuele 185, 186, 187, 194
Barezzi, Antonio 13, 203, 221; *12, 13, 15, 16, 27, 37, 226–30*; friendship with Verdi 147, 150, 186; financial aid to Verdi 148; letters to 149, 151, 159, 160–2, 164–5, 167, 169, 171, 172, 173, 176; death of his daughter 153; *Macbeth* dedicated to 170; visits Verdi in Paris 174; goes to Naples with Verdi 178; view of Verdi's relationship with Giuseppina 184–5; appearance 185–6; remarries 206; death 219
Barezzi, Giovannino 154–5, 159, 169, 184
Barezzi, Maddalena 206
Barezzi, Margherita 11, 12–13, 147, 149, 150–1, 152, 153; *13, 30, 33, 34, 46, 55, 285*
Barezzi, Stefano *31–2, 33*
Barsani, Barbara 145
Bartolini, Lorenzo 169, 177; *96*
Basevi, Abramo 198
Basily, Francesco 148; *23*
Bassi, Calisto *13*
Battista, Vincenzo 164
Baucardé, Carlo 188
Bazzini, Antonio 236

Beaumont, A. 214
Beethoven, Ludwig van 148
Belgiojoso, Count Pompeo 12
Bellaigue, Camille 248, 252
Bellini, Vincenzo 153, 156, 163, 164, 166; *50, 107*
Bellinzaghi, Giovannina 14
Bellinzaghi, Giulio 231
Benelli, J. B. 165
Bennett, William Sterndale 209
Berlioz, Hector 195, 229
Bertoja, Giuseppe *54, 61–3, 82–3, 89–90*; and Pietro *117–19, 123–4, 134, 147–8*
Biazzi, Giovanni 146
Bismarck, Prince Otto von 224
Boito, Arrigo *231, 252, 262, 264–5*; writes text for *Inno delle nazioni* 209–10; *167*; friendship with Verdi 212, 251, *239*; 'Alla salute dell'Arte italiana!' 213; projected libretto for *Nerone* 226; writes *Amleto* for Faccio 243; and *Otello* 11, 237–9, 241–3, 244; *190*; and composition of *Quattro pezzi sacri* 244–5; and *Falstaff* 245, 246, 247; *248–50*; friendship with Bellaigue 248; on Verdi's death 252
Boito, Camillo 245–6; *263–5*
Boldini, Giovanni *200, 235–8*
Boninsegna, Celestina *286*
Bonnehée, Marc 195
Bonoldi, Claudio 11
Borrani, President of Verdi Hospital 244
Borromeo, Count Renato 12
Bottesini, Giovanni 228; *189*
Bouché, Lucien 172
Bourgeois, Eugène 179
Brambilla, Teresa *116*
Brambilla, Teresita *116*
Brenna, Guglielmo 158, 179, 182
Bülow, Hans von 232, 247
Burckhardt, Jakob 236

Cahen, Albert 252
Calzado, Torribio 196
Cammarano, Salvatore *85*; libretto for *Alzira* 159, 163; libretto for *La battaglia di Legnano* 175–6; libretto for *Luisa Miller* 176–7; and projected libretto for *Re Lear* 178, 179; libretto for *Il trovatore* 182–3, 184, 185; death 185
Campanini, Italo *188*
Canti, Giovanni 151, 152; *51*
Caponi, Jacopo *see* Folchetto
Capponi, Gino *98*

Capponi, Giuseppe 169, 232; *208*
Carcano, Giulio 179
Carlo Alberto, King 176; *175*
Carrara family 250
Carrara, Alberto 236; *232*
Carrara, Angelo 216
Carrara-Verdi, Filomena *see* Verdi
Carvalho, Léon 214
Casali, Pietro 145
Casarini, Camillo 227
Casati, Giovanni 229–30
Cassioli, Amos *112*
Catalani, Alfredo *193, 252*
Catone 154
Cavalletti, Stefano 146
Cavour, Count Camillo Benso di 203–4, 205, 207–8; *161, 163, 165*
Cesari, Gaetano 229–30
Chaperon, Philippe *199, 201*
Chigi, Prince Agostino 161
Chopin, Frédéric 234
Christina, Queen *120*
Coccia, Carlo *41–4*
Coletti, Filippo 159, 172, 184, 199
Colini, Filippo 184
Corelli, Arcangelo 149
Corio, L. 203–4
Coronaro, Gaetano 237
Corte, Clemente 204
Corticelli, Mauro 205–6, 207, 208, 210, 216, 234
Costa, Michele (Sir Michael) 219
Costantini, Natale 165, 166
Crispi, Francesco 249
Crosnier, François Louis 194–5
Cruvelli, Sophie 193, 194, 195; *139, 140*

D'Albertis, Enrico *270–1*
D'Annunzio, Gabriele 252
De Amicis, Edmondo 249–50
De Bassini, Achille 161, 178
De Giovanni, Nicola 251
De Giuli-Borsi, Teresa 184
Dejean, J. 202
Delfico, Melchiorre 145–6, 147; *7, 153, 154, 158, 215*
Del Signore, Carlino 227
Demaldè, Giuseppe 145, 146–7; *14*
Demaldè, Maria 150
Derivis, Prosper 14
De Sanctis, Caterina 200
De Sanctis, Cesarino, letters to 182–3, 185, 193–4, 195–6, 197, 202, 204, 211, 216–17, 219; and libretto for *Il trovatore* 186–7; Verdi shows libretto for *Adelia degli Adimari* to 200
Destinn, Marie *188*

253

VERDI'S WORKS

PHOTO CREDITS